DEMON FLOWERS

KURUIZAKI NO HANA

Volume One

By
Mizuki Hakase

TOKYOPOP®

HAMBURG // LONDON // LOS ANGELES // TOKYO

MIZUKI HAKASE
Presents
KURUIZAKI NO HANA

CONTENTS

NO.01   Kuruizaki no Hana   007

NO.02   Partners
          ~Three people and one animal~ 053

NO.03   Conflicted   093

NO.04   Attack   133

NO.00   Dream   173

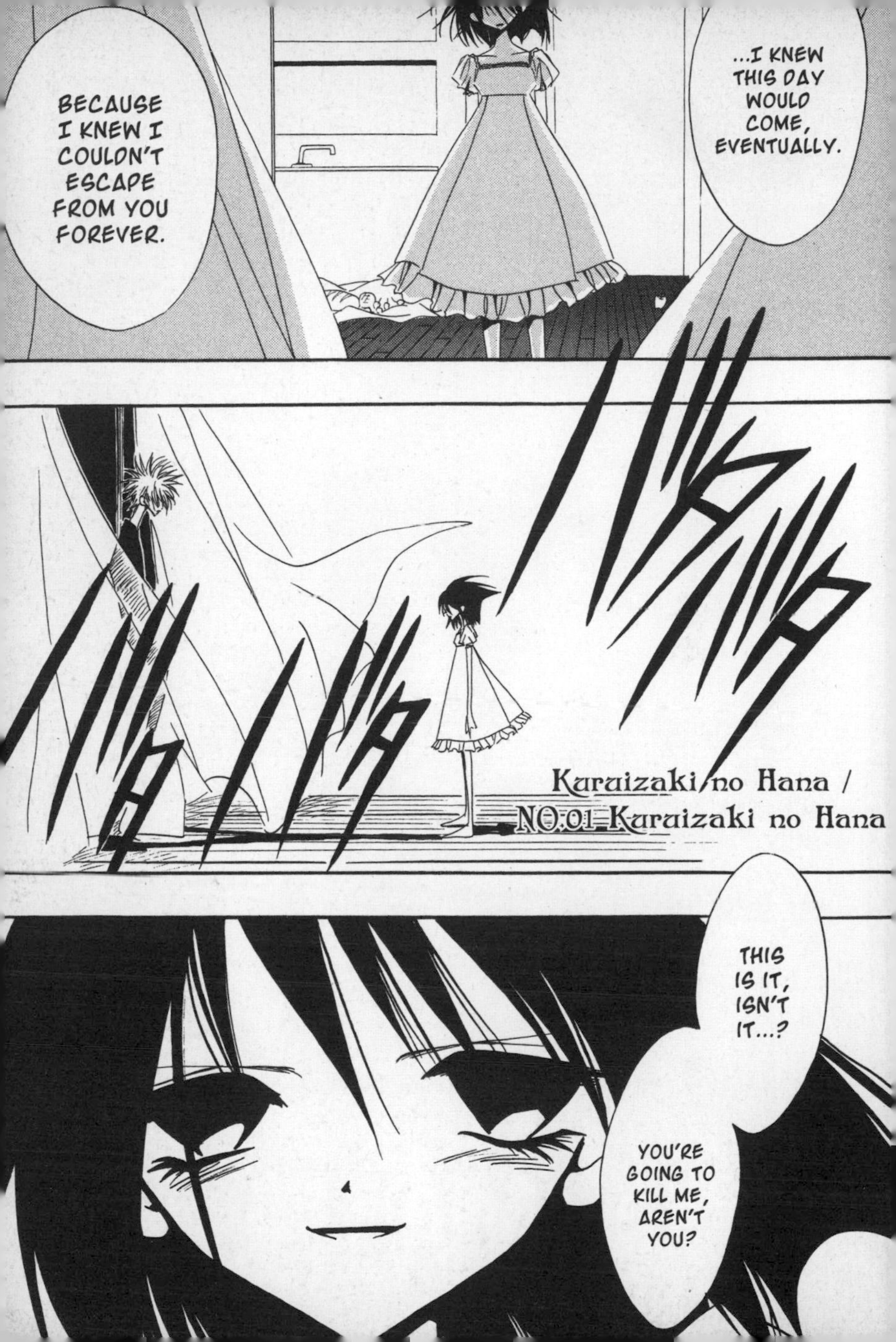
...I KNEW THIS DAY WOULD COME, EVENTUALLY.
BECAUSE I KNEW I COULDN'T ESCAPE FROM YOU FOREVER.
Kuruizaki no Hana /
NO.01 Kuruizaki no Hana
THIS IS IT, ISN'T IT...?
YOU'RE GOING TO KILL ME, AREN'T YOU?

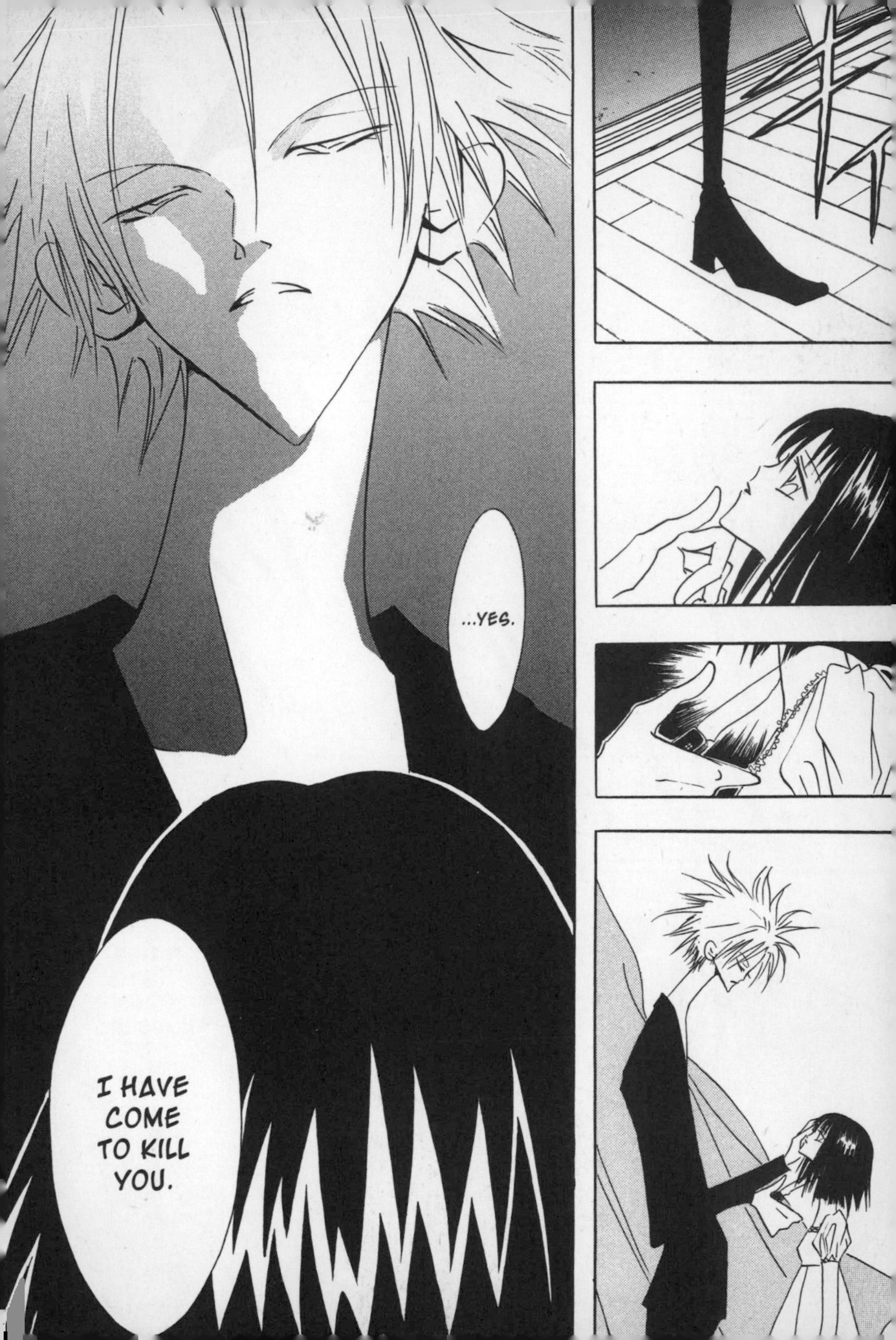
...YES.
I HAVE COME TO KILL YOU.

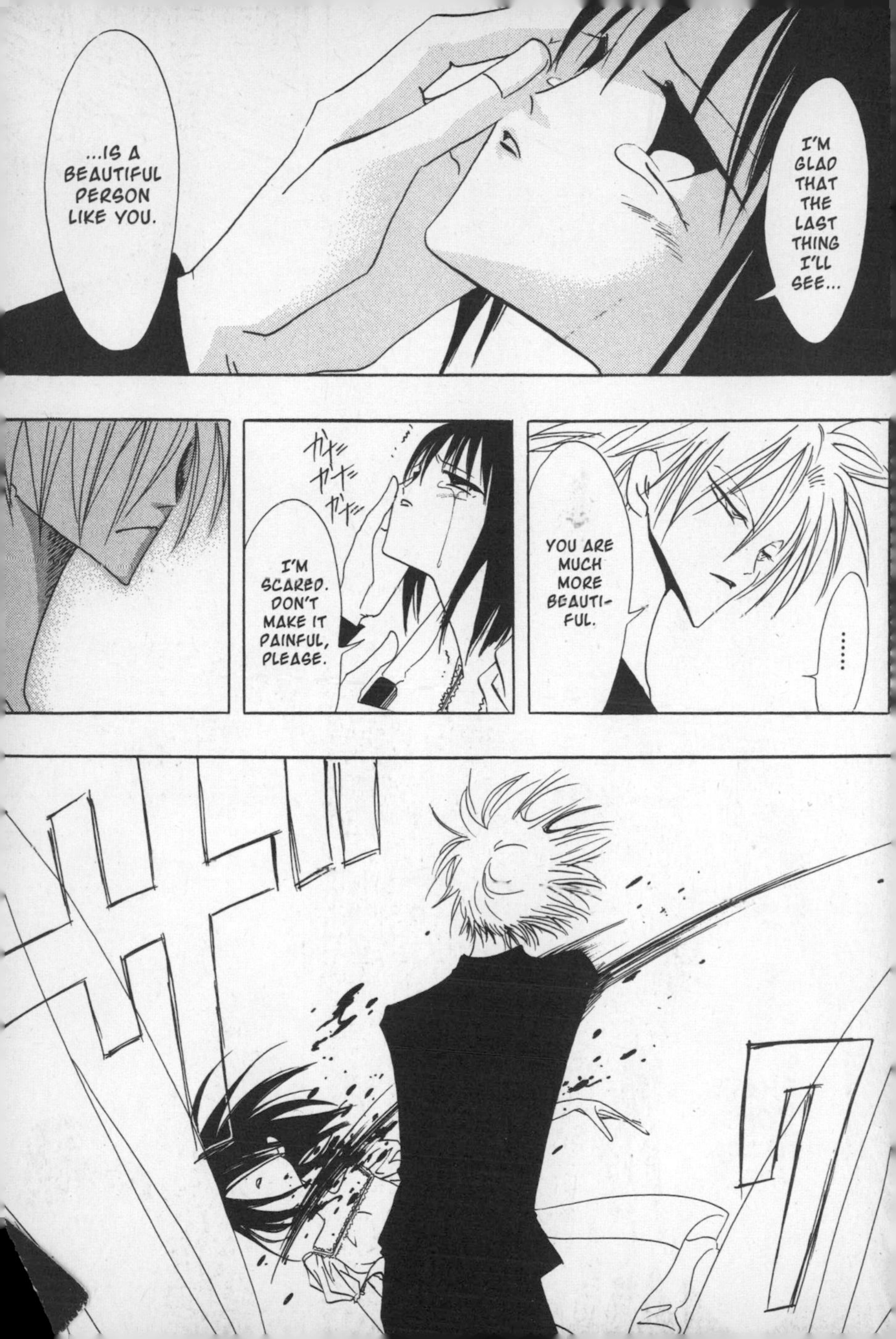
I'M GLAD THAT THE LAST THING I'LL SEE...
...IS A BEAUTIFUL PERSON LIKE YOU.
......
YOU ARE MUCH MORE BEAUTI-FUL.
I'M SCARED. DON'T MAKE IT PAINFUL, PLEASE.

DEMONS DEVOURED THE
GODS THAT ONCE GUARDED
JAPAN AND KEPT IT SAFE.

BY CONSUMING THE FLESH
OF THE GODS, THE DEMONS
ASSIMILATED THEIR POWERS.

THE DEMONS HAVE DISCOVERED
THAT SOME OF THE GODS
BORE HUMAN CHILDREN
WITH SPECIAL POWERS.

THE DEMONS ARE LOOKING
FOR THESE CHILDREN...

TO CONSUME THEM...

TO TAKE THEIR POWERS.

THEY CALL THESE CHILDREN...

"KURUIZAKI NO HANA"--FLOWERS OUT OF SEASON.

DEMON FLOWERS
KURUIZAKI NO HANA

NO.01 Kuruizaki no Hana

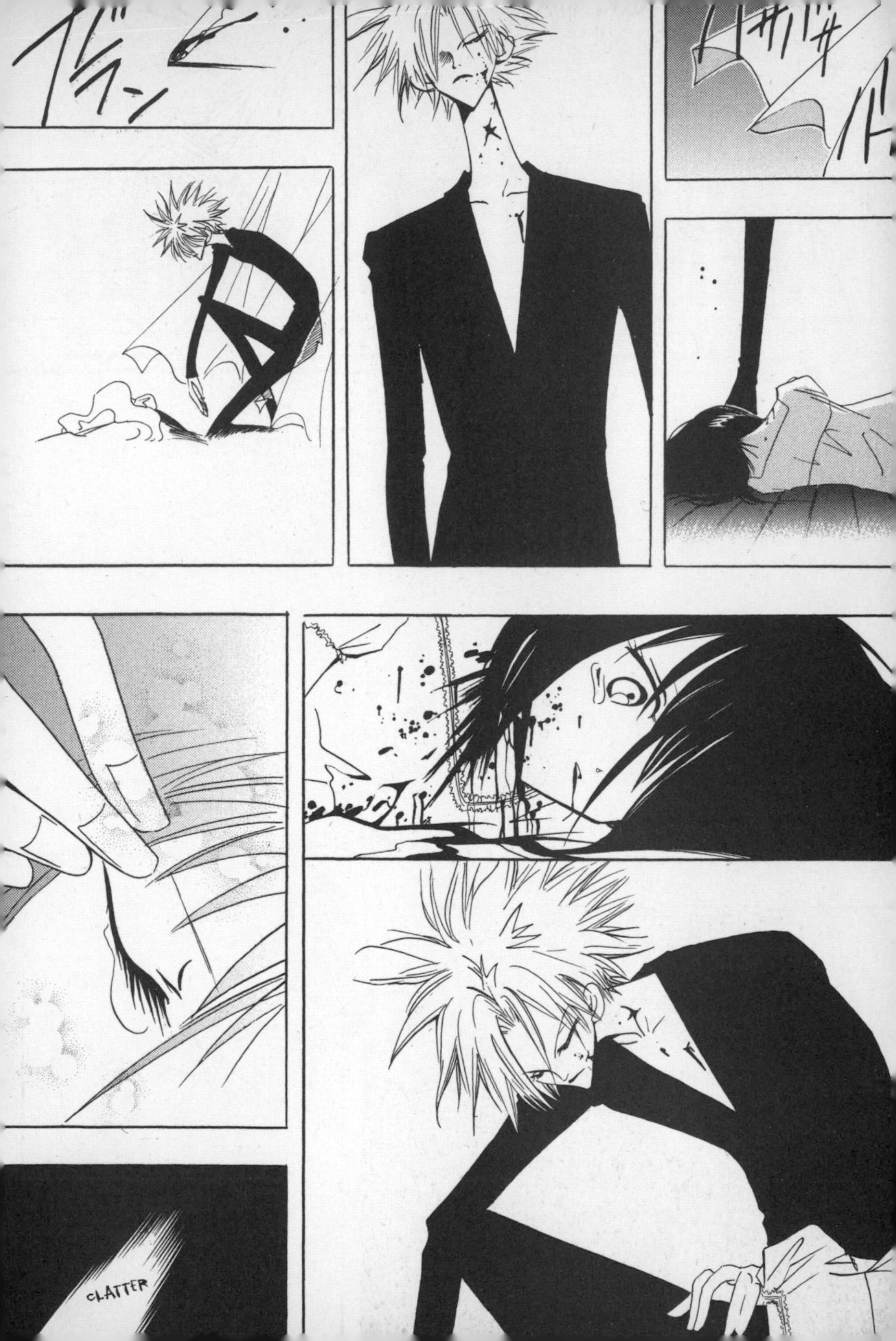
CLATTER

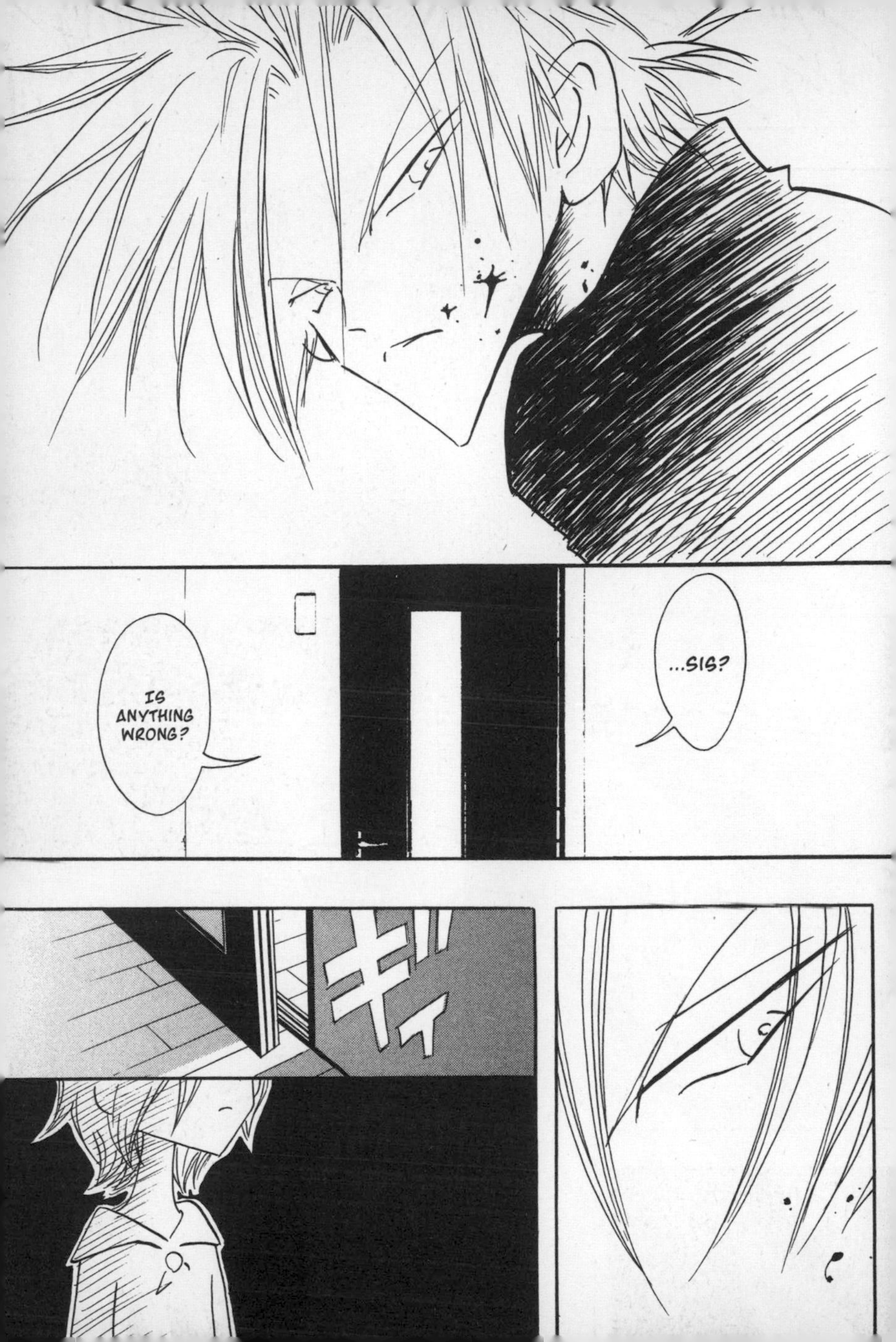
...SIS?
IS ANYTHING WRONG?
ギィ

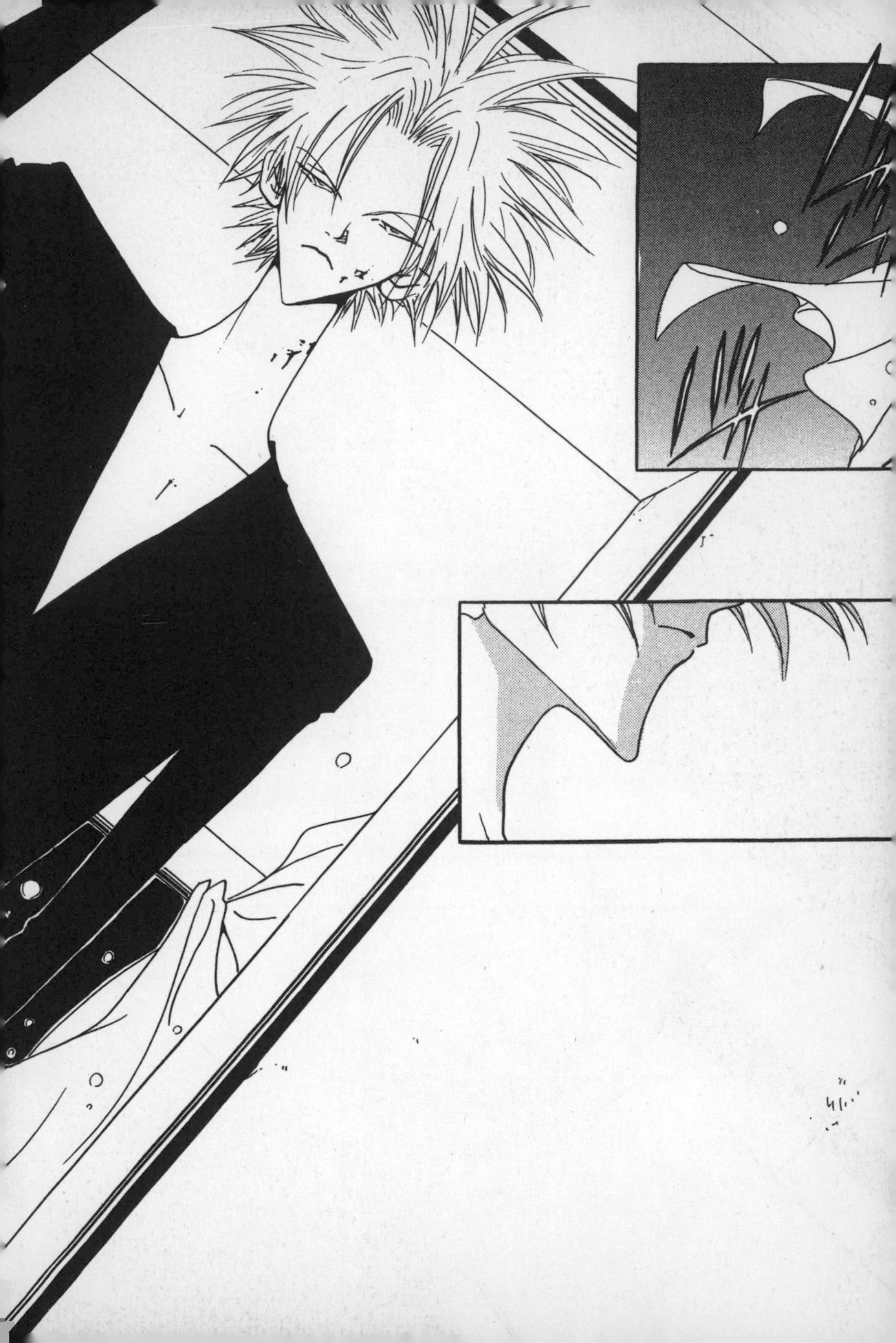

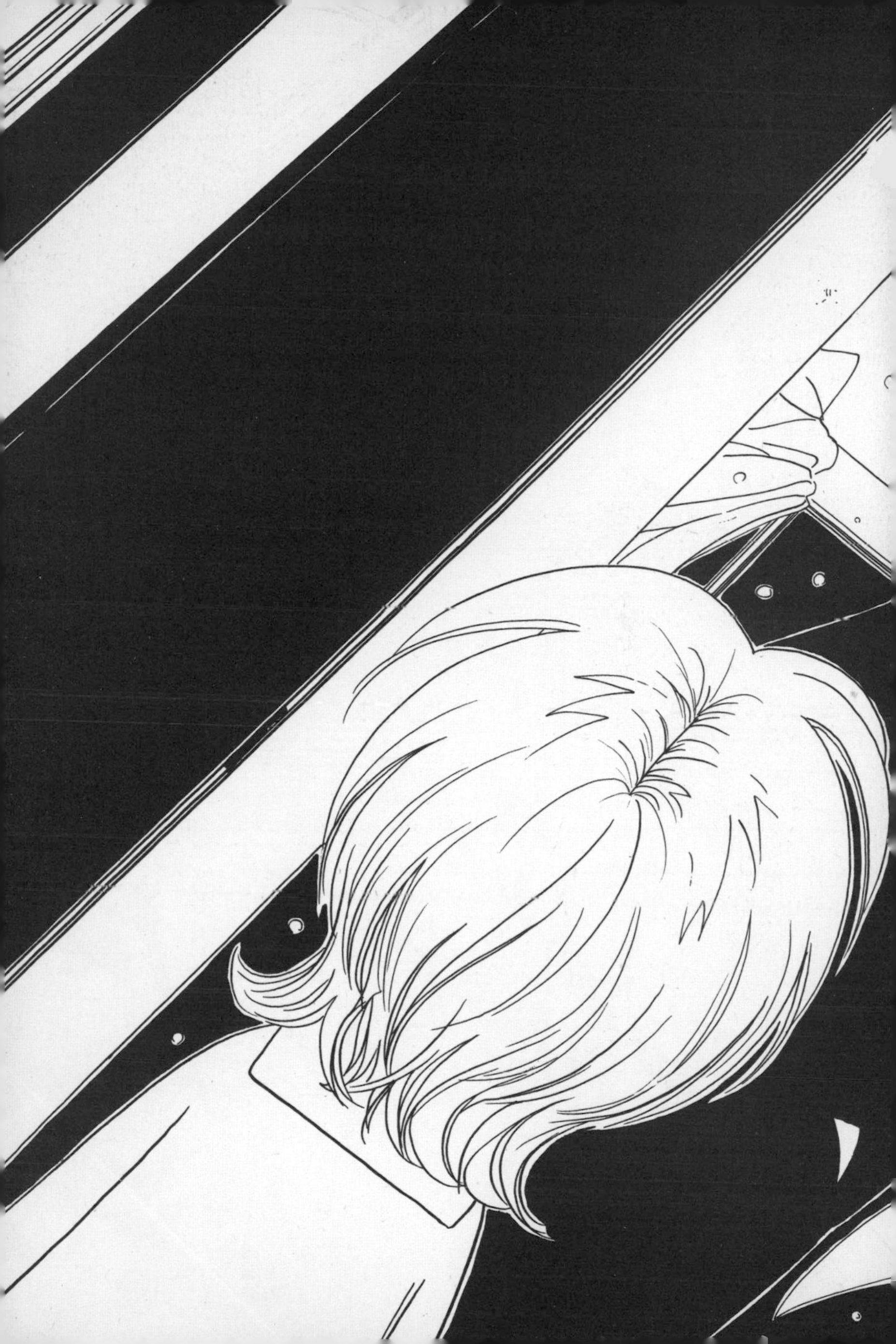

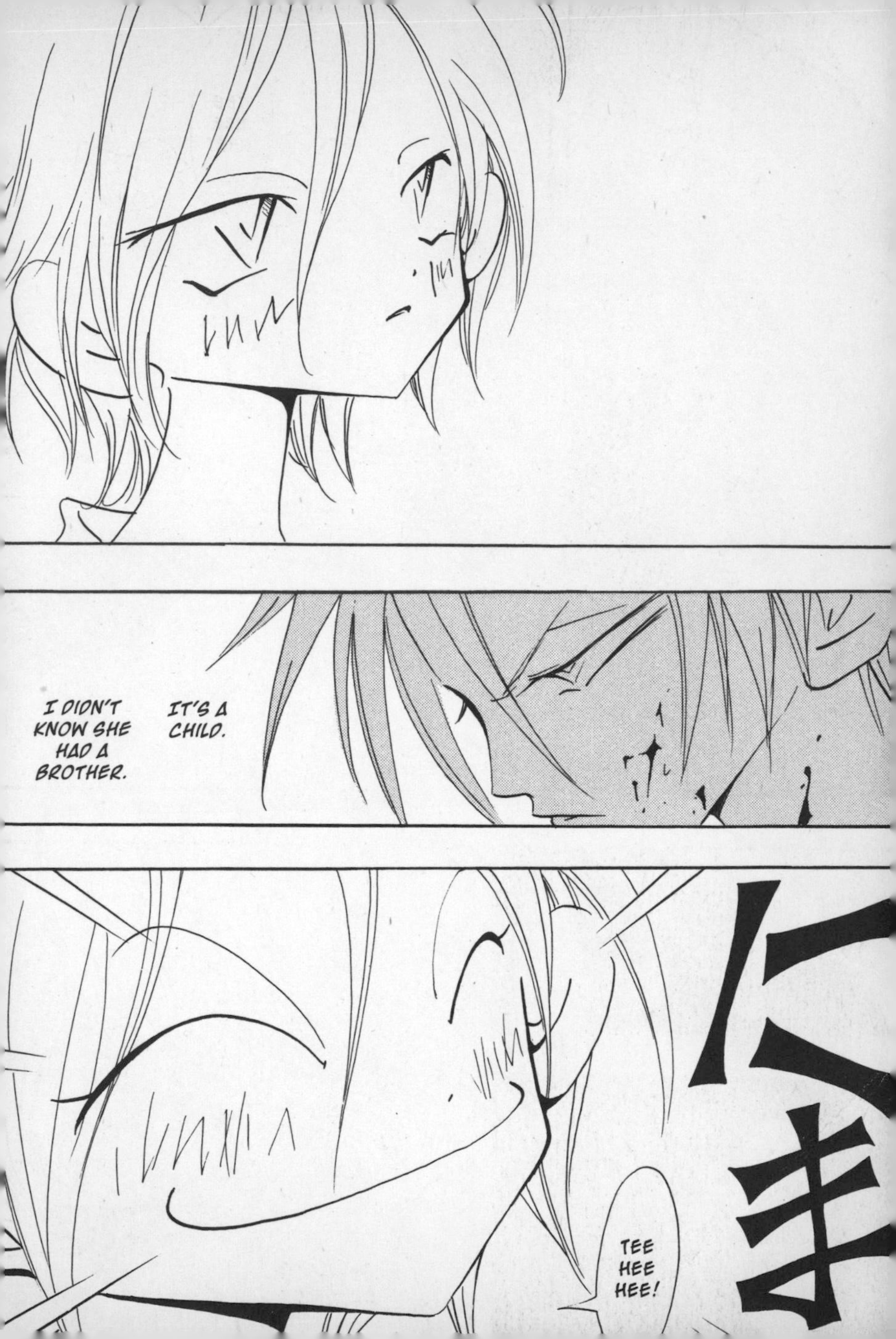
IT'S A CHILD.
I DIDN'T KNOW SHE HAD A BROTHER.
にま
TEE HEE HEE!

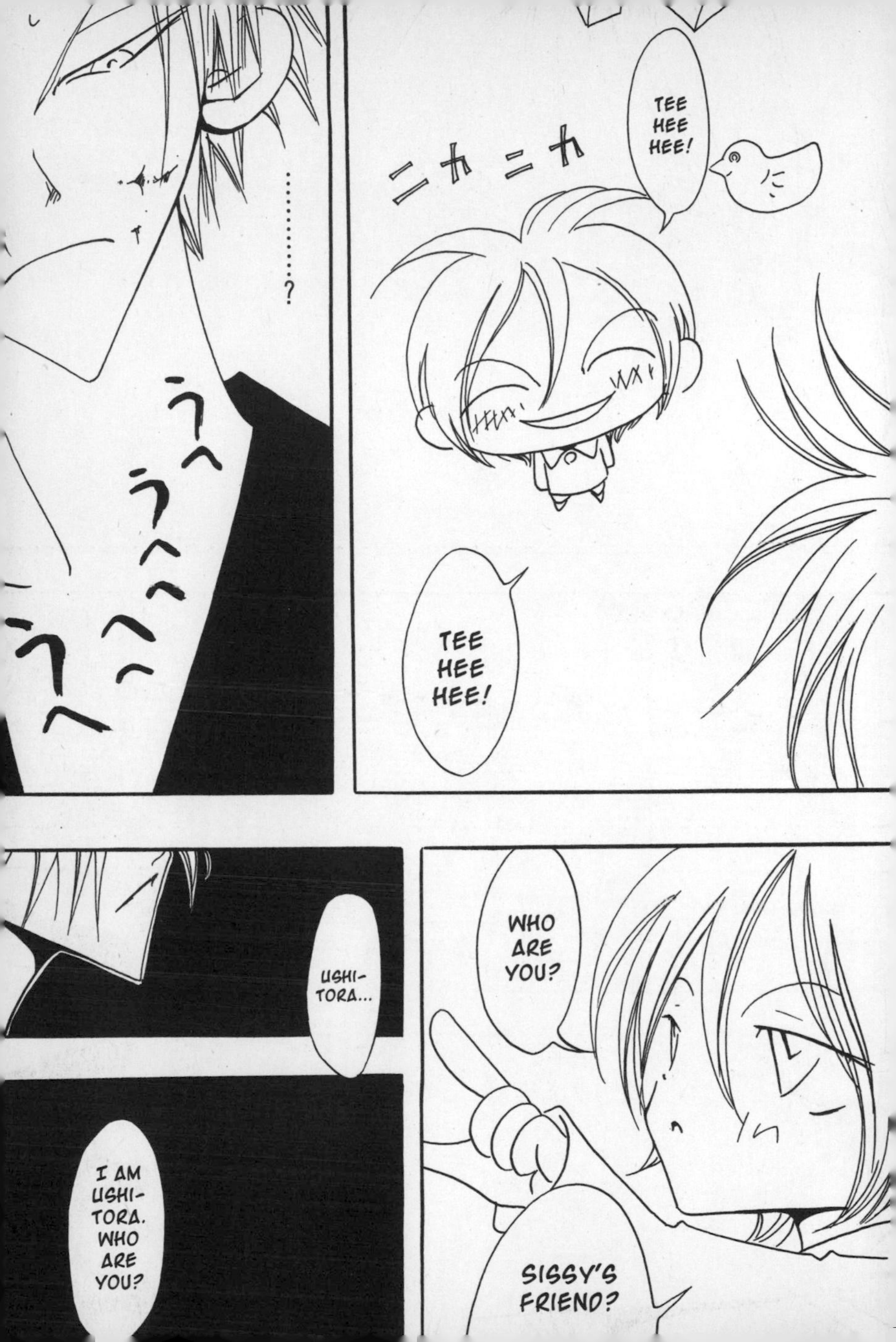
ニカニカ
TEE HEE HEE!
TEE HEE HEE!
......?
WHO ARE YOU?
SISSY'S FRIEND?
USHI-TORA...
I AM USHI-TORA. WHO ARE YOU?

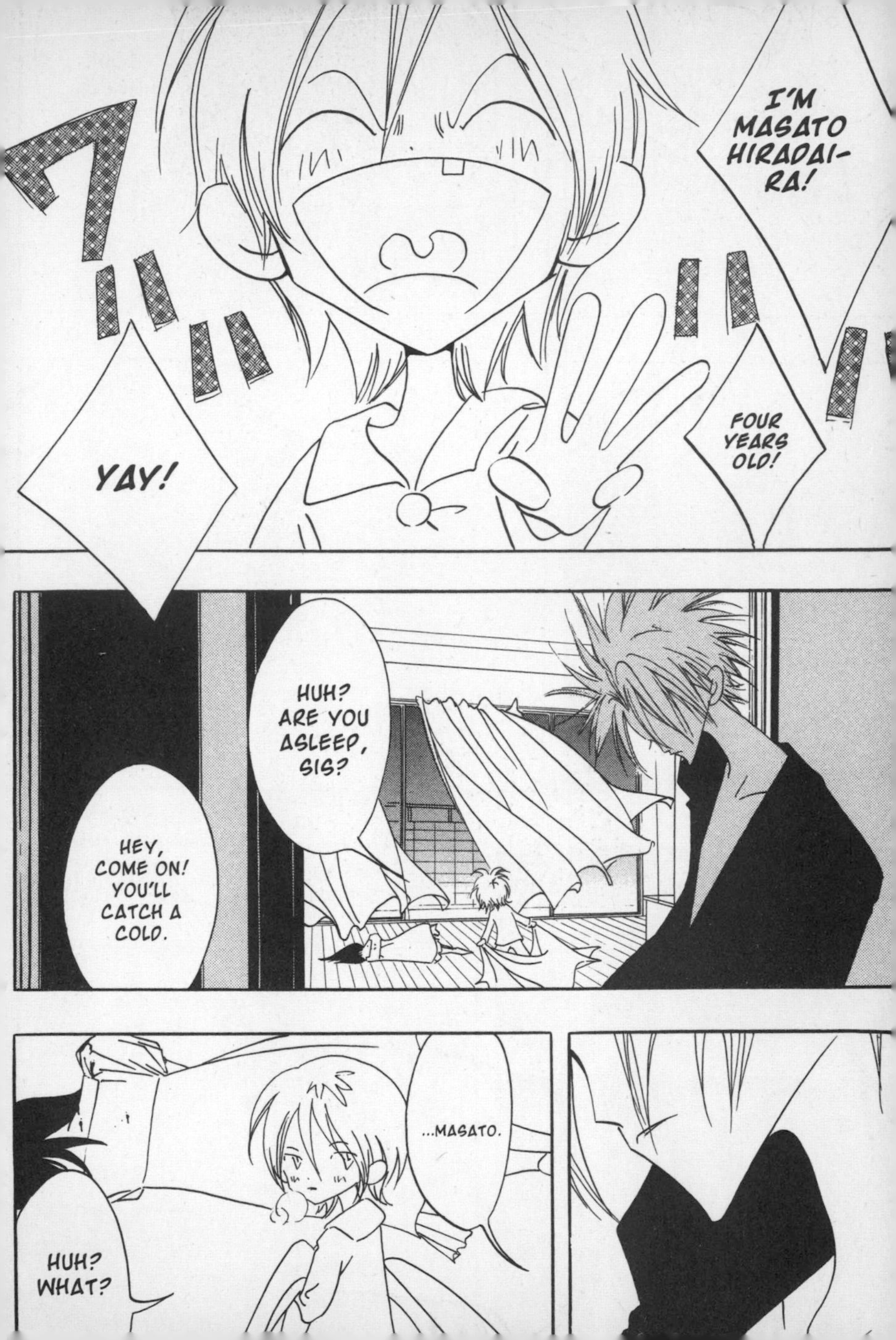
I'M MASATO HIRADAI-RA!
FOUR YEARS OLD!
YAY!
HUH? ARE YOU ASLEEP, SIS?
HEY, COME ON! YOU'LL CATCH A COLD.
...MASATO.
HUH? WHAT?

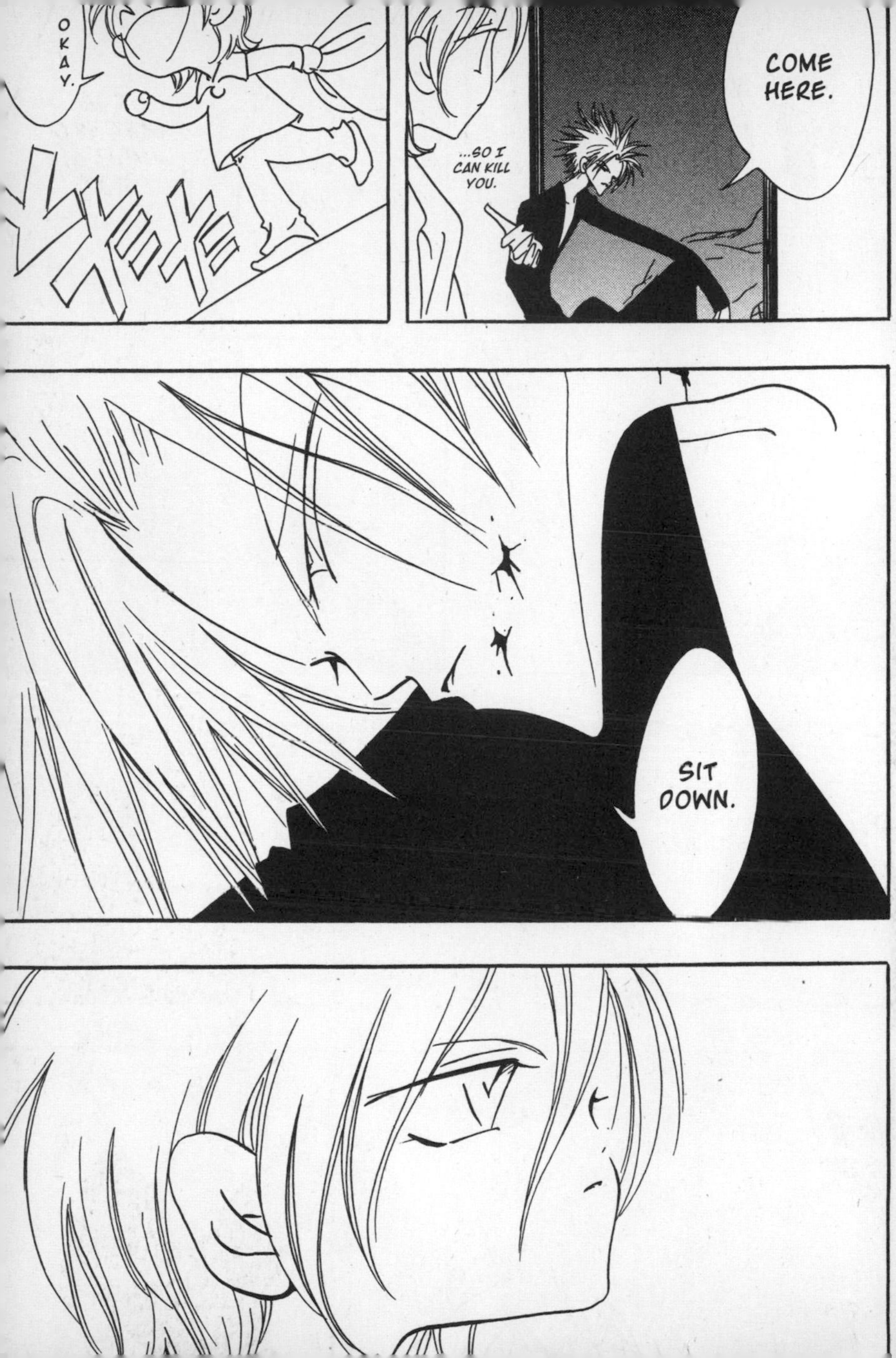
COME HERE.
...SO I CAN KILL YOU.
OKAY.
SIT DOWN.

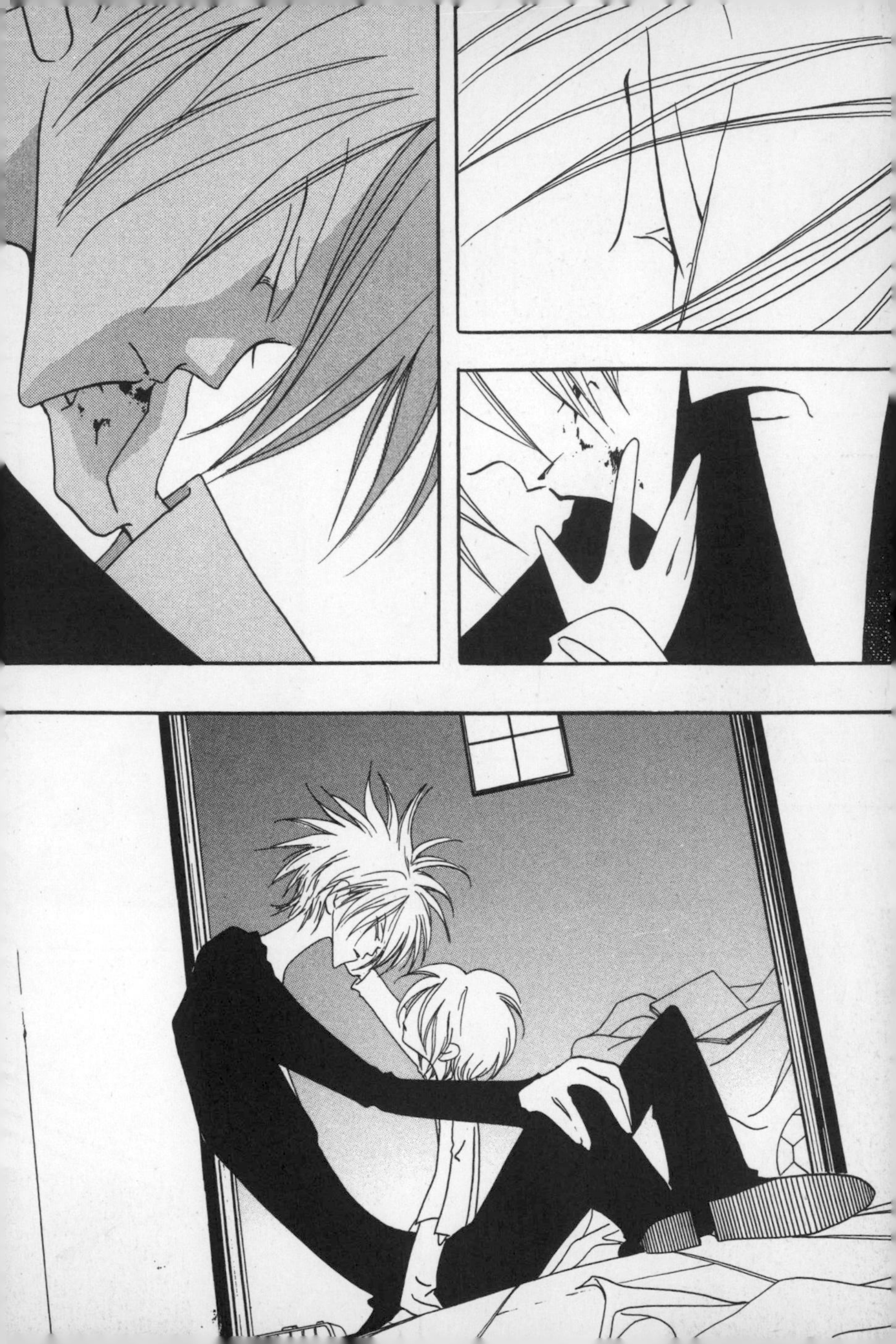

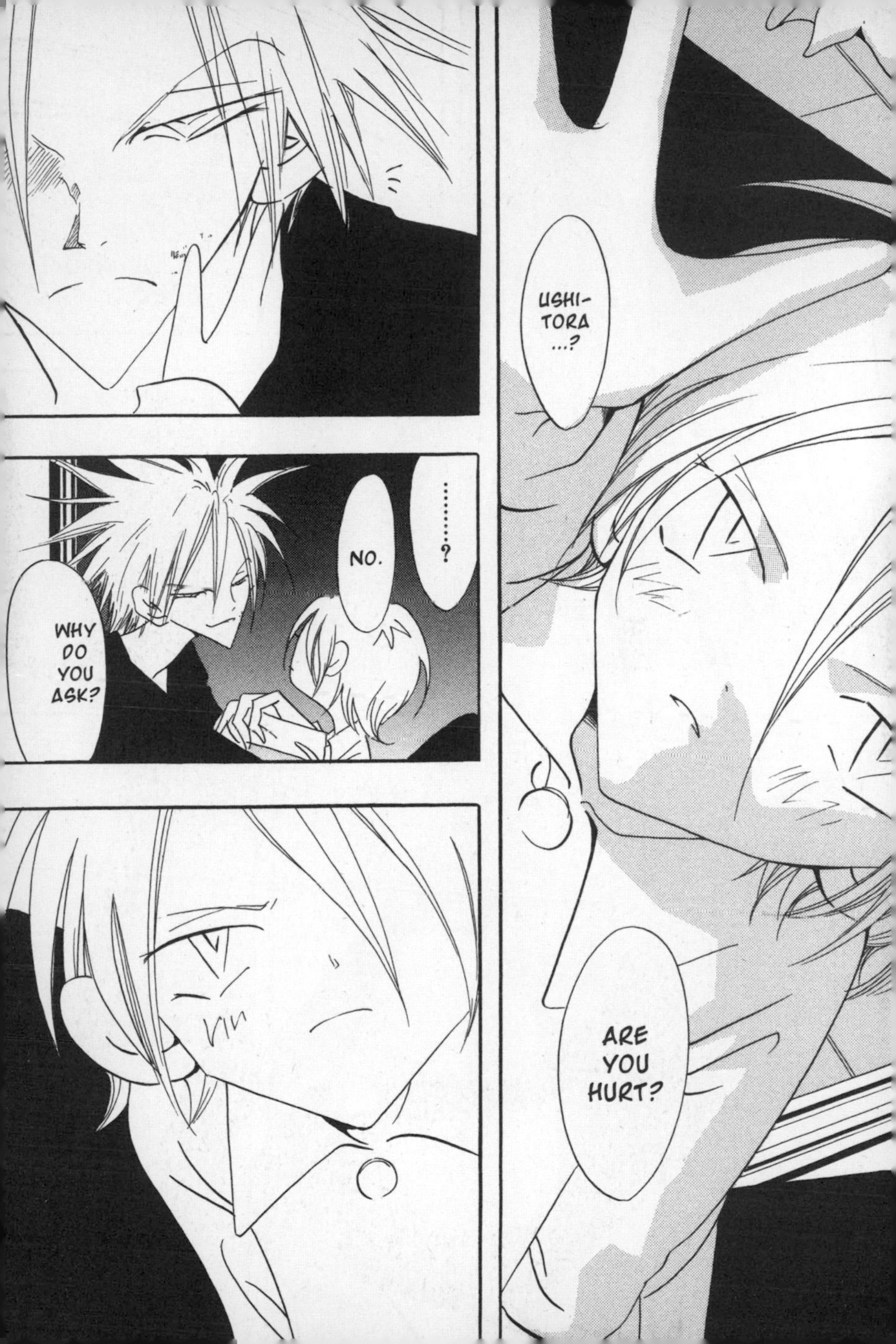
USHI-TORA ...?
ARE YOU HURT?
......?
NO.
WHY DO YOU ASK?

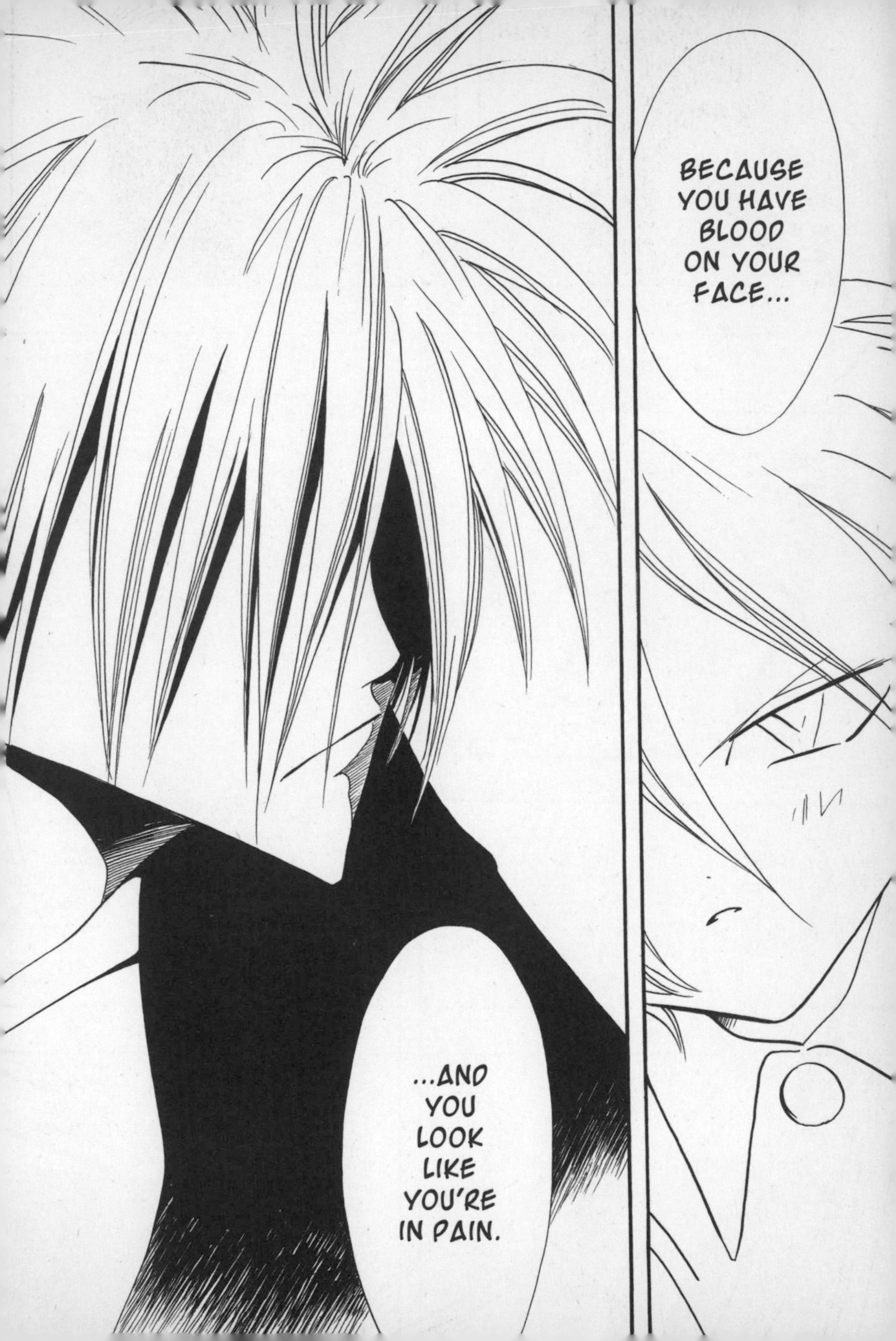
BECAUSE YOU HAVE BLOOD ON YOUR FACE...
...AND YOU LOOK LIKE YOU'RE IN PAIN.

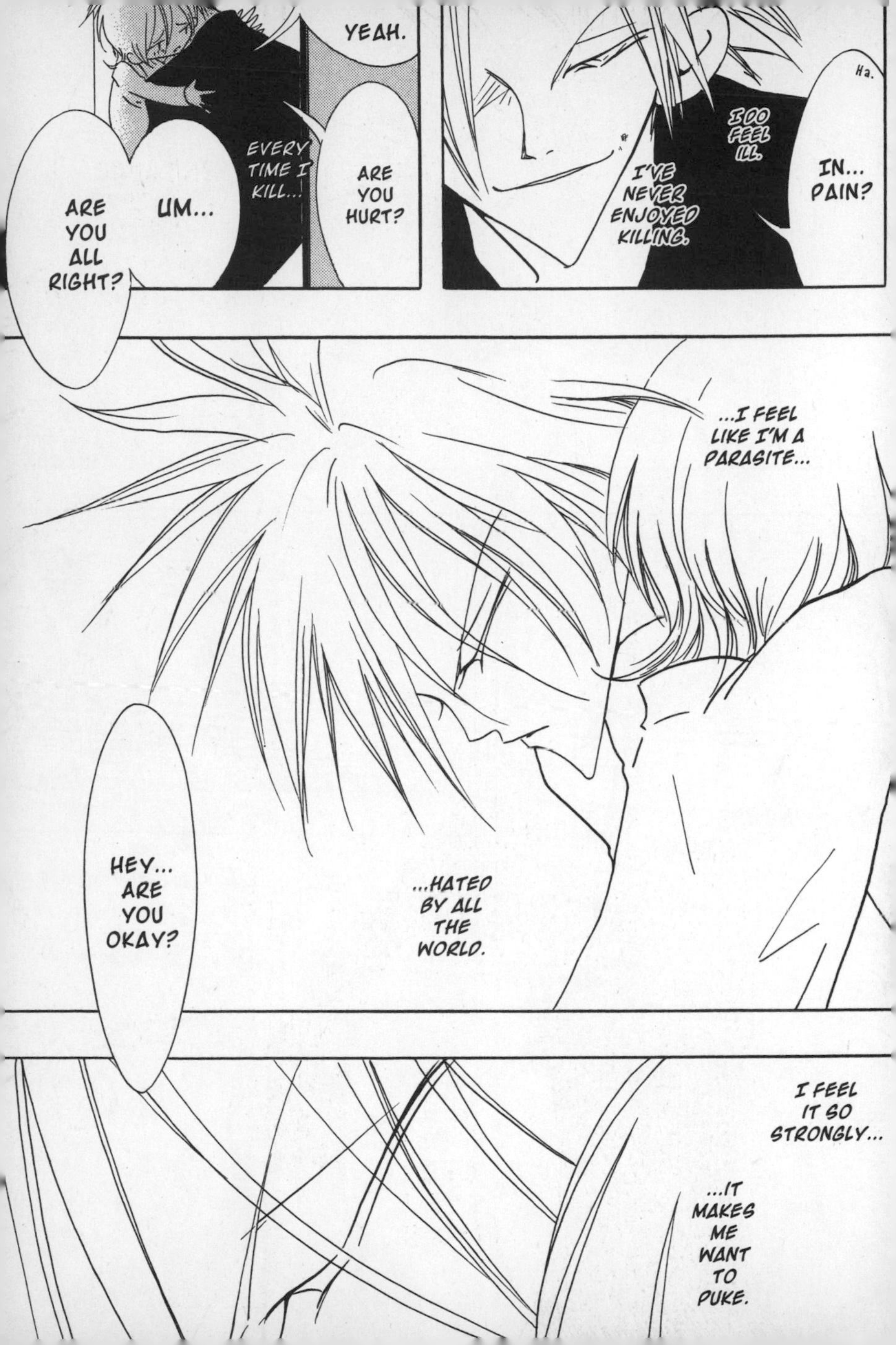
Ha.
IN... PAIN?
I DO FEEL ILL.
I'VE NEVER ENJOYED KILLING.
YEAH.
ARE YOU HURT?
EVERY TIME I KILL...
UM...
ARE YOU ALL RIGHT?
...I FEEL LIKE I'M A PARASITE...
...HATED BY ALL THE WORLD.
HEY... ARE YOU OKAY?
I FEEL IT SO STRONGLY...
...IT MAKES ME WANT TO PUKE.

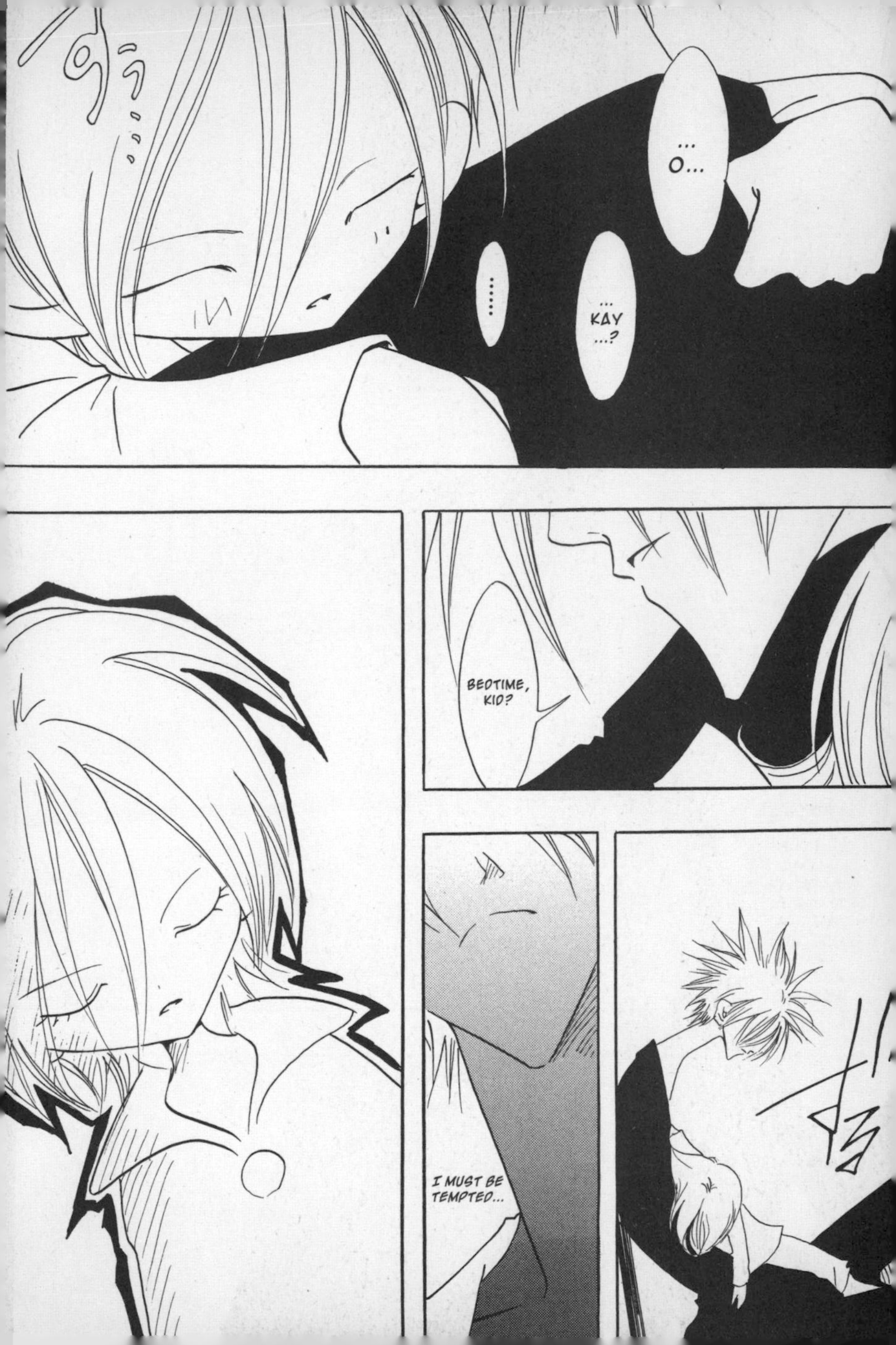
...
O...
...
KAY
...?
......
BEDTIME,
KID?
I MUST BE
TEMPTED...

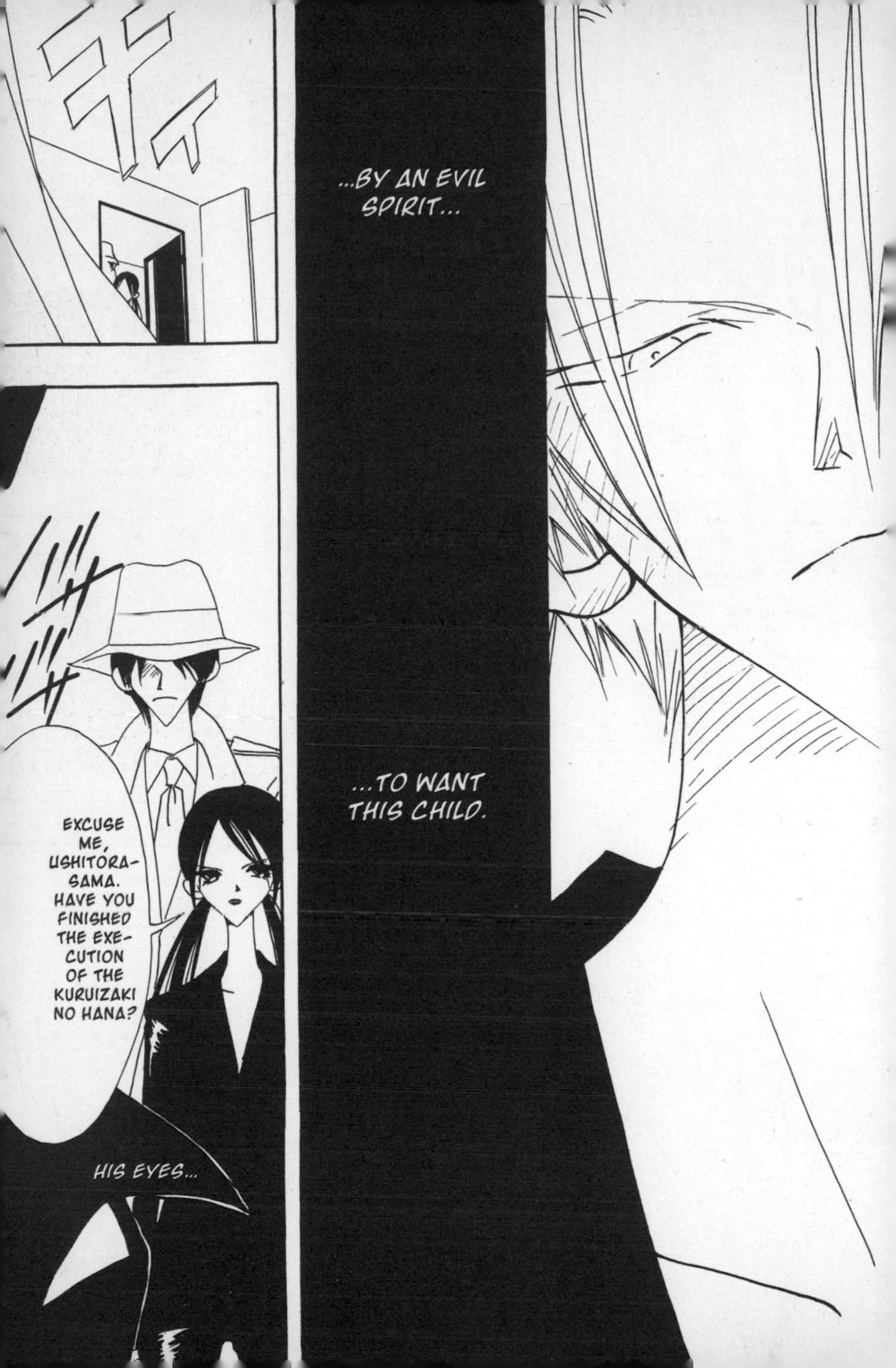
...BY AN EVIL SPIRIT...
...TO WANT THIS CHILD.
EXCUSE ME, USHITORA-SAMA. HAVE YOU FINISHED THE EXE-CUTION OF THE KURUIZAKI NO HANA?
HIS EYES...

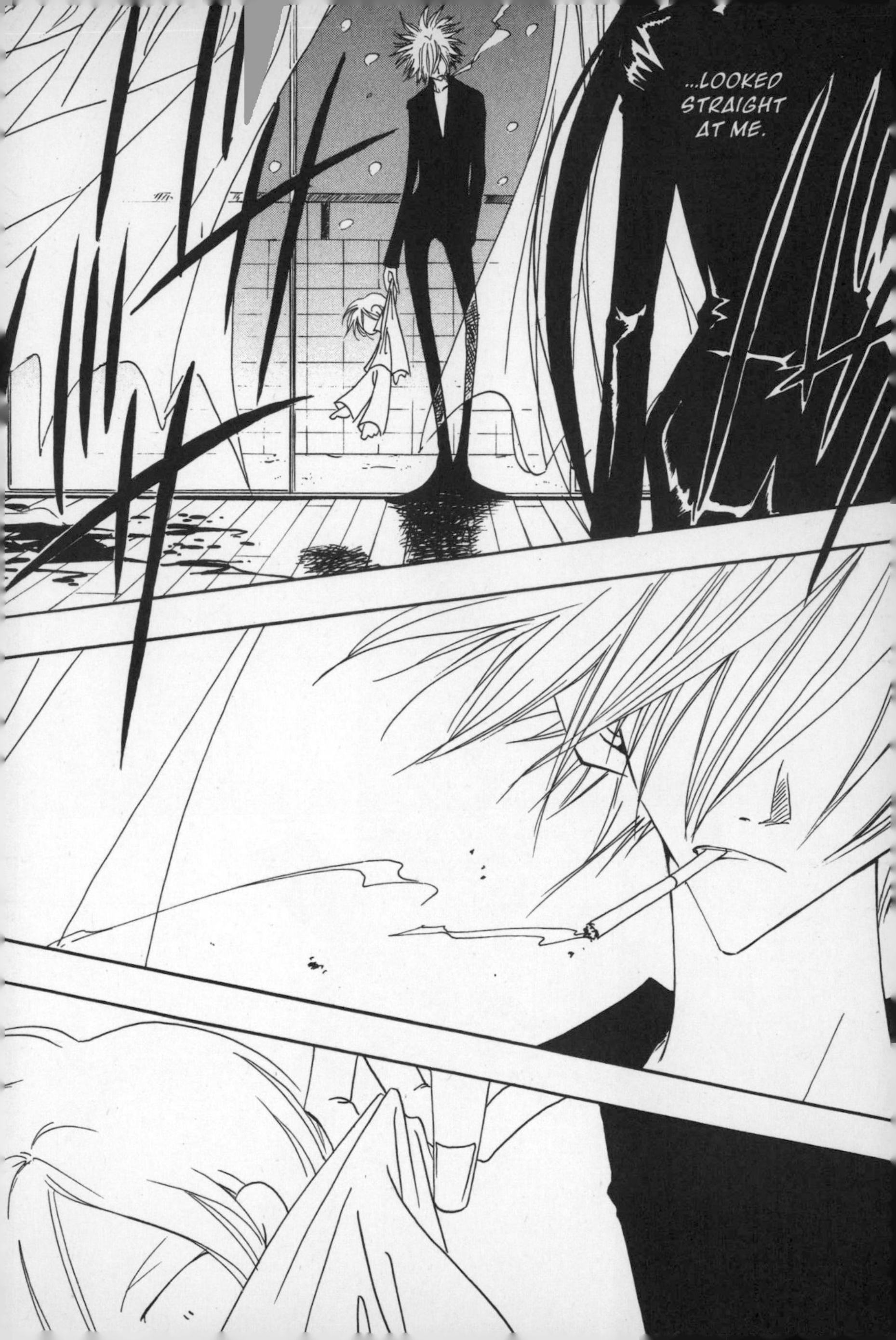
...LOOKED
STRAIGHT
AT ME.

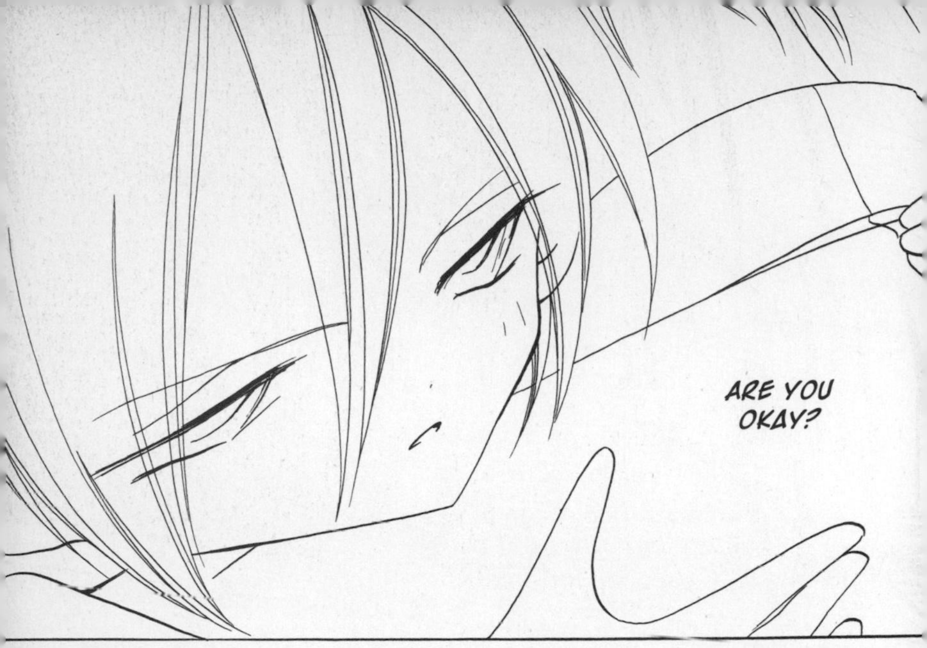
ARE YOU OKAY?
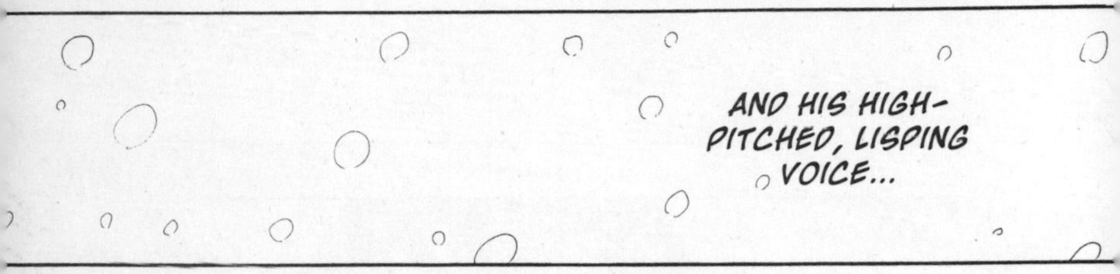
AND HIS HIGH-PITCHED, LISPING VOICE...
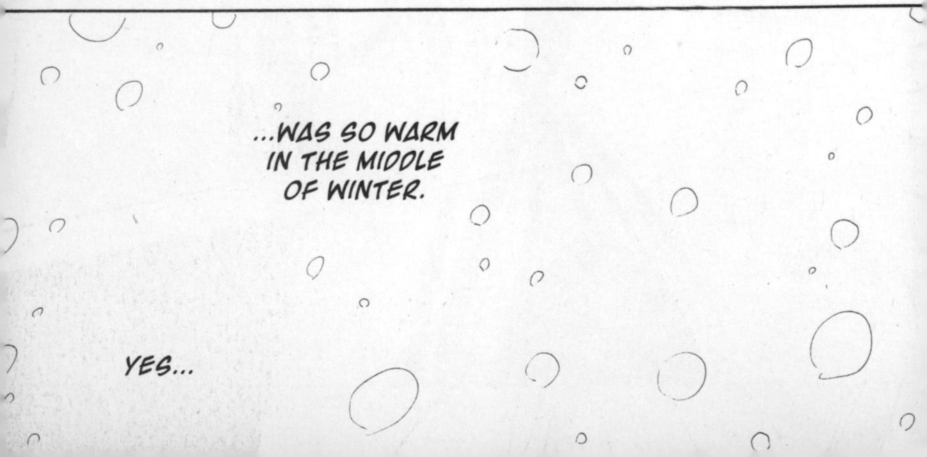
...WAS SO WARM IN THE MIDDLE OF WINTER.
YES...

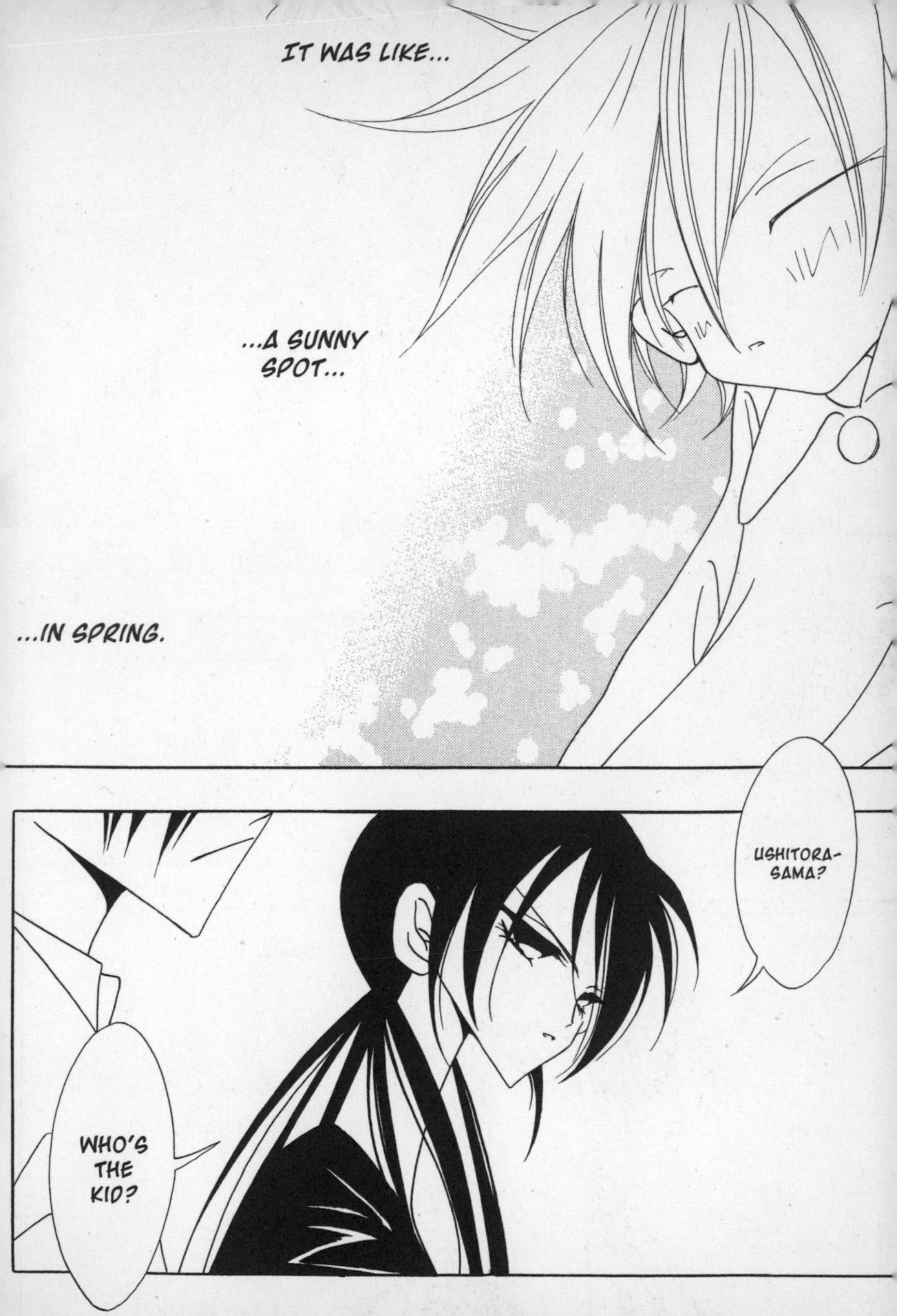
IT WAS LIKE...
...A SUNNY SPOT...
...IN SPRING.
USHITORA-SAMA?
WHO'S THE KID?

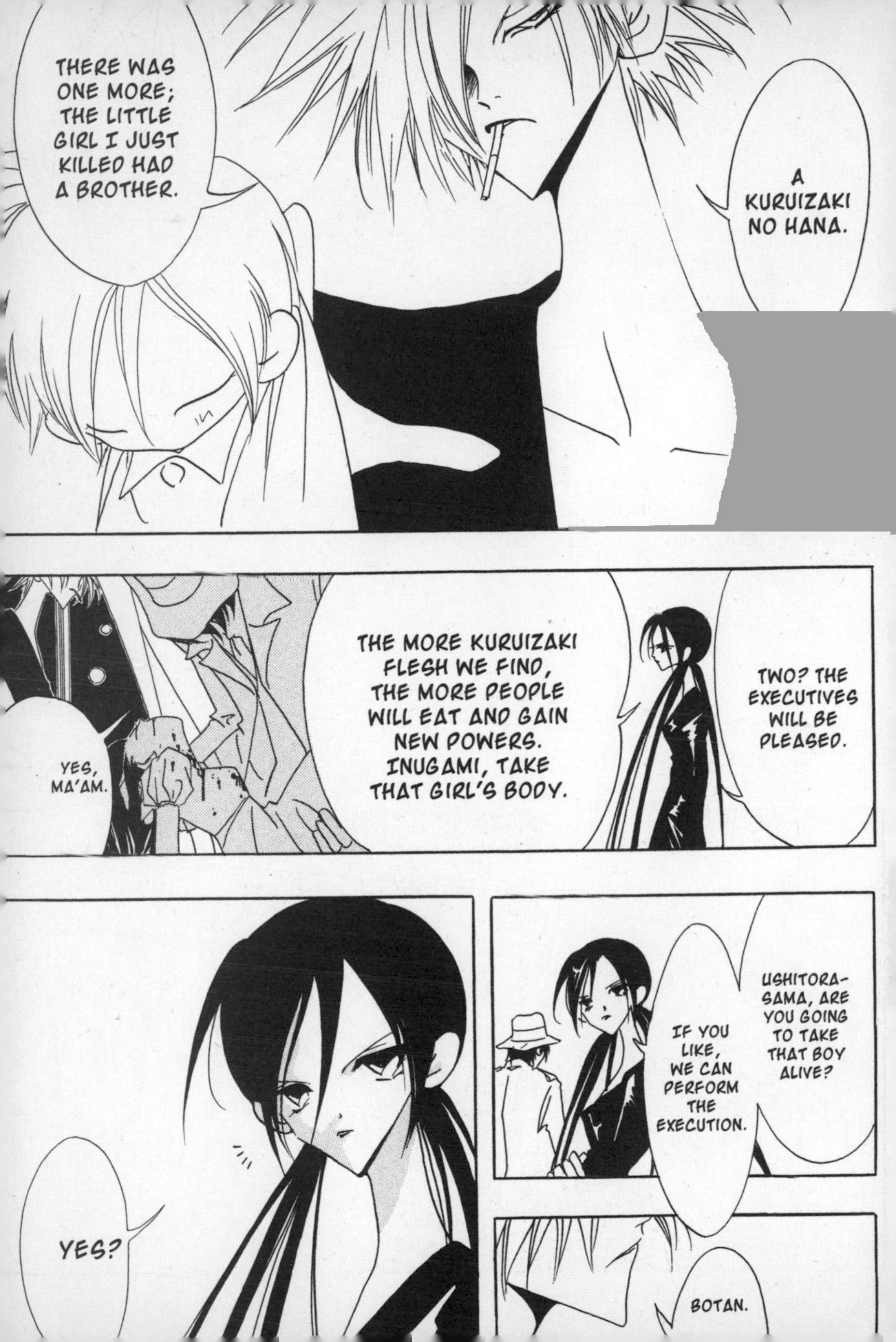
A KURUIZAKI NO HANA.
THERE WAS ONE MORE; THE LITTLE GIRL I JUST KILLED HAD A BROTHER.
TWO? THE EXECUTIVES WILL BE PLEASED.
THE MORE KURUIZAKI FLESH WE FIND, THE MORE PEOPLE WILL EAT AND GAIN NEW POWERS. INUGAMI, TAKE THAT GIRL'S BODY.
YES, MA'AM.
USHITORA-SAMA, ARE YOU GOING TO TAKE THAT BOY ALIVE?
IF YOU LIKE, WE CAN PERFORM THE EXECUTION.
BOTAN.
YES?

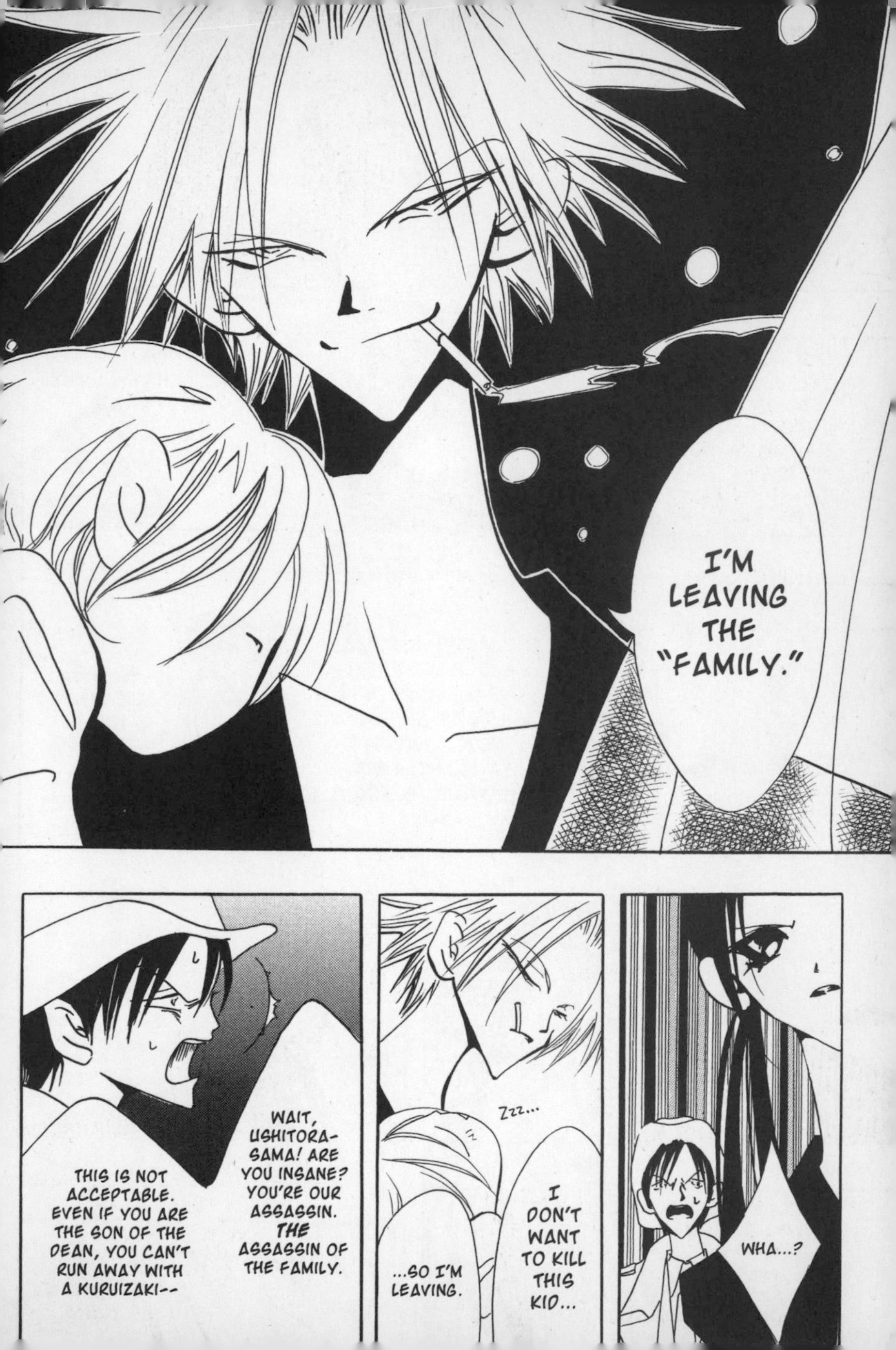
I'M LEAVING THE "FAMILY."
WHA...?
Zzz...
I DON'T WANT TO KILL THIS KID...
...SO I'M LEAVING.
WAIT, USHITORA-SAMA! ARE YOU INSANE? YOU'RE OUR ASSASSIN. *THE* ASSASSIN OF THE FAMILY.
THIS IS NOT ACCEPTABLE. EVEN IF YOU ARE THE SON OF THE DEAN, YOU CAN'T RUN AWAY WITH A KURUIZAKI--

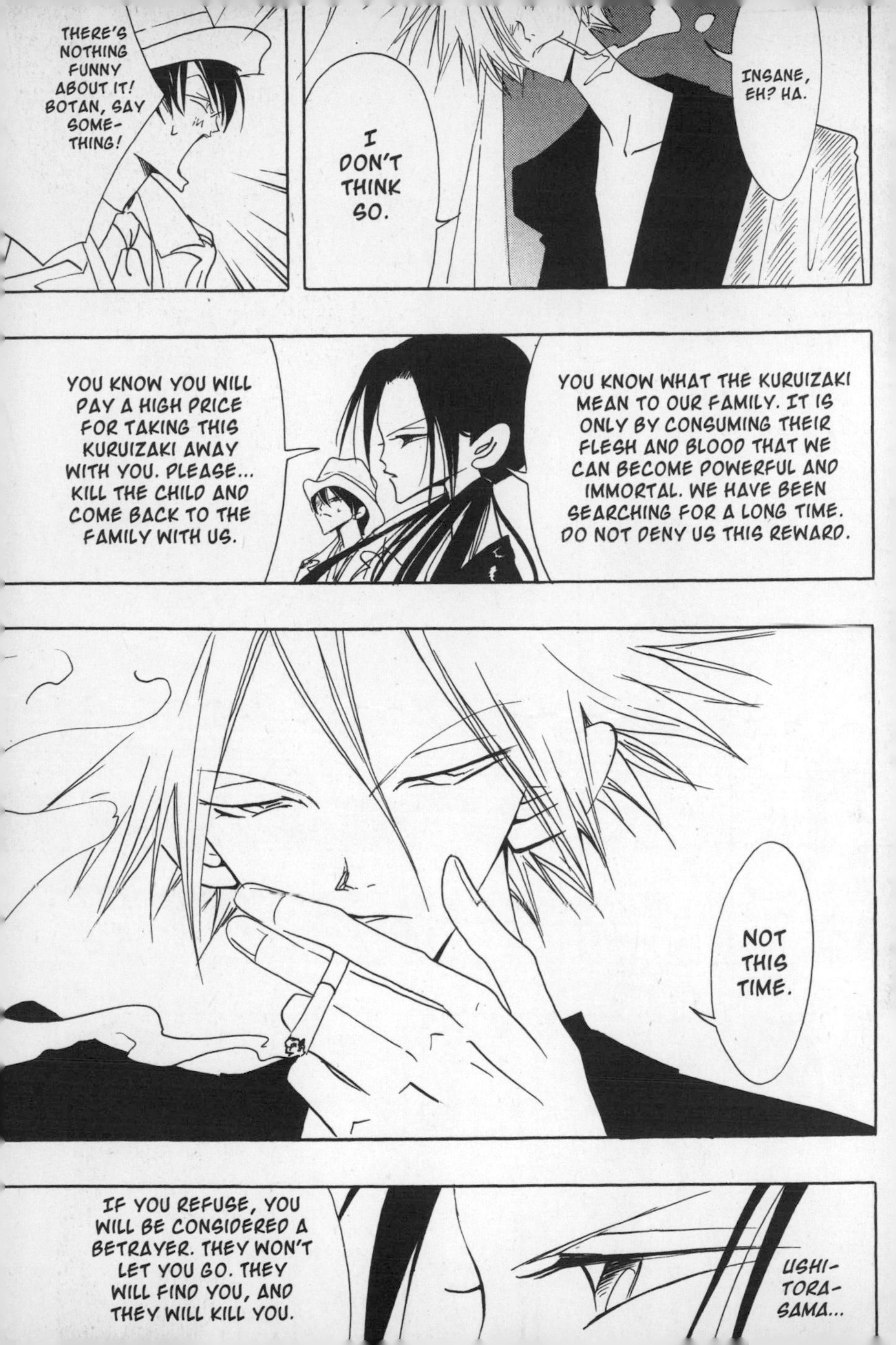
INSANE, EH? HA.
I DON'T THINK SO.
THERE'S NOTHING FUNNY ABOUT IT! BOTAN, SAY SOME-THING!
YOU KNOW WHAT THE KURUIZAKI MEAN TO OUR FAMILY. IT IS ONLY BY CONSUMING THEIR FLESH AND BLOOD THAT WE CAN BECOME POWERFUL AND IMMORTAL. WE HAVE BEEN SEARCHING FOR A LONG TIME. DO NOT DENY US THIS REWARD.
YOU KNOW YOU WILL PAY A HIGH PRICE FOR TAKING THIS KURUIZAKI AWAY WITH YOU. PLEASE... KILL THE CHILD AND COME BACK TO THE FAMILY WITH US.
NOT THIS TIME.
USHI-TORA-SAMA...
IF YOU REFUSE, YOU WILL BE CONSIDERED A BETRAYER. THEY WON'T LET YOU GO. THEY WILL FIND YOU, AND THEY WILL KILL YOU.

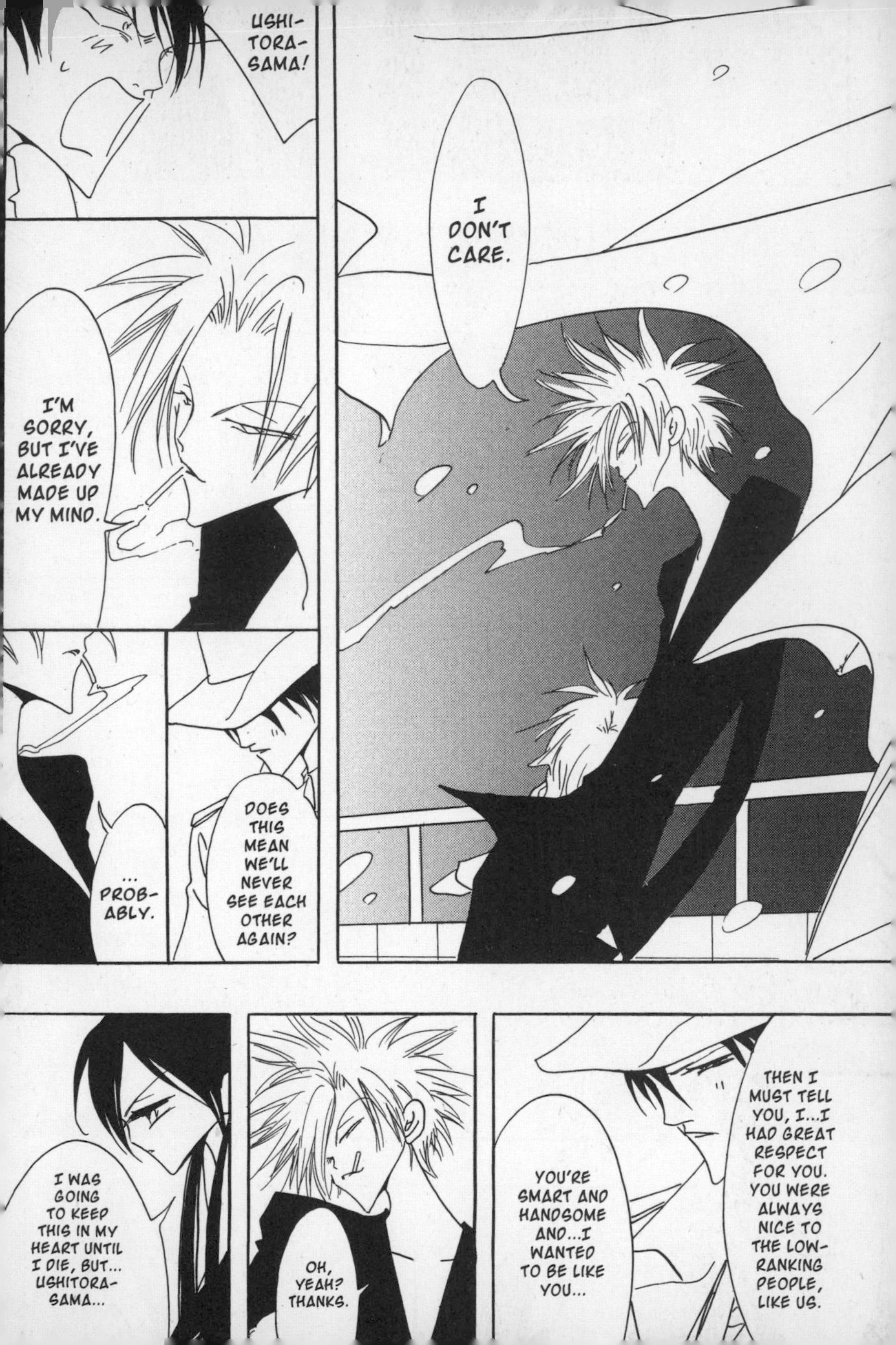
I DON'T CARE.
USHITORA-SAMA!
I'M SORRY, BUT I'VE ALREADY MADE UP MY MIND.
DOES THIS MEAN WE'LL NEVER SEE EACH OTHER AGAIN?
... PROBABLY.
THEN I MUST TELL YOU, I...I HAD GREAT RESPECT FOR YOU. YOU WERE ALWAYS NICE TO THE LOW-RANKING PEOPLE, LIKE US.
YOU'RE SMART AND HANDSOME AND...I WANTED TO BE LIKE YOU...
OH, YEAH? THANKS.
I WAS GOING TO KEEP THIS IN MY HEART UNTIL I DIE, BUT... USHITORA-SAMA...

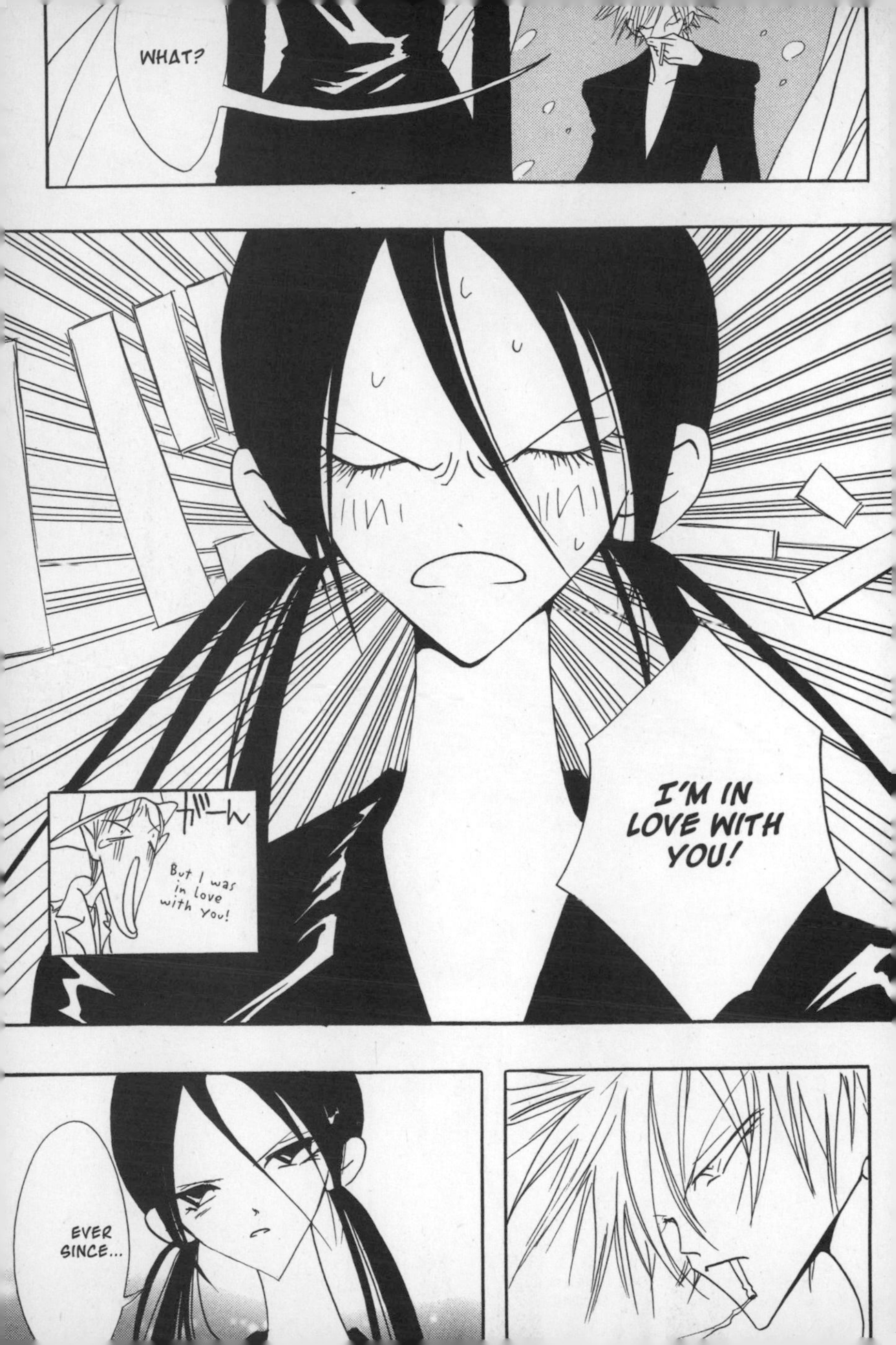
WHAT?
I'M IN LOVE WITH YOU!
がーん
But I was in love with you!
EVER SINCE...

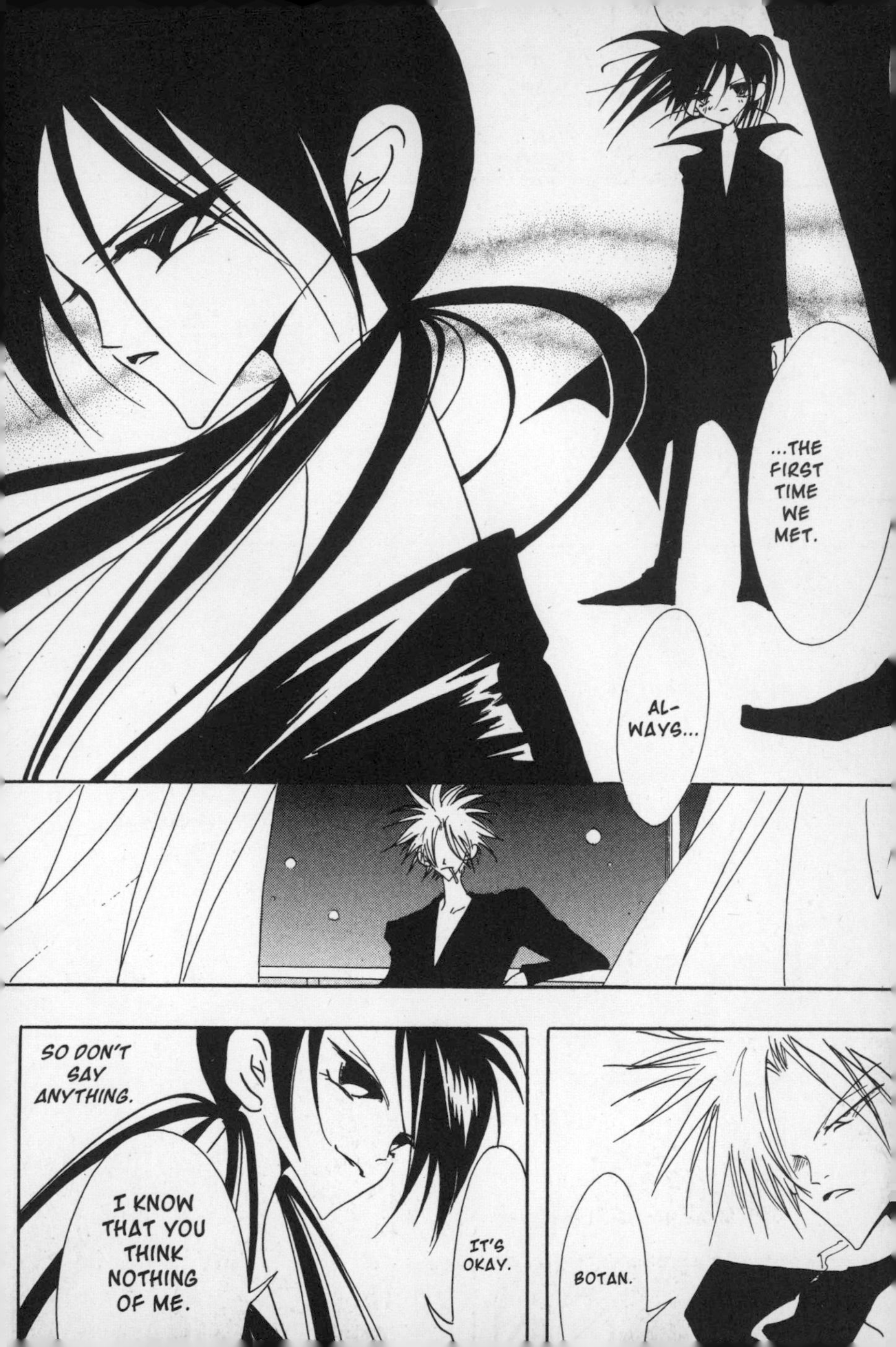
...THE FIRST TIME WE MET.
AL-WAYS...
BOTAN.
IT'S OKAY.
I KNOW THAT YOU THINK NOTHING OF ME.
SO DON'T SAY ANYTHING.

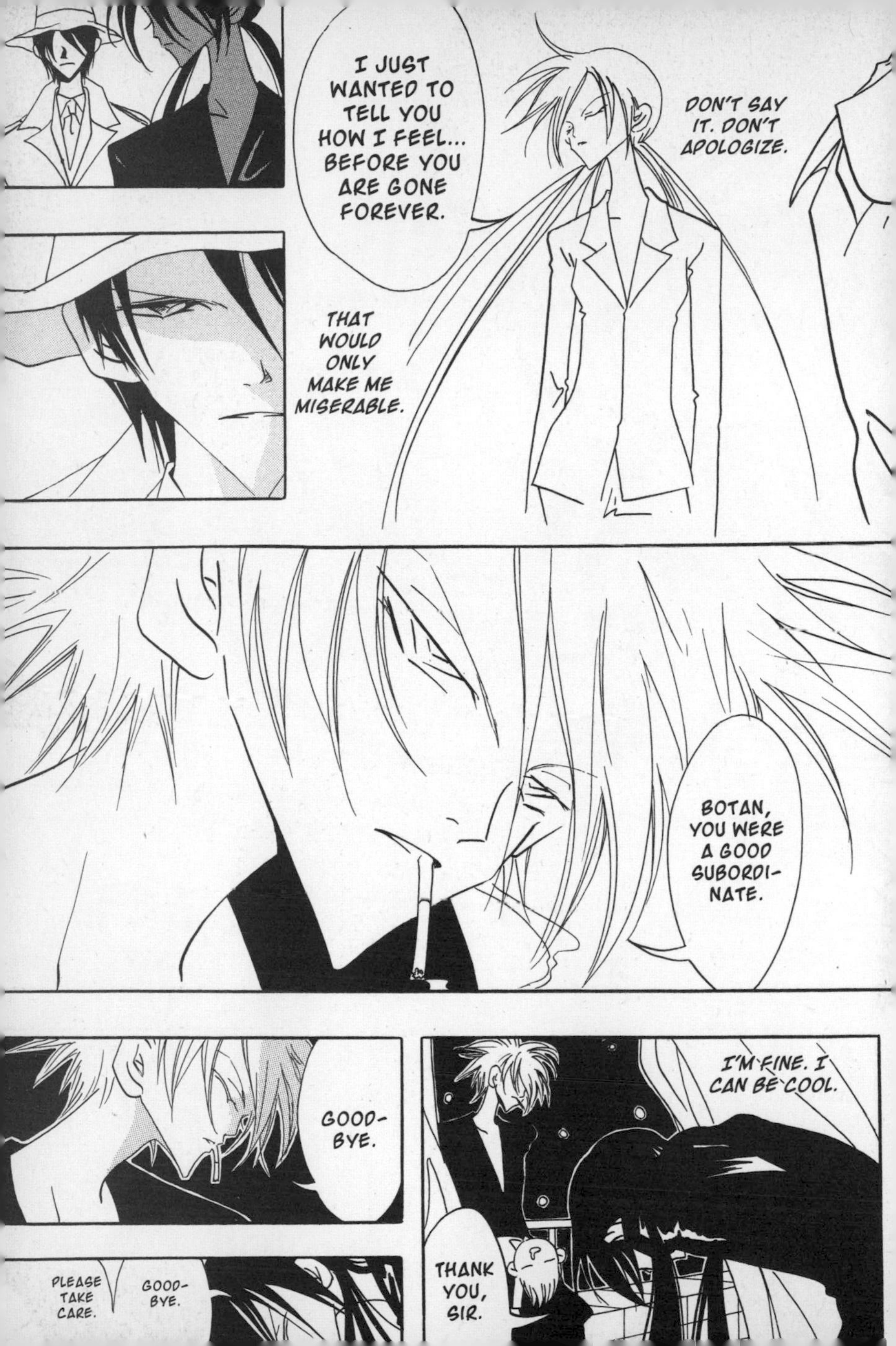
I JUST WANTED TO TELL YOU HOW I FEEL... BEFORE YOU ARE GONE FOREVER.
DON'T SAY IT. DON'T APOLOGIZE.
THAT WOULD ONLY MAKE ME MISERABLE.
BOTAN, YOU WERE A GOOD SUBORDI-NATE.
I'M FINE. I CAN BE COOL.
THANK YOU, SIR.
GOOD-BYE.
GOOD-BYE.
PLEASE TAKE CARE.

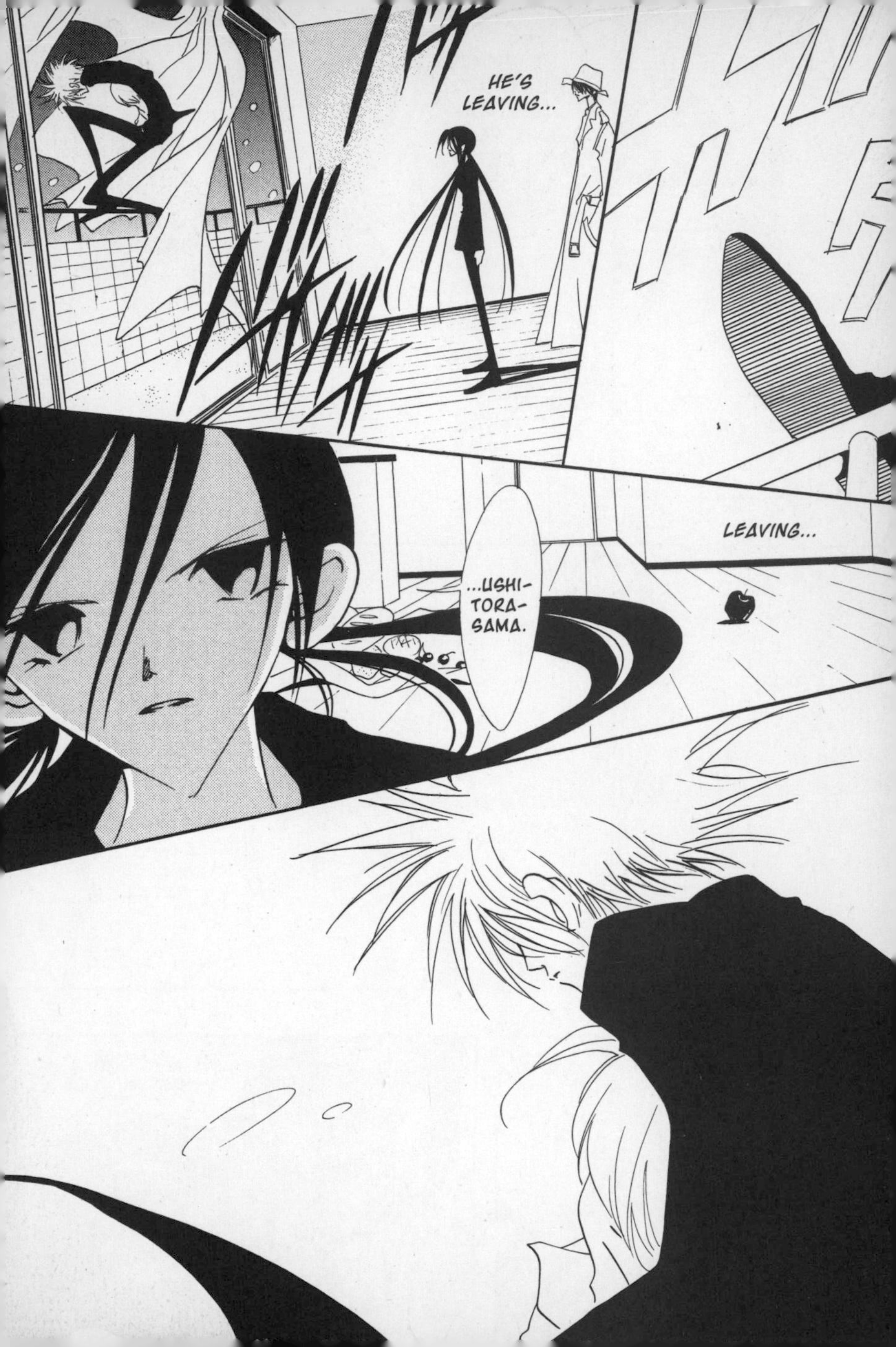

HE'S LEAVING...
LEAVING...
...USHI-TORA-SAMA.

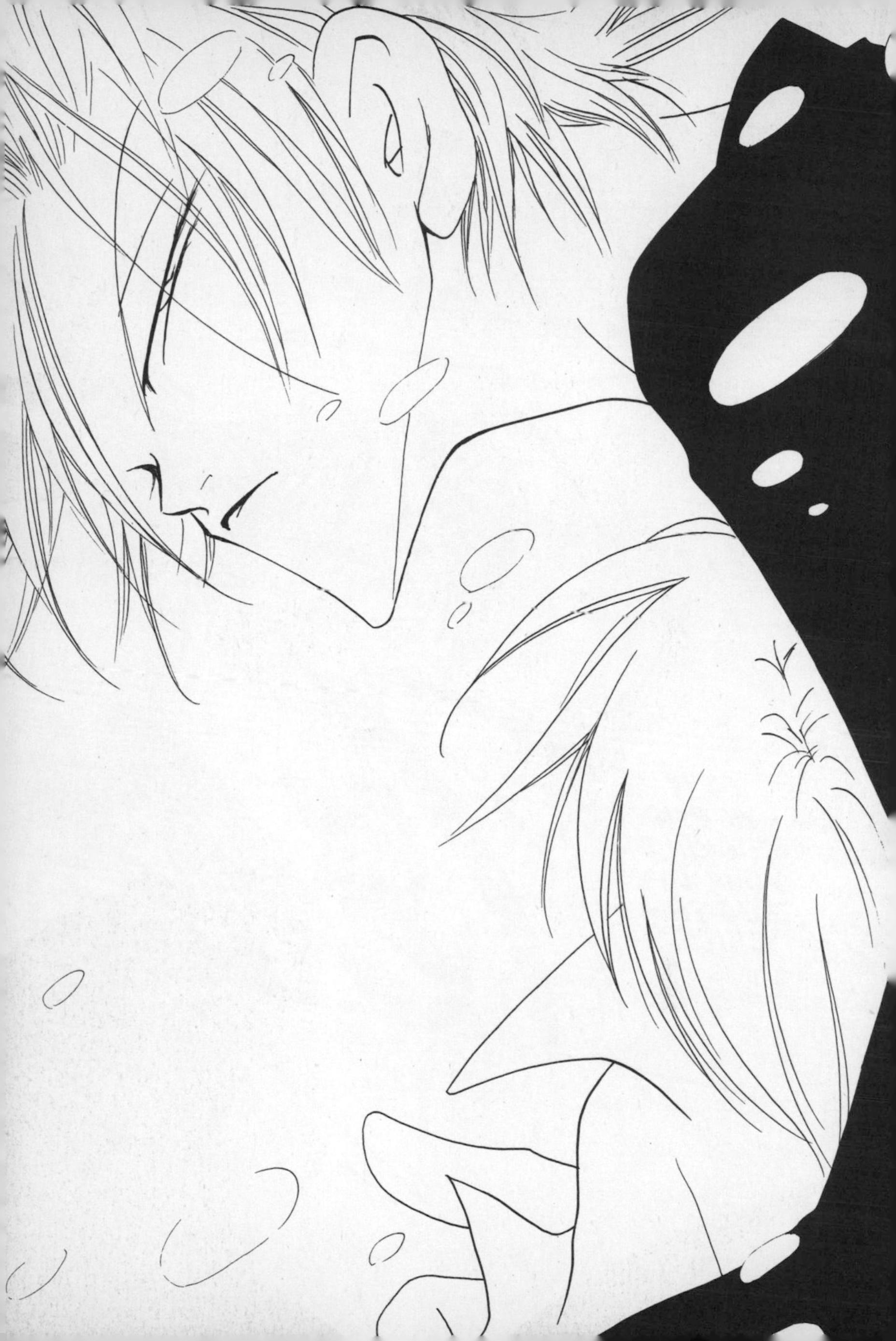

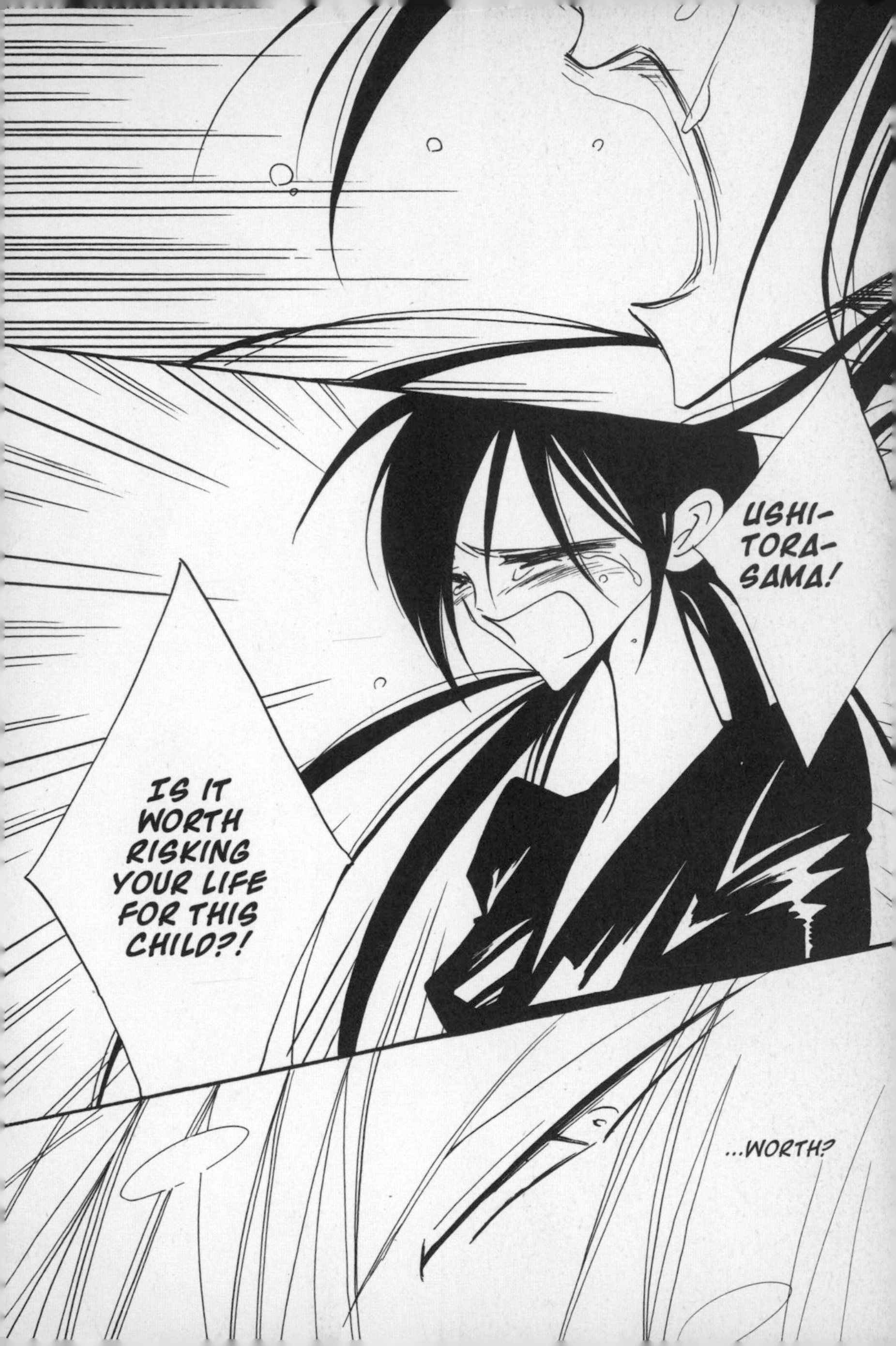
USHI-TORA-SAMA!
IS IT WORTH RISKING YOUR LIFE FOR THIS CHILD?!
...WORTH?

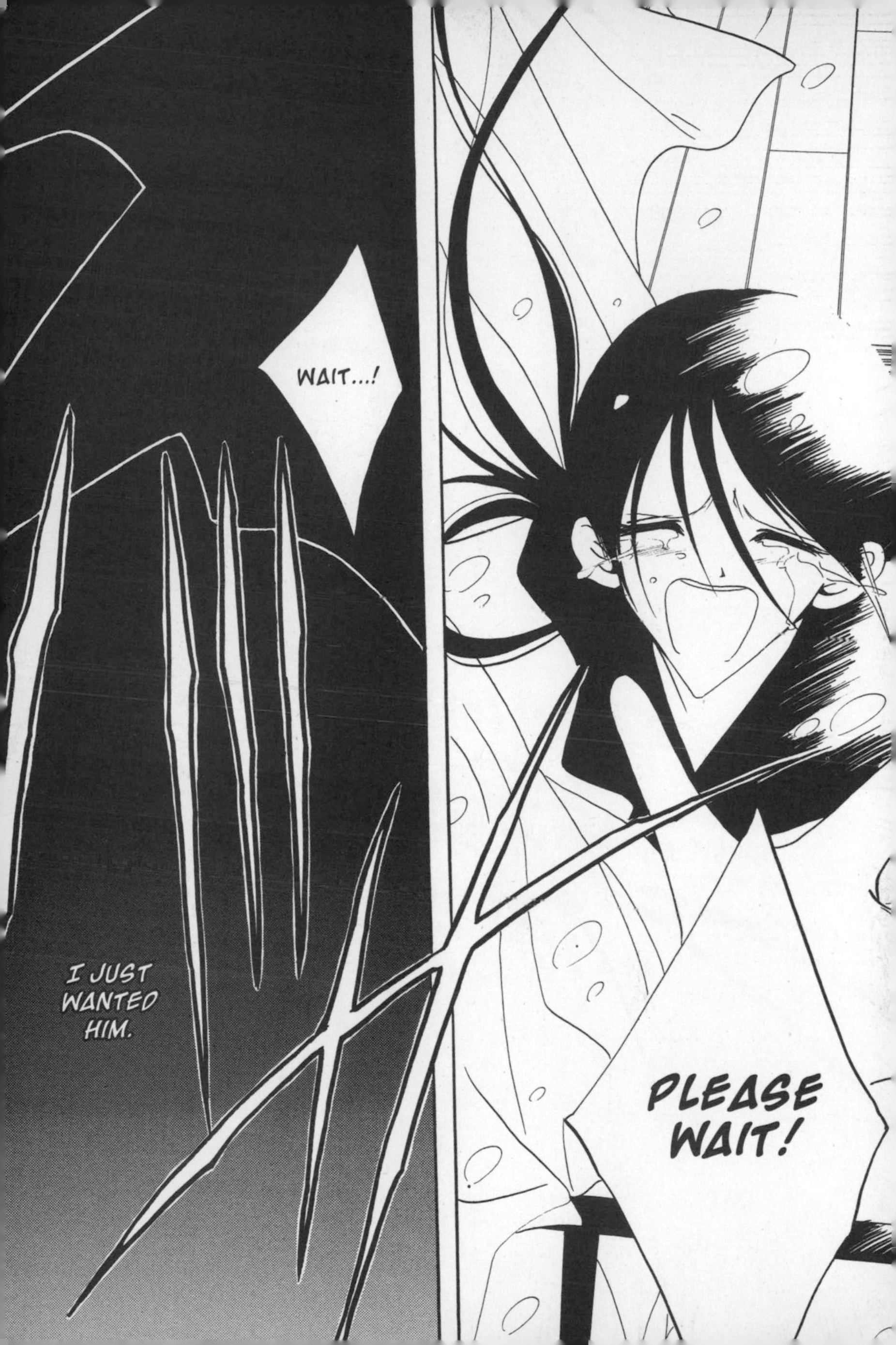
PLEASE WAIT!
WAIT...!
I JUST WANTED HIM.

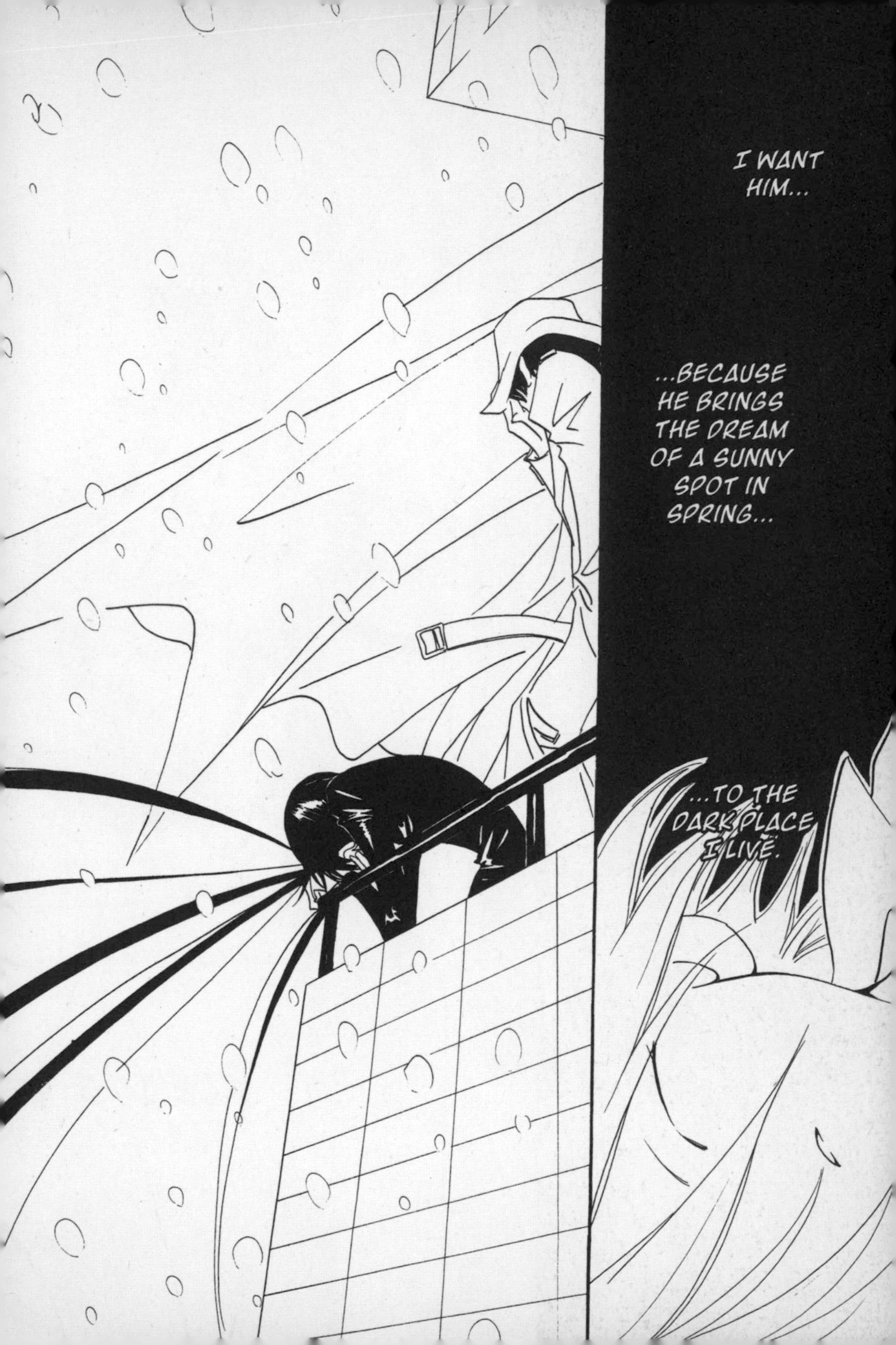
I WANT HIM...
...BECAUSE HE BRINGS THE DREAM OF A SUNNY SPOT IN SPRING...
...TO THE DARK PLACE I LIVE.

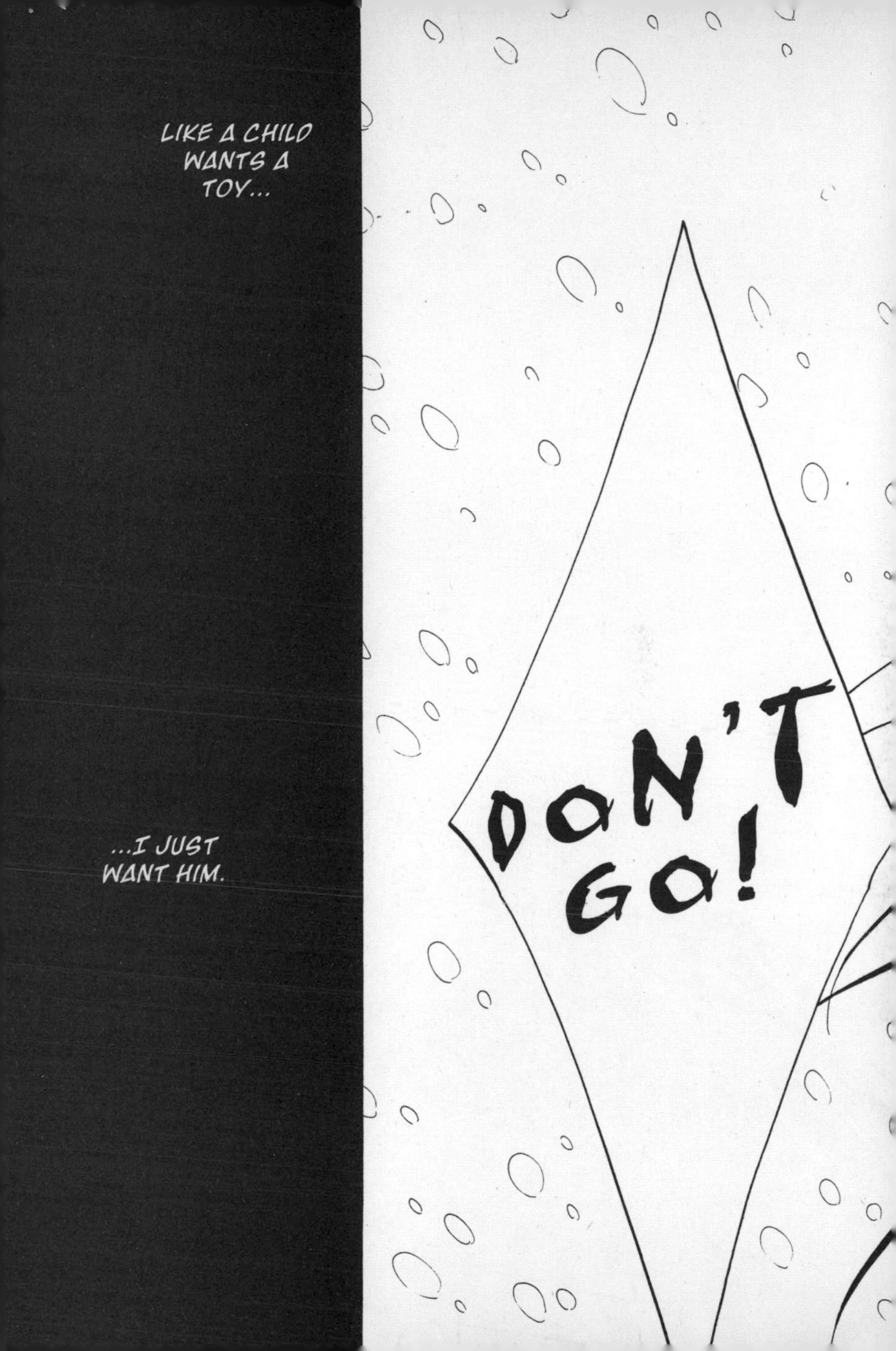
DON'T GO!
LIKE A CHILD WANTS A TOY...
...I JUST WANT HIM.

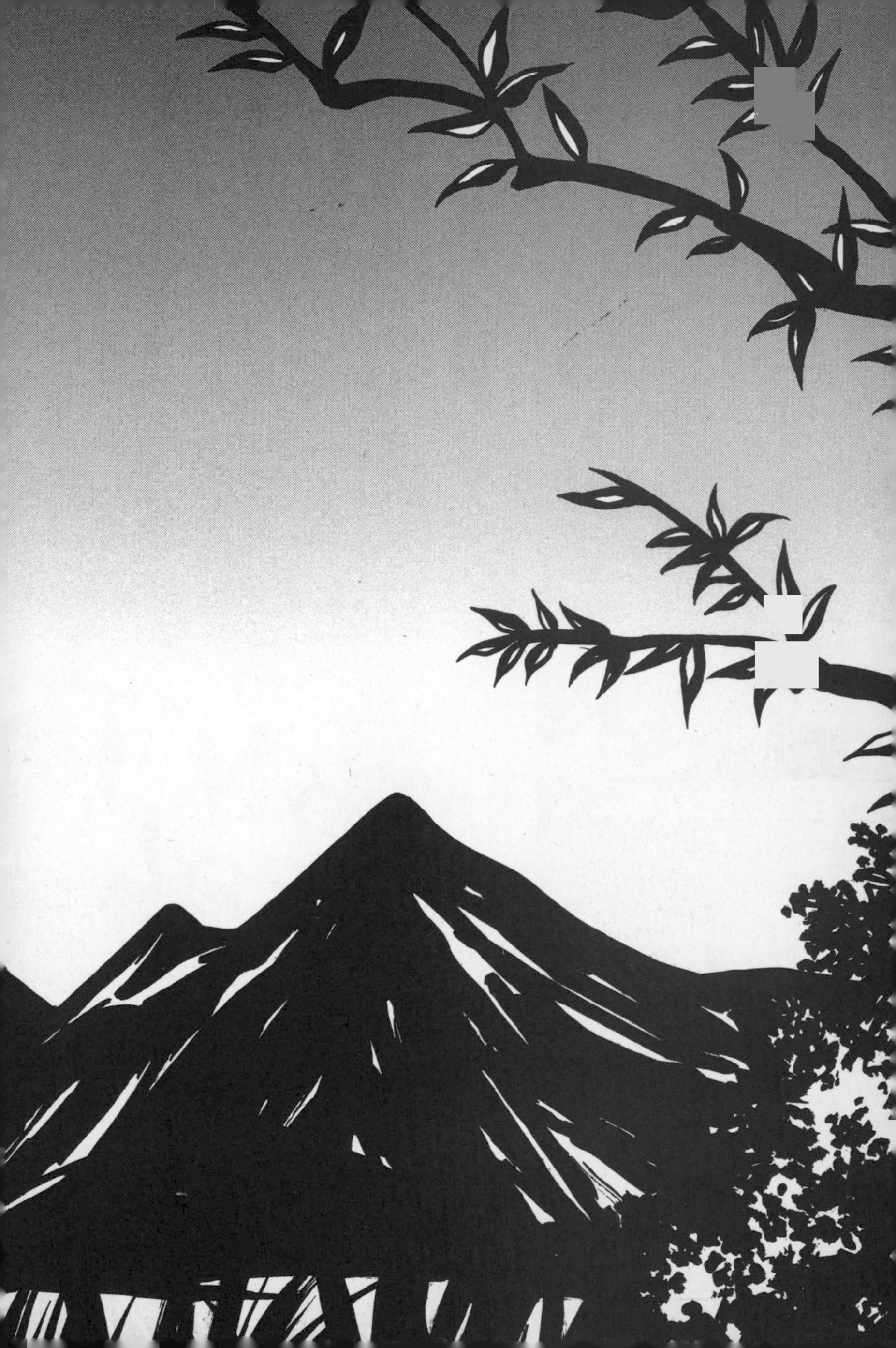

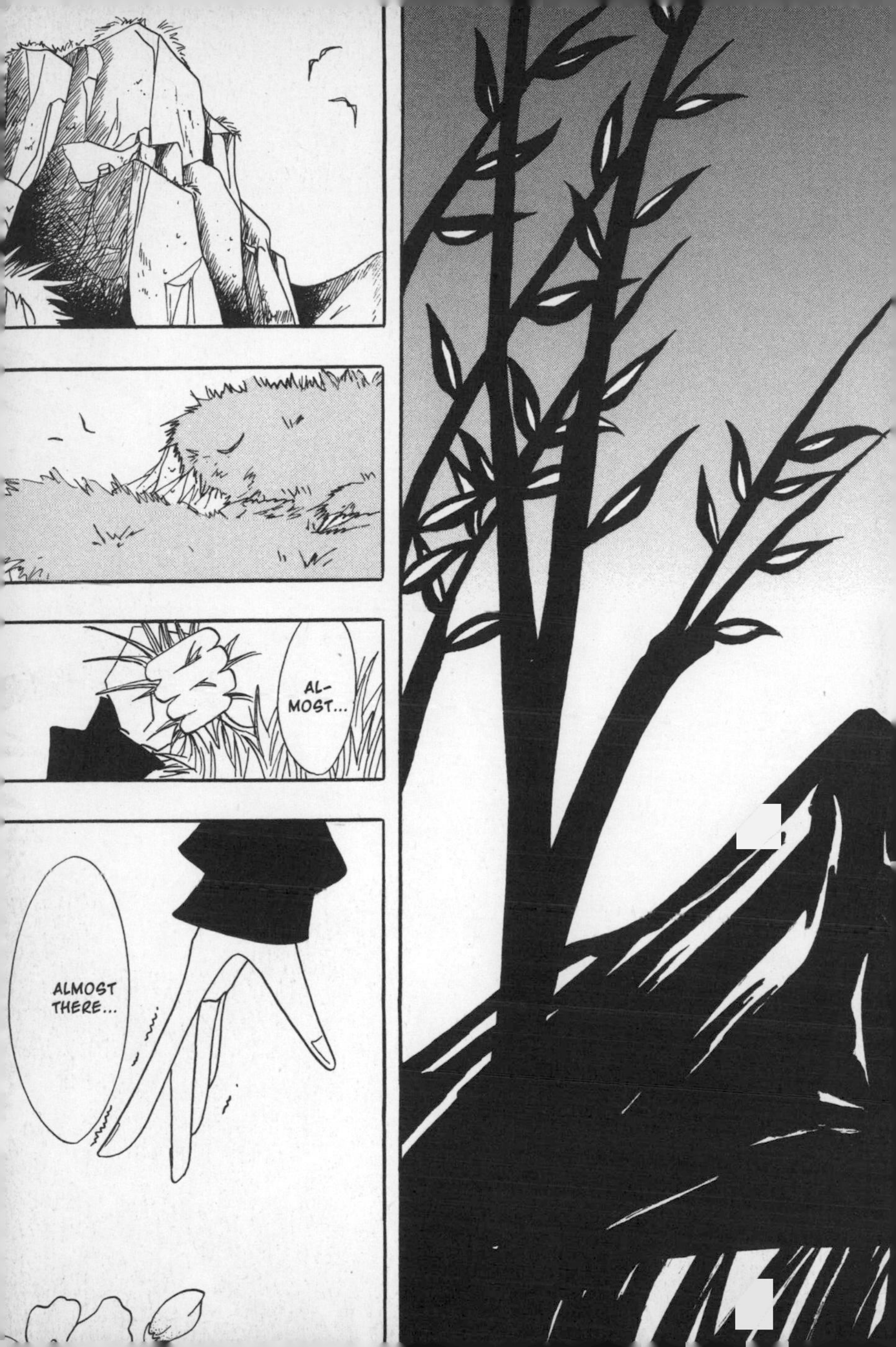
AL-
MOST...
ALMOST
THERE...

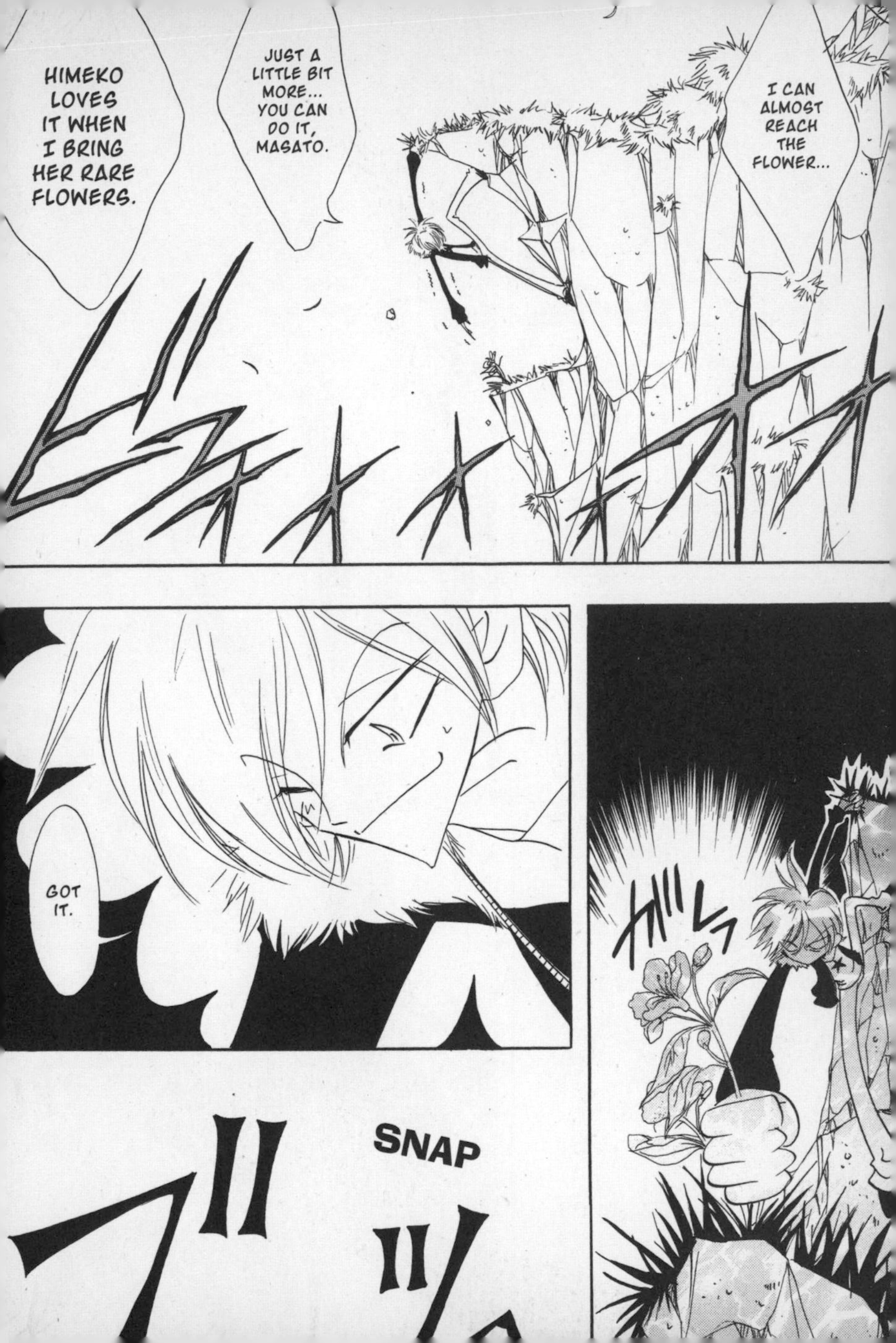
I CAN ALMOST REACH THE FLOWER...
JUST A LITTLE BIT MORE... YOU CAN DO IT, MASATO.
HIMEKO LOVES IT WHEN I BRING HER RARE FLOWERS.
GOT IT.
SNAP

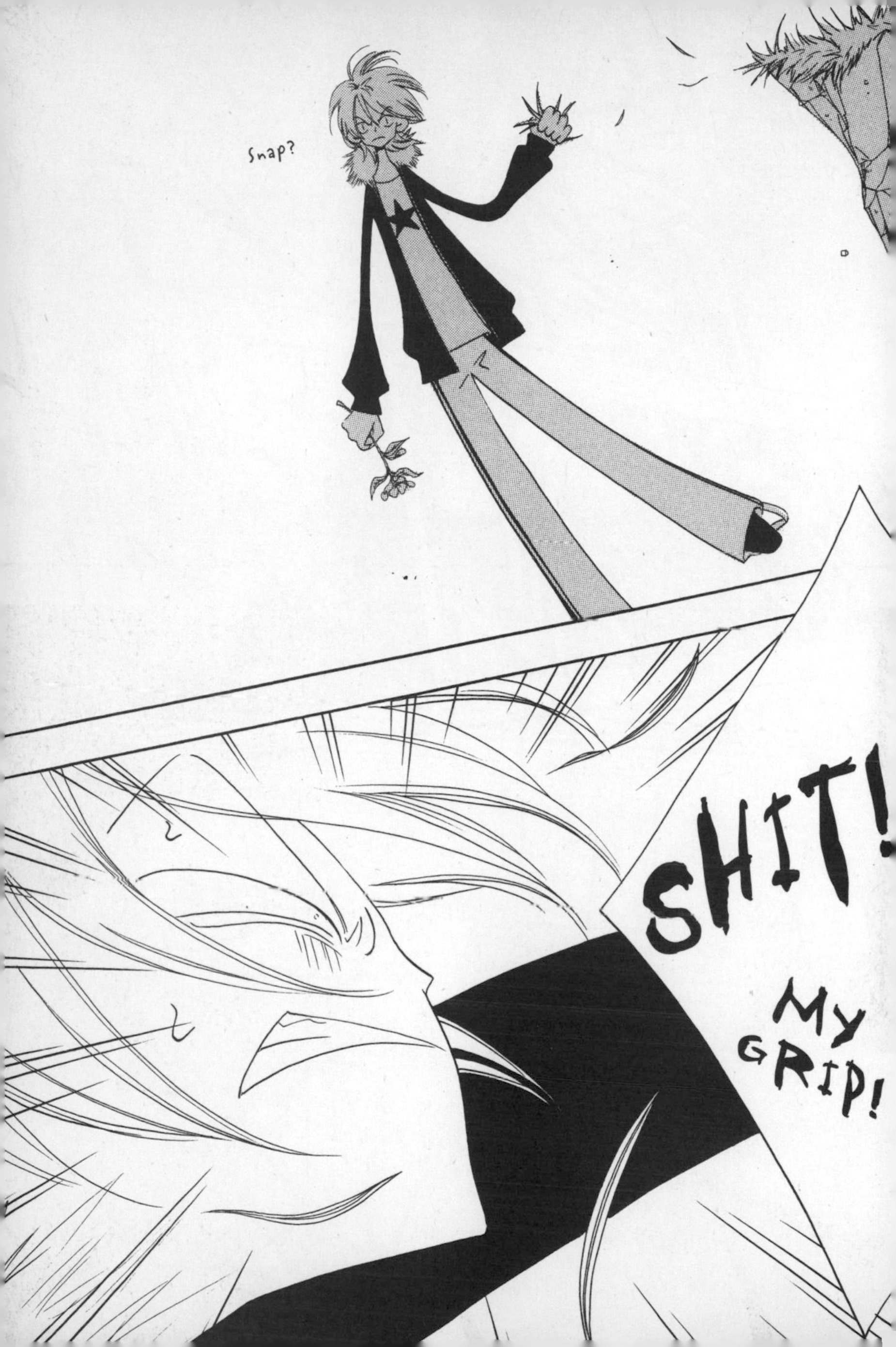
Snap?
...
SHIT!
MY GRIP!

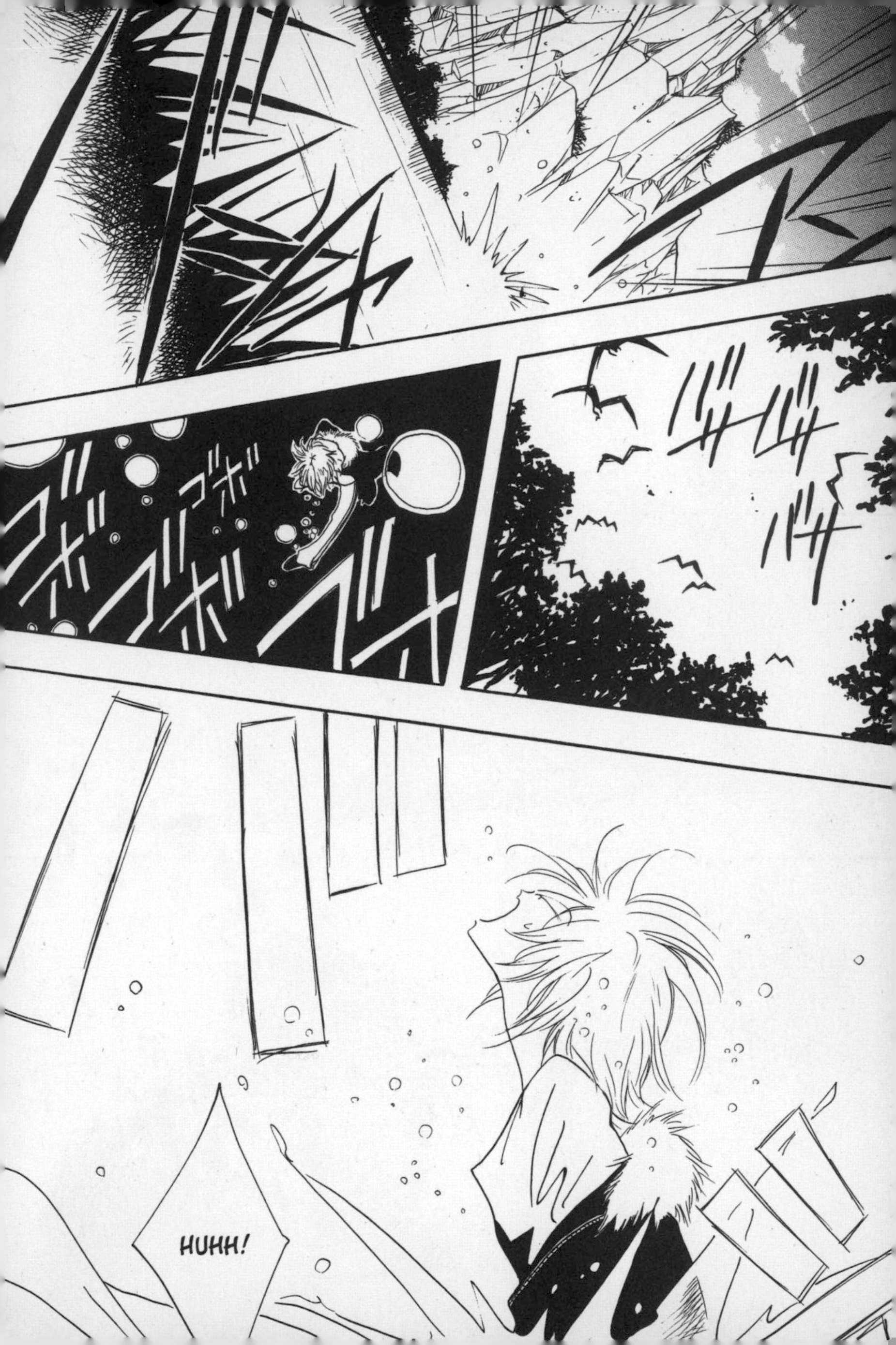
バサバサ
バサ
ゴボゴボ
ゴボゴボ
ゴボ
HUHH!

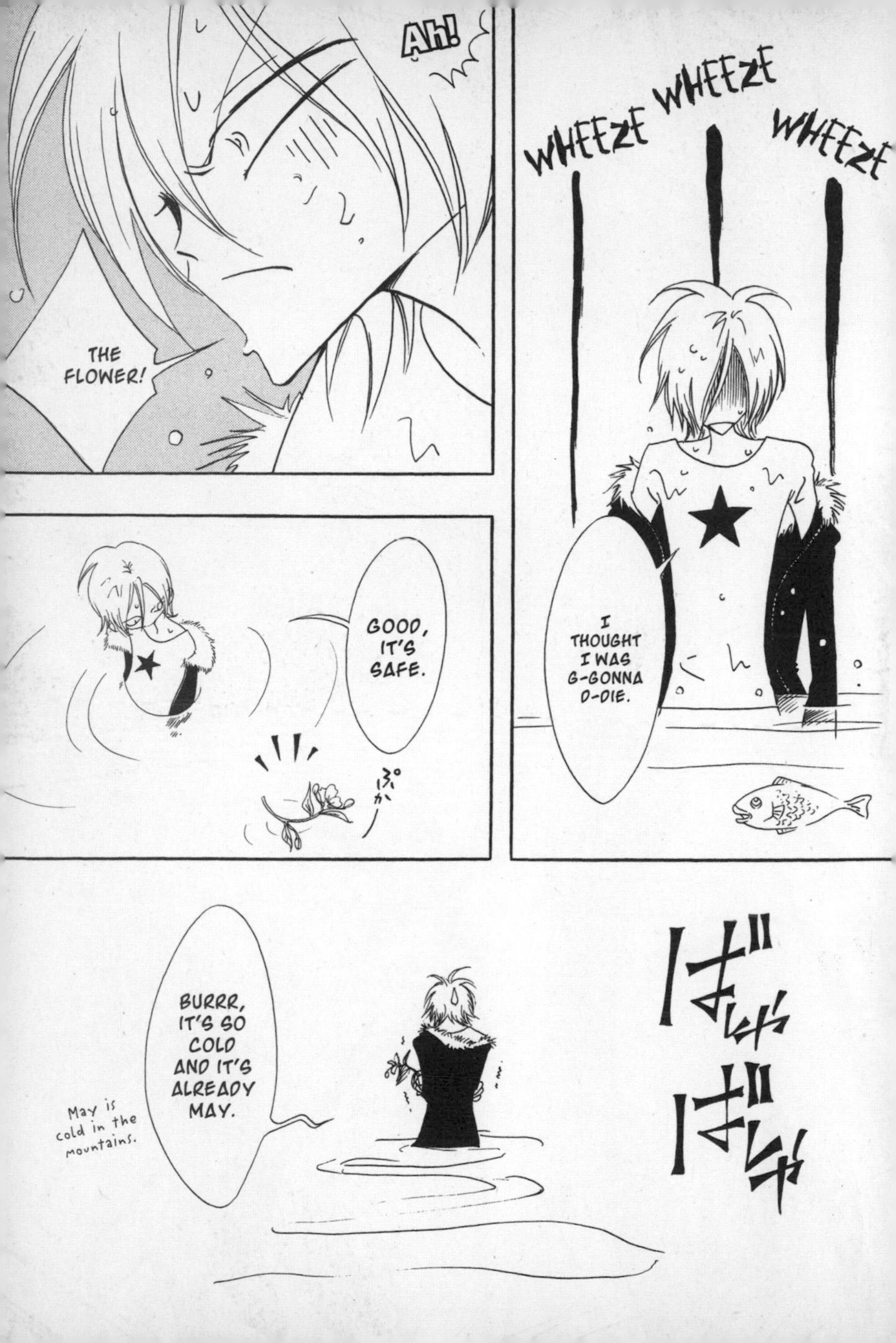

WHEEZE WHEEZE WHEEZE
I THOUGHT I WAS G-GONNA D-DIE.
Ah!
THE FLOWER!
GOOD, IT'S SAFE.
ぷか
ばしゃばしゃ
BURRR, IT'S SO COLD AND IT'S ALREADY MAY.
May is cold in the mountains.

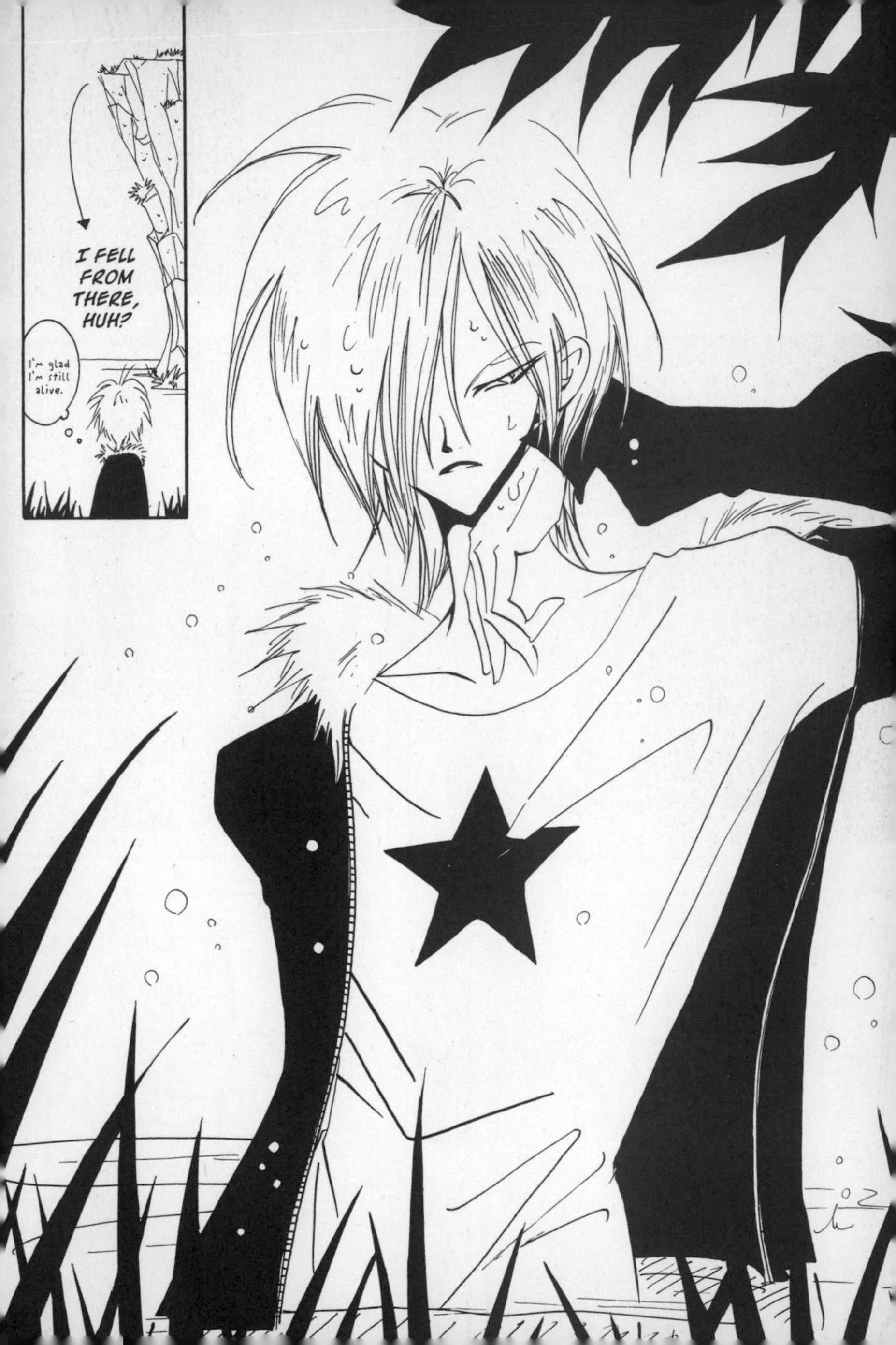
I FELL FROM THERE, HUH?
I'm glad I'm still alive.

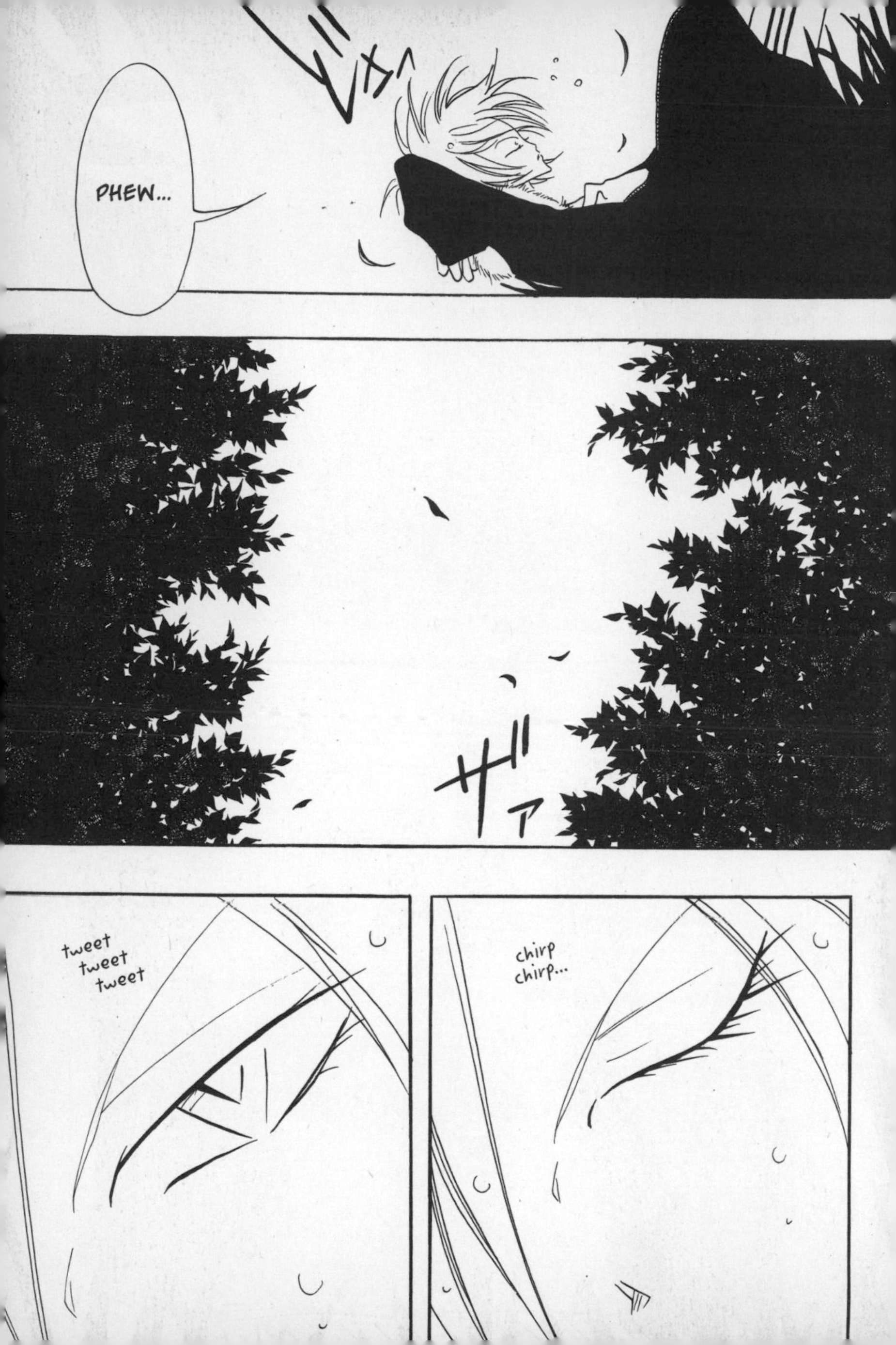
PHEW...
chirp chirp...
tweet tweet tweet

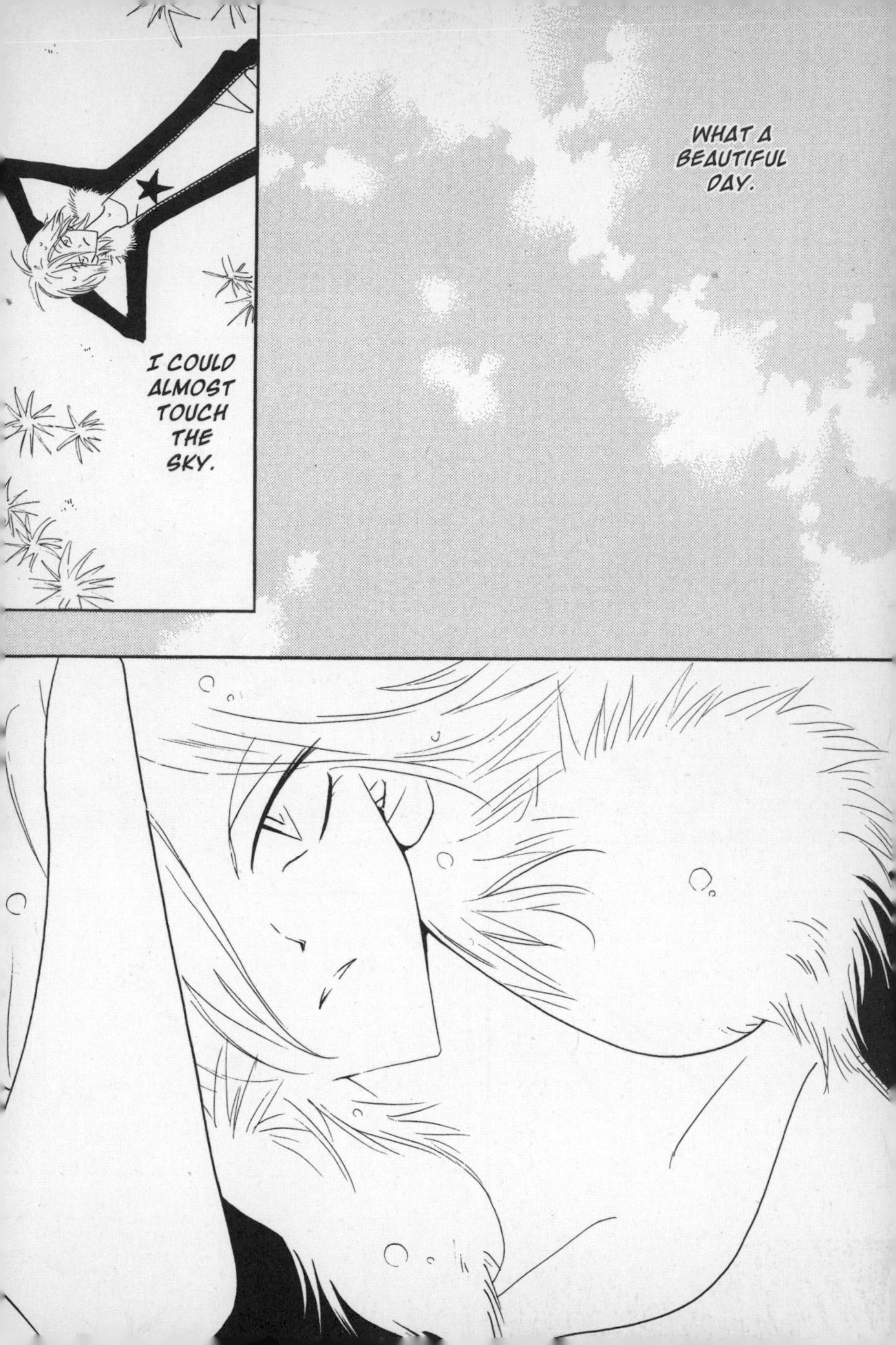
WHAT A BEAUTIFUL DAY.
I COULD ALMOST TOUCH THE SKY.

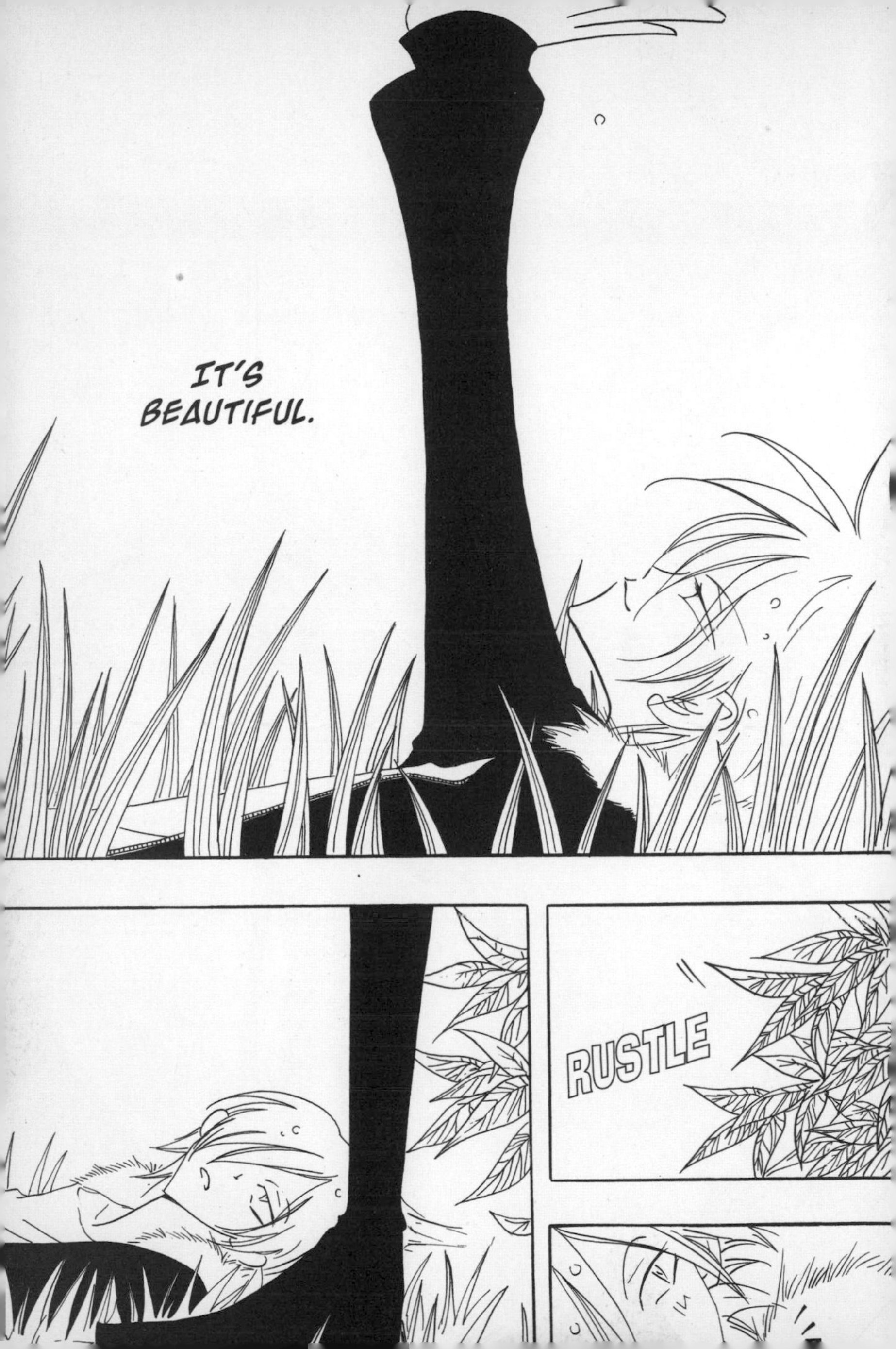
IT'S BEAUTIFUL.
RUSTLE

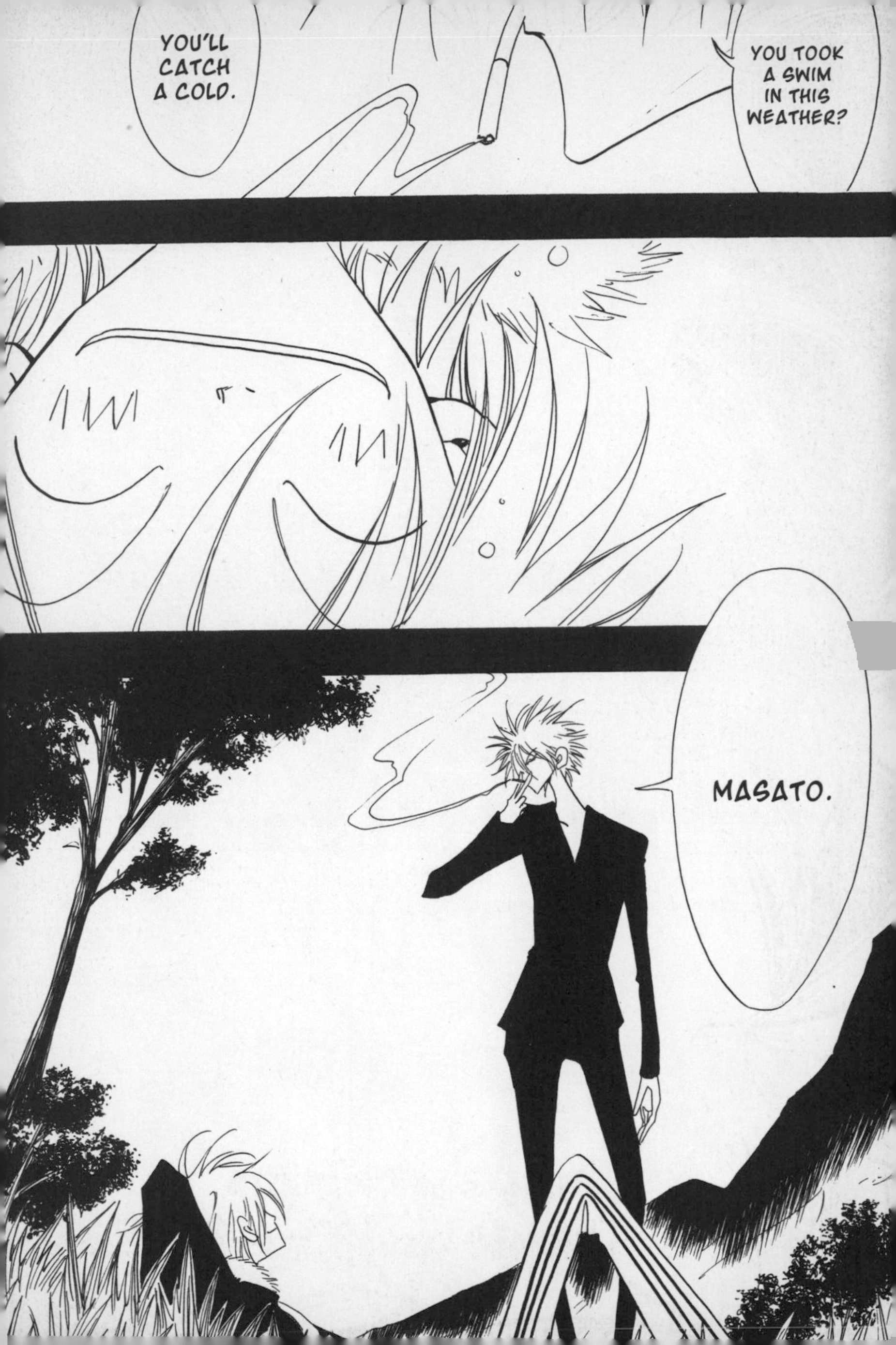
YOU TOOK A SWIM IN THIS WEATHER?
YOU'LL CATCH A COLD.
MASATO.

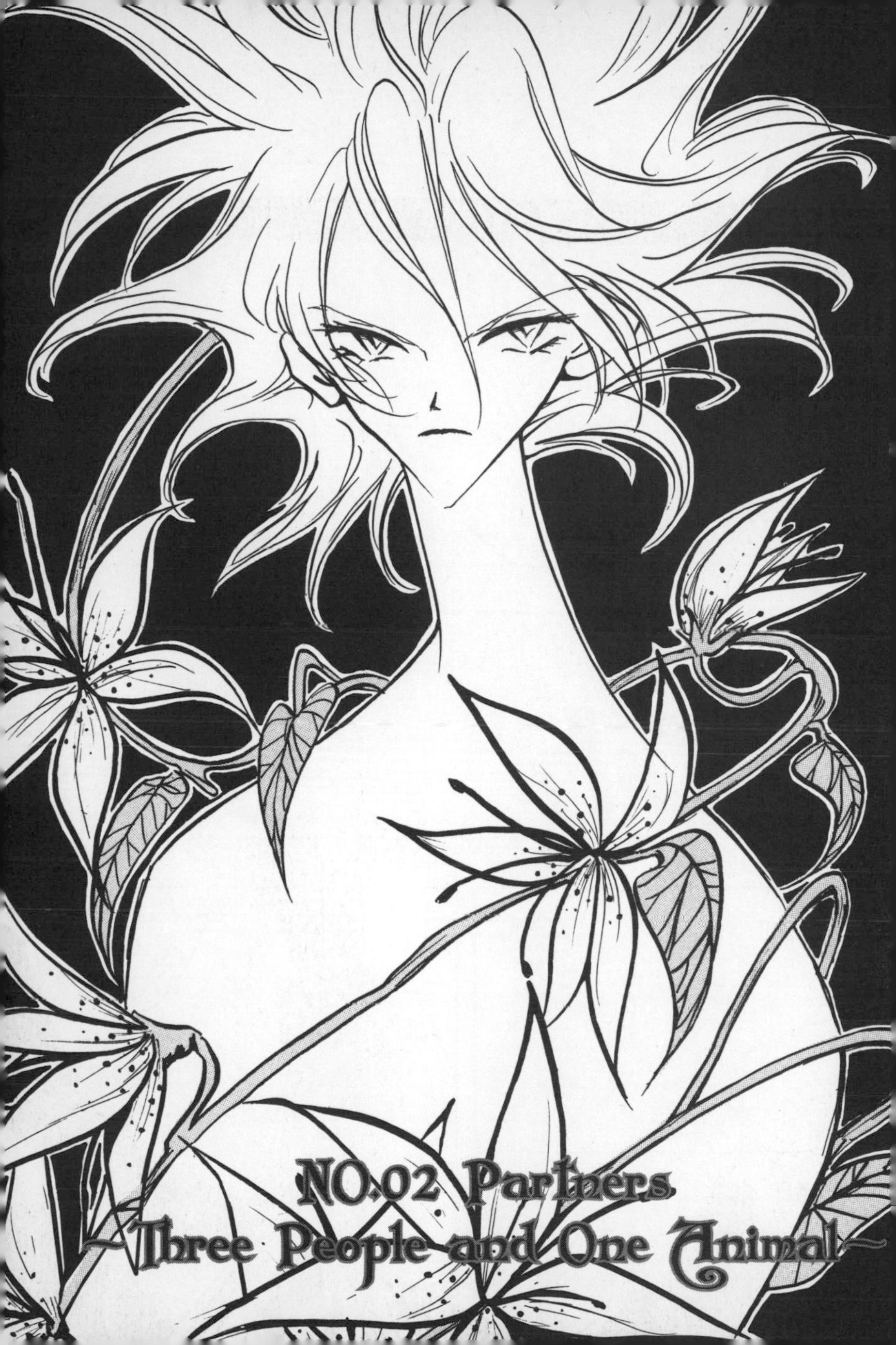
NO.02 Partners
~Three People and One Animal~

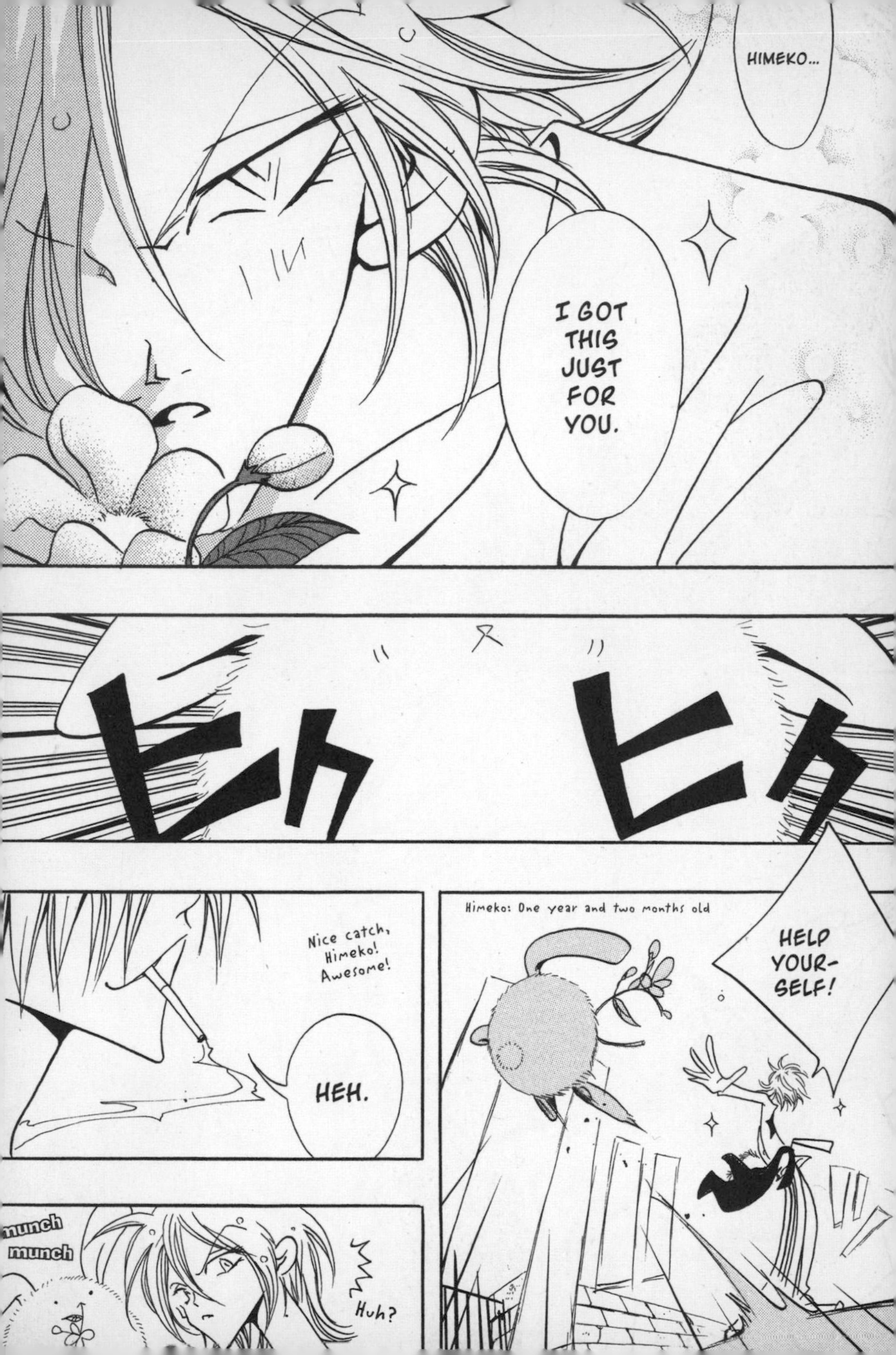
HIMEKO...
I GOT THIS JUST FOR YOU.
ヒクヒク
Himeko: One year and two months old
HELP YOURSELF!
Nice catch, Himeko! Awesome!
HEH.
munch munch
Huh?

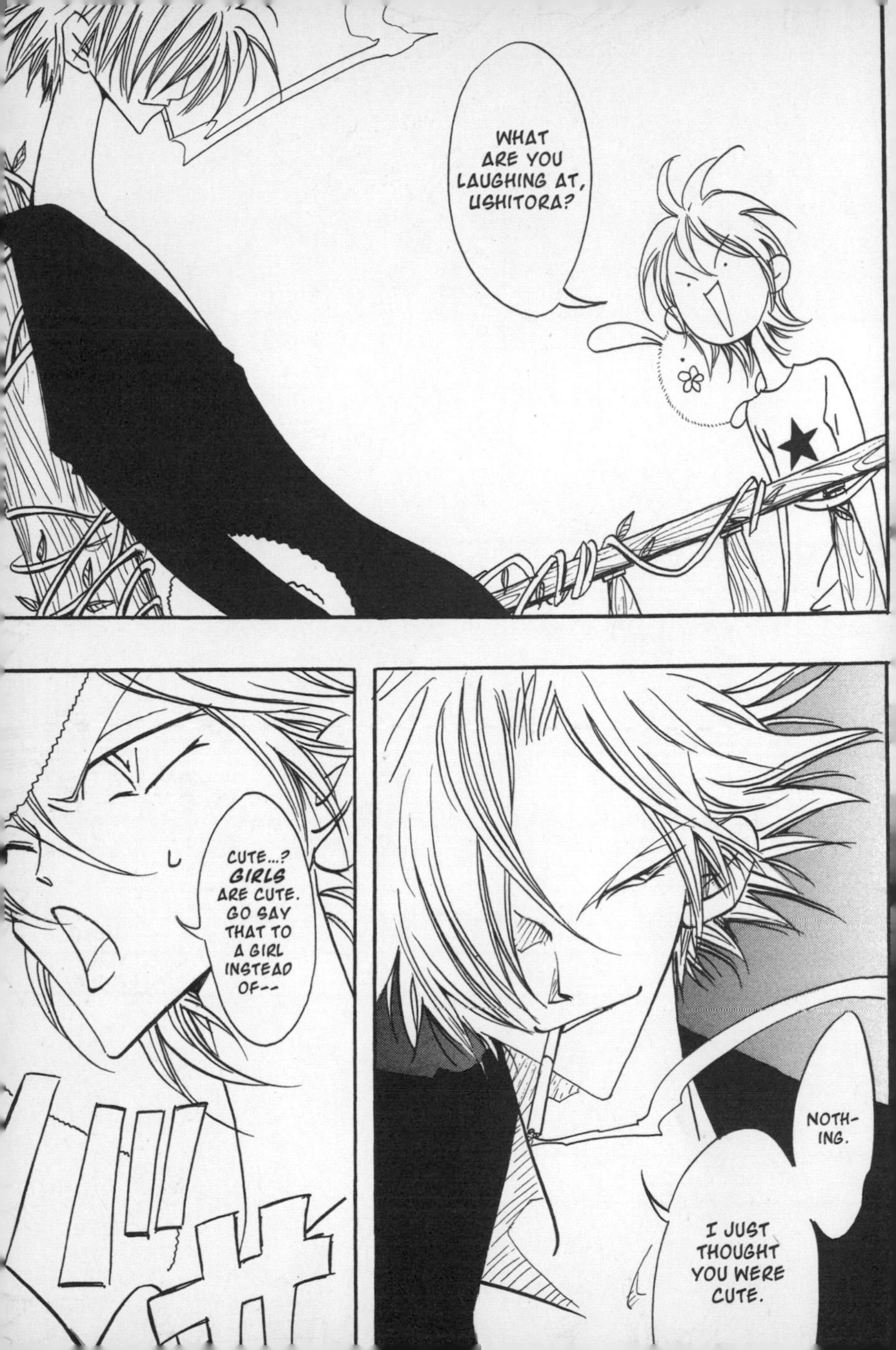
WHAT ARE YOU LAUGHING AT, USHITORA?
NOTHING.
I JUST THOUGHT YOU WERE CUTE.
CUTE...? **GIRLS** ARE CUTE. GO SAY THAT TO A GIRL INSTEAD OF--

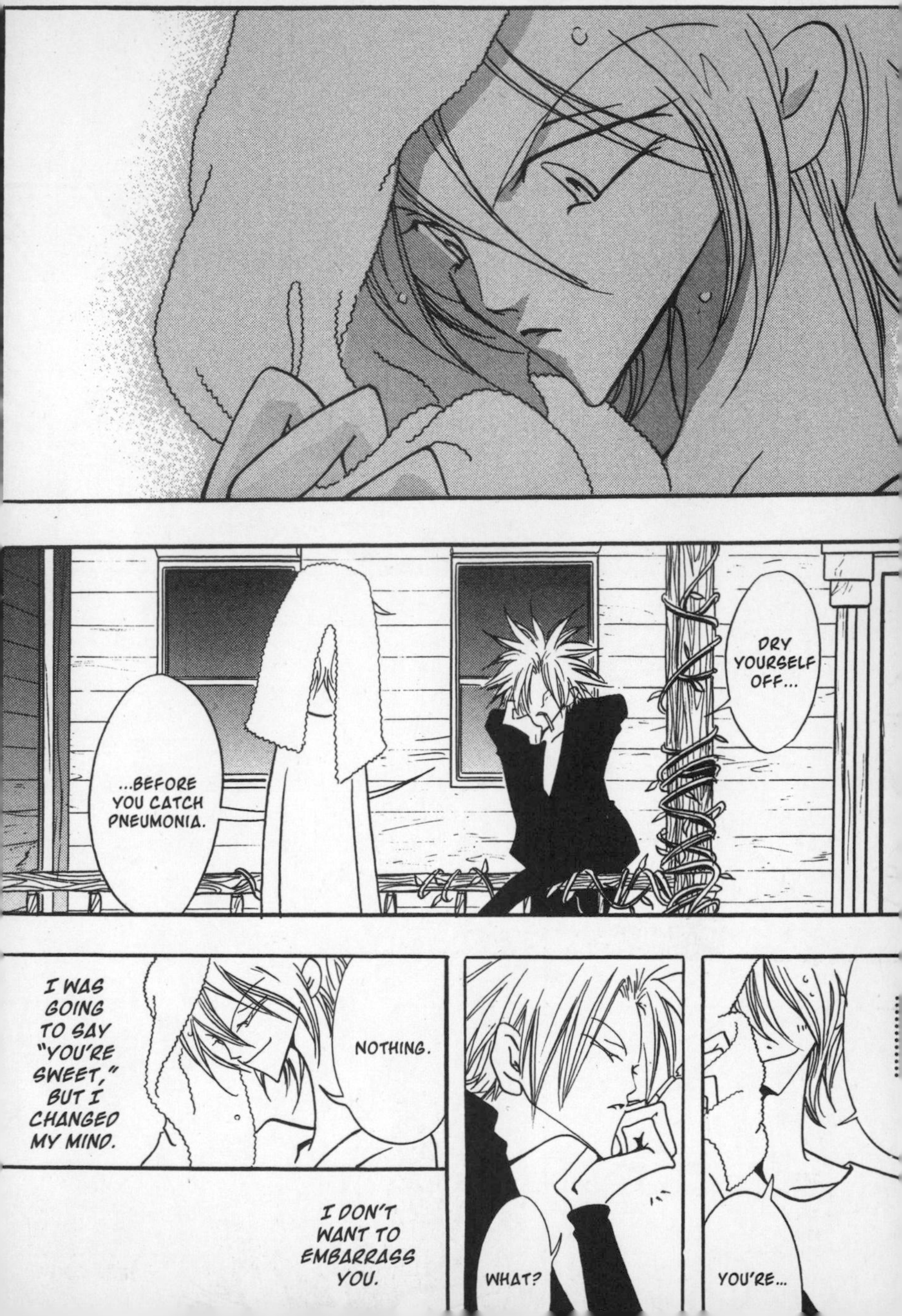
DRY YOURSELF OFF...
...BEFORE YOU CATCH PNEUMONIA.
YOU'RE...
WHAT?
NOTHING.
I WAS GOING TO SAY "YOU'RE SWEET," BUT I CHANGED MY MIND.
I DON'T WANT TO EMBARRASS YOU.

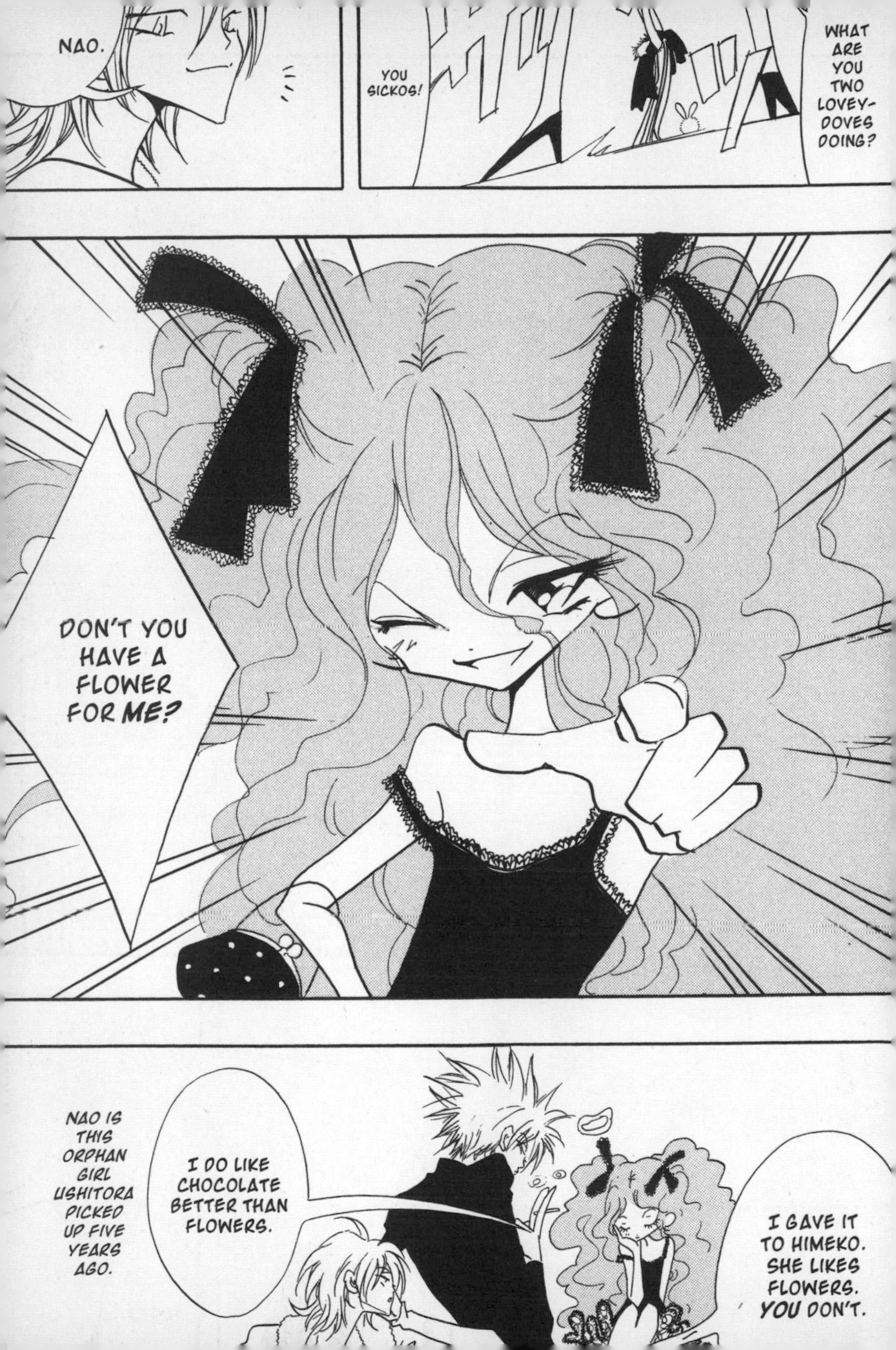
WHAT ARE YOU TWO LOVEY-DOVES DOING?
YOU SICKOS!
NAO.
DON'T YOU HAVE A FLOWER FOR ME?
I GAVE IT TO HIMEKO. SHE LIKES FLOWERS. YOU DON'T.
I DO LIKE CHOCOLATE BETTER THAN FLOWERS.
NAO IS THIS ORPHAN GIRL USHITORA PICKED UP FIVE YEARS AGO.

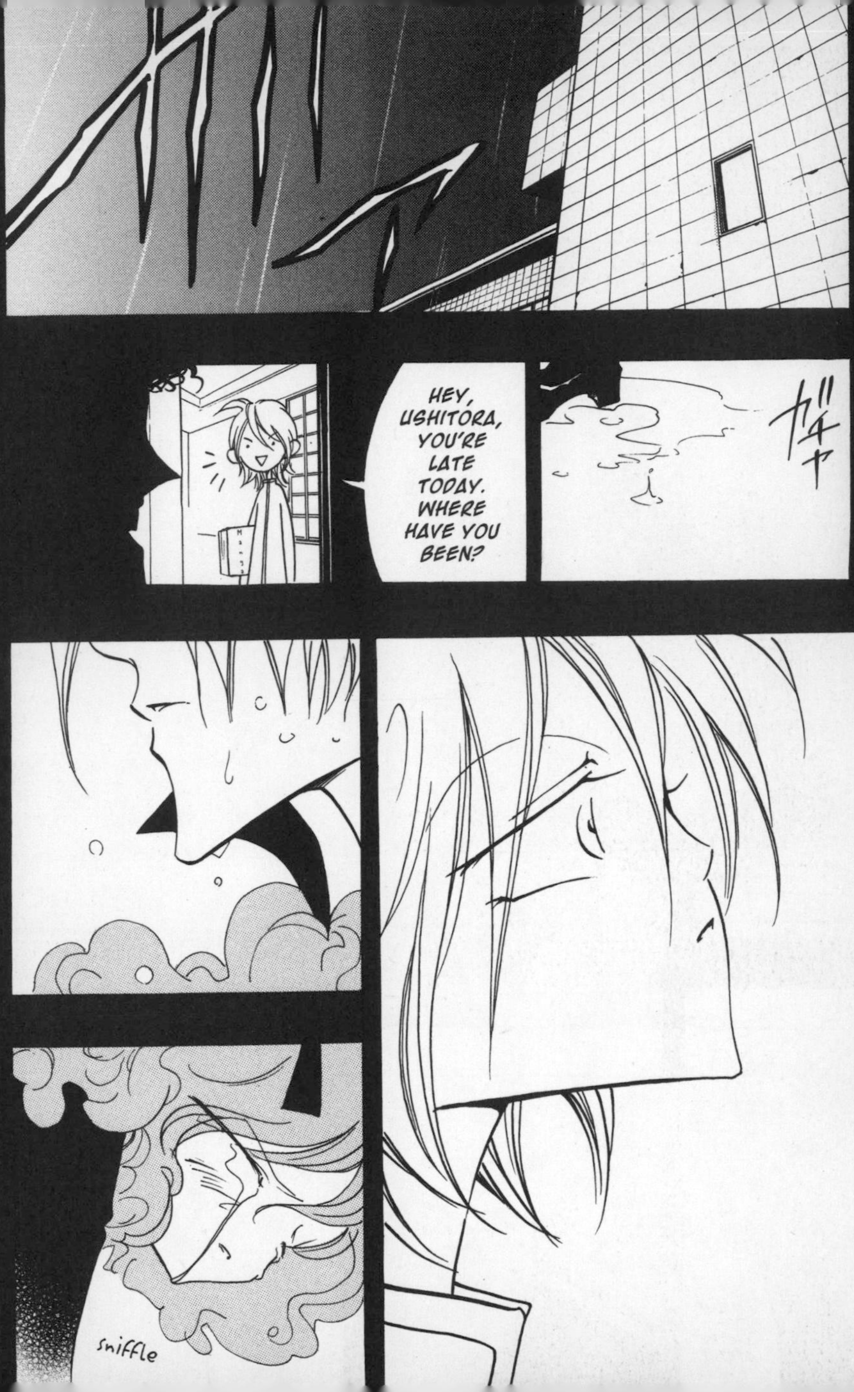
ガチャ
HEY, USHITORA, YOU'RE LATE TODAY. WHERE HAVE YOU BEEN?
sniffle

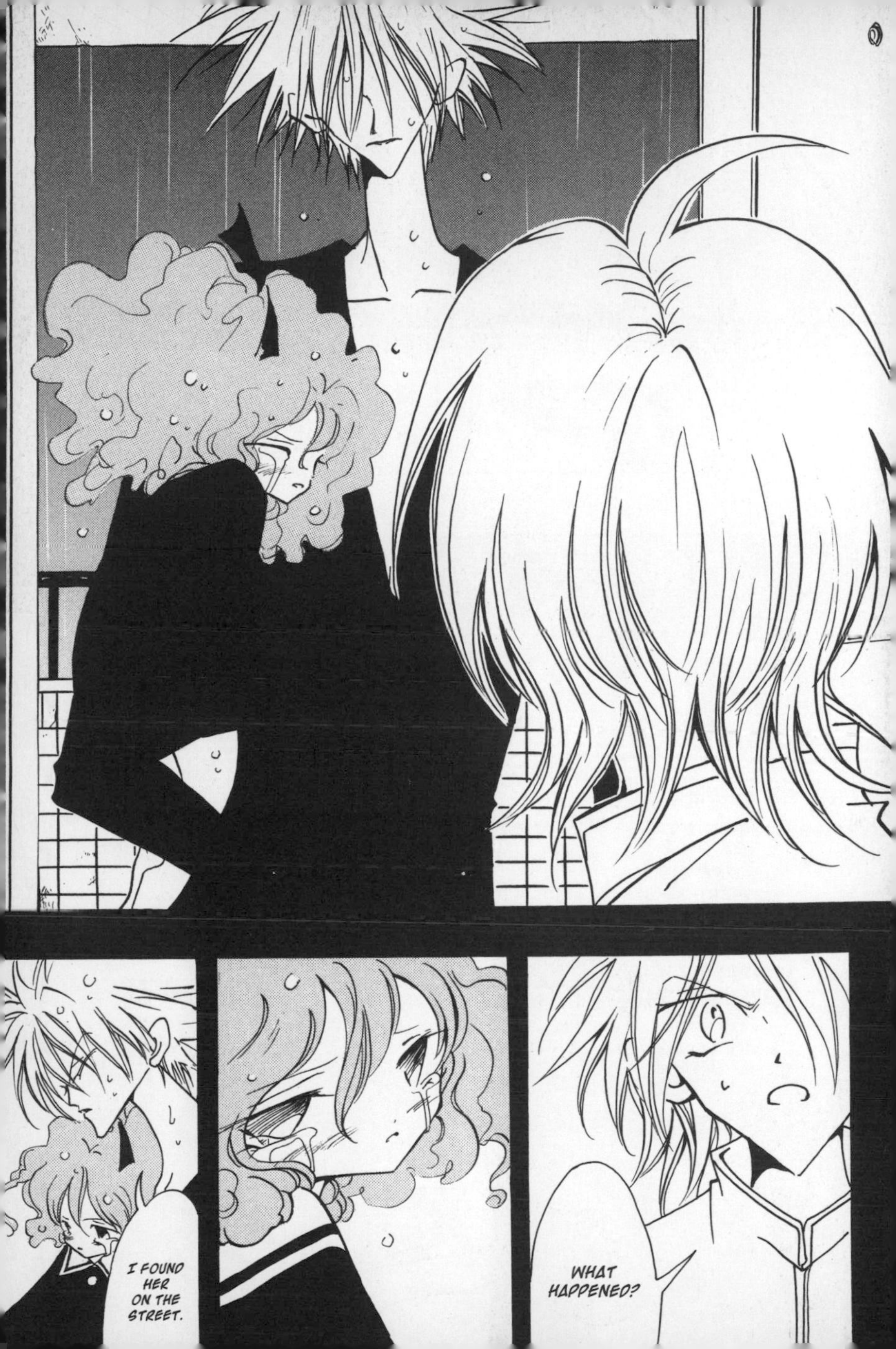
WHAT HAPPENED?
I FOUND HER ON THE STREET.

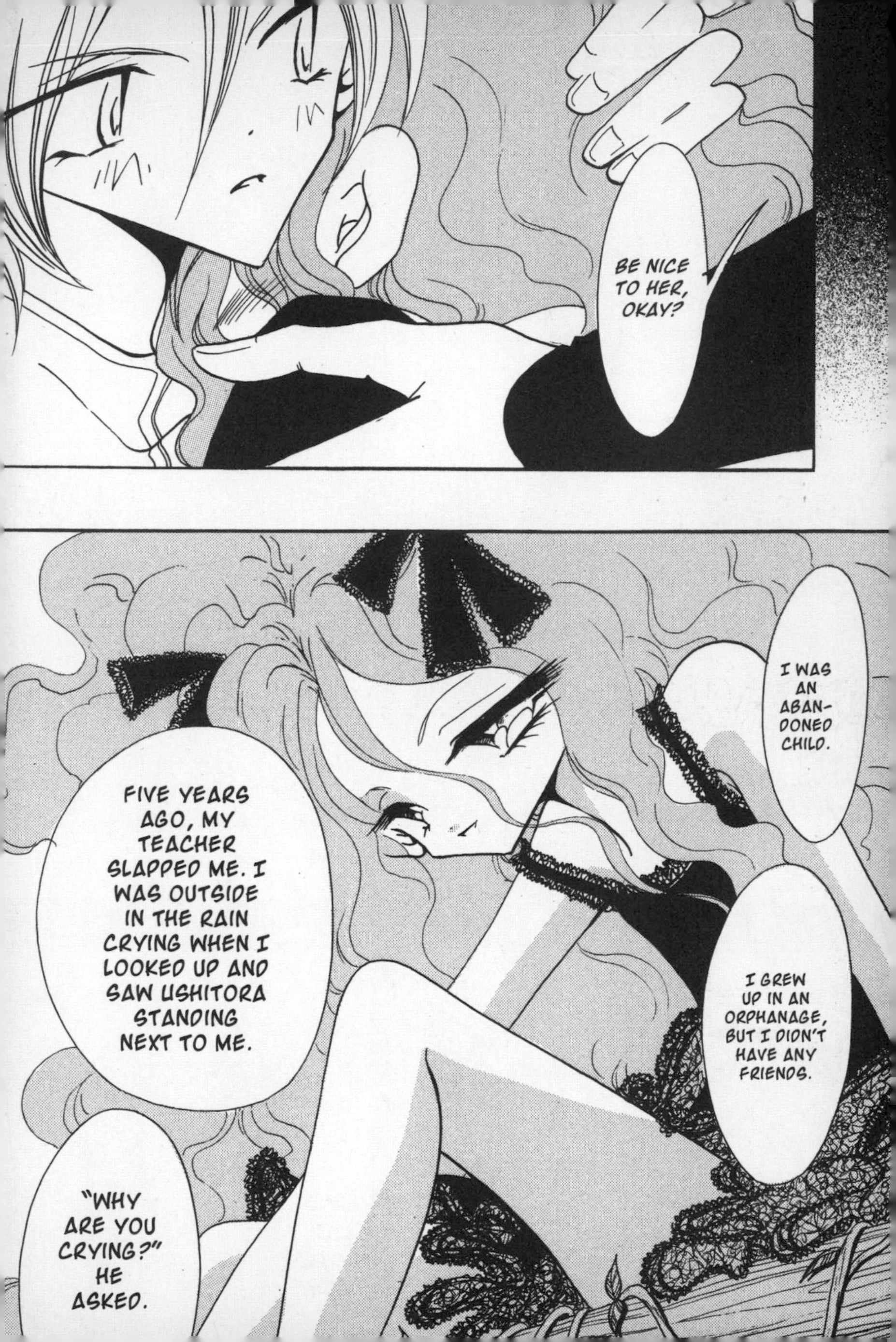
BE NICE TO HER, OKAY?
I WAS AN ABAN-DONED CHILD.
I GREW UP IN AN ORPHANAGE, BUT I DIDN'T HAVE ANY FRIENDS.
FIVE YEARS AGO, MY TEACHER SLAPPED ME. I WAS OUTSIDE IN THE RAIN CRYING WHEN I LOOKED UP AND SAW USHITORA STANDING NEXT TO ME.
"WHY ARE YOU CRYING?" HE ASKED.

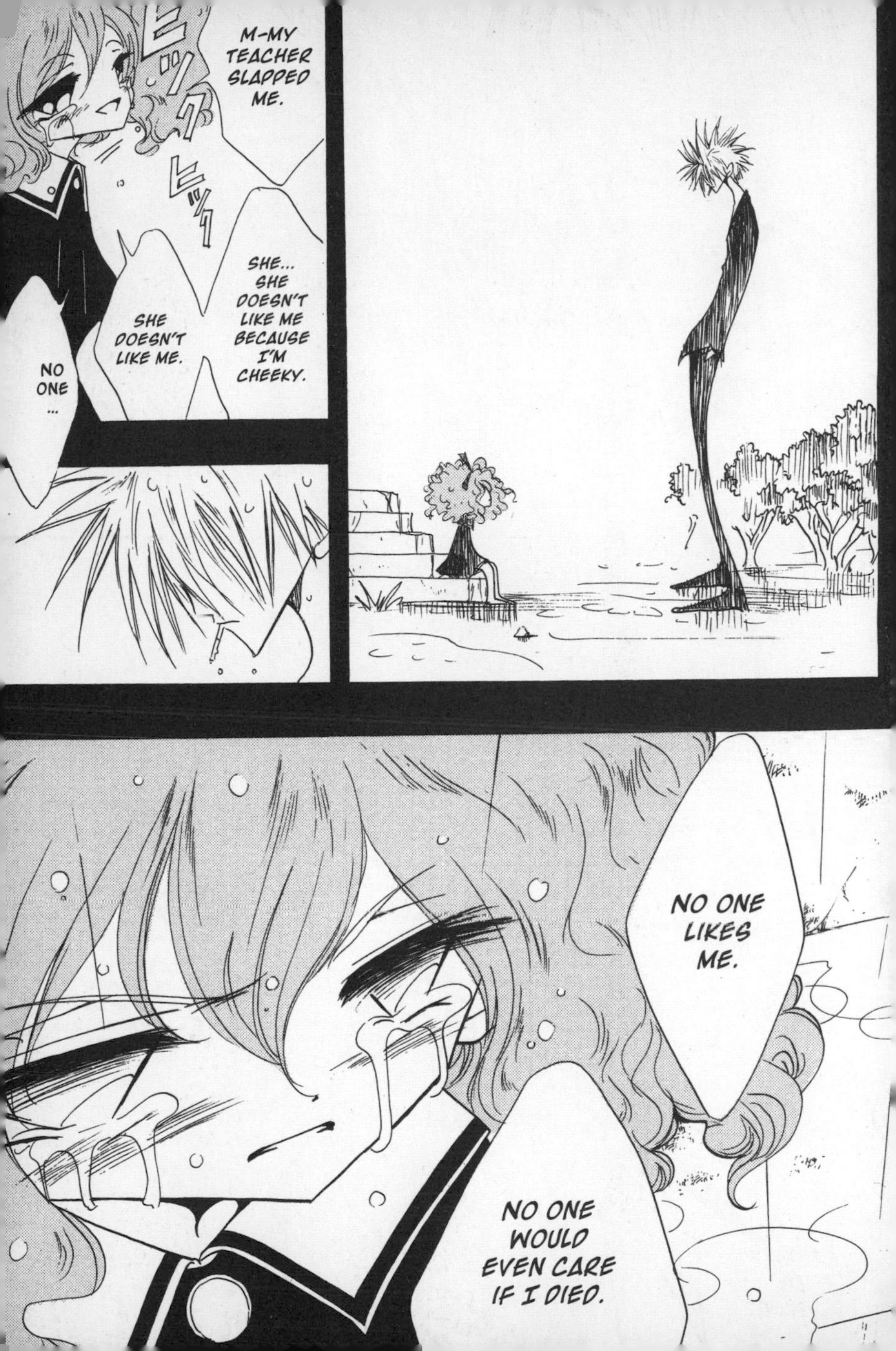
M-MY TEACHER SLAPPED ME.
ヒック
ヒック
SHE... SHE DOESN'T LIKE ME BECAUSE I'M CHEEKY.
SHE DOESN'T LIKE ME.
NO ONE ...
NO ONE LIKES ME.
NO ONE WOULD EVEN CARE IF I DIED.

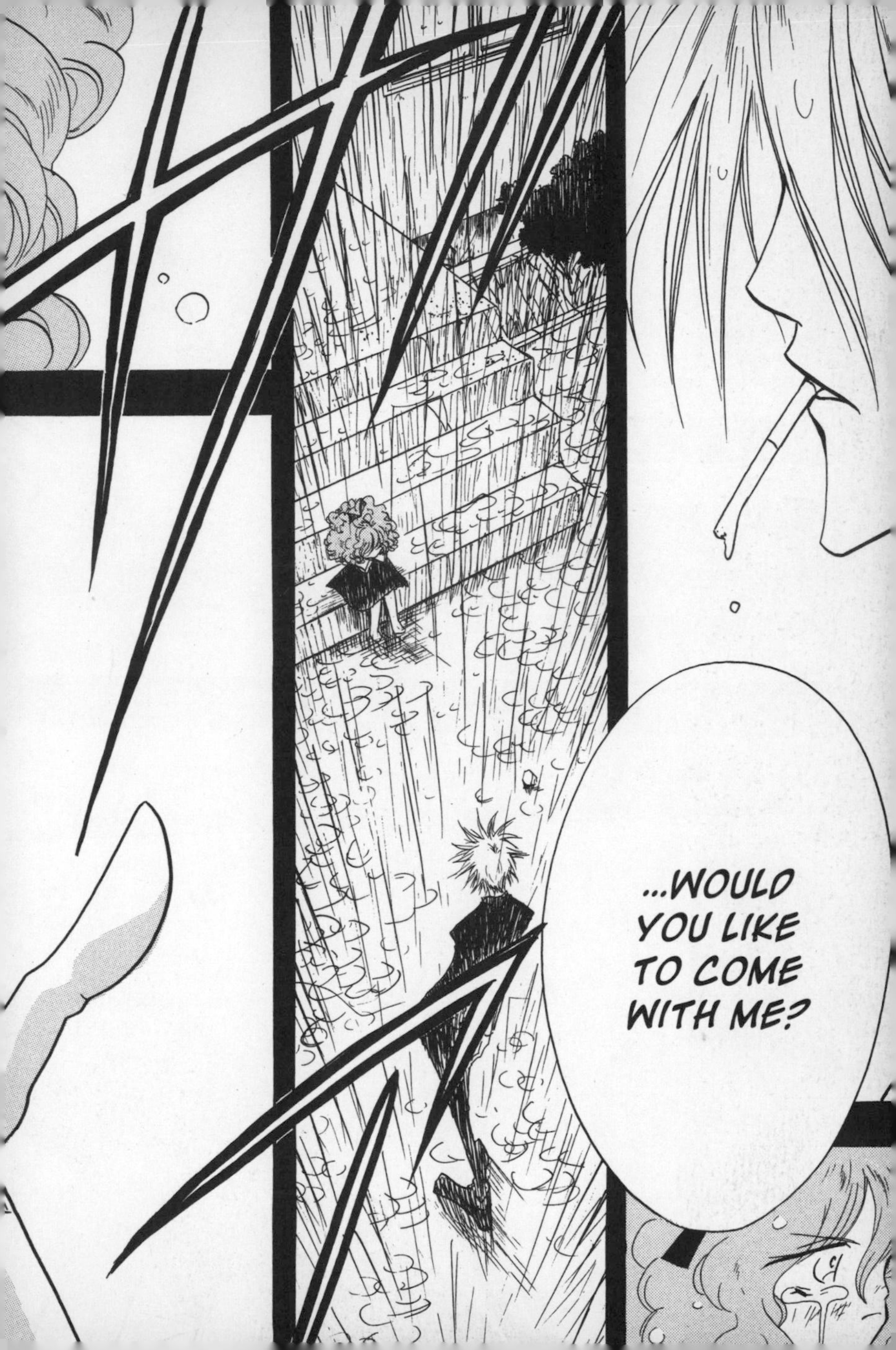
...WOULD YOU LIKE TO COME WITH ME?

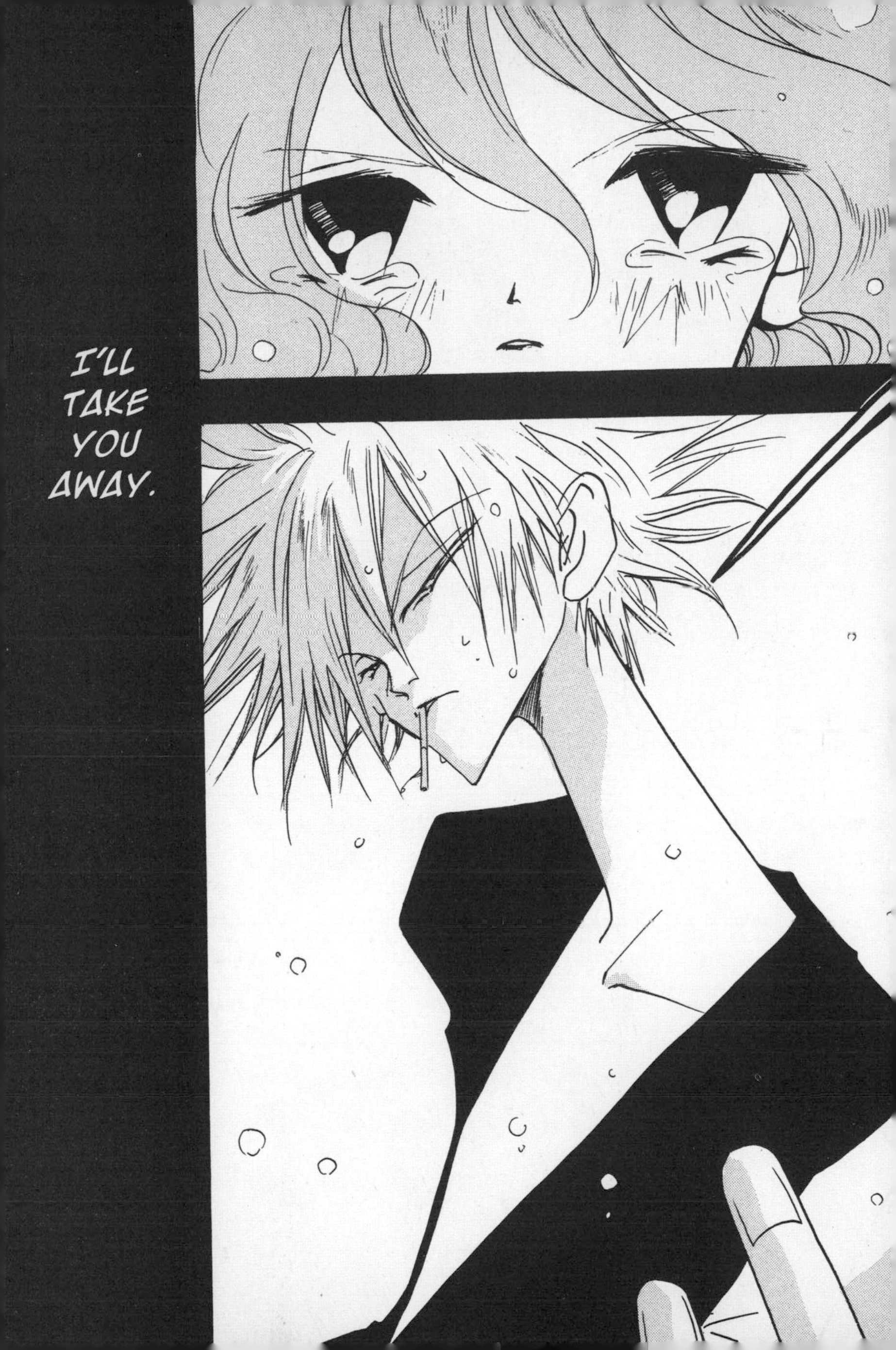
I'LL TAKE YOU AWAY.

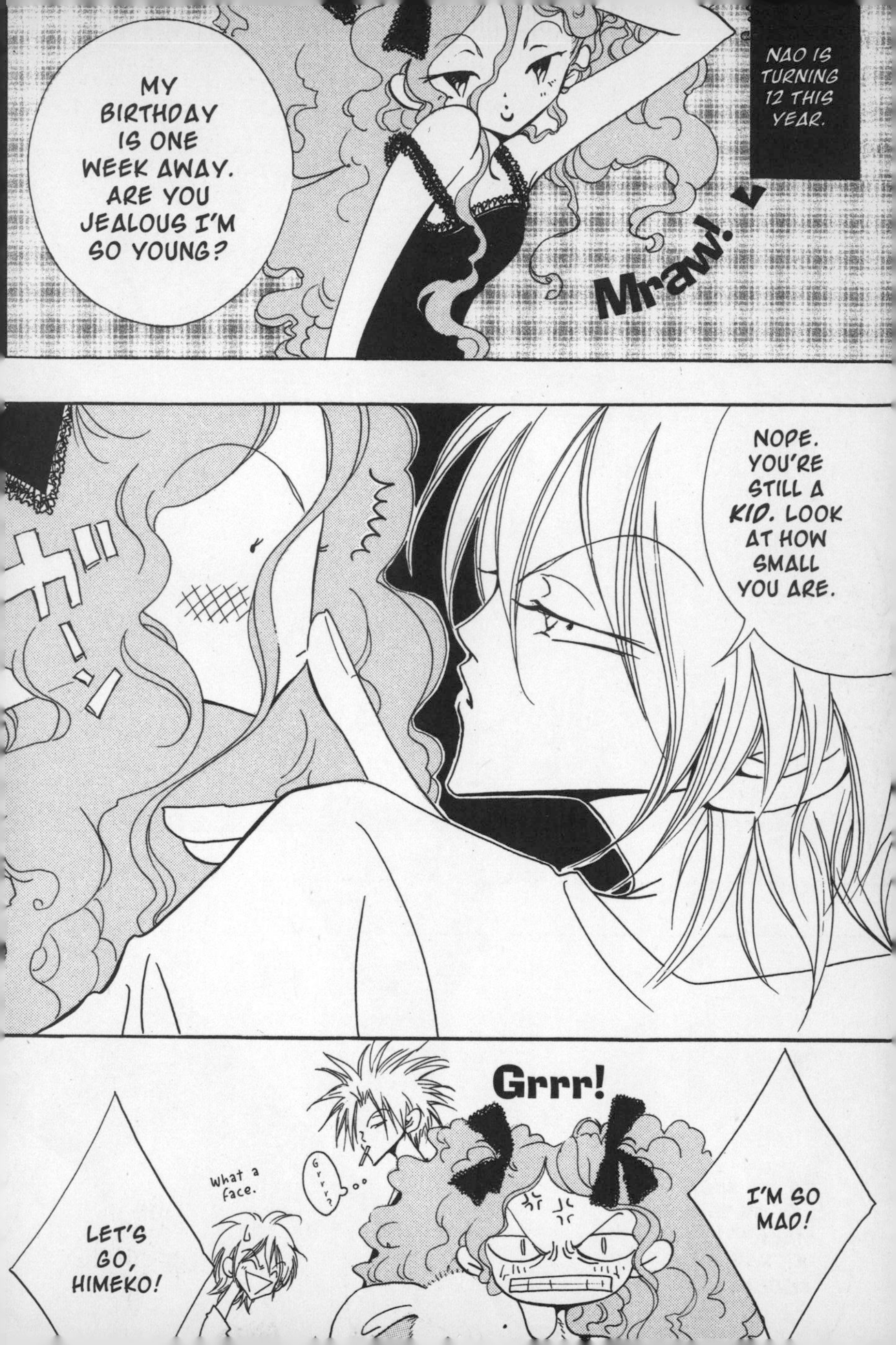
NAO IS TURNING 12 THIS YEAR.
Mraw!
MY BIRTHDAY IS ONE WEEK AWAY. ARE YOU JEALOUS I'M SO YOUNG?
NOPE. YOU'RE STILL A KID. LOOK AT HOW SMALL YOU ARE.
I'M SO MAD!
Grrr!
Grrr?
What a face.
LET'S GO, HIMEKO!

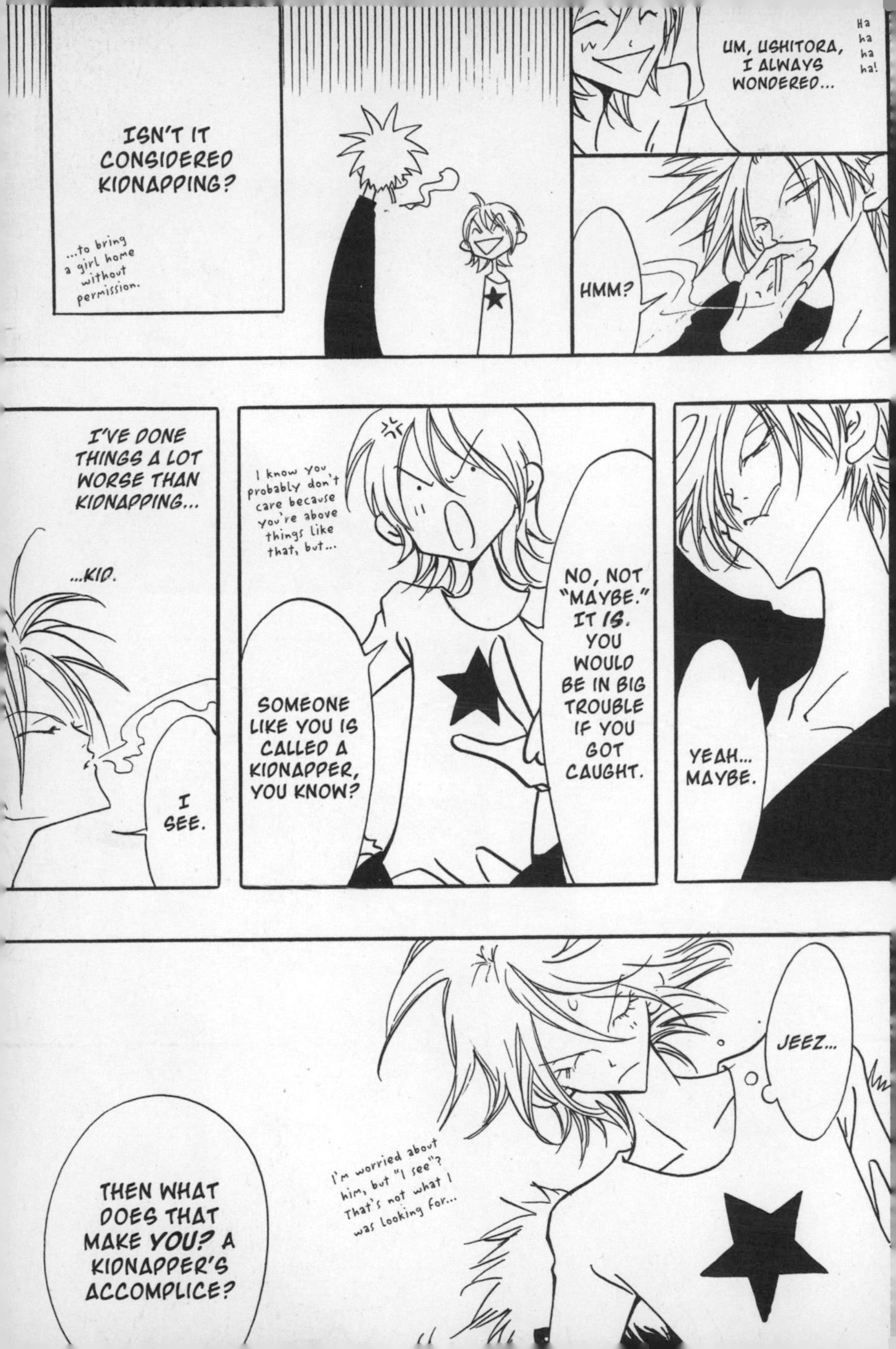
UM, USHITORA, I ALWAYS WONDERED...
Ha ha ha ha!
HMM?
ISN'T IT CONSIDERED KIDNAPPING?
...to bring a girl home without permission.
YEAH... MAYBE.
NO, NOT "MAYBE." IT IS. YOU WOULD BE IN BIG TROUBLE IF YOU GOT CAUGHT.
I know you probably don't care because you're above things like that, but...
SOMEONE LIKE YOU IS CALLED A KIDNAPPER, YOU KNOW?
I SEE.
I'VE DONE THINGS A LOT WORSE THAN KIDNAPPING...
...KID.
JEEZ...
I'm worried about him, but "I see"? That's not what I was looking for...
THEN WHAT DOES THAT MAKE YOU? A KIDNAPPER'S ACCOMPLICE?

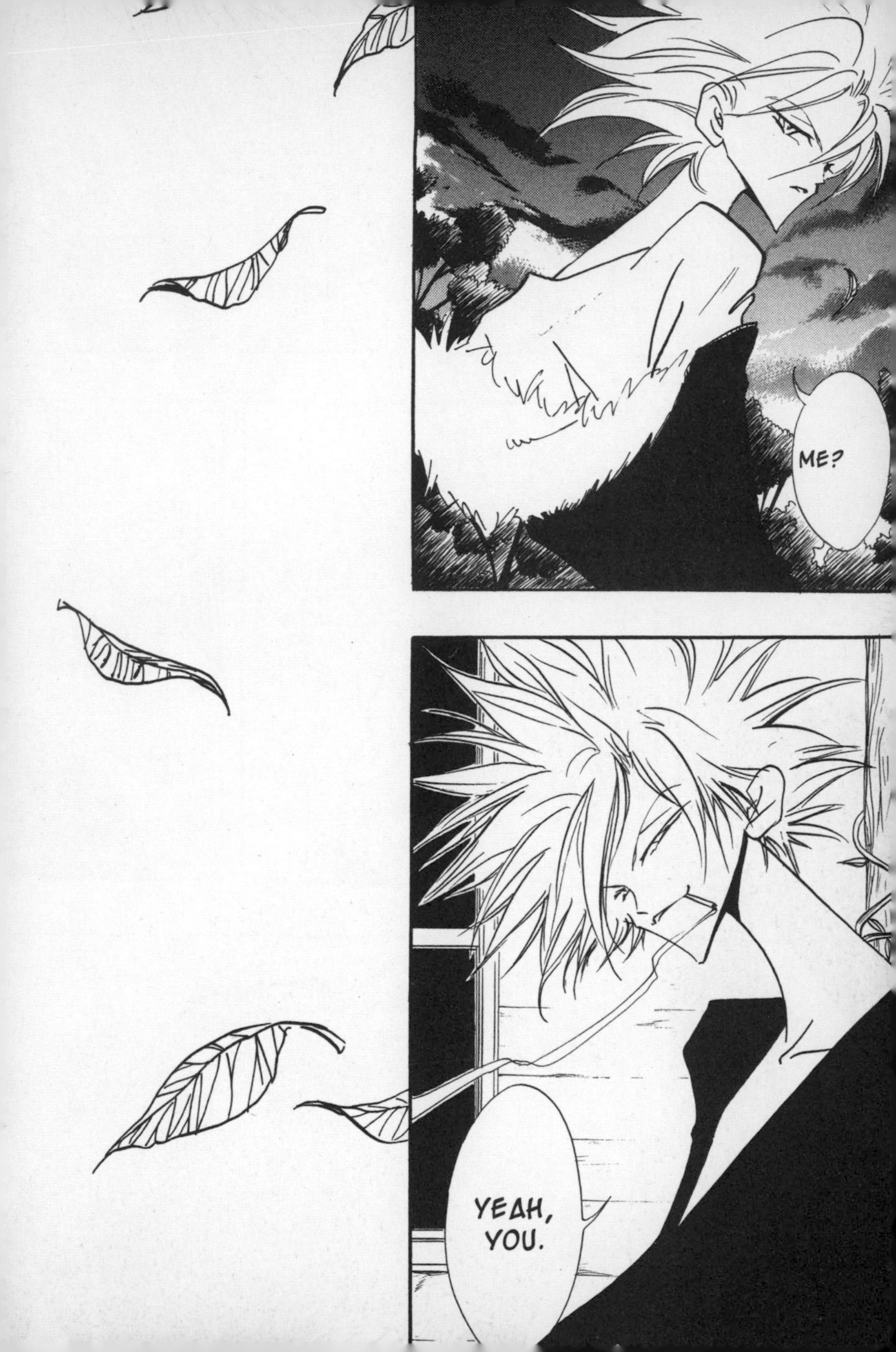
ME?
YEAH, YOU.

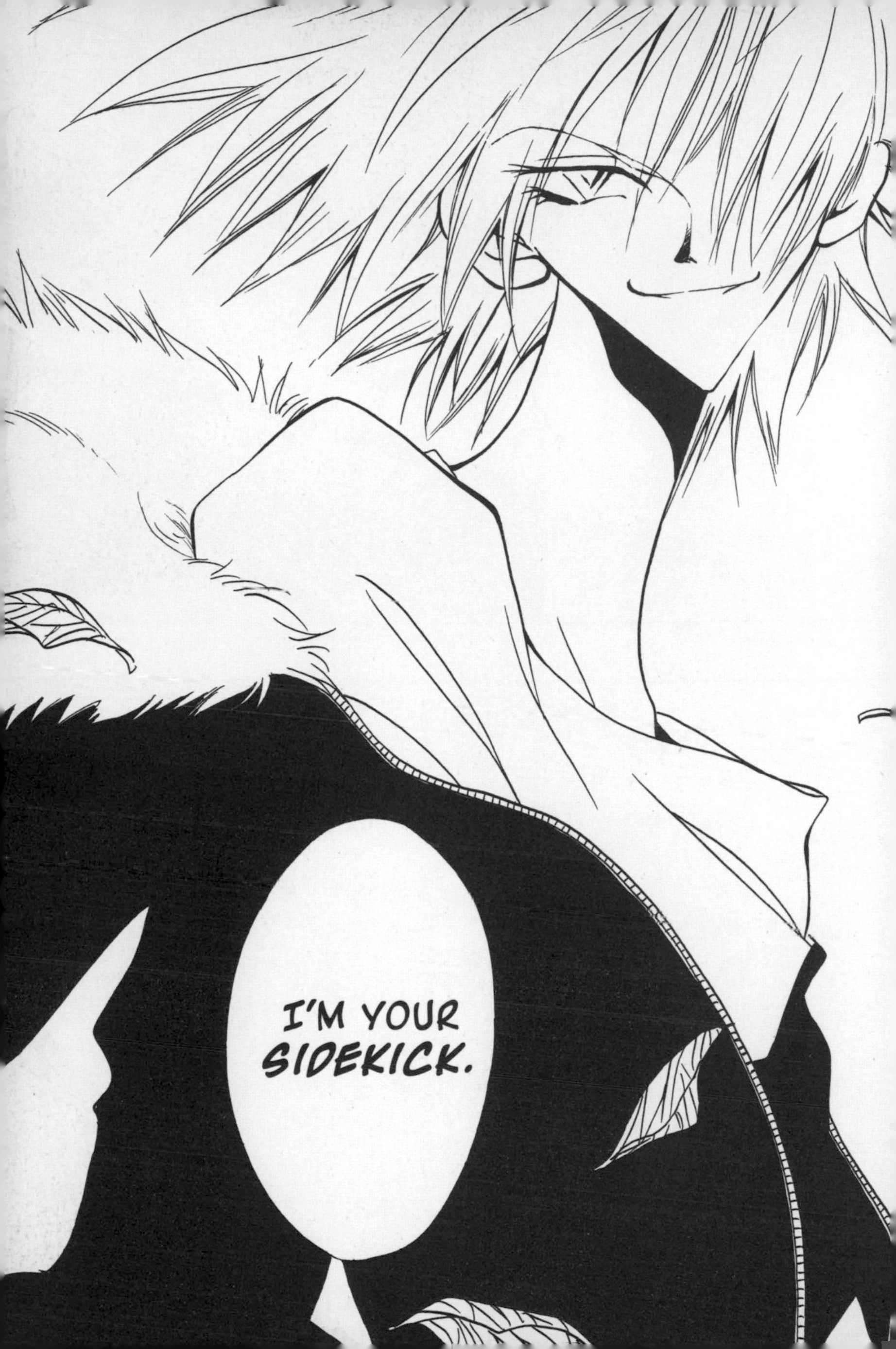
I'M YOUR SIDEKICK.

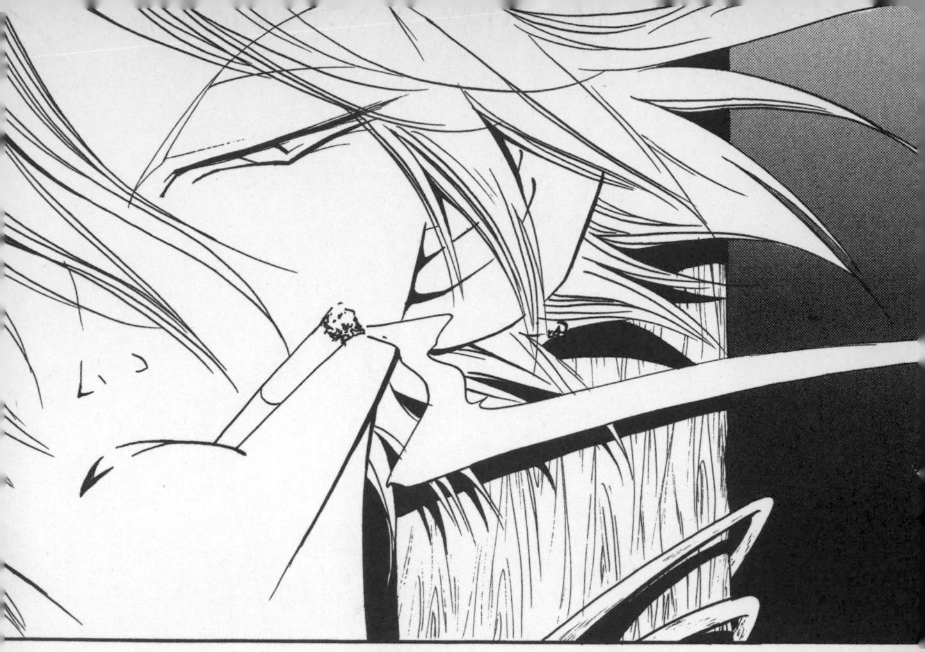
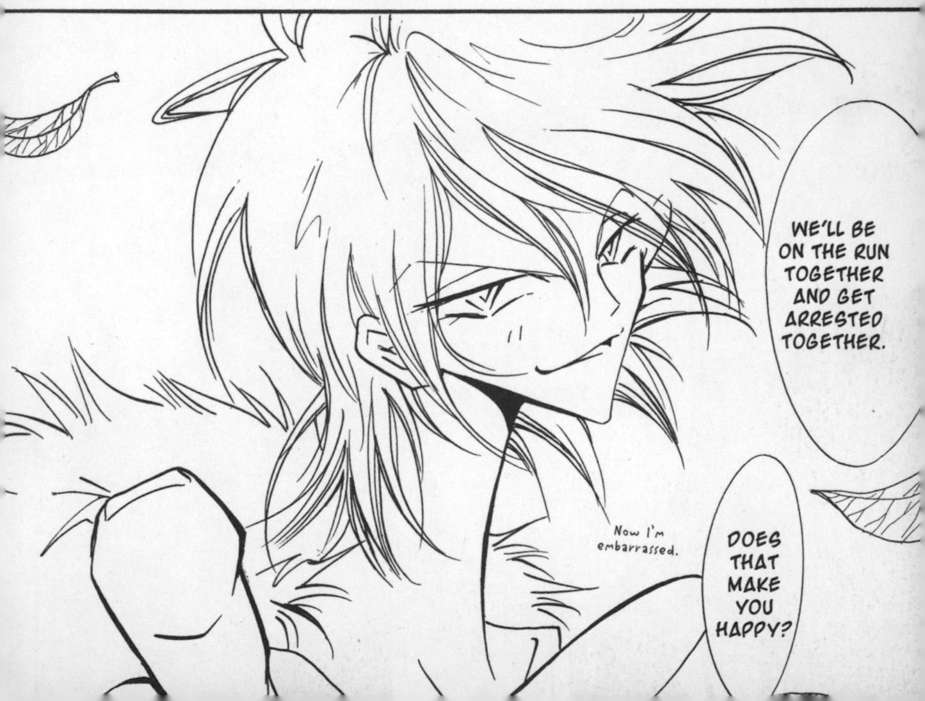
WE'LL BE ON THE RUN TOGETHER AND GET ARRESTED TOGETHER.
DOES THAT MAKE YOU HAPPY?
Now I'm embarrassed.

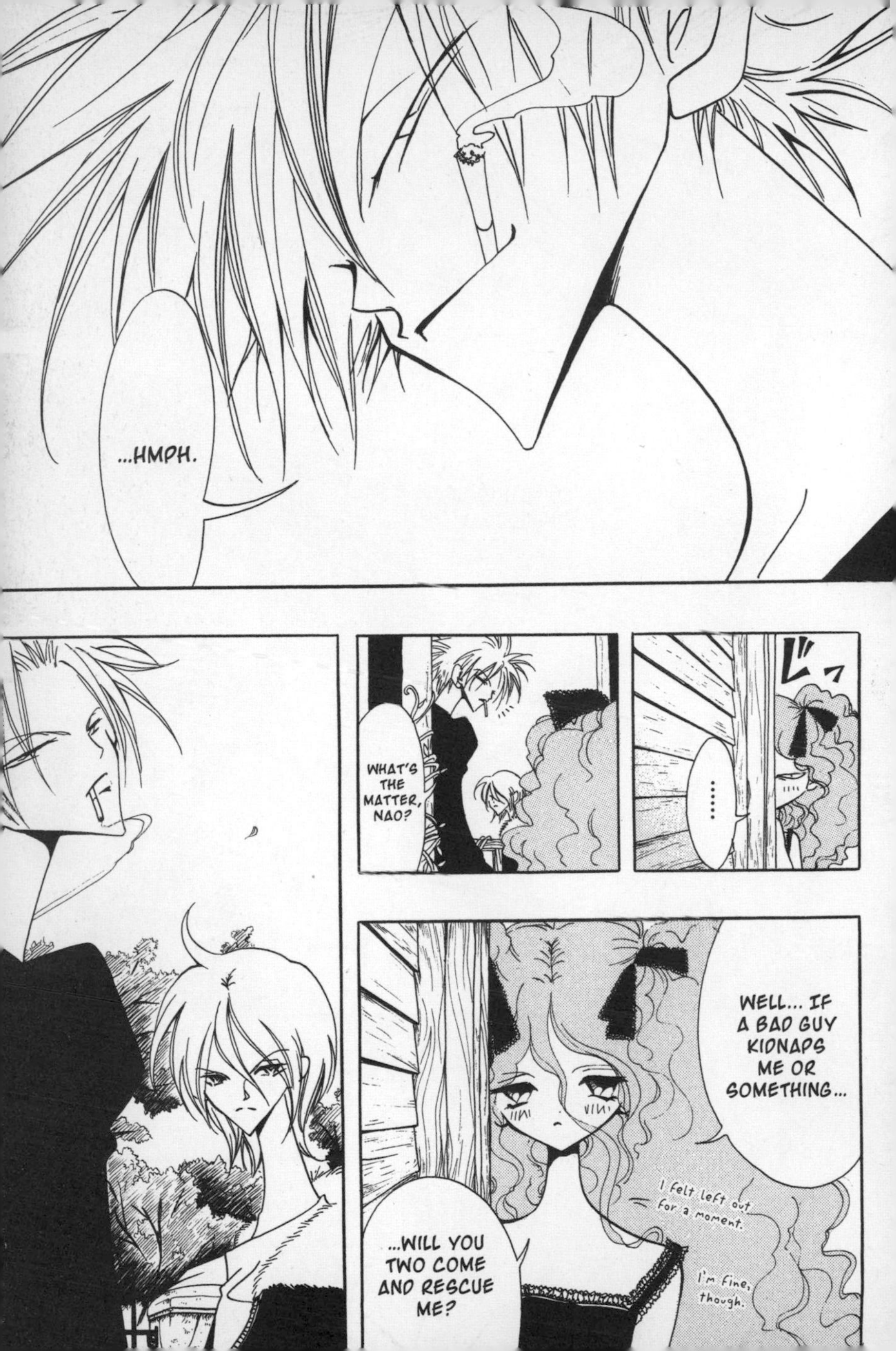
...HMPH.
ジッ
......
WHAT'S THE MATTER, NAO?
WELL... IF A BAD GUY KIDNAPS ME OR SOMETHING...
I felt left out for a moment.
...WILL YOU TWO COME AND RESCUE ME?
I'm fine, though.

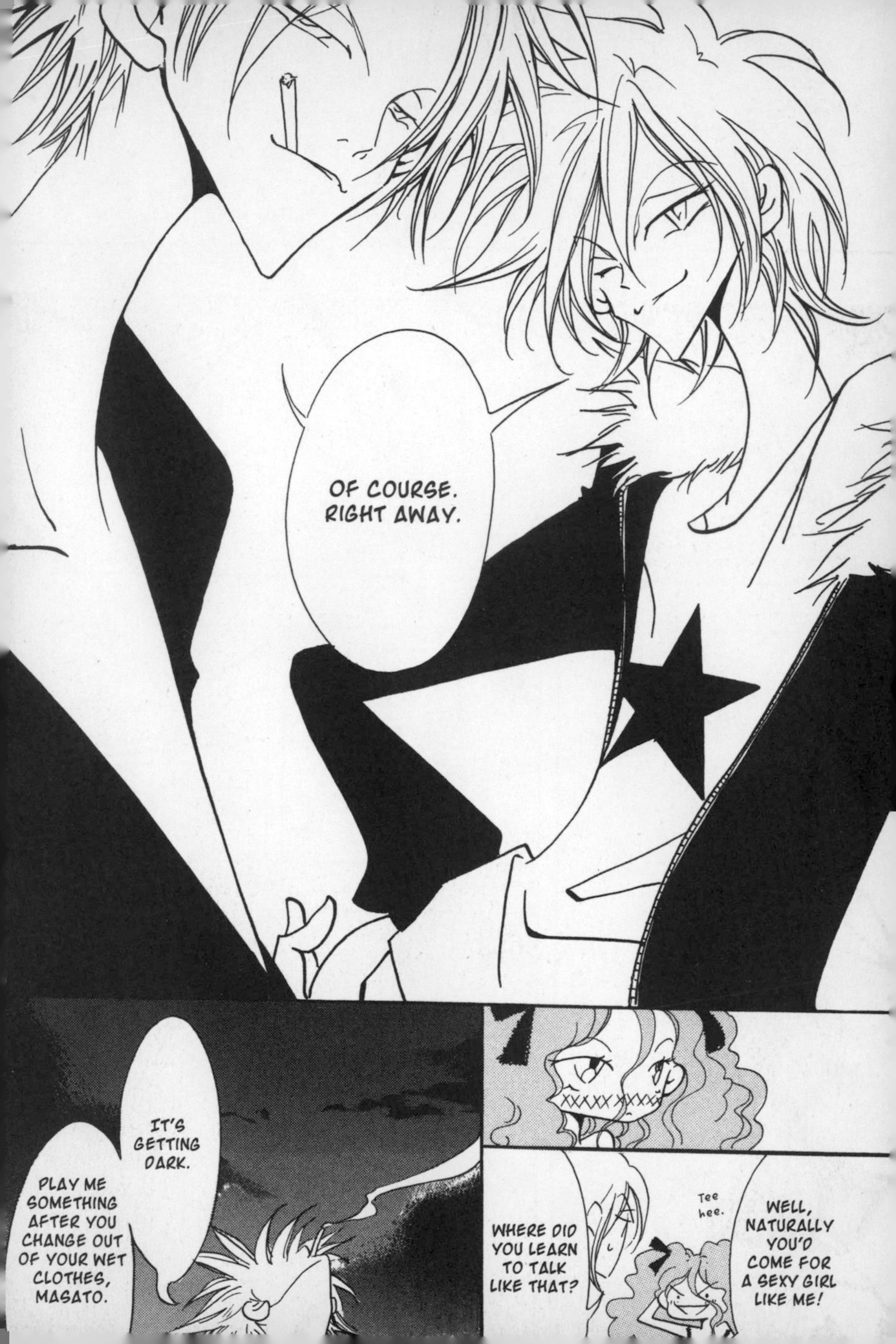
OF COURSE. RIGHT AWAY.
WELL, NATURALLY YOU'D COME FOR A SEXY GIRL LIKE ME!
Tee hee.
WHERE DID YOU LEARN TO TALK LIKE THAT?
IT'S GETTING DARK.
PLAY ME SOMETHING AFTER YOU CHANGE OUT OF YOUR WET CLOTHES, MASATO.

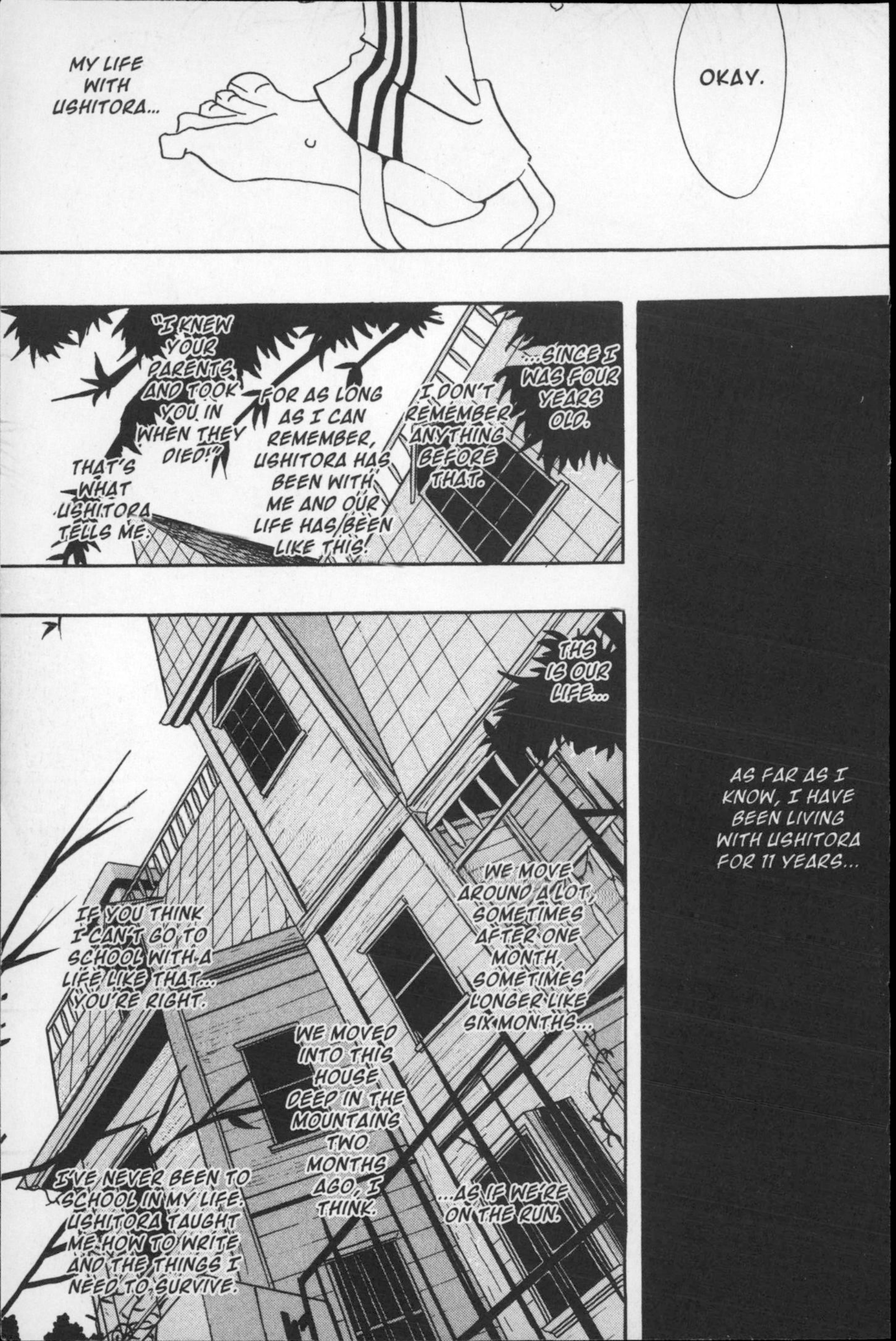
OKAY.
MY LIFE WITH USHITORA...
AS FAR AS I KNOW, I HAVE BEEN LIVING WITH USHITORA FOR 11 YEARS...
...SINCE I WAS FOUR YEARS OLD.
I DON'T REMEMBER ANYTHING BEFORE THAT.
FOR AS LONG AS I CAN REMEMBER, USHITORA HAS BEEN WITH ME AND OUR LIFE HAS BEEN LIKE THIS!
"I KNEW YOUR PARENTS AND TOOK YOU IN WHEN THEY DIED!"
THAT'S WHAT USHITORA TELLS ME.
THS IS OUR LIFE...
WE MOVE AROUND A LOT, SOMETIMES AFTER ONE MONTH, SOMETIMES LONGER LIKE SIX MONTHS...
...AS IF WE'RE ON THE RUN.
WE MOVED INTO THIS HOUSE DEEP IN THE MOUNTAINS TWO MONTHS AGO, I THINK.
IF YOU THINK I CAN'T GO TO SCHOOL WITH A LIFE LIKE THAT... YOU'RE RIGHT.
I'VE NEVER BEEN TO SCHOOL IN MY LIFE. USHITORA TAUGHT ME HOW TO WRITE AND THE THINGS I NEED TO SURVIVE.

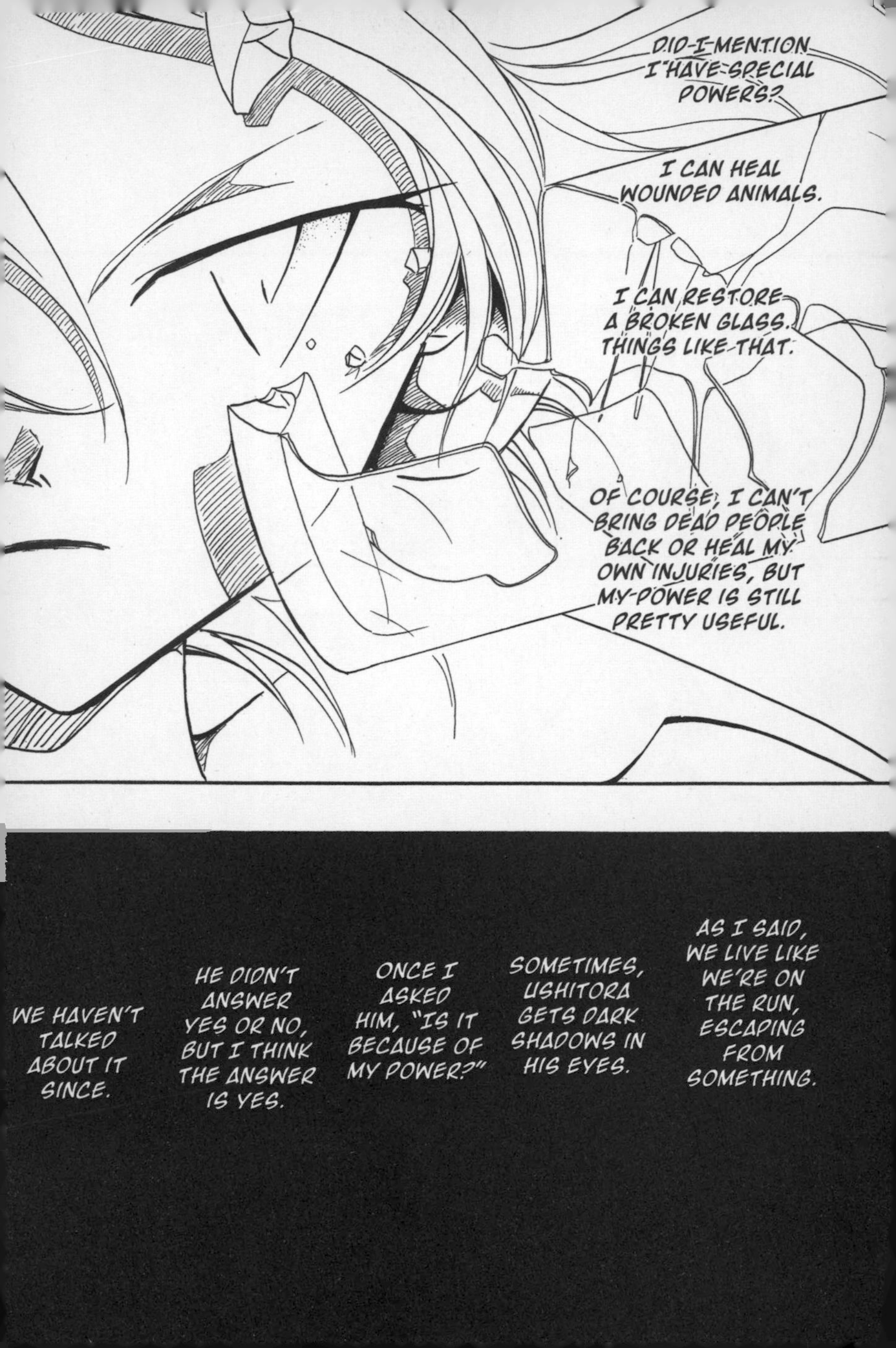
DID I MENTION I HAVE SPECIAL POWERS?
I CAN HEAL WOUNDED ANIMALS.
I CAN RESTORE A BROKEN GLASS. THINGS LIKE THAT.
OF COURSE, I CAN'T BRING DEAD PEOPLE BACK OR HEAL MY OWN INJURIES, BUT MY POWER IS STILL PRETTY USEFUL.
AS I SAID, WE LIVE LIKE WE'RE ON THE RUN, ESCAPING FROM SOMETHING.
SOMETIMES, USHITORA GETS DARK SHADOWS IN HIS EYES.
ONCE I ASKED HIM, "IS IT BECAUSE OF MY POWER?"
HE DIDN'T ANSWER YES OR NO, BUT I THINK THE ANSWER IS YES.
WE HAVEN'T TALKED ABOUT IT SINCE.

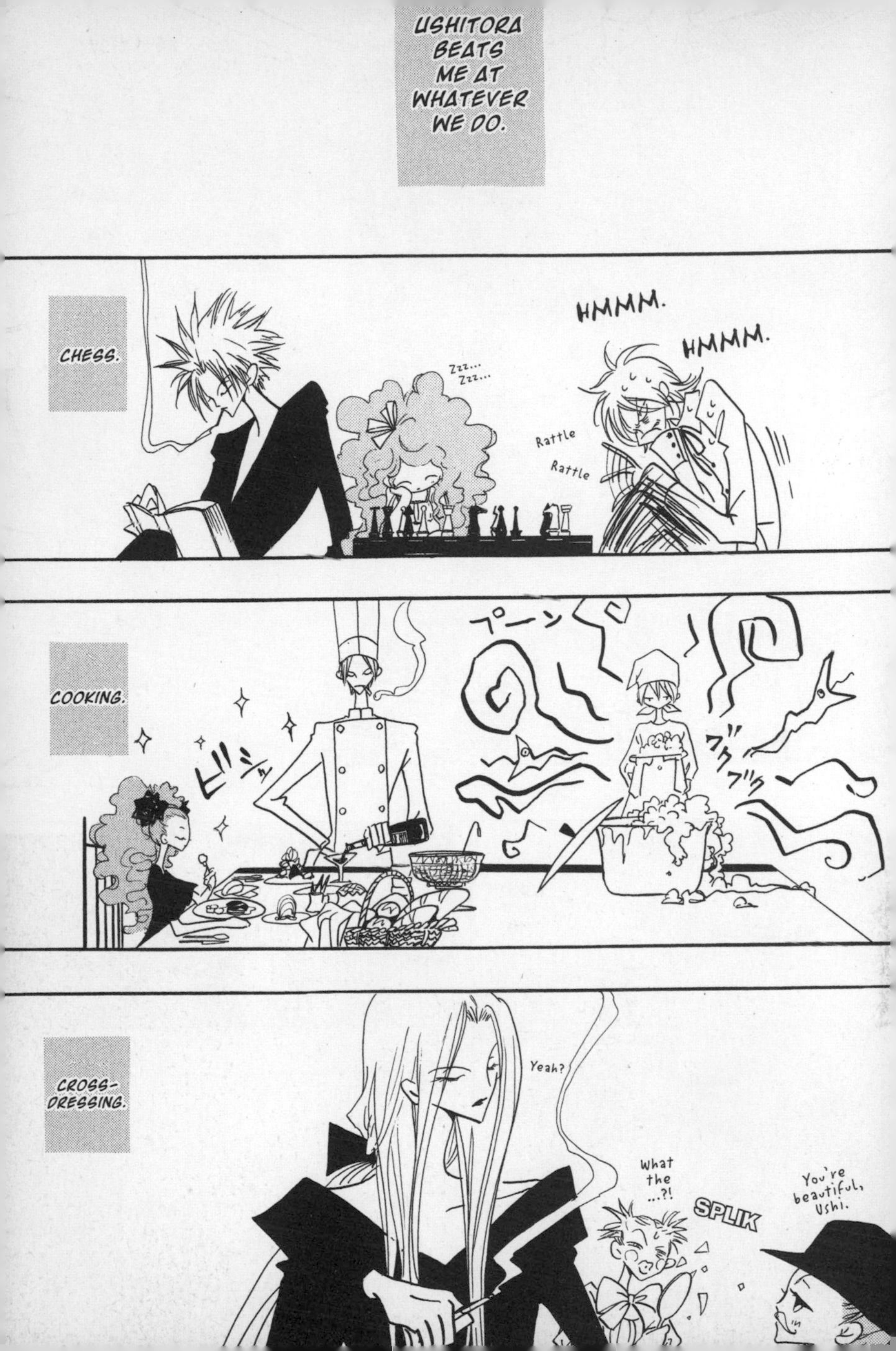
USHITORA BEATS ME AT WHATEVER WE DO.
HMMM.
HMMM.
Rattle
Rattle
Zzz... Zzz...
CHESS.
ブクブク
プーン
COOKING.
You're beautiful, Ushi.
SPLIK
What the ...?!
Yeah?
CROSS-DRESSING.

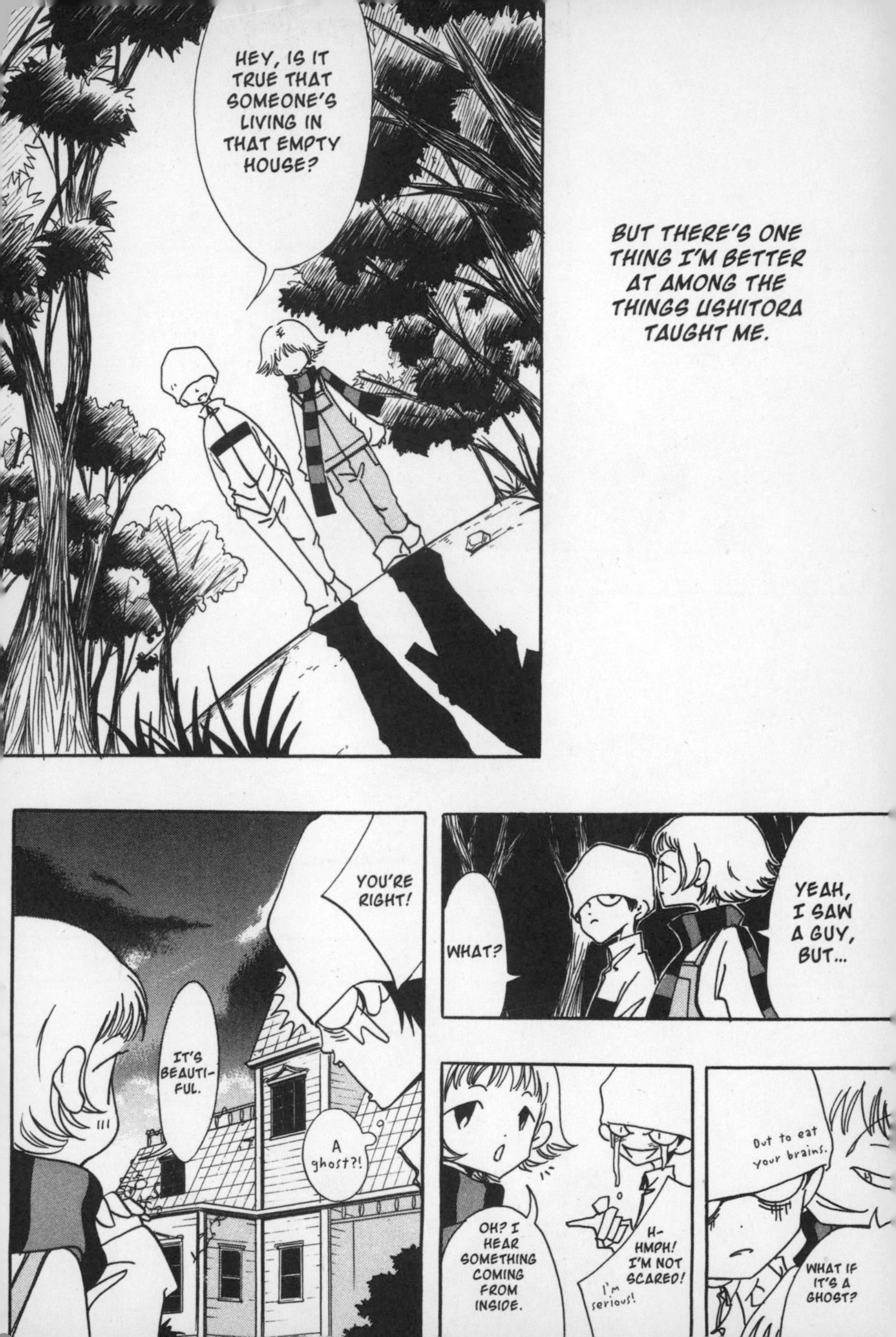
BUT THERE'S ONE THING I'M BETTER AT AMONG THE THINGS USHITORA TAUGHT ME.
HEY, IS IT TRUE THAT SOMEONE'S LIVING IN THAT EMPTY HOUSE?
YEAH, I SAW A GUY, BUT...
WHAT?
WHAT IF IT'S A GHOST?
Out to eat your brains.
H-HMPH! I'M NOT SCARED!
I'm serious!
OH? I HEAR SOMETHING COMING FROM INSIDE.
YOU'RE RIGHT!
IT'S BEAUTI-FUL.
A ghost?!

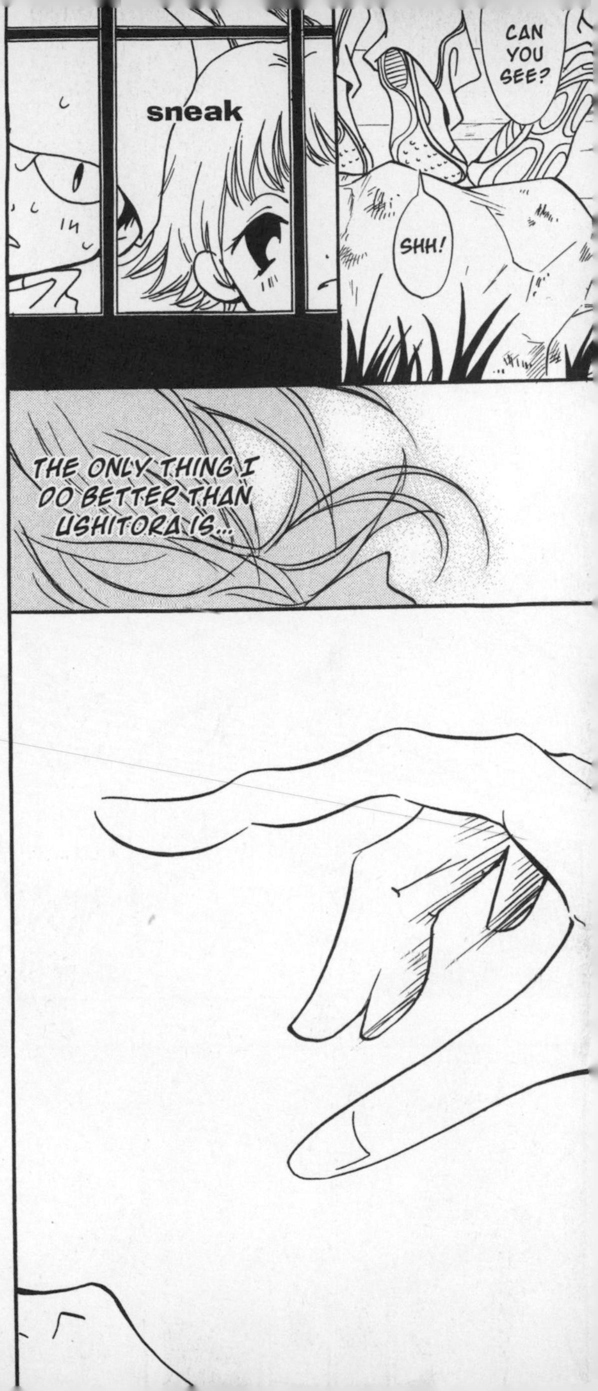
CAN YOU SEE?
SHH!
sneak
THE ONLY THING I DO BETTER THAN USHITORA IS...

...PLAY PIANO.

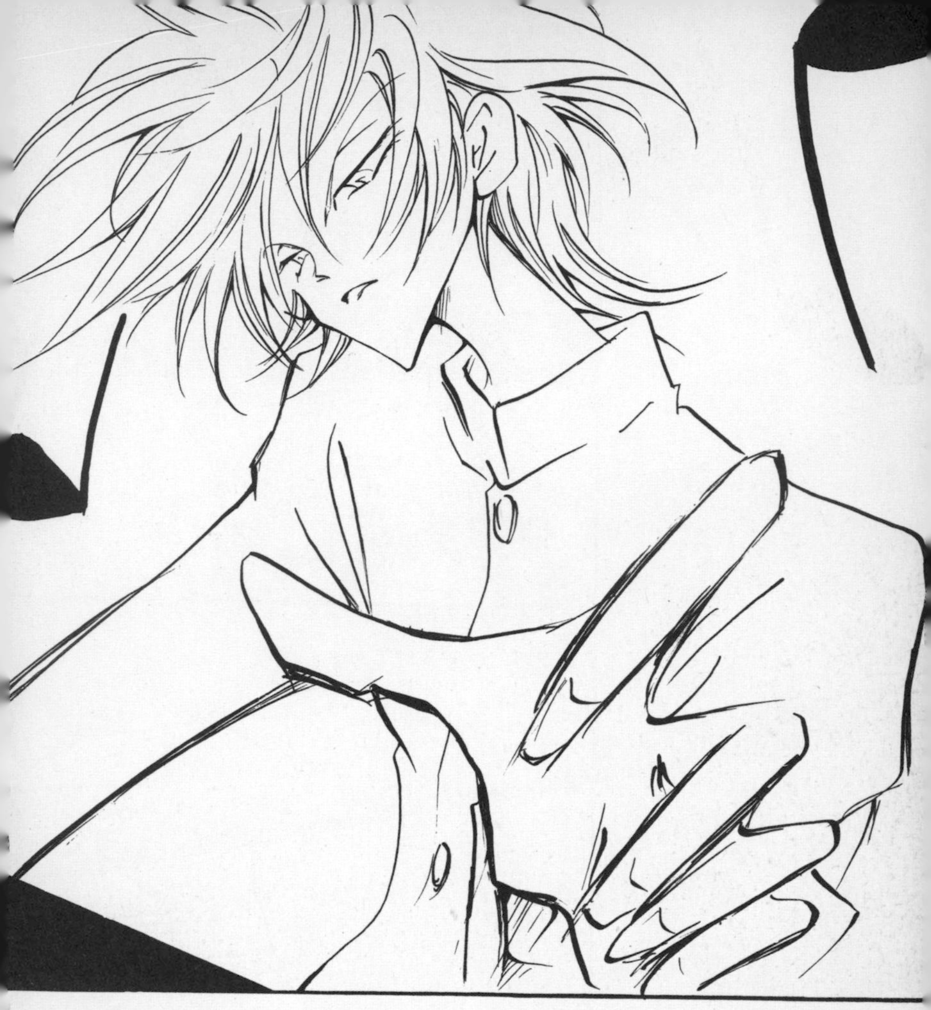
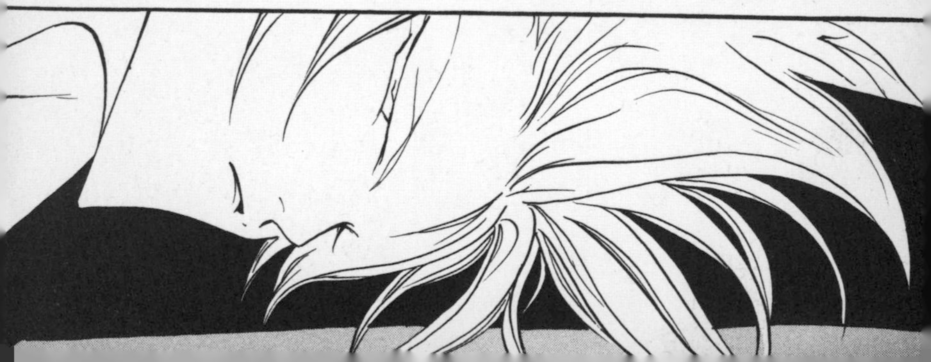

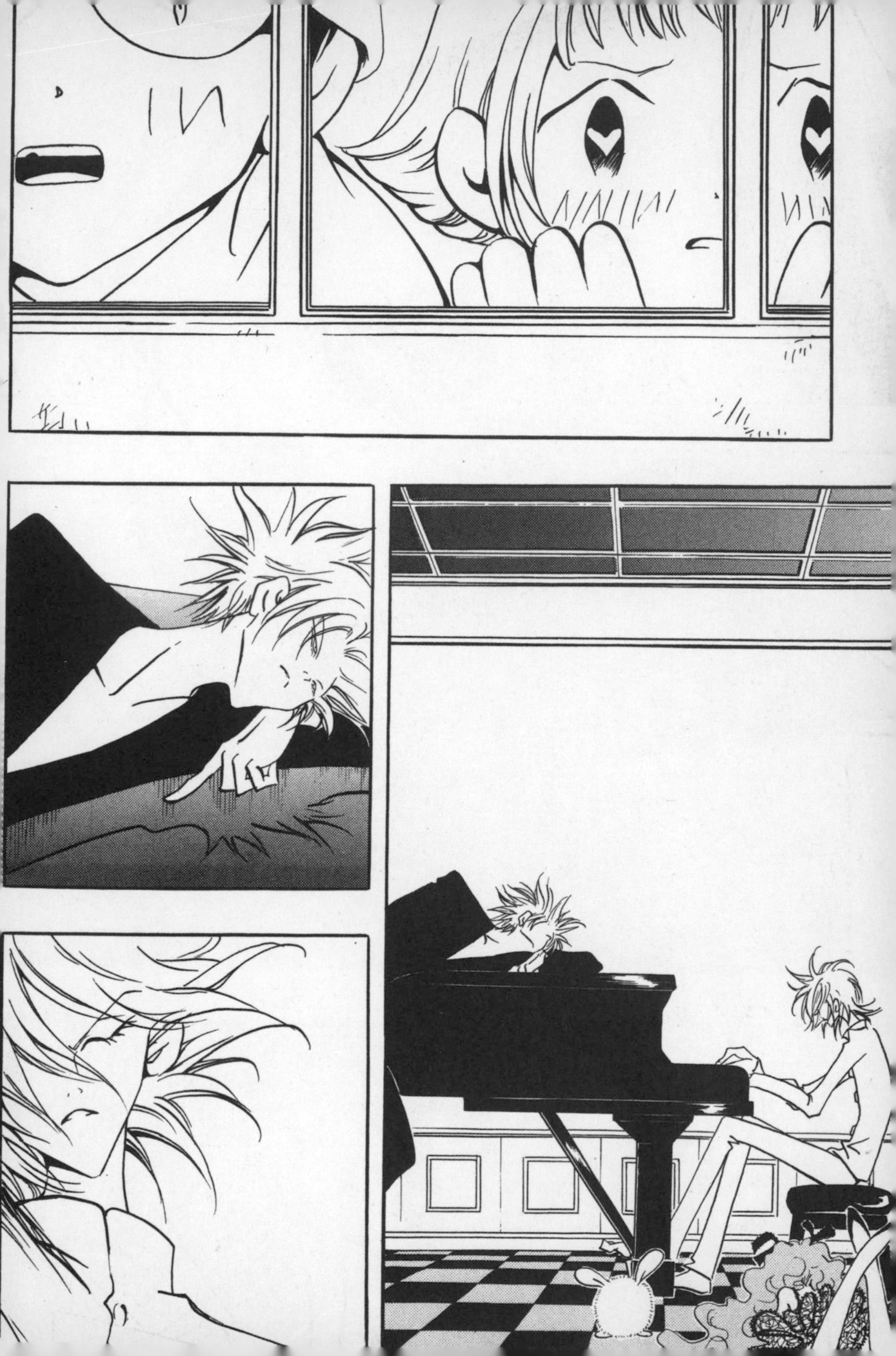

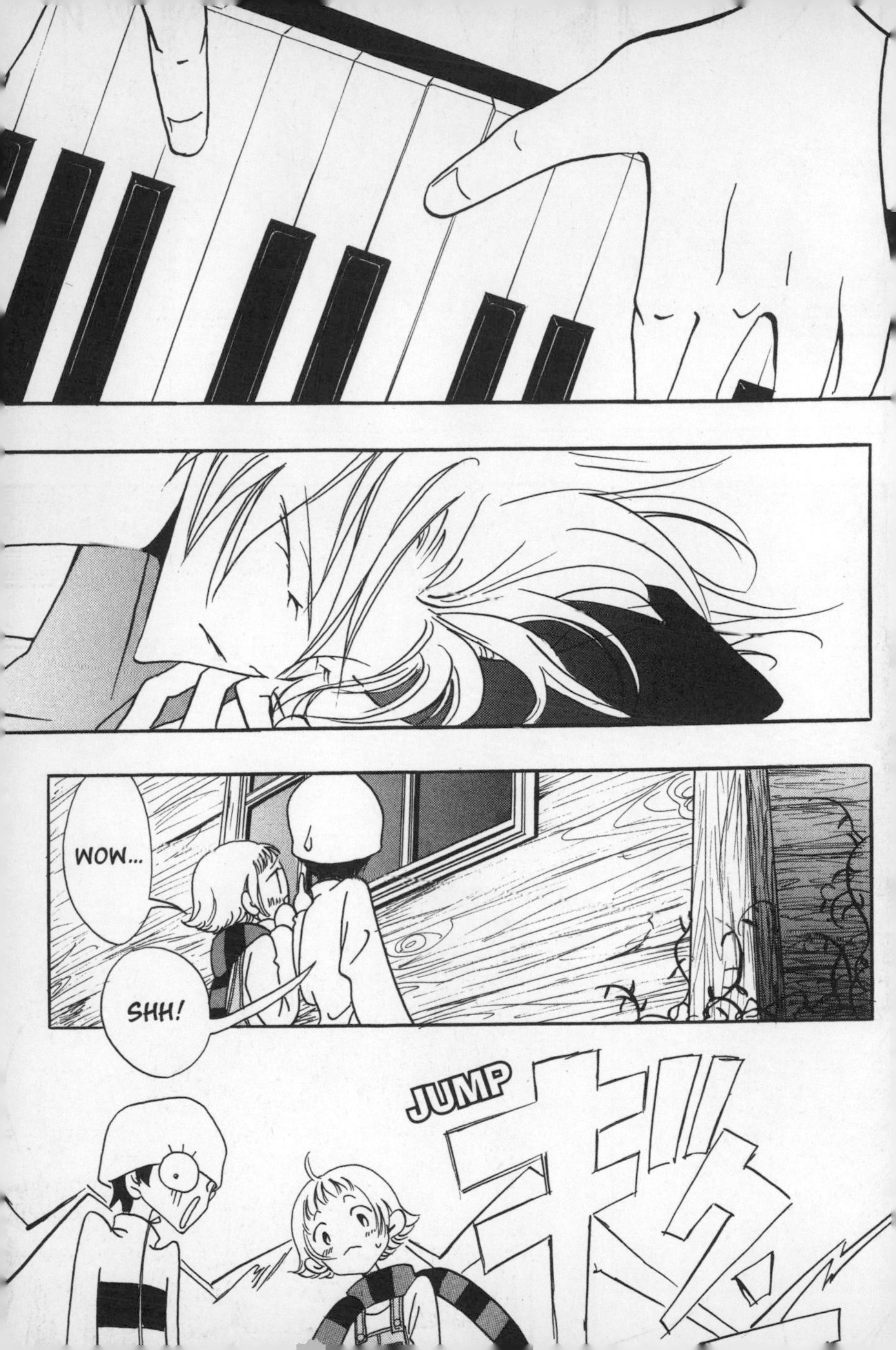
WOW...
SHH!
JUMP

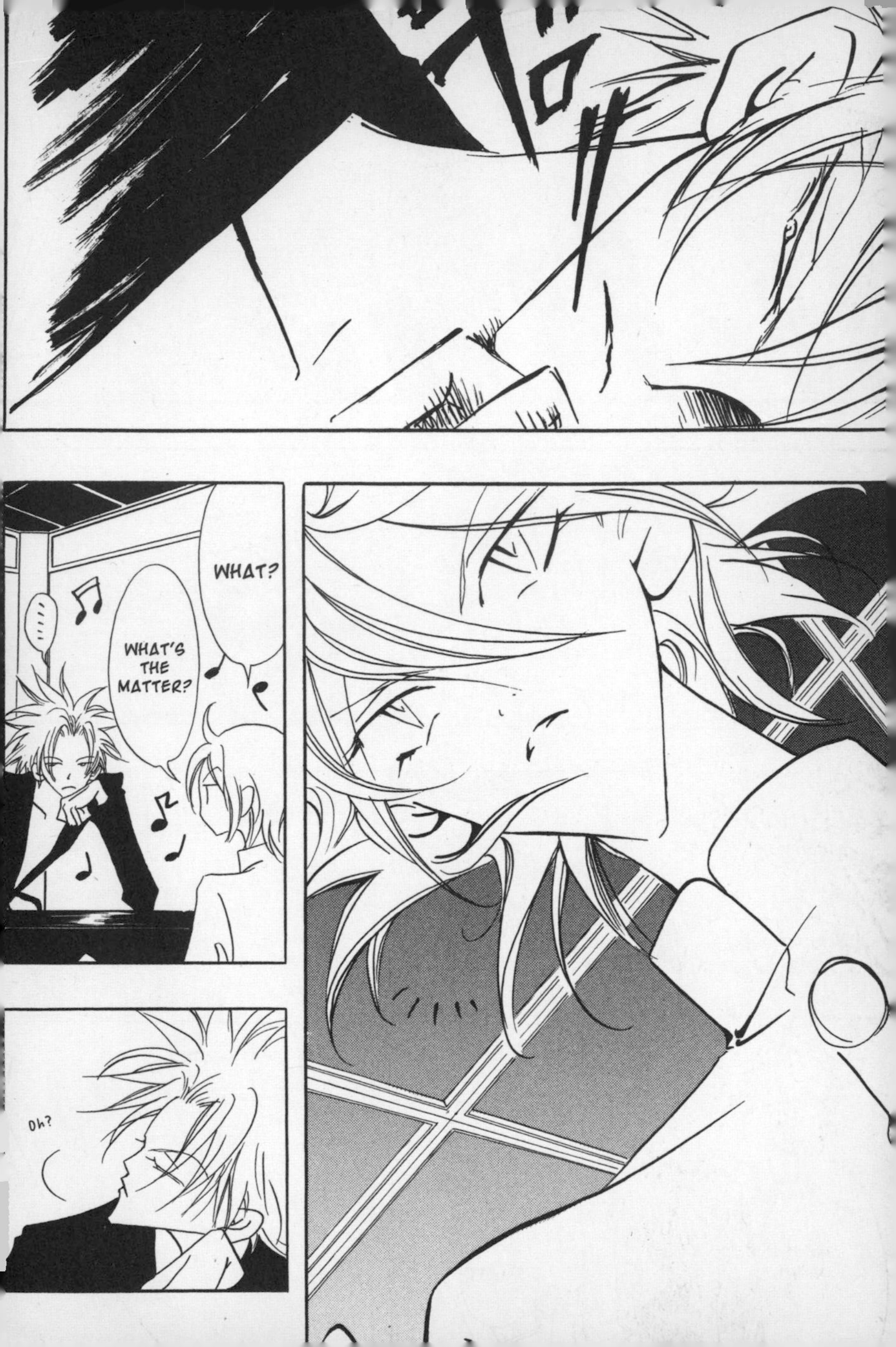
WHAT?
WHAT'S THE MATTER?
......
Oh?

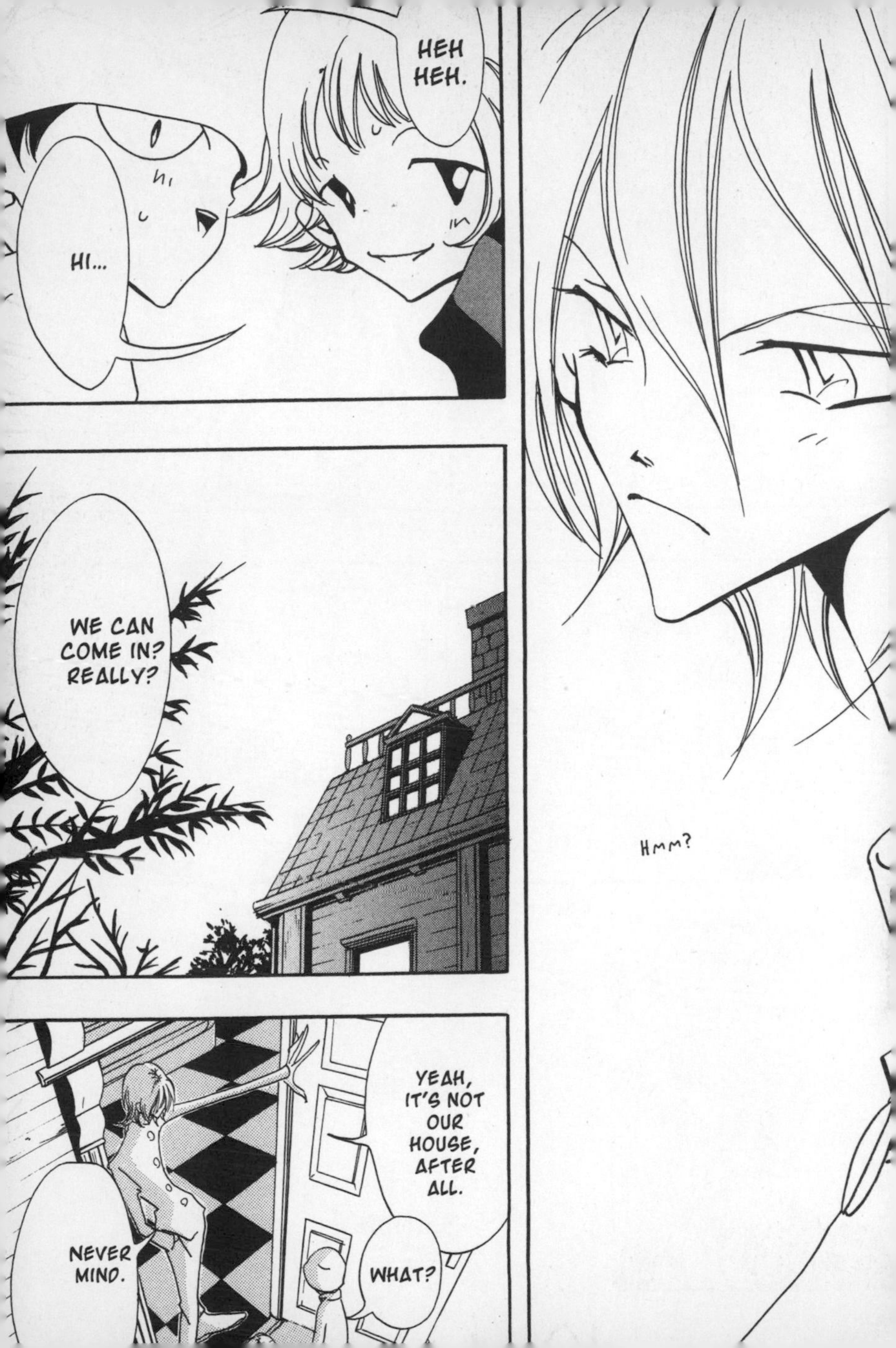
HMM?
HEH HEH.
HI...
WE CAN COME IN? REALLY?
YEAH, IT'S NOT OUR HOUSE, AFTER ALL.
WHAT?
NEVER MIND.

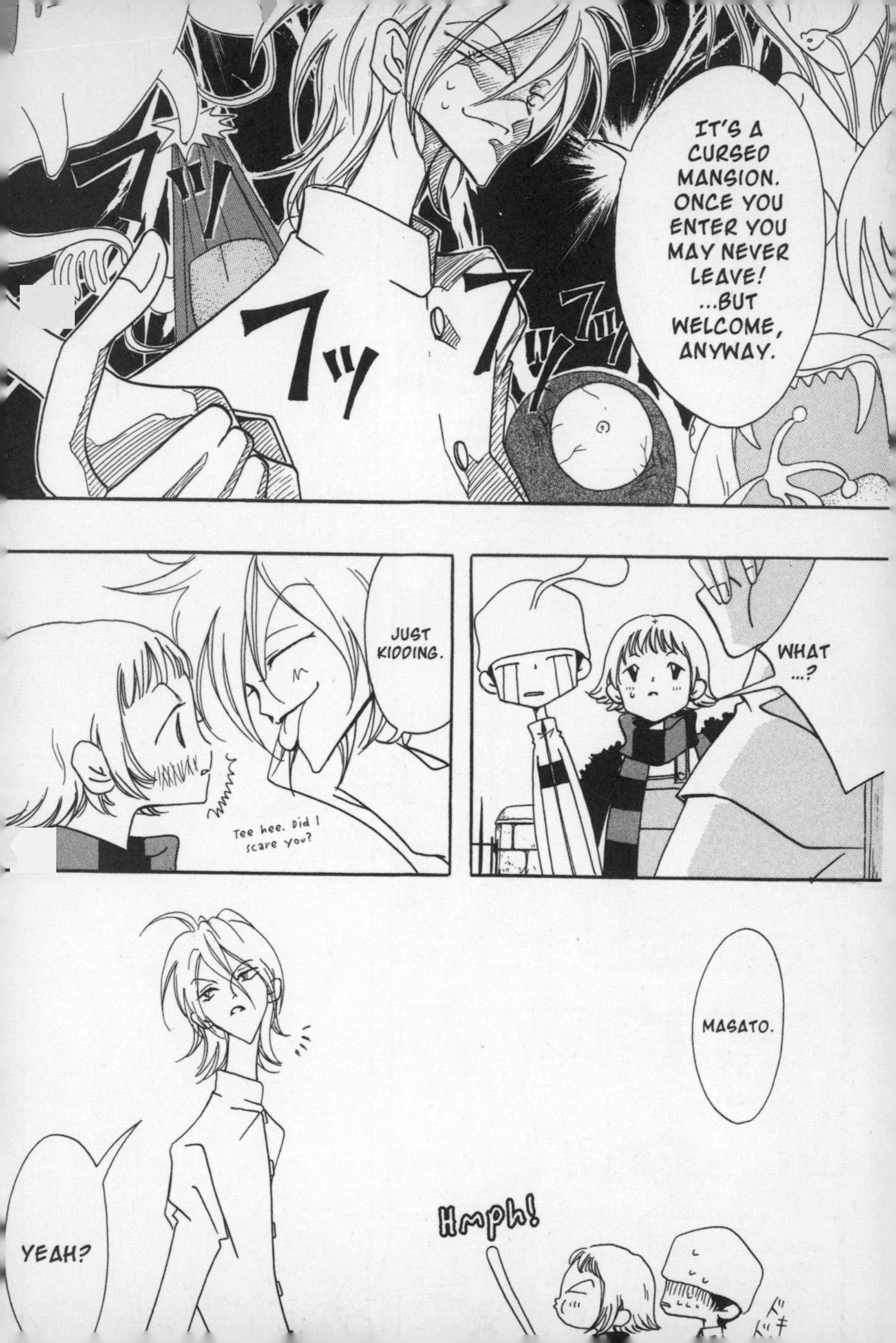
IT'S A CURSED MANSION. ONCE YOU ENTER YOU MAY NEVER LEAVE! ...BUT WELCOME, ANYWAY.
WHAT ...?
JUST KIDDING.
Tee hee. Did I scare you?
MASATO.
YEAH?
Hmph!

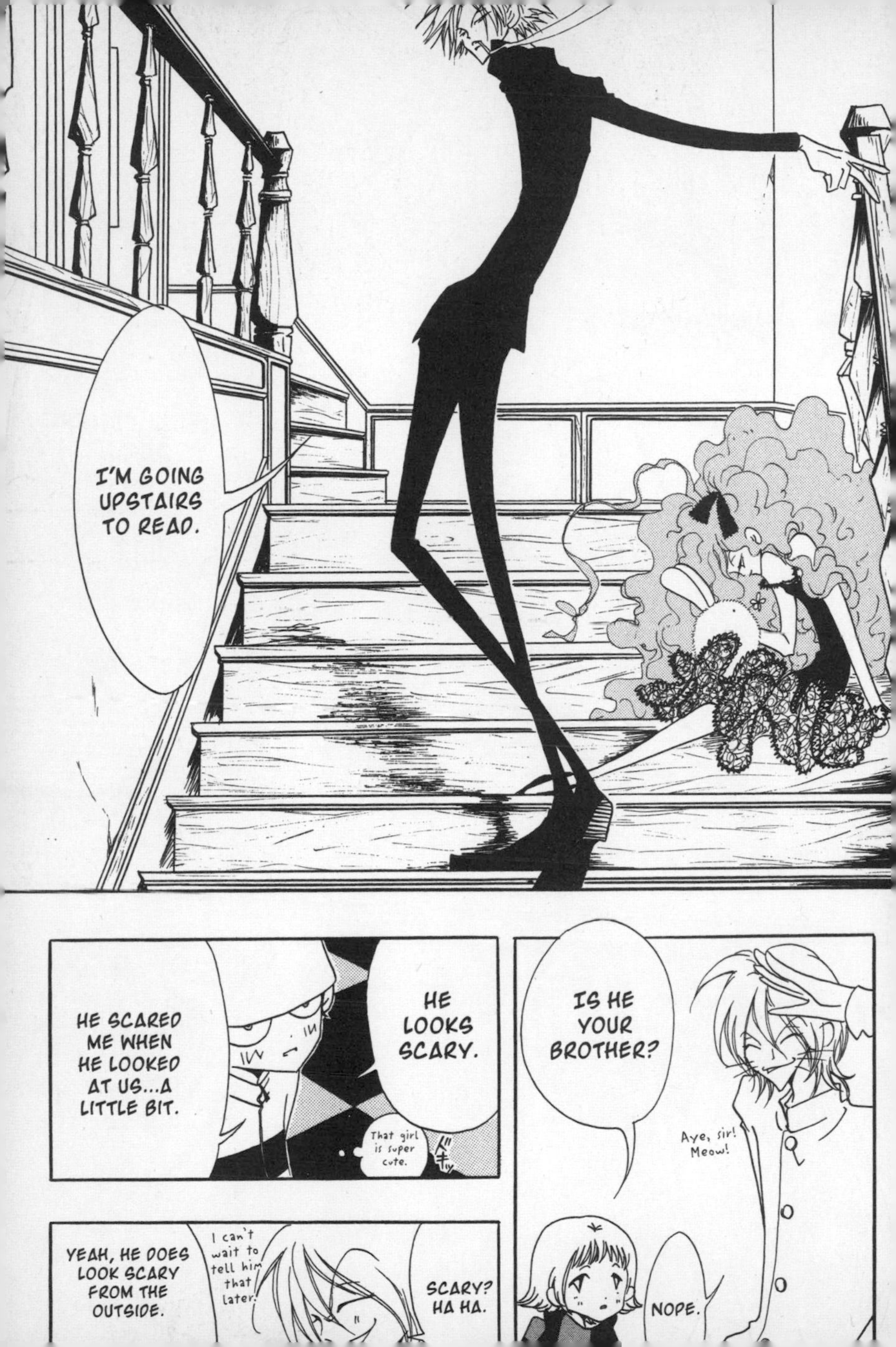
I'M GOING UPSTAIRS TO READ.
IS HE YOUR BROTHER?
Aye, sir! Meow!
NOPE.
HE LOOKS SCARY.
That girl is super cute.
HE SCARED ME WHEN HE LOOKED AT US...A LITTLE BIT.
SCARY? HA HA.
I can't wait to tell him that later.
YEAH, HE DOES LOOK SCARY FROM THE OUTSIDE.

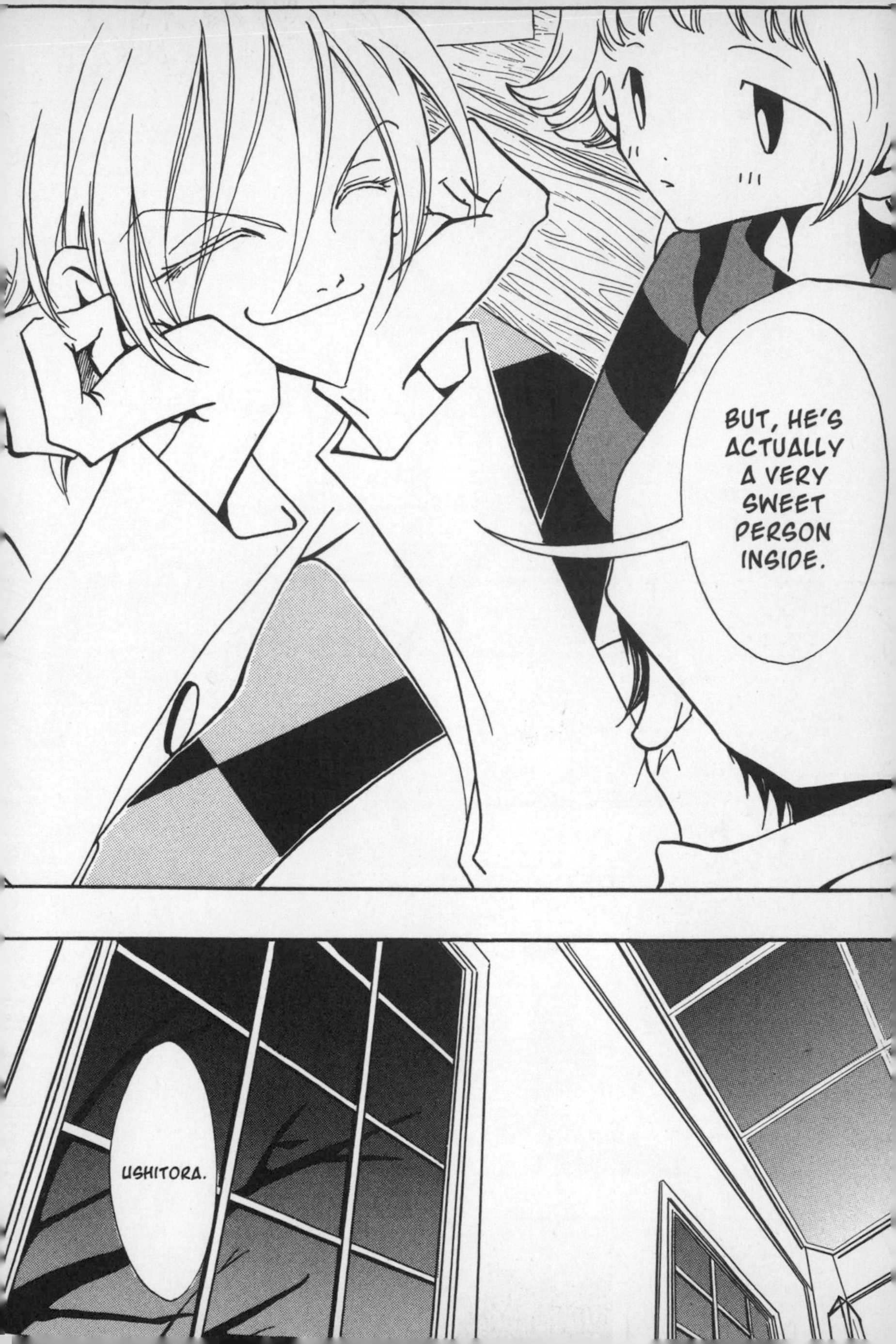
BUT, HE'S ACTUALLY A VERY SWEET PERSON INSIDE.
USHITORA.

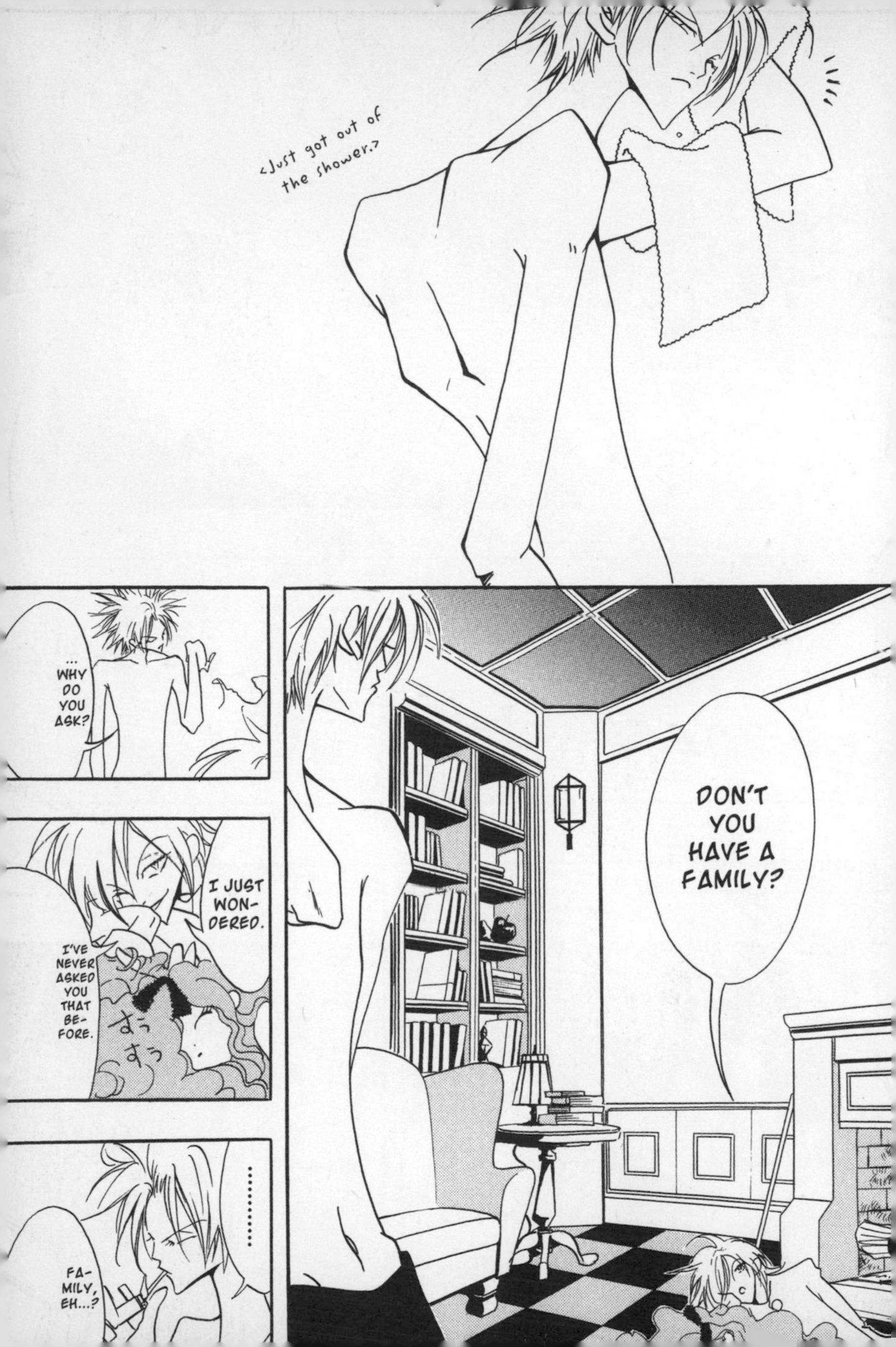
<Just got out of the shower.>
DON'T YOU HAVE A FAMILY?
...WHY DO YOU ASK?
I JUST WONDERED.
I'VE NEVER ASKED YOU THAT BEFORE.
すぅ すぅ
....
FAMILY, EH...?

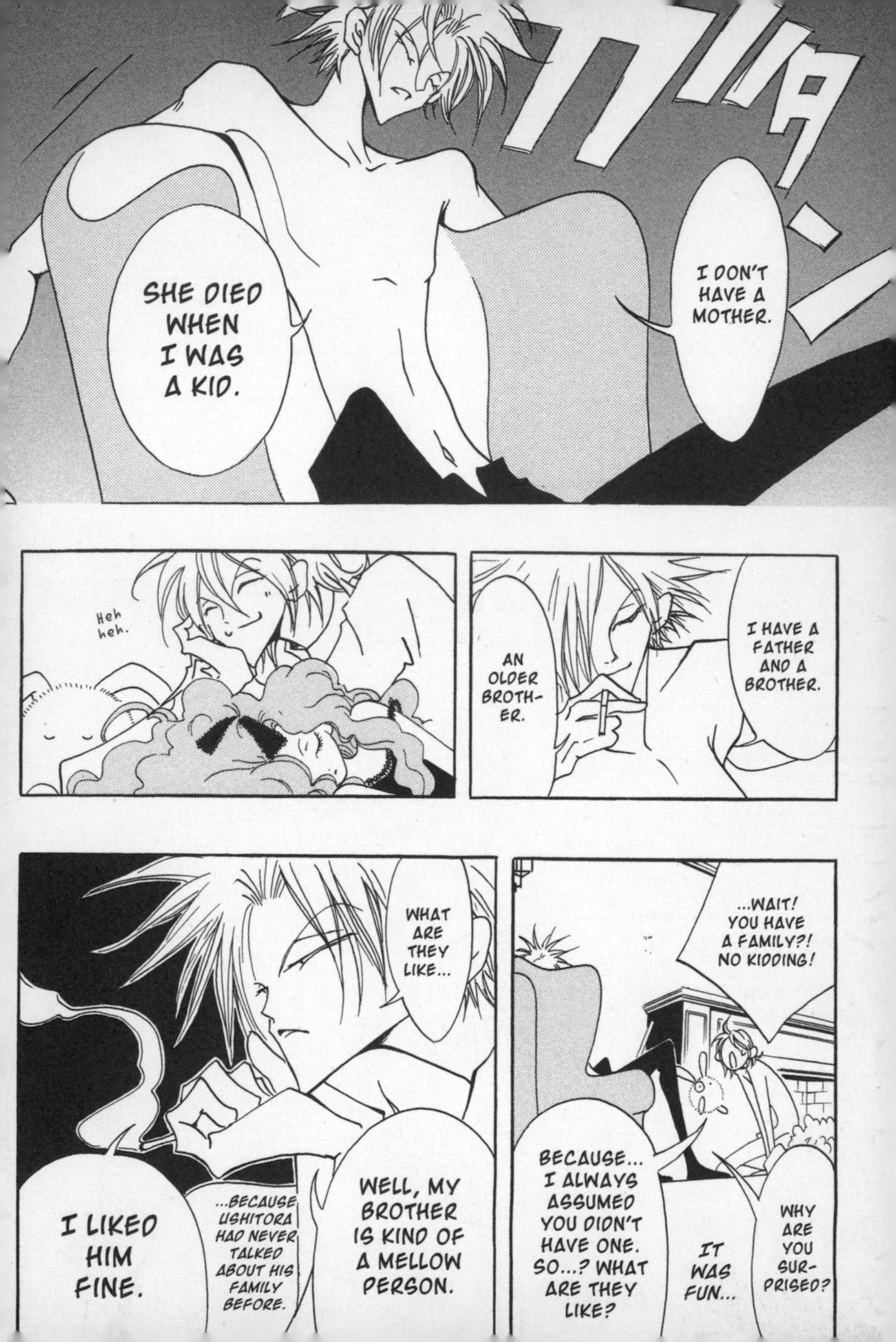
I DON'T HAVE A MOTHER.
SHE DIED WHEN I WAS A KID.
I HAVE A FATHER AND A BROTHER.
AN OLDER BROTH-ER.
Heh heh.
...WAIT! YOU HAVE A FAMILY?! NO KIDDING!
WHY ARE YOU SUR-PRISED?
IT WAS FUN...
BECAUSE... I ALWAYS ASSUMED YOU DIDN'T HAVE ONE. SO...? WHAT ARE THEY LIKE?
WHAT ARE THEY LIKE...
WELL, MY BROTHER IS KIND OF A MELLOW PERSON.
...BECAUSE USHITORA HAD NEVER TALKED ABOUT HIS FAMILY BEFORE.
I LIKED HIM FINE.

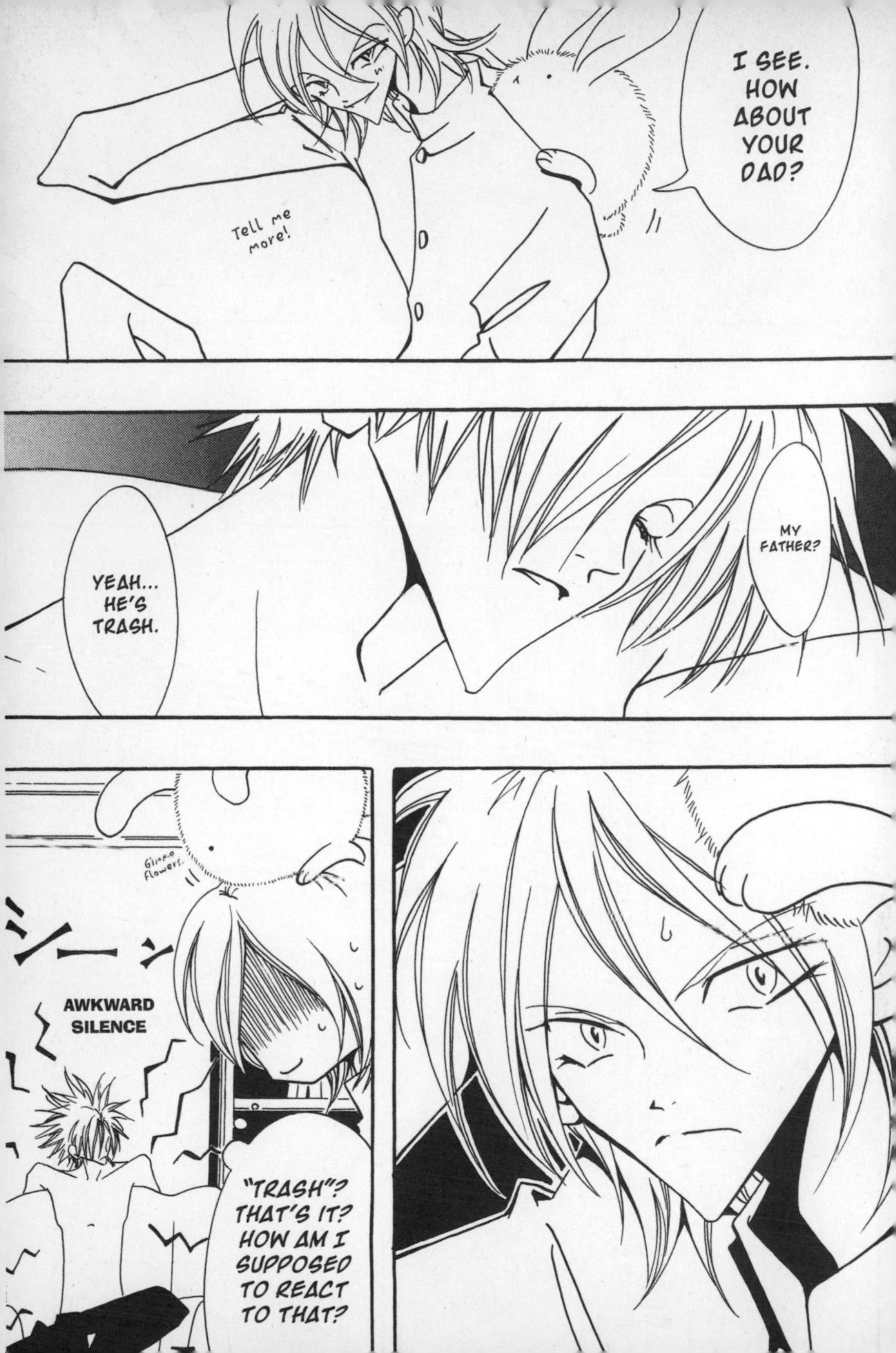

I SEE. HOW ABOUT YOUR DAD?
Tell me more!
MY FATHER?
YEAH... HE'S TRASH.
AWKWARD SILENCE
"TRASH"? THAT'S IT? HOW AM I SUPPOSED TO REACT TO THAT?

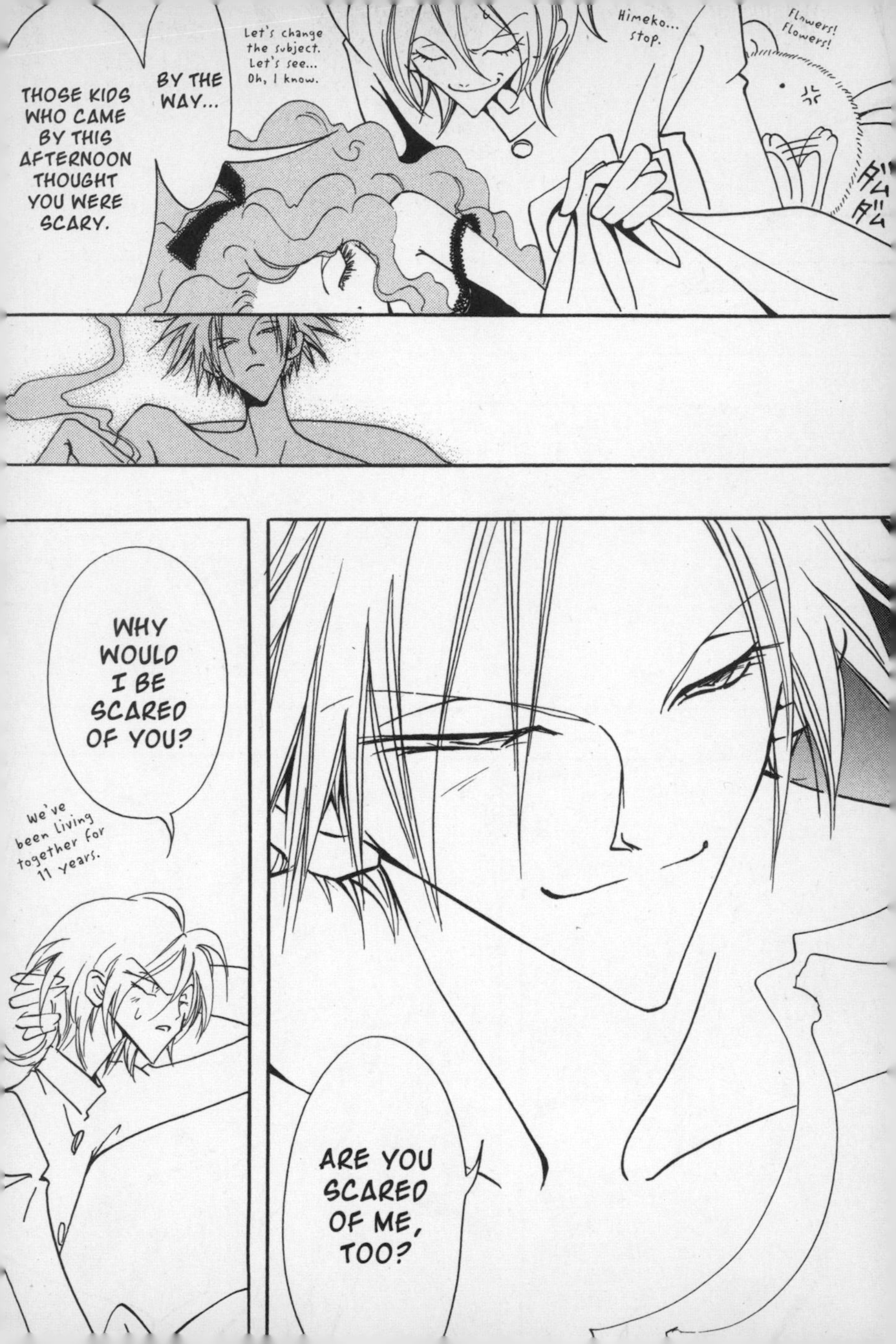
Flowers! Flowers!
Himeko... stop.
ダムダム
Let's change the subject. Let's see... Oh, I know.
BY THE WAY...
THOSE KIDS WHO CAME BY THIS AFTERNOON THOUGHT YOU WERE SCARY.
ARE YOU SCARED OF ME, TOO?
WHY WOULD I BE SCARED OF YOU?
We've been living together for 11 years.

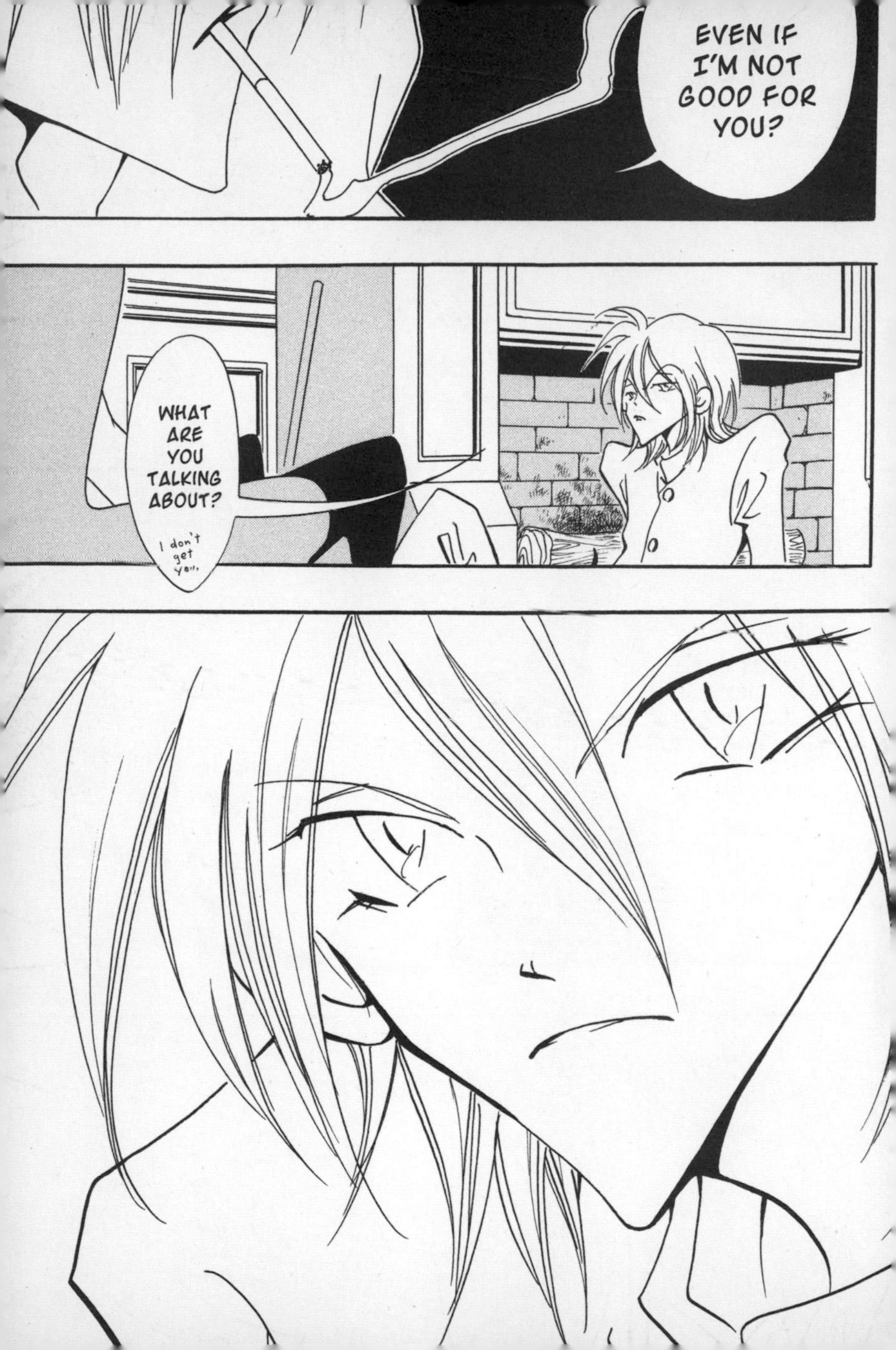
EVEN IF I'M NOT GOOD FOR YOU?
WHAT ARE YOU TALKING ABOUT?
I don't get you.

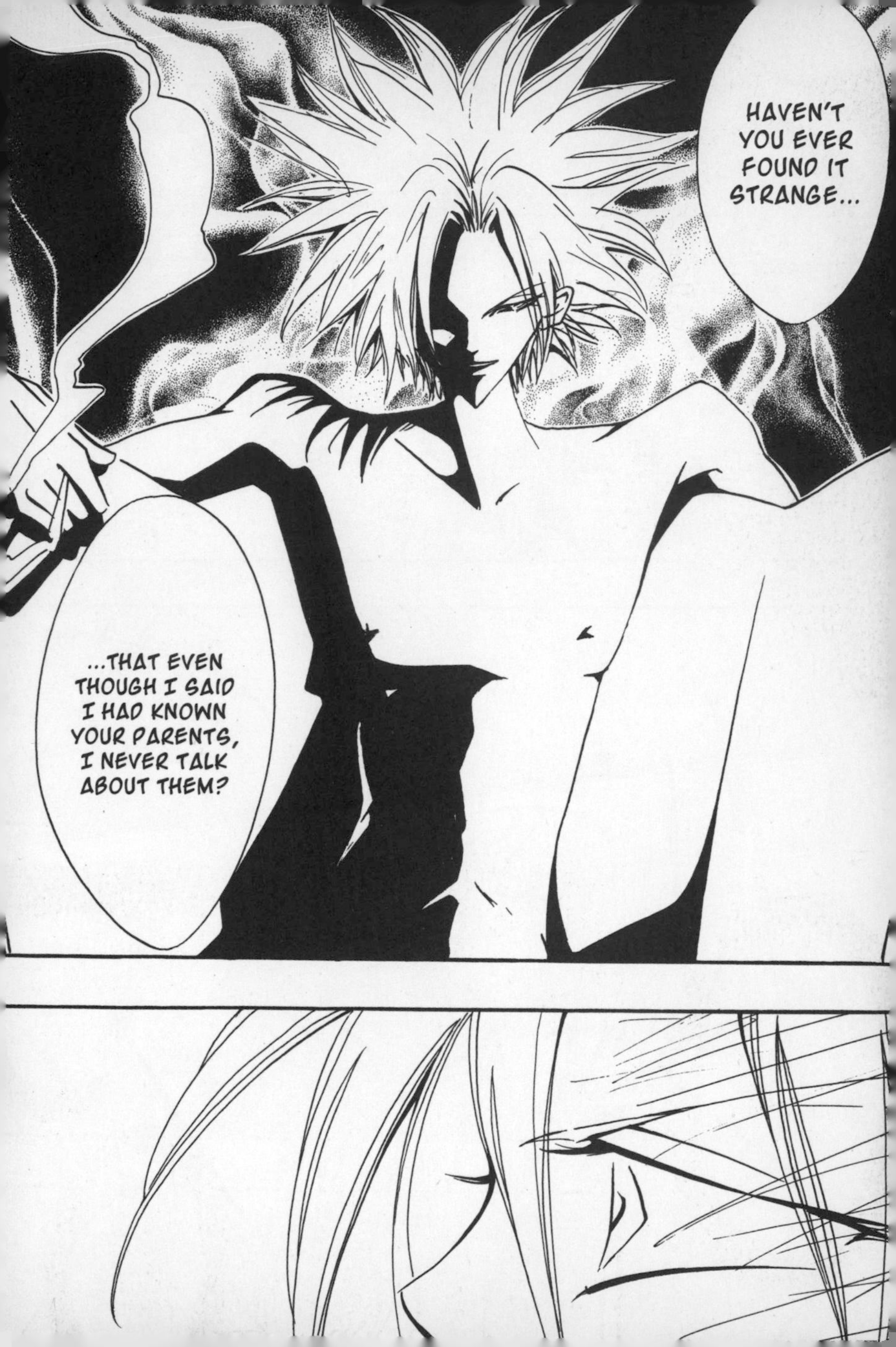
HAVEN'T YOU EVER FOUND IT STRANGE...
...THAT EVEN THOUGH I SAID I HAD KNOWN YOUR PARENTS, I NEVER TALK ABOUT THEM?

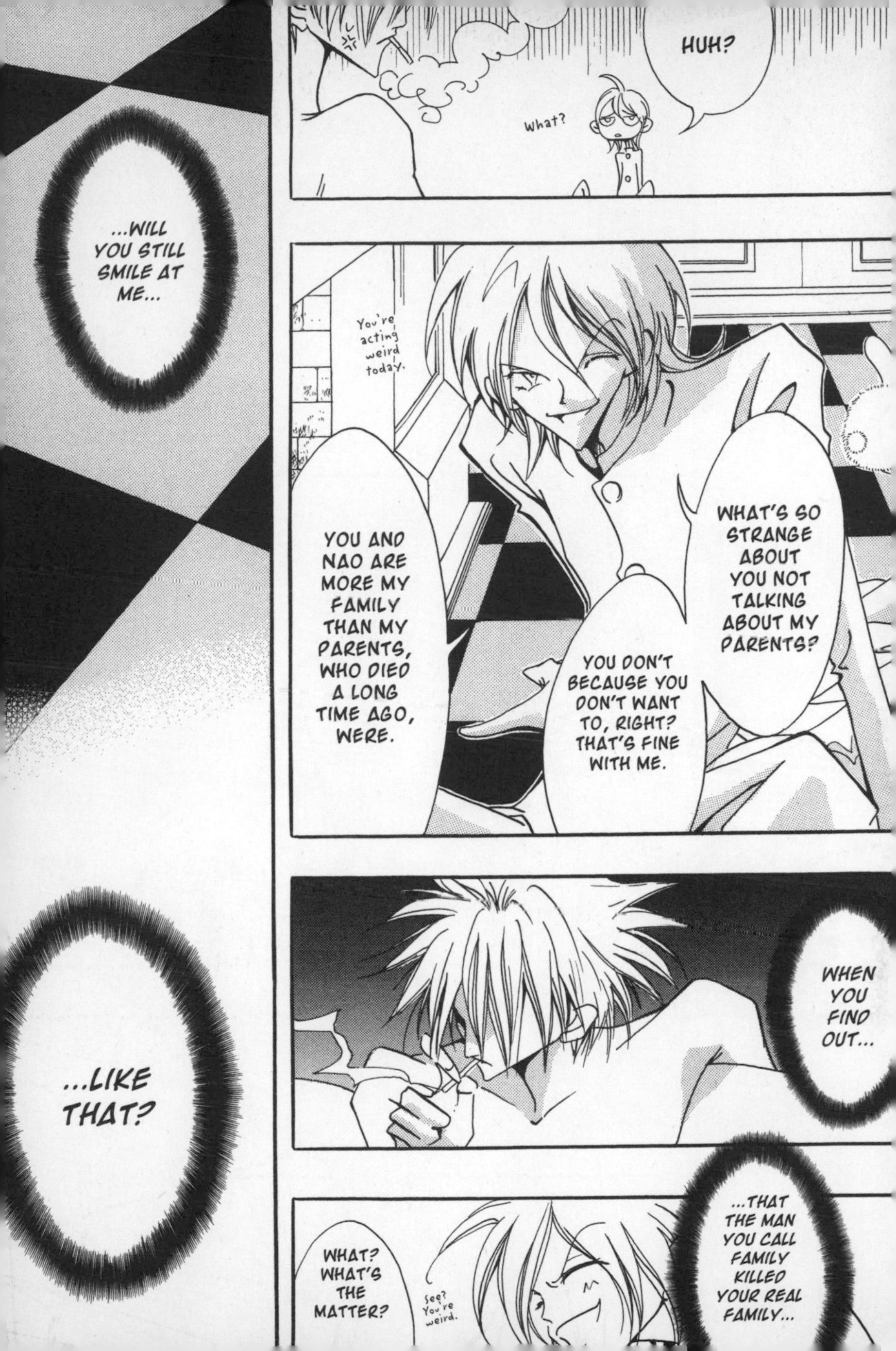
HUH?
What?
WHAT'S SO STRANGE ABOUT YOU NOT TALKING ABOUT MY PARENTS?
YOU DON'T BECAUSE YOU DON'T WANT TO, RIGHT? THAT'S FINE WITH ME.
YOU AND NAO ARE MORE MY FAMILY THAN MY PARENTS, WHO DIED A LONG TIME AGO, WERE.
You're acting weird today.
WHEN YOU FIND OUT...
...THAT THE MAN YOU CALL FAMILY KILLED YOUR REAL FAMILY...
See? You're weird.
WHAT? WHAT'S THE MATTER?
...WILL YOU STILL SMILE AT ME...
...LIKE THAT?

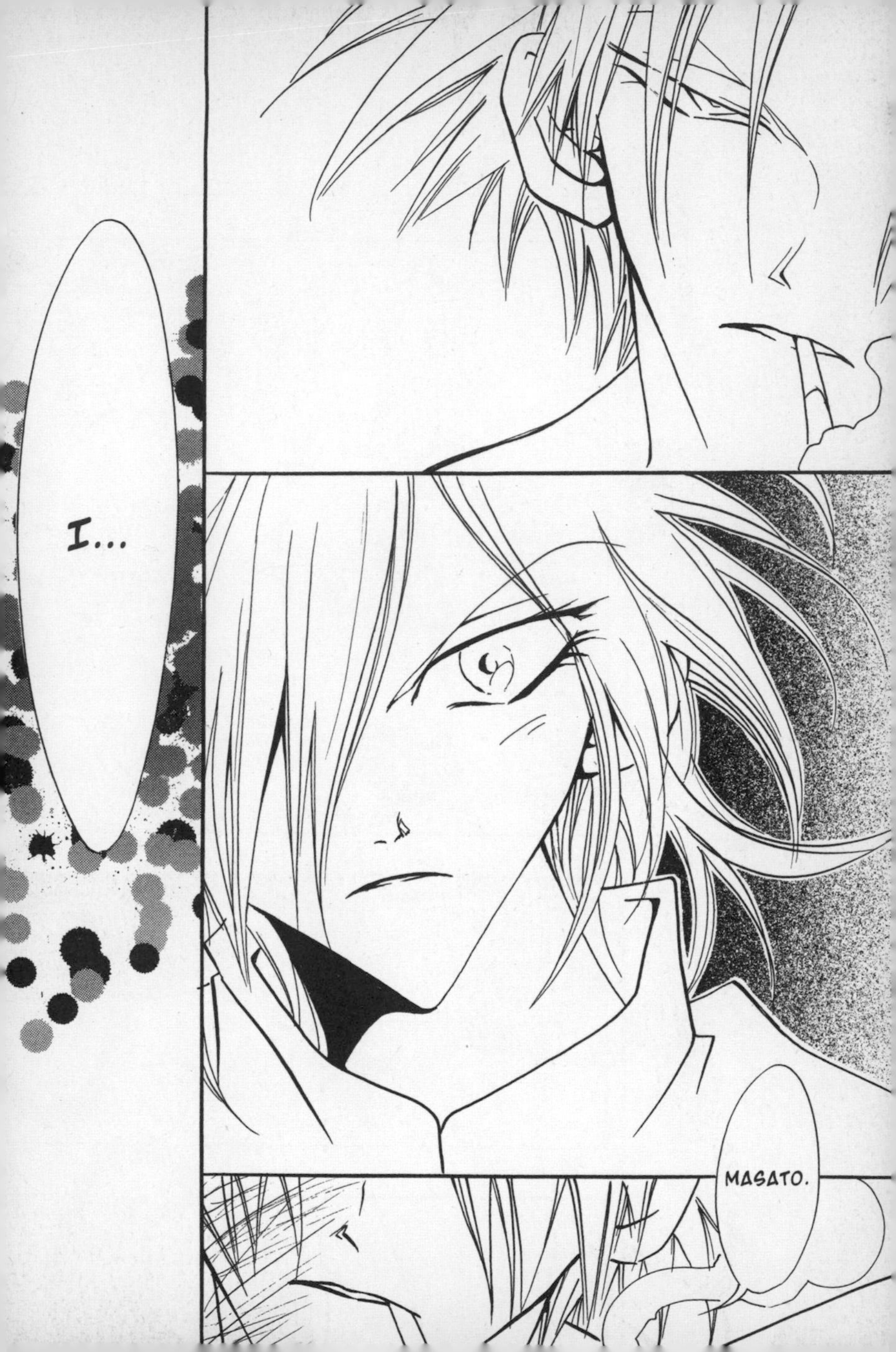
MASATO.
I...

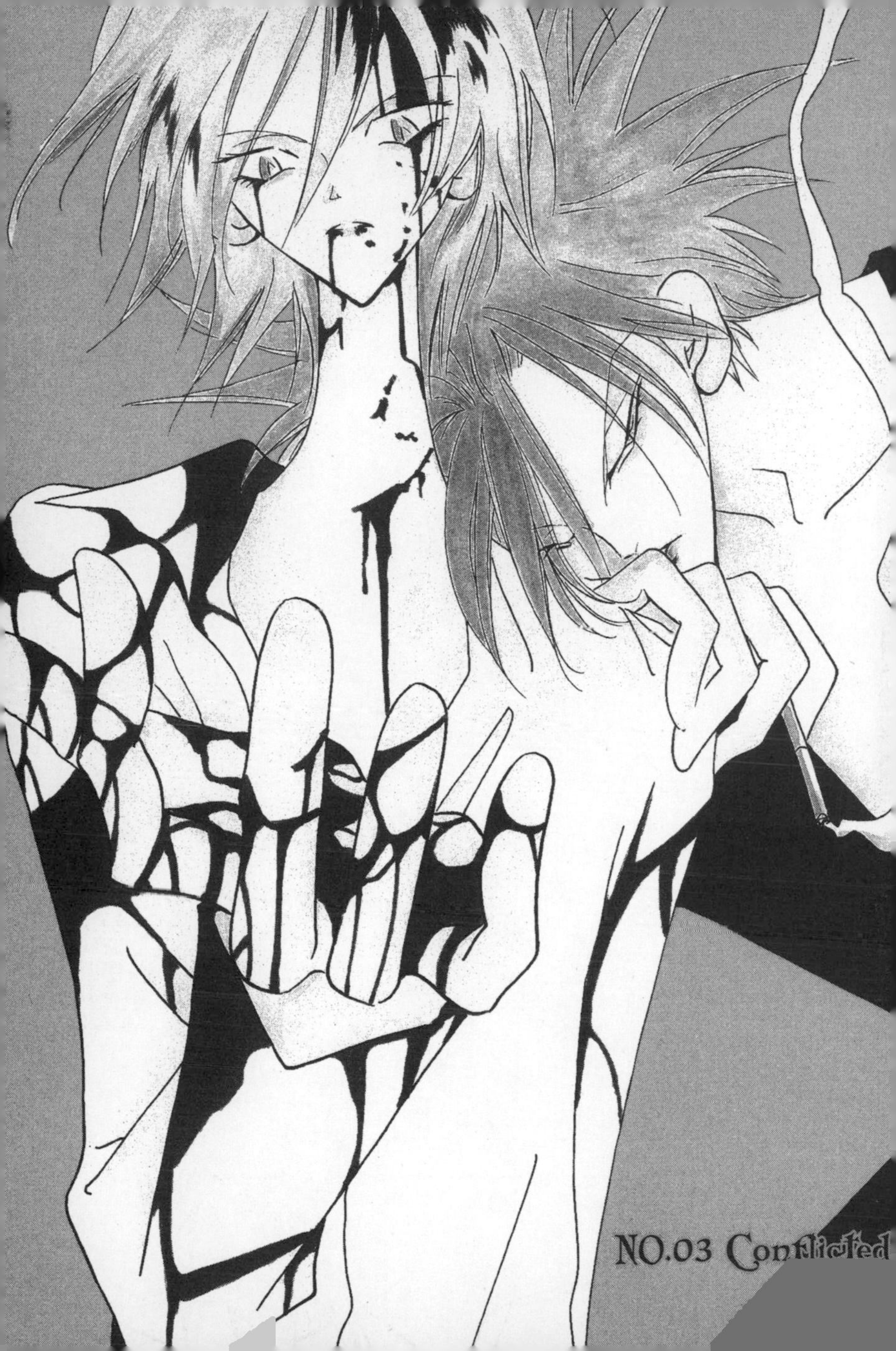
NO.03 Conflicted

NO.03

Conflicted

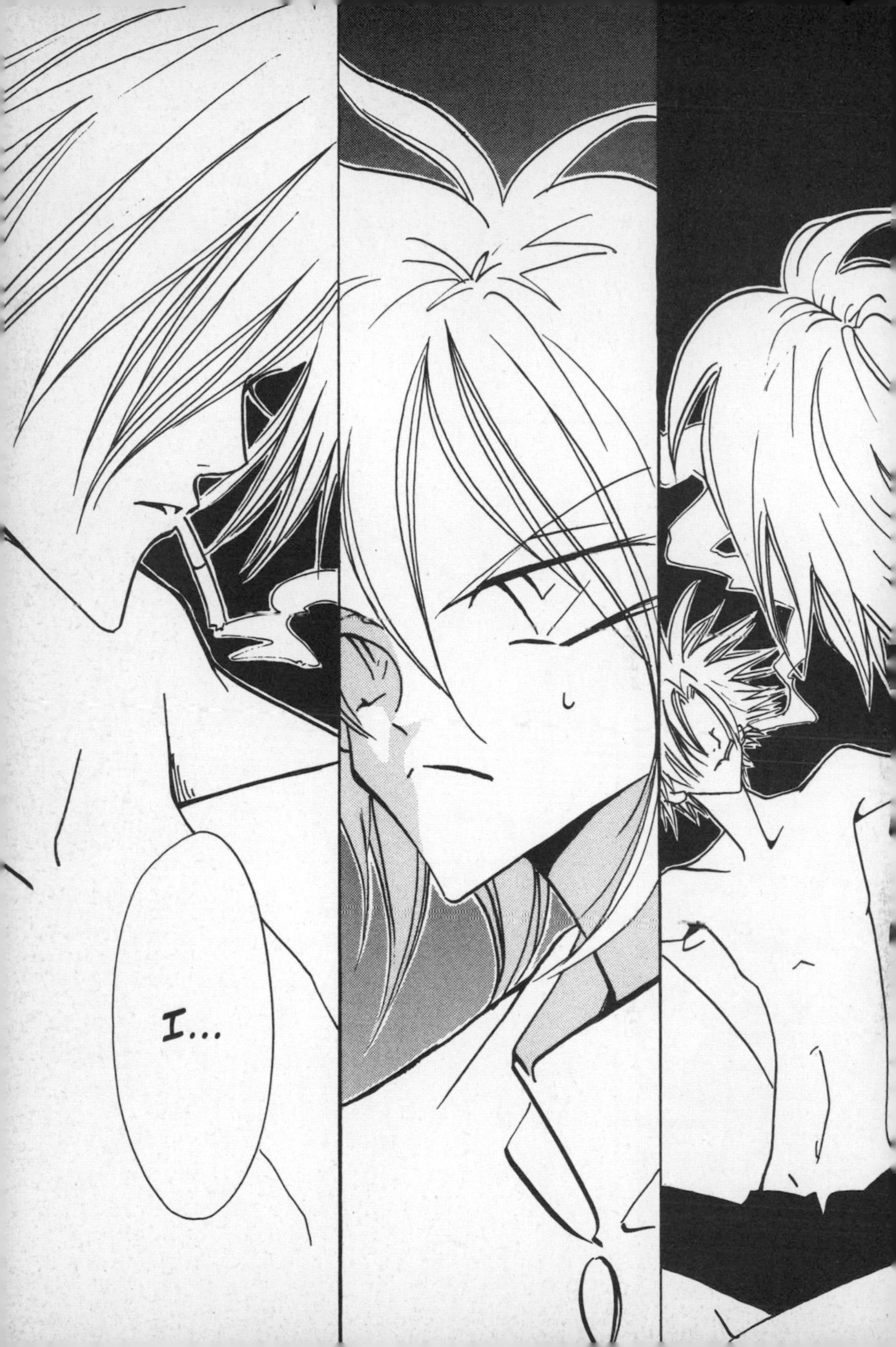
I...

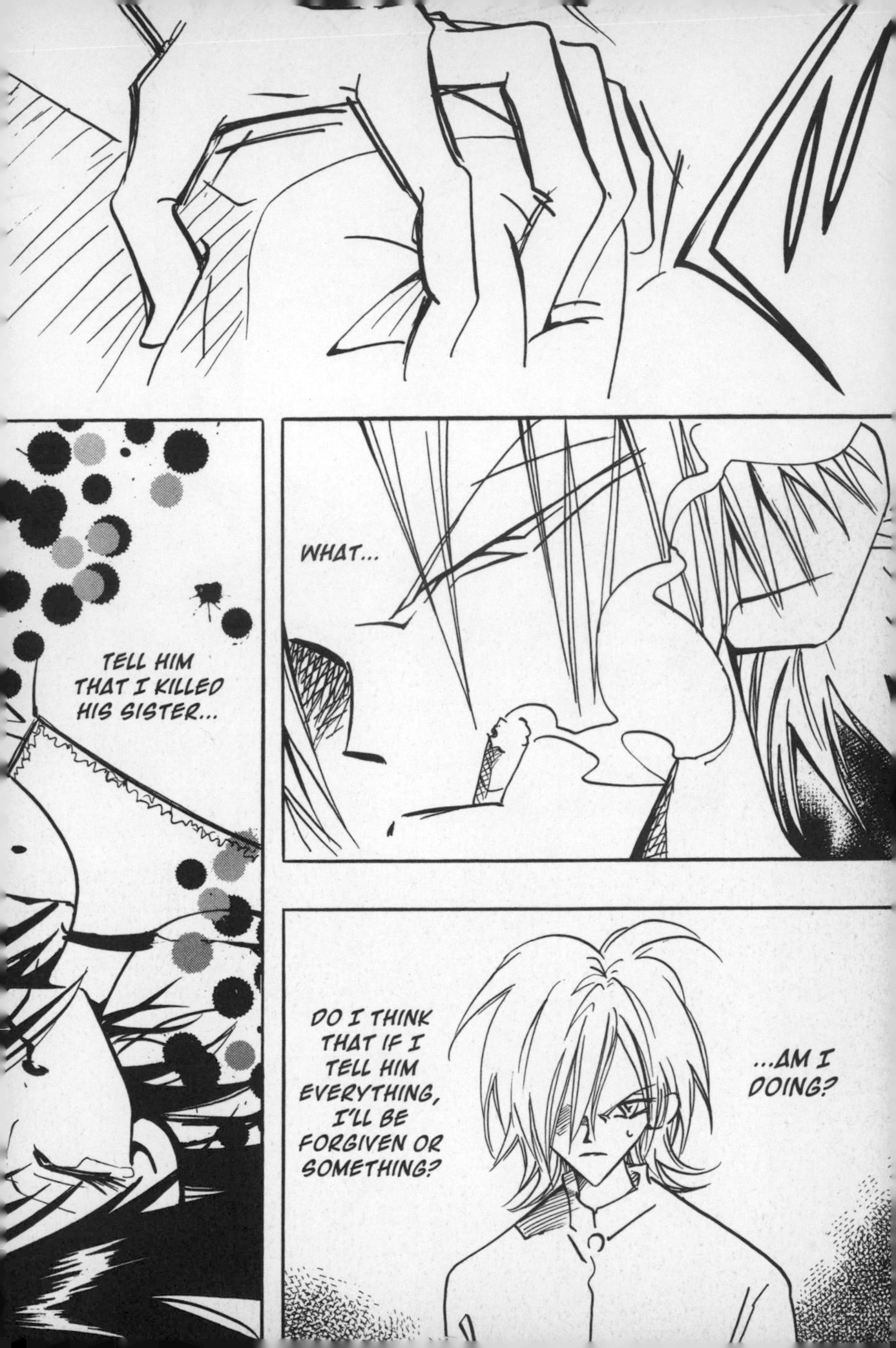
WHAT...
...AM I DOING?
DO I THINK THAT IF I TELL HIM EVERYTHING, I'LL BE FORGIVEN OR SOMETHING?
TELL HIM THAT I KILLED HIS SISTER...

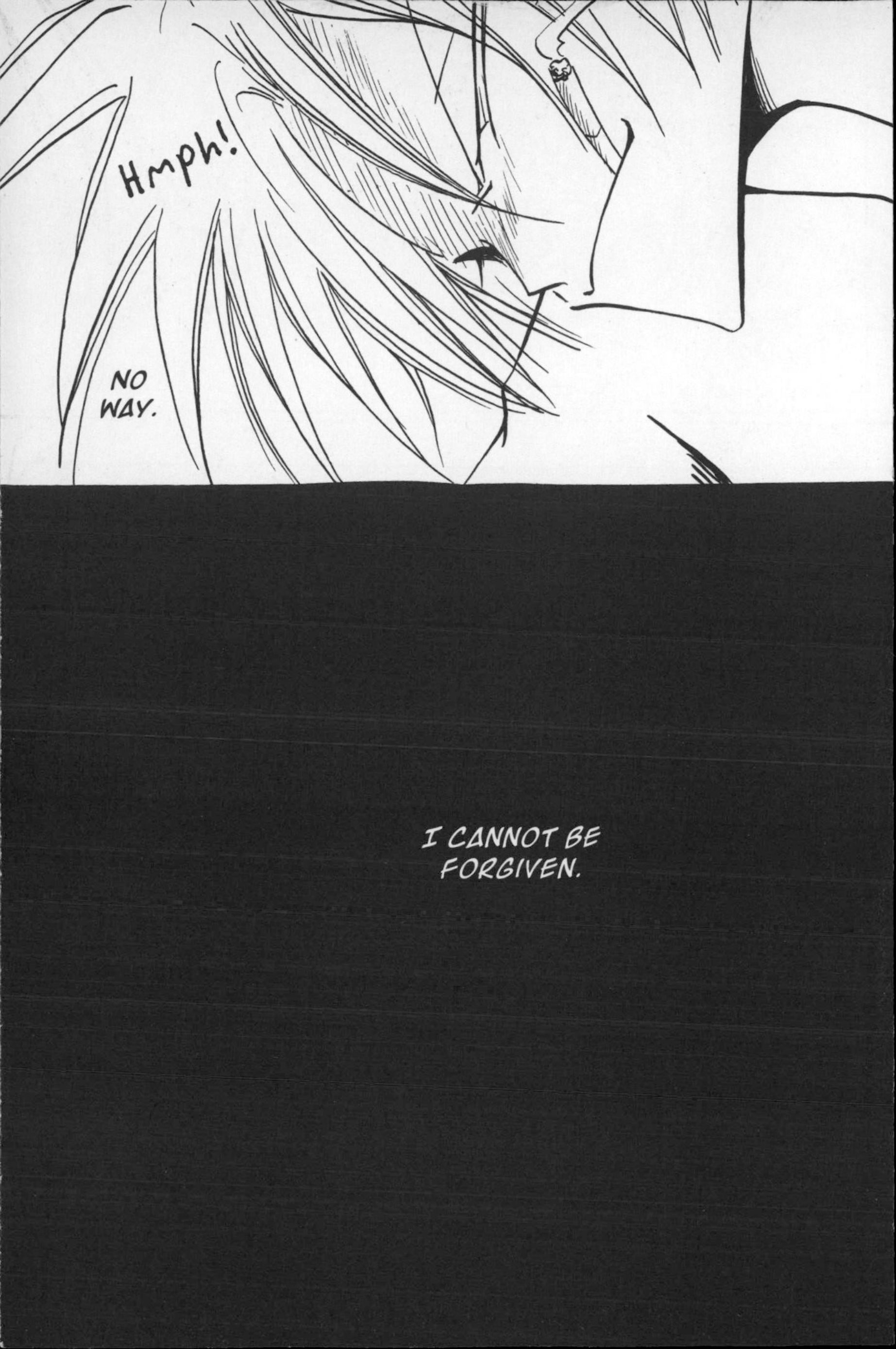
Hmph!
NO WAY.
I CANNOT BE FORGIVEN.

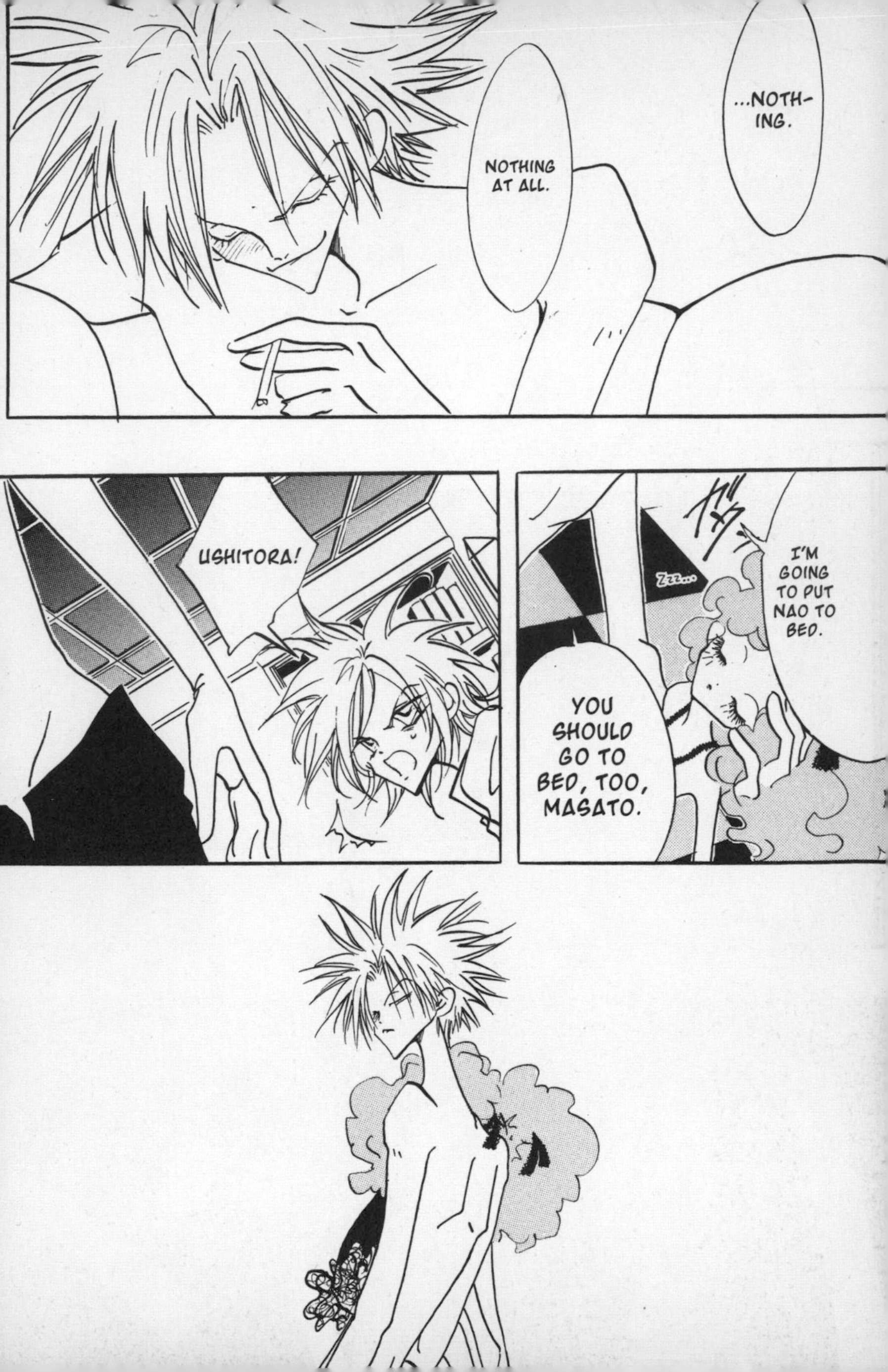
...NOTH-ING.
NOTHING AT ALL.
I'M GOING TO PUT NAO TO BED.
Zzz...
YOU SHOULD GO TO BED, TOO, MASATO.
USHITORA!

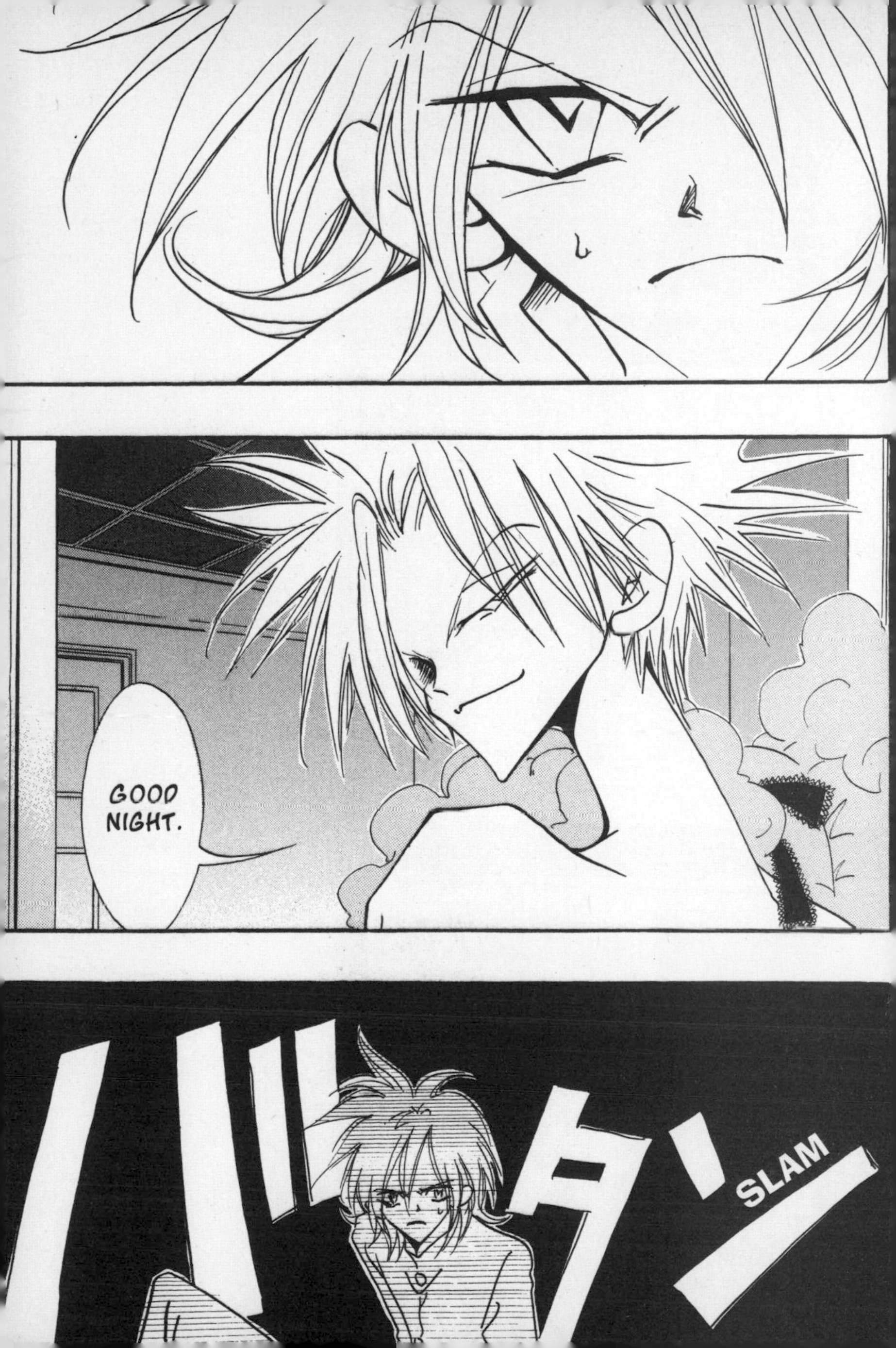
GOOD NIGHT.
バタン
SLAM

SIS?

ARE YOU ASLEEP?

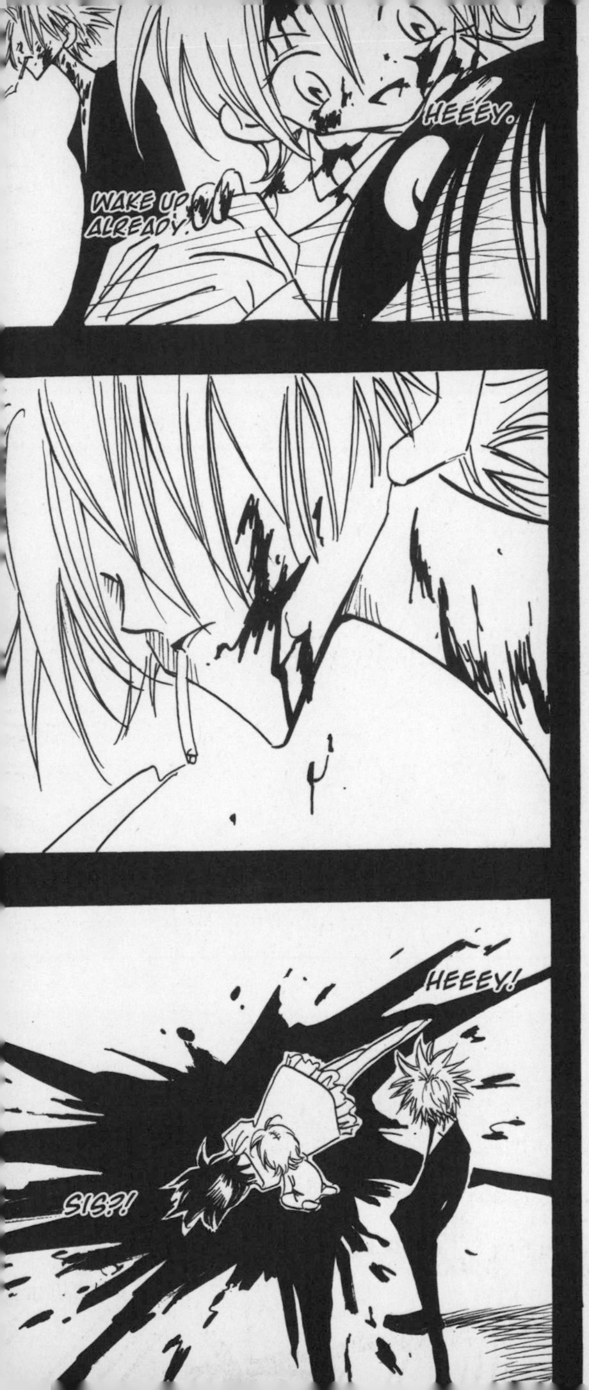
HEEEY.
WAKE UP ALREADY.
HEEEY!
SIS?!

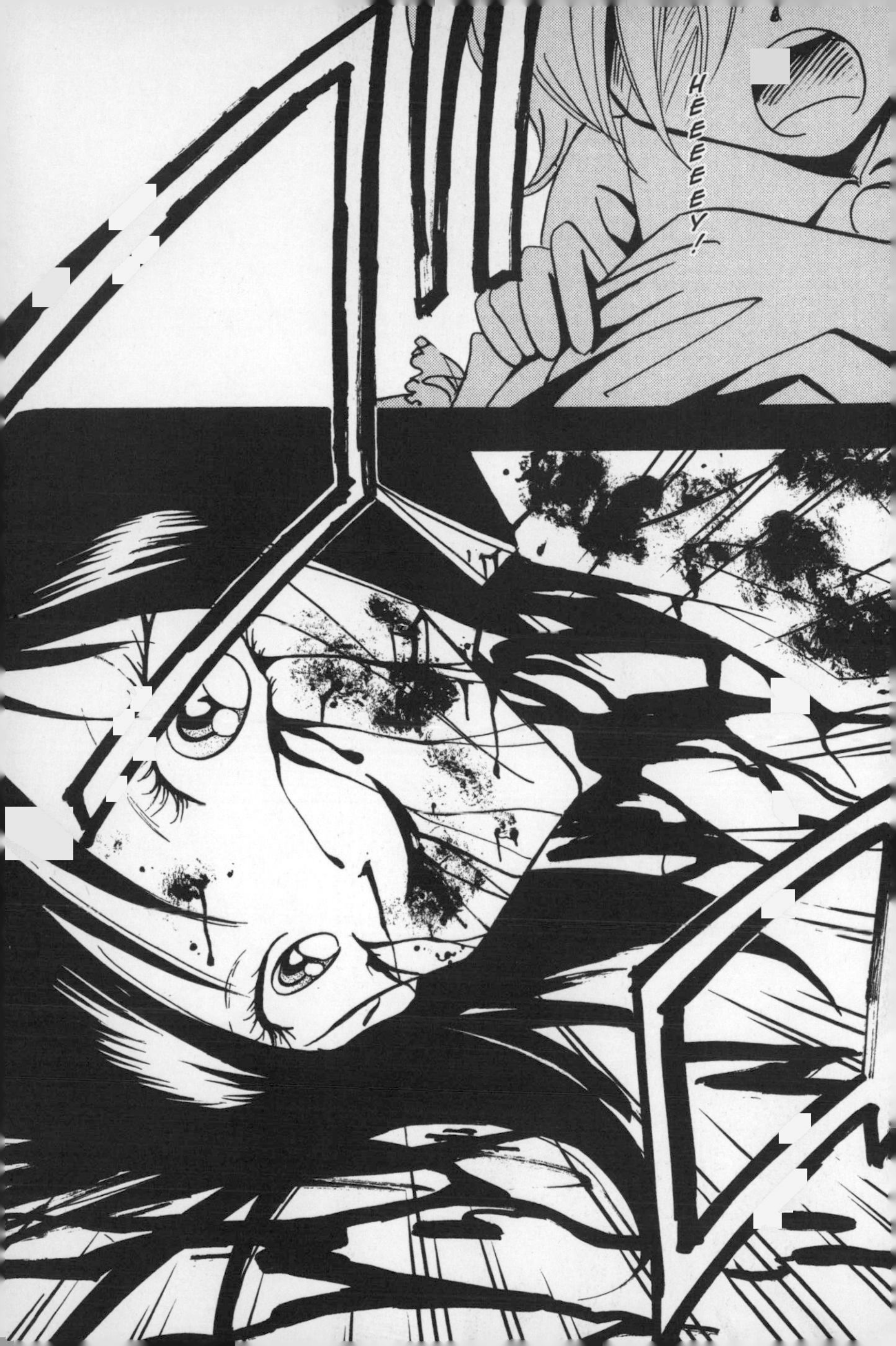
HEEEEEY!

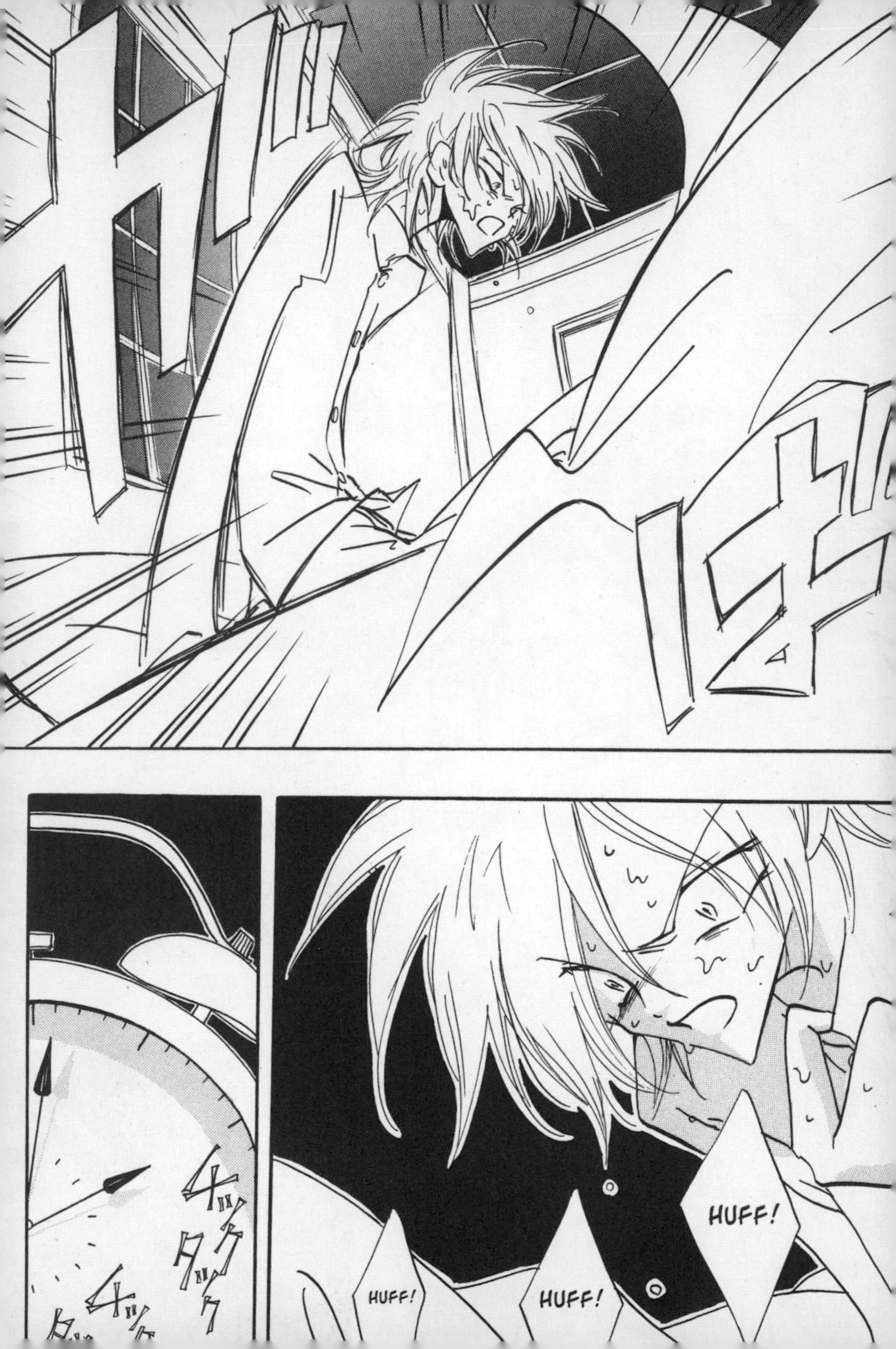
HUFF!
HUFF!
HUFF!

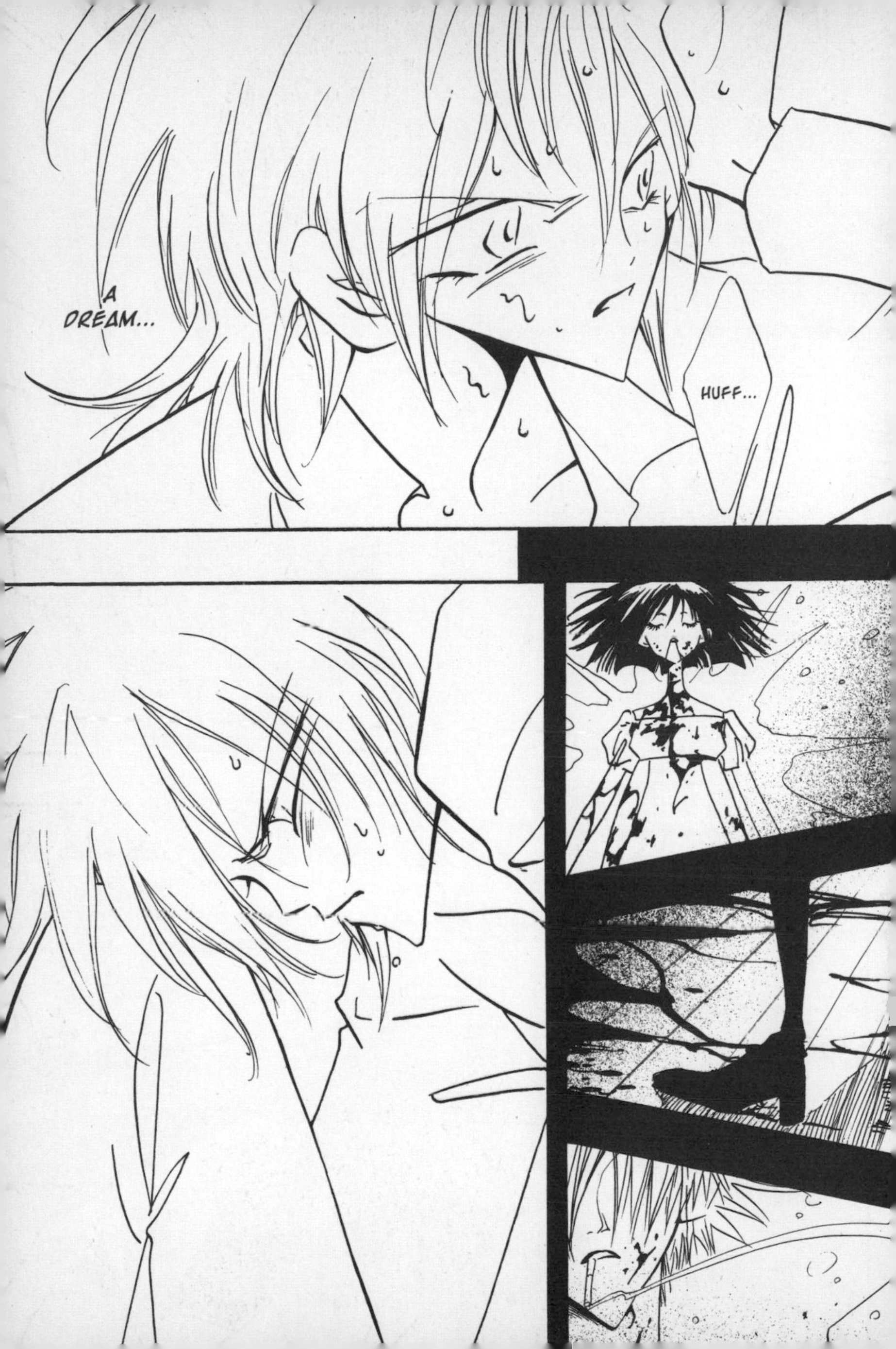
HUFF...
A DREAM...

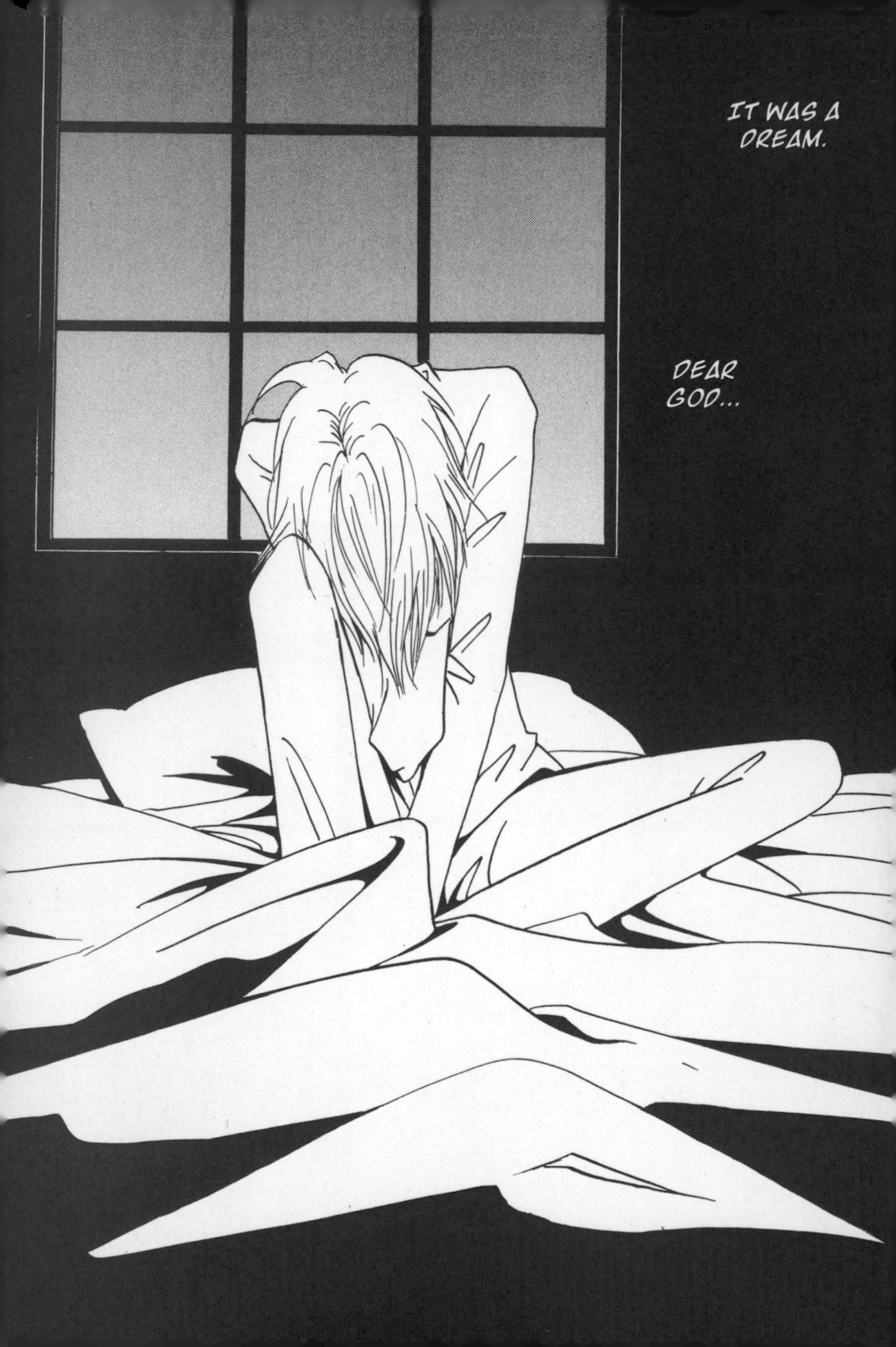
IT WAS A DREAM.
DEAR GOD...

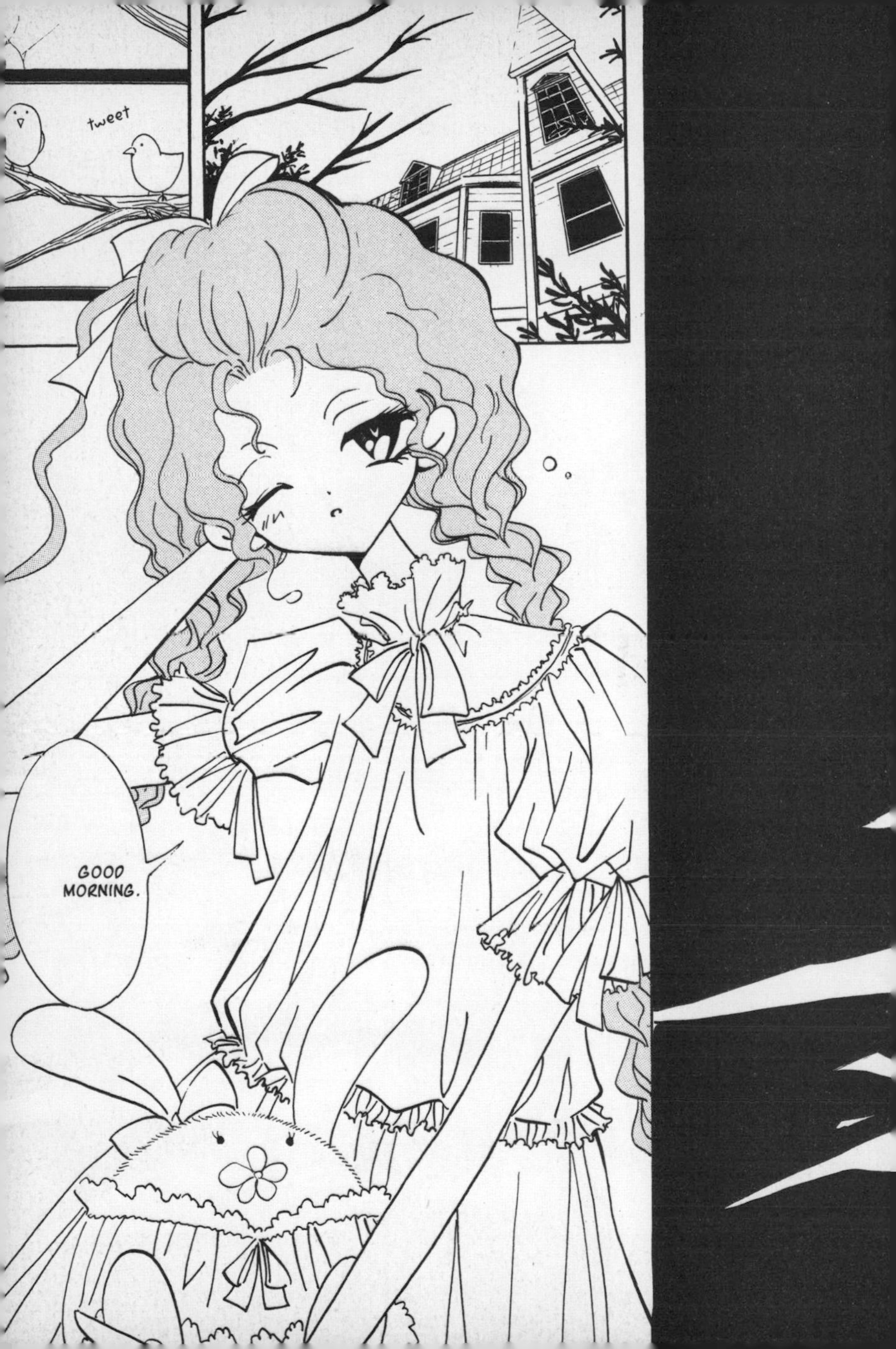
tweet
GOOD MORNING.

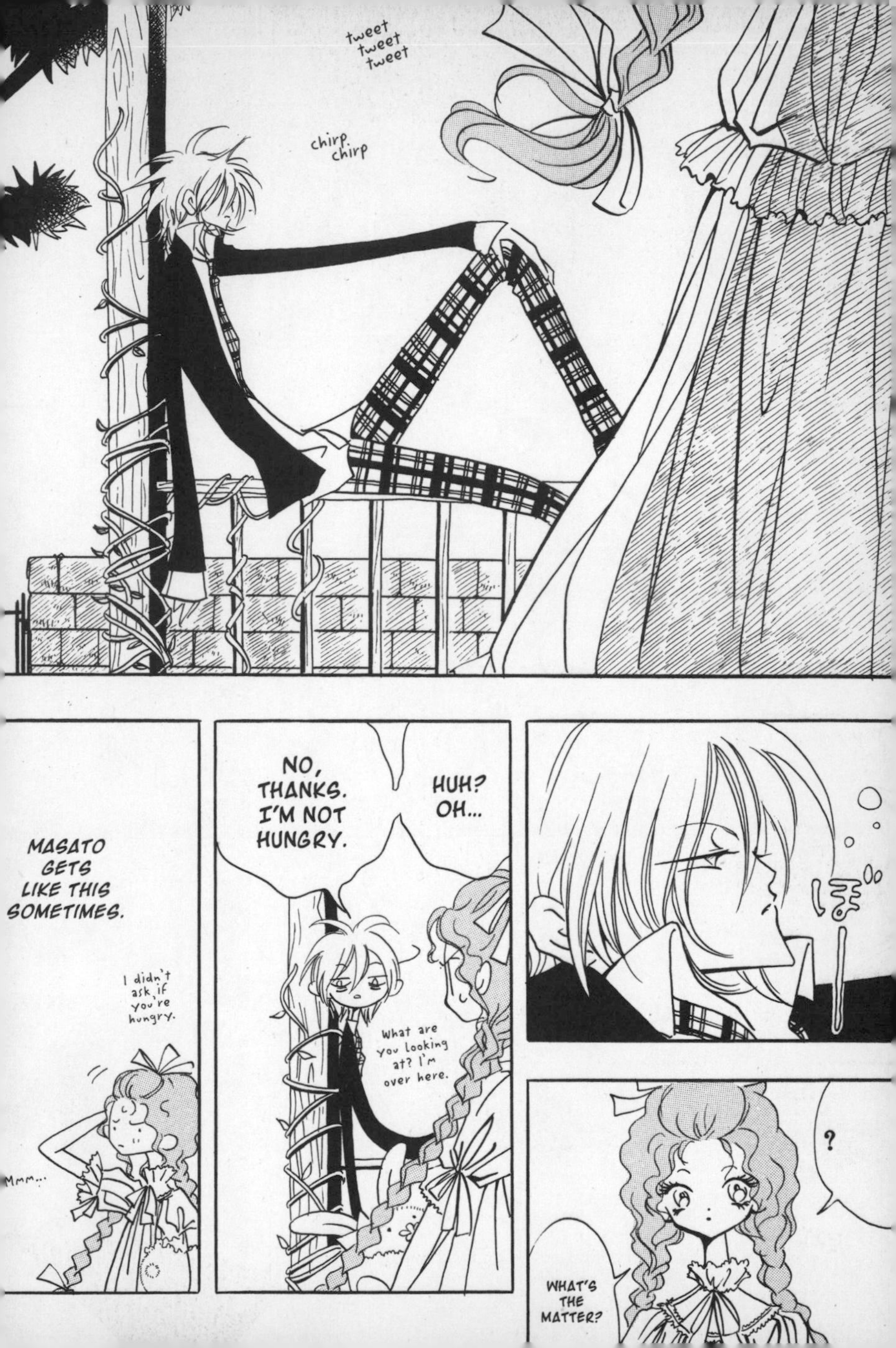
tweet tweet tweet
chirp. chirp
?
WHAT'S THE MATTER?
HUH? OH...
NO, THANKS. I'M NOT HUNGRY.
What are you looking at? I'm over here.
MASATO GETS LIKE THIS SOMETIMES.
I didn't ask if you're hungry.
Mmm...

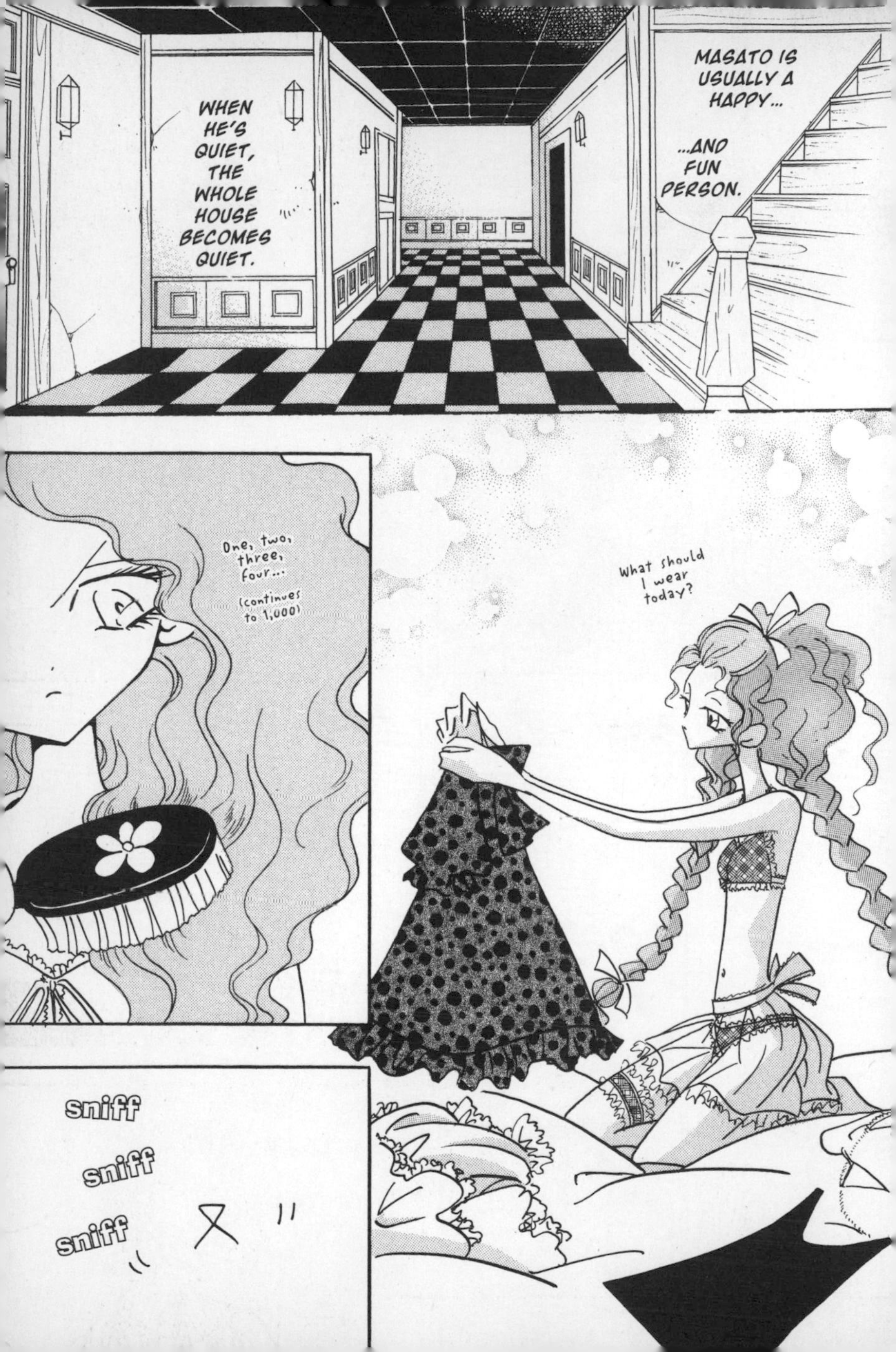
MASATO IS USUALLY A HAPPY...
...AND FUN PERSON.
WHEN HE'S QUIET, THE WHOLE HOUSE BECOMES QUIET.
What should I wear today?
One, two, three, four...
(continues to 1,000)
sniff
sniff
sniff

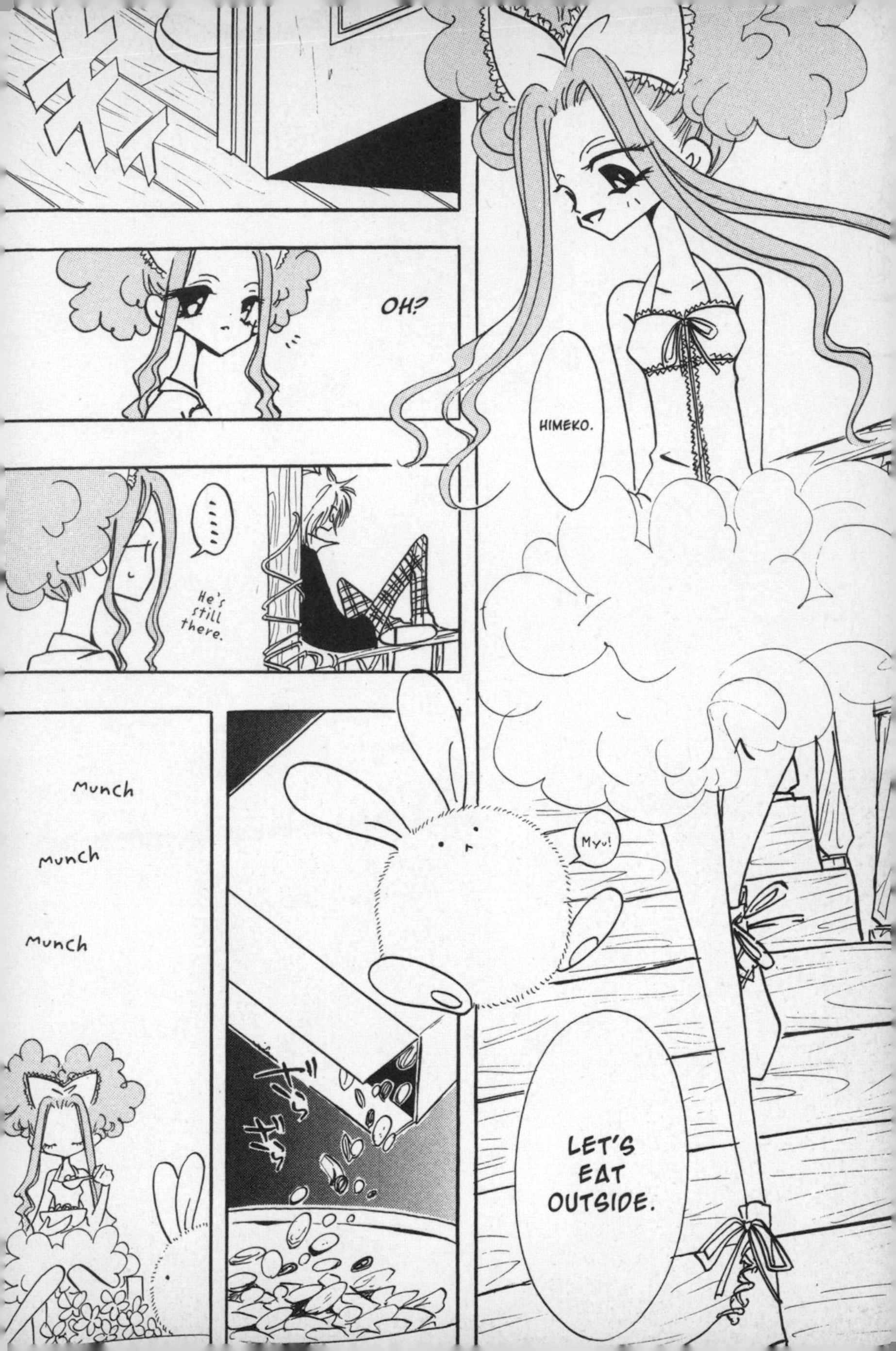
HIMEKO.
Myu!
LET'S EAT OUTSIDE.
OH?
......
He's still there.
Munch
Munch
Munch

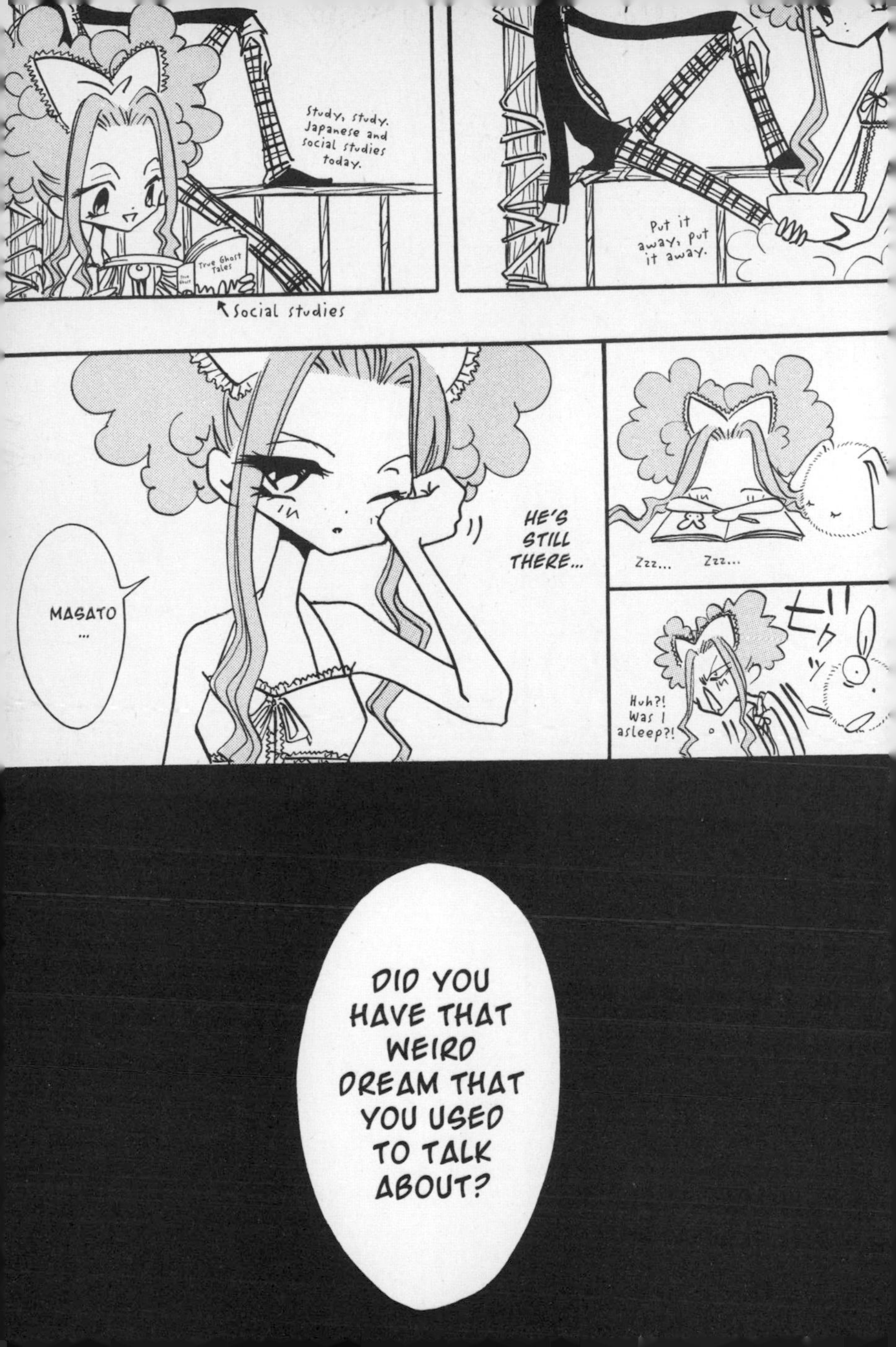
Put it away, put it away.
Study, study. Japanese and social studies today.
True Ghost Tales
Social studies
Zzz... Zzz...
Huh?! Was I asleep?!
HE'S STILL THERE...
MASATO ...
DID YOU HAVE THAT WEIRD DREAM THAT YOU USED TO TALK ABOUT?

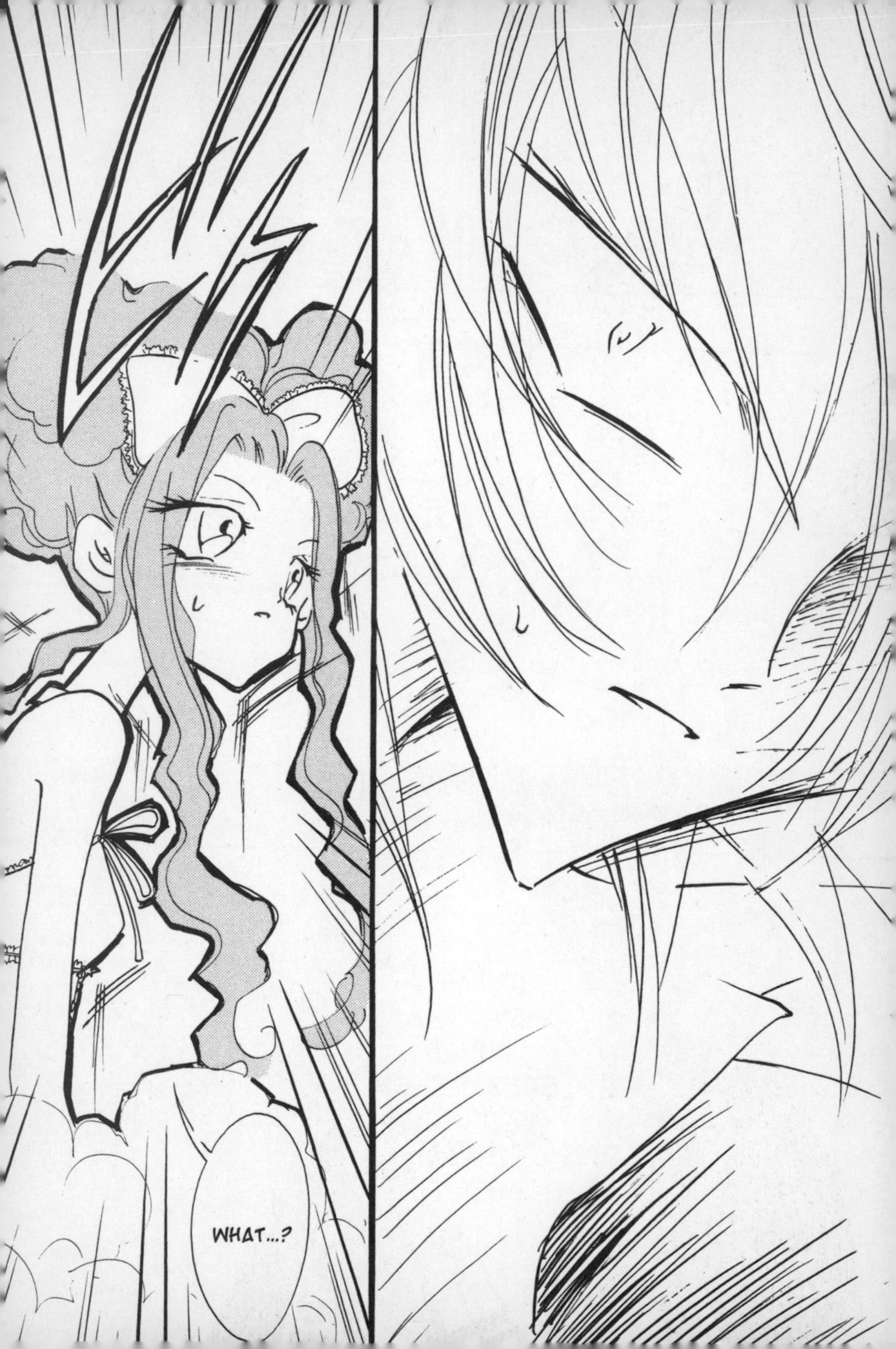
WHAT...?

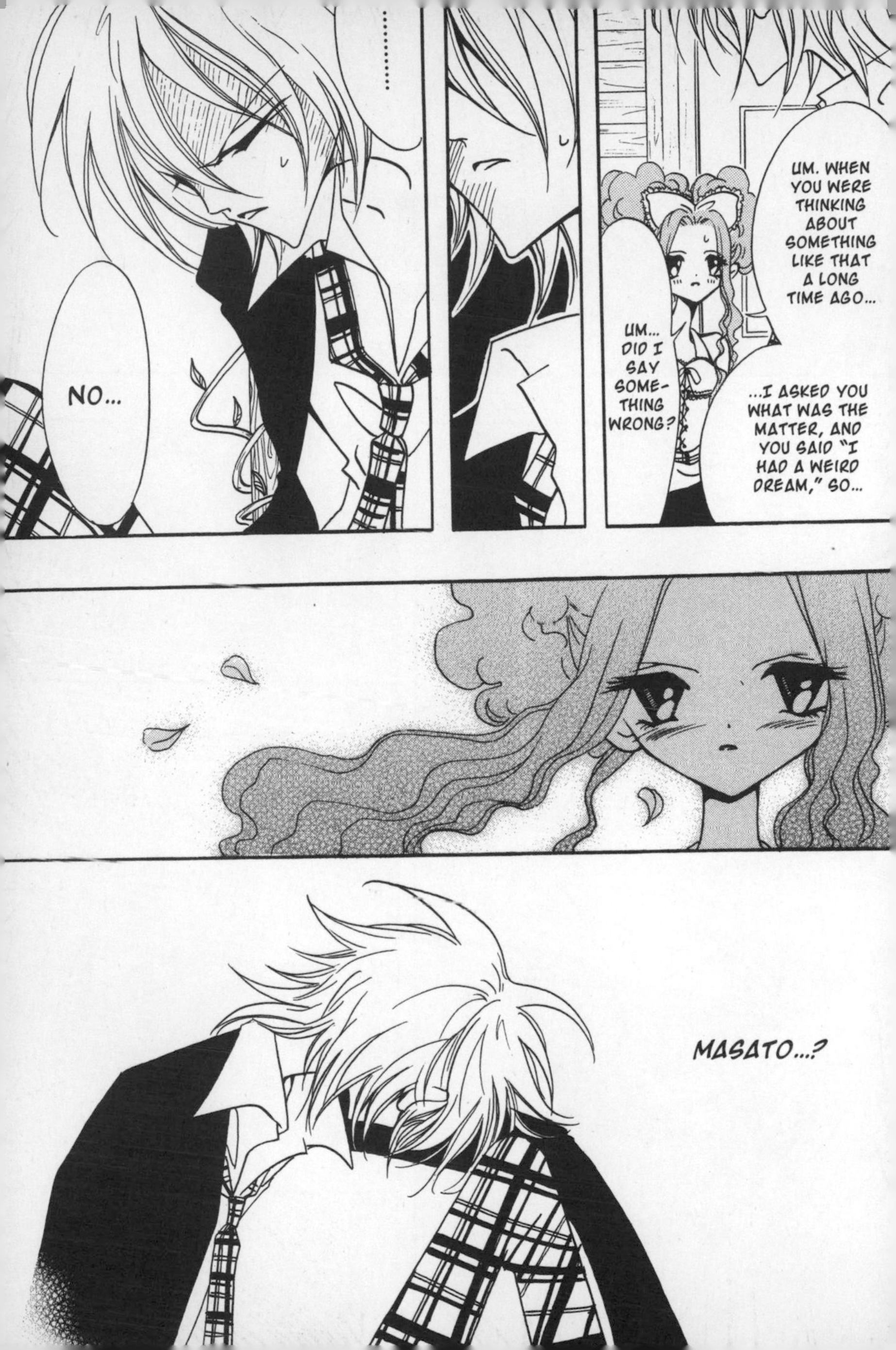
UM. WHEN YOU WERE THINKING ABOUT SOMETHING LIKE THAT A LONG TIME AGO...
...I ASKED YOU WHAT WAS THE MATTER, AND YOU SAID "I HAD A WEIRD DREAM," SO...
UM... DID I SAY SOME-THING WRONG?
NO...
MASATO...?

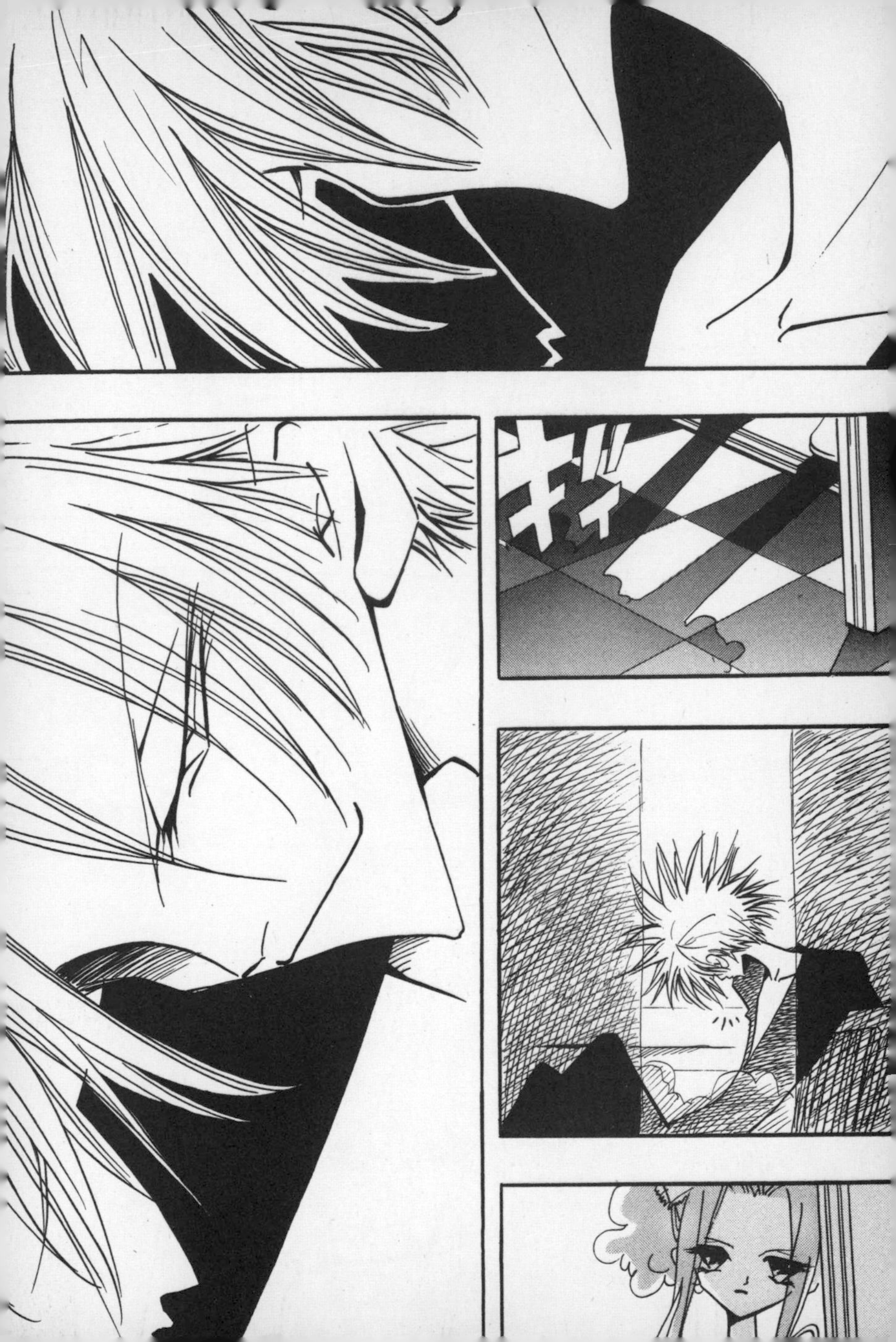
ギィ

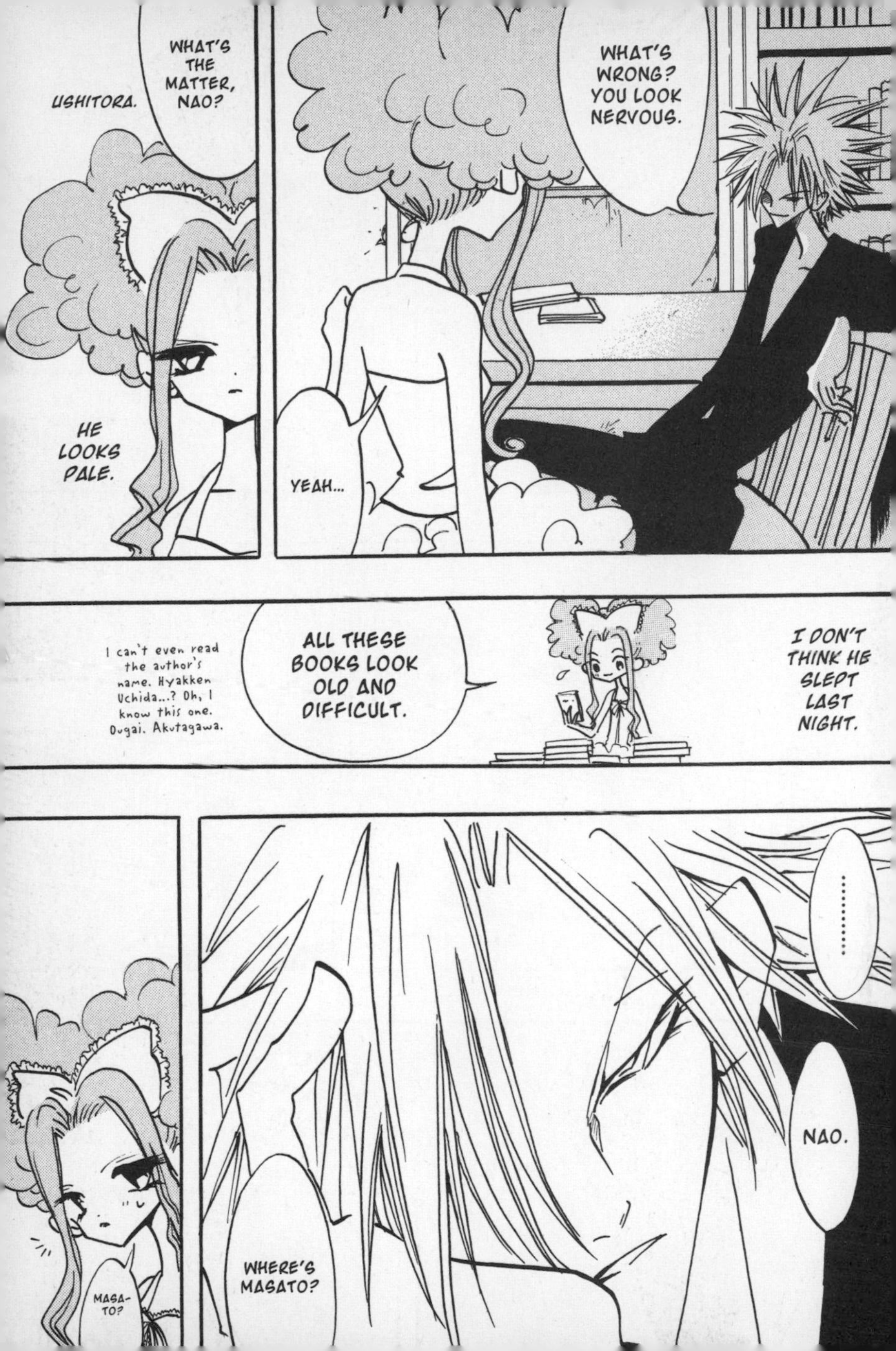
WHAT'S WRONG? YOU LOOK NERVOUS.
YEAH...
WHAT'S THE MATTER, NAO?
USHITORA.
HE LOOKS PALE.
I DON'T THINK HE SLEPT LAST NIGHT.
ALL THESE BOOKS LOOK OLD AND DIFFICULT.
I can't even read the author's name. Hyakken Uchida...? Oh, I know this one. Ougai. Akutagawa.
....
NAO.
WHERE'S MASATO?
MASA-TO?

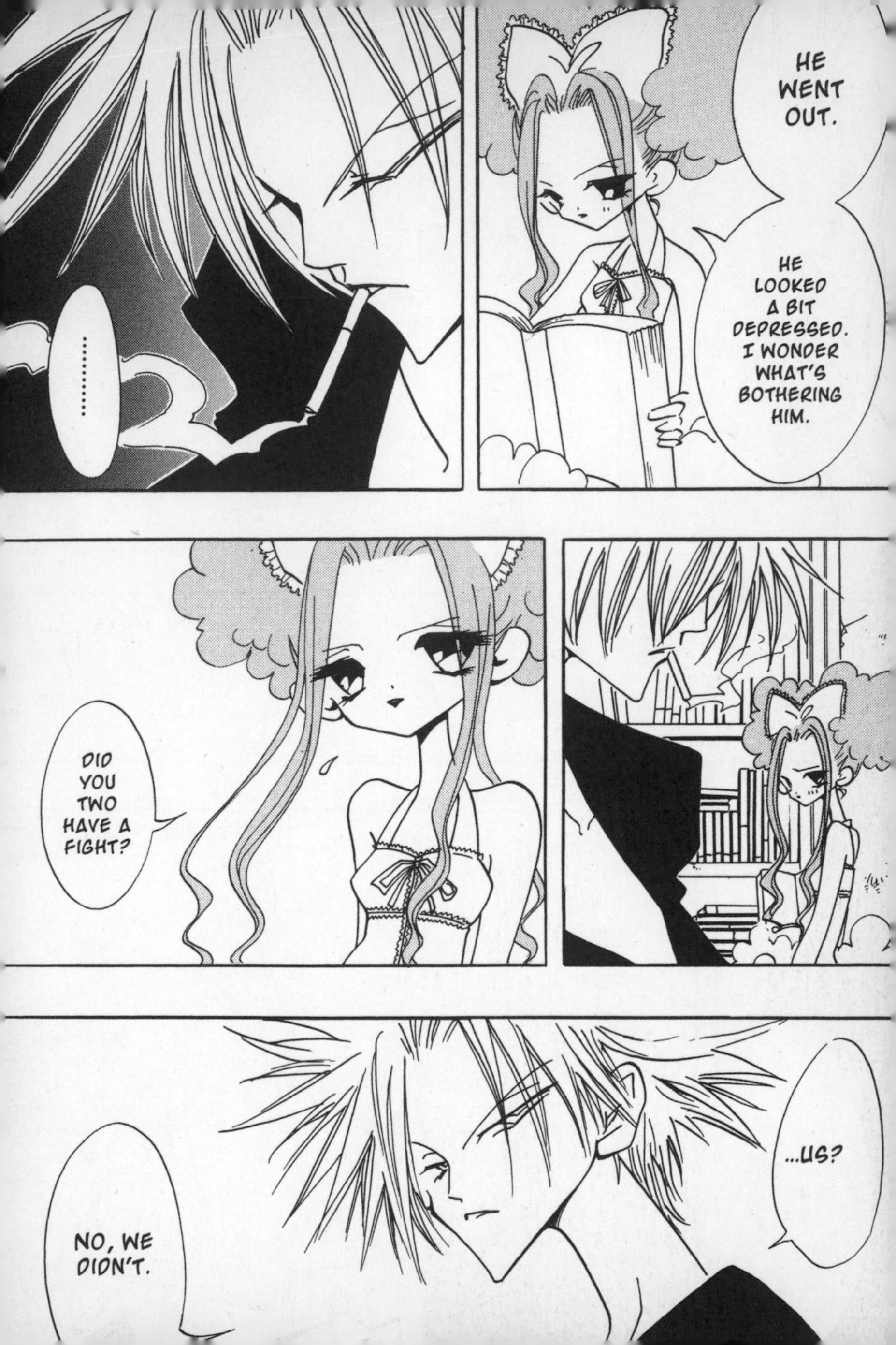
HE WENT OUT.
HE LOOKED A BIT DEPRESSED. I WONDER WHAT'S BOTHERING HIM.
....
DID YOU TWO HAVE A FIGHT?
...US?
NO, WE DIDN'T.

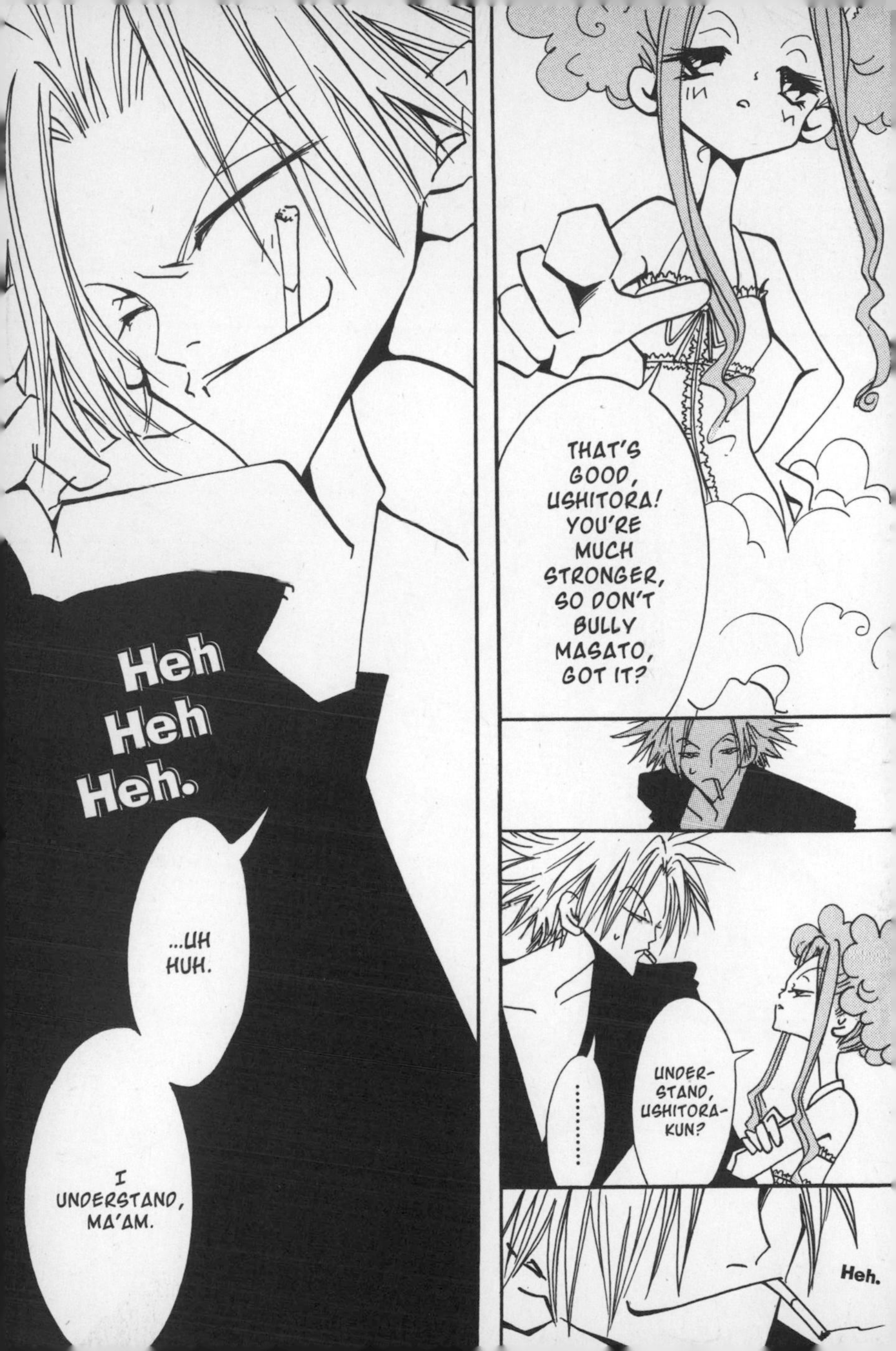
THAT'S GOOD, USHITORA! YOU'RE MUCH STRONGER, SO DON'T BULLY MASATO, GOT IT?
UNDER-STAND, USHITORA-KUN?
....
Heh.
Heh Heh Heh.
...UH HUH.
I UNDERSTAND, MA'AM.

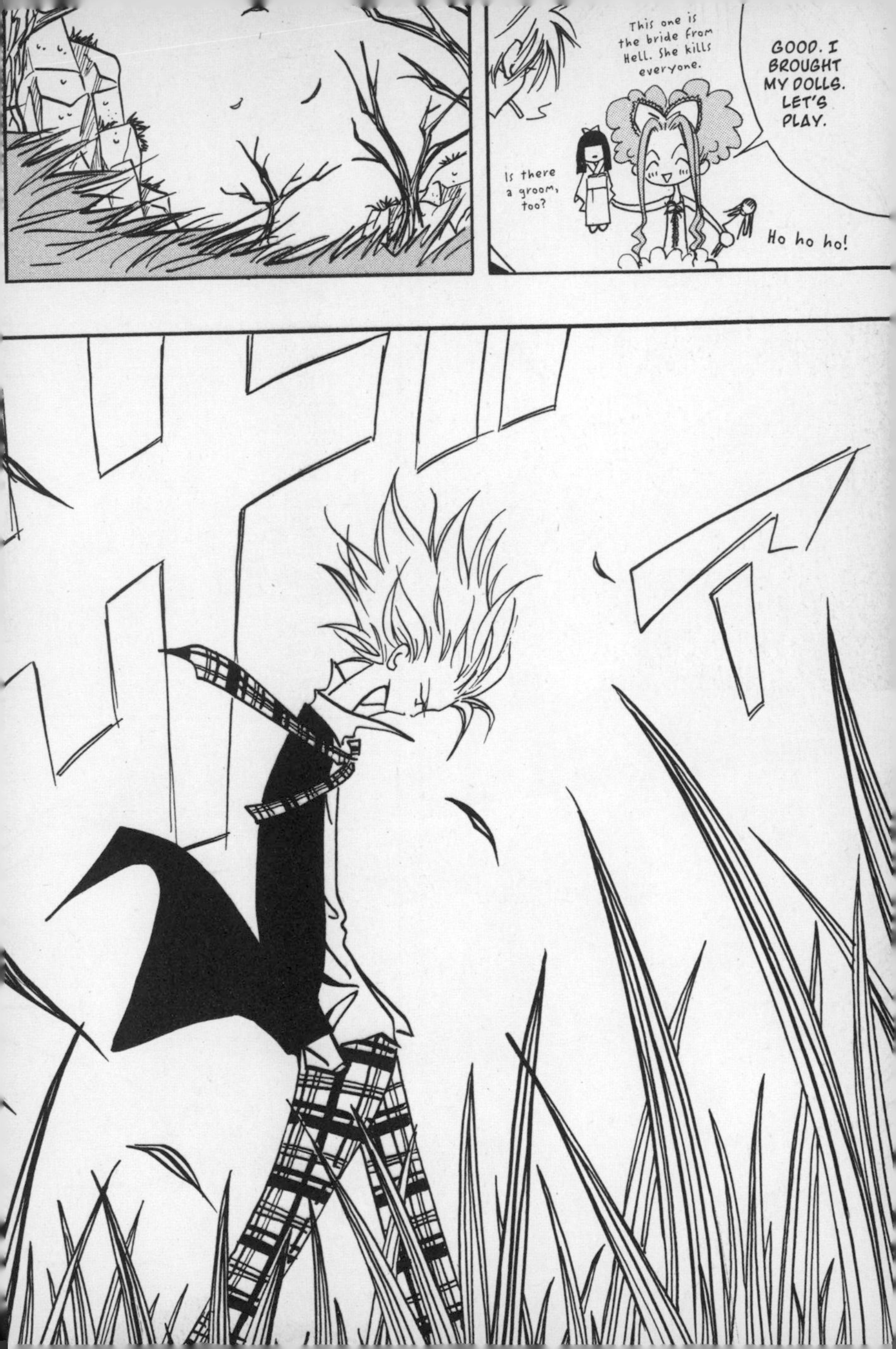
GOOD. I BROUGHT MY DOLLS. LET'S PLAY.
Ho ho ho!
This one is the bride from Hell. She kills everyone.
Is there a groom, too?

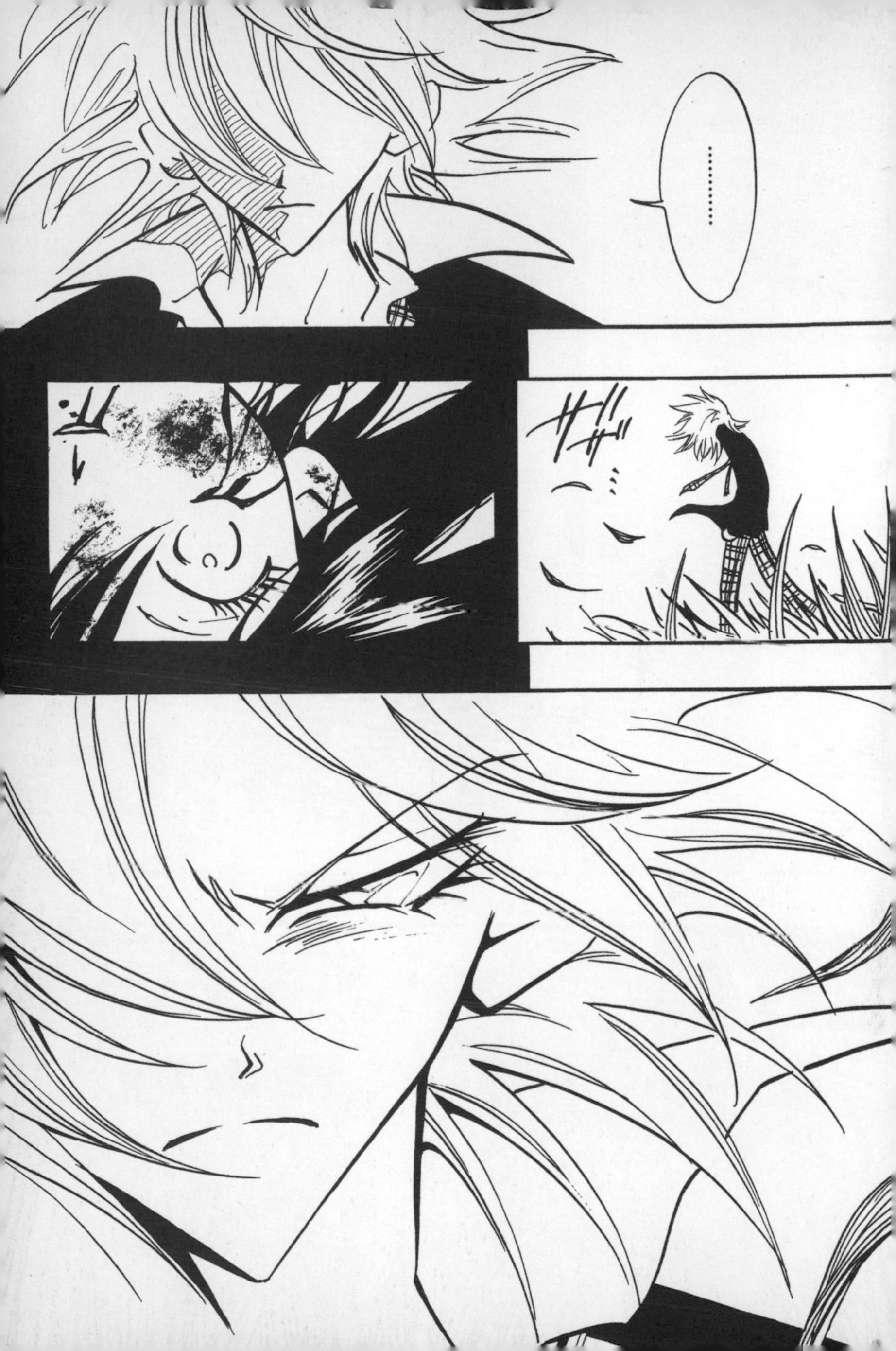
……

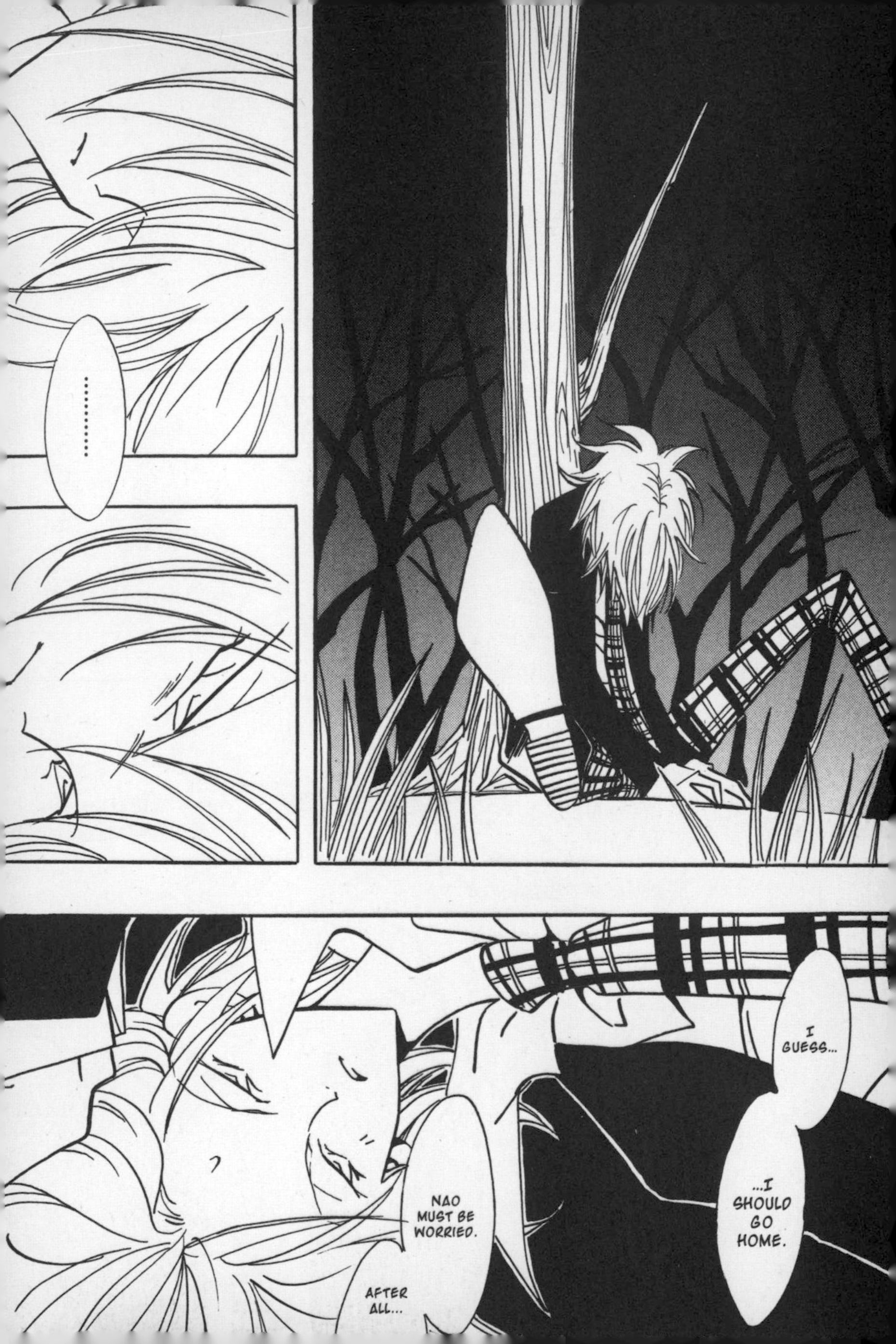
......
I GUESS...
...I SHOULD GO HOME.
NAO MUST BE WORRIED.
AFTER ALL...

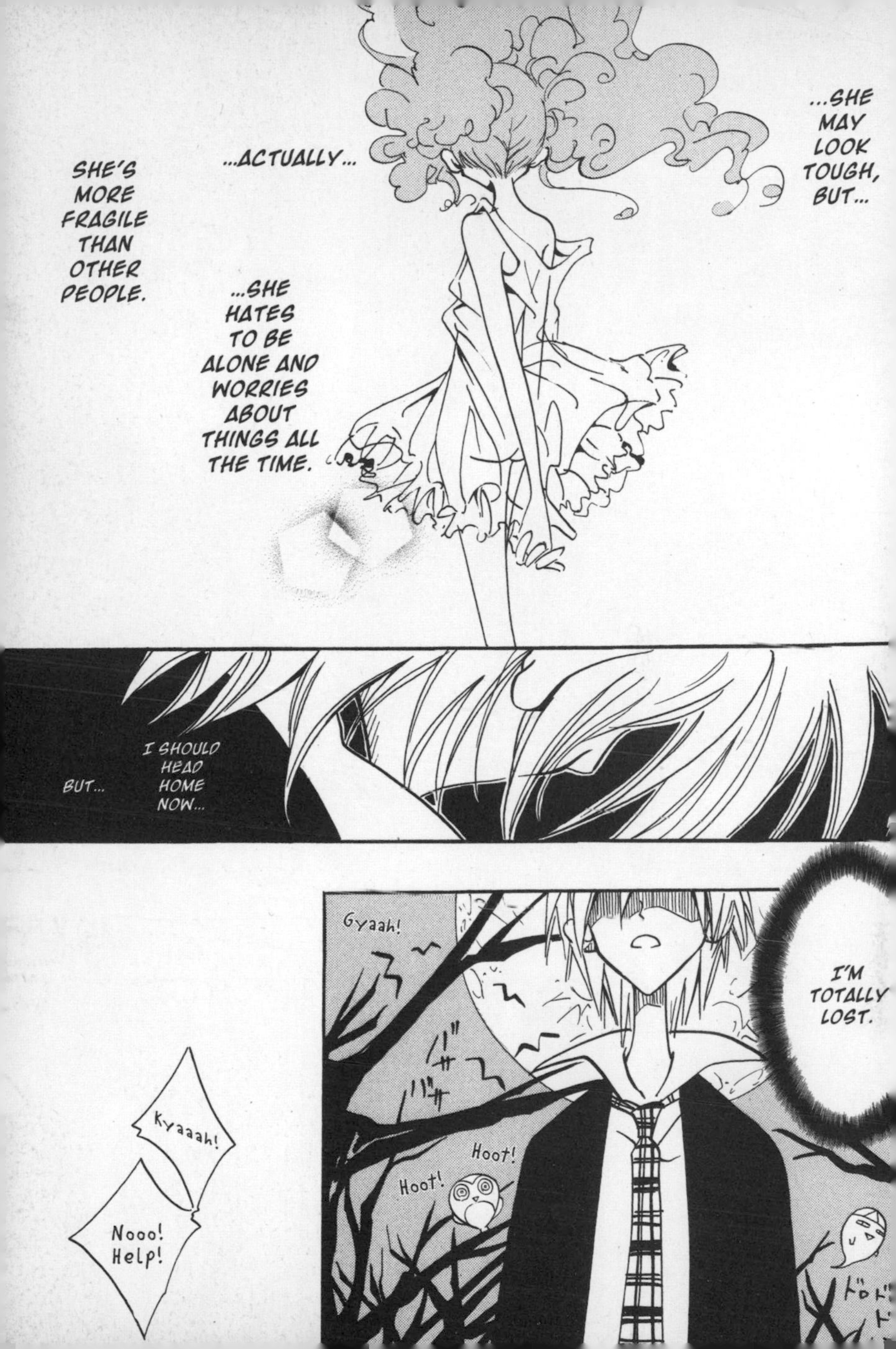
...SHE MAY LOOK TOUGH, BUT...
...ACTUALLY...
...SHE HATES TO BE ALONE AND WORRIES ABOUT THINGS ALL THE TIME.
SHE'S MORE FRAGILE THAN OTHER PEOPLE.
I SHOULD HEAD HOME NOW...
BUT...
I'M TOTALLY LOST.
Gyaah!
Hoot!
Hoot!
Kyaaah!
Nooo! Help!

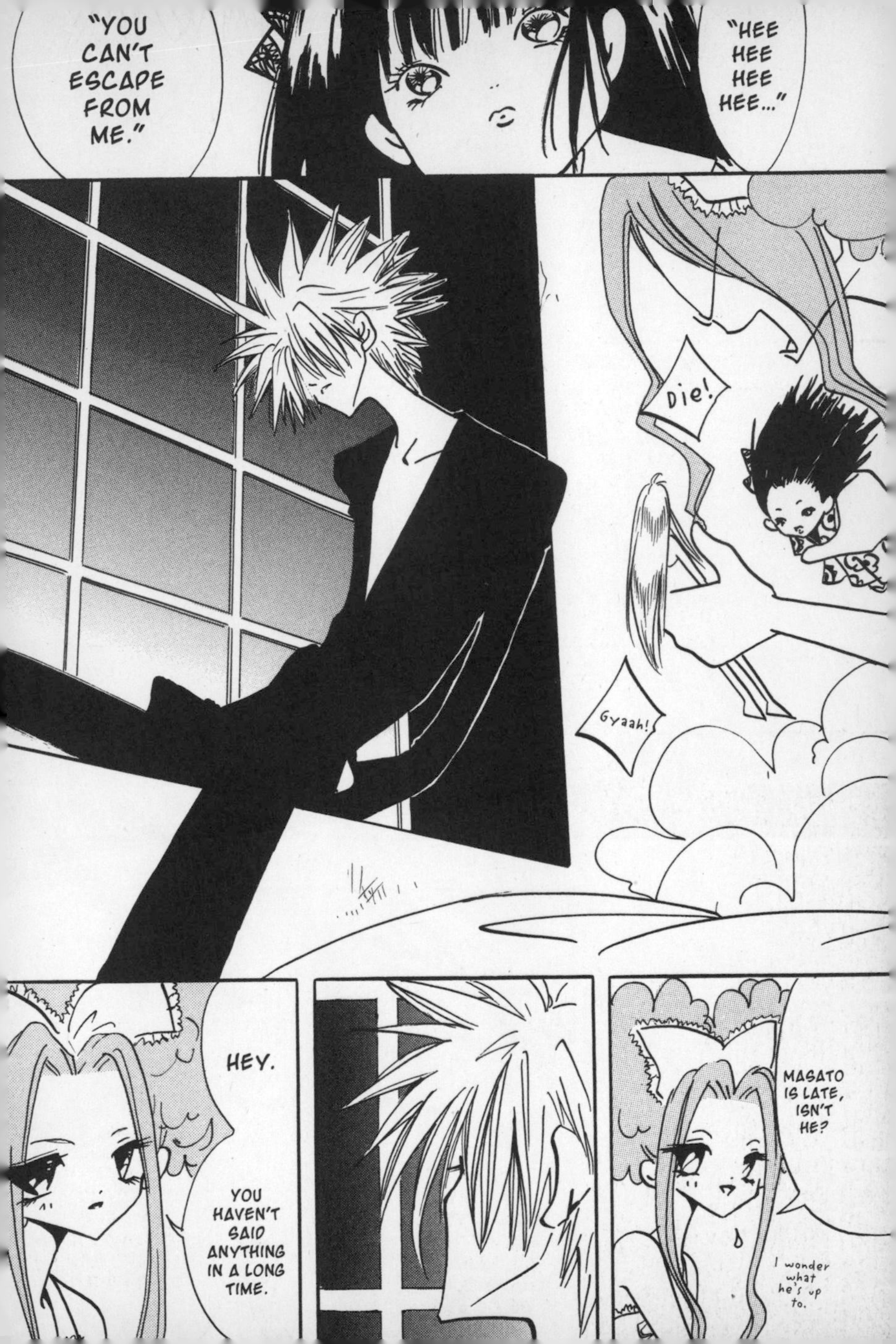
"HEE HEE HEE HEE..."
"YOU CAN'T ESCAPE FROM ME."
Die!
Gyaah!
MASATO IS LATE, ISN'T HE?
I wonder what he's up to.
HEY.
YOU HAVEN'T SAID ANYTHING IN A LONG TIME.

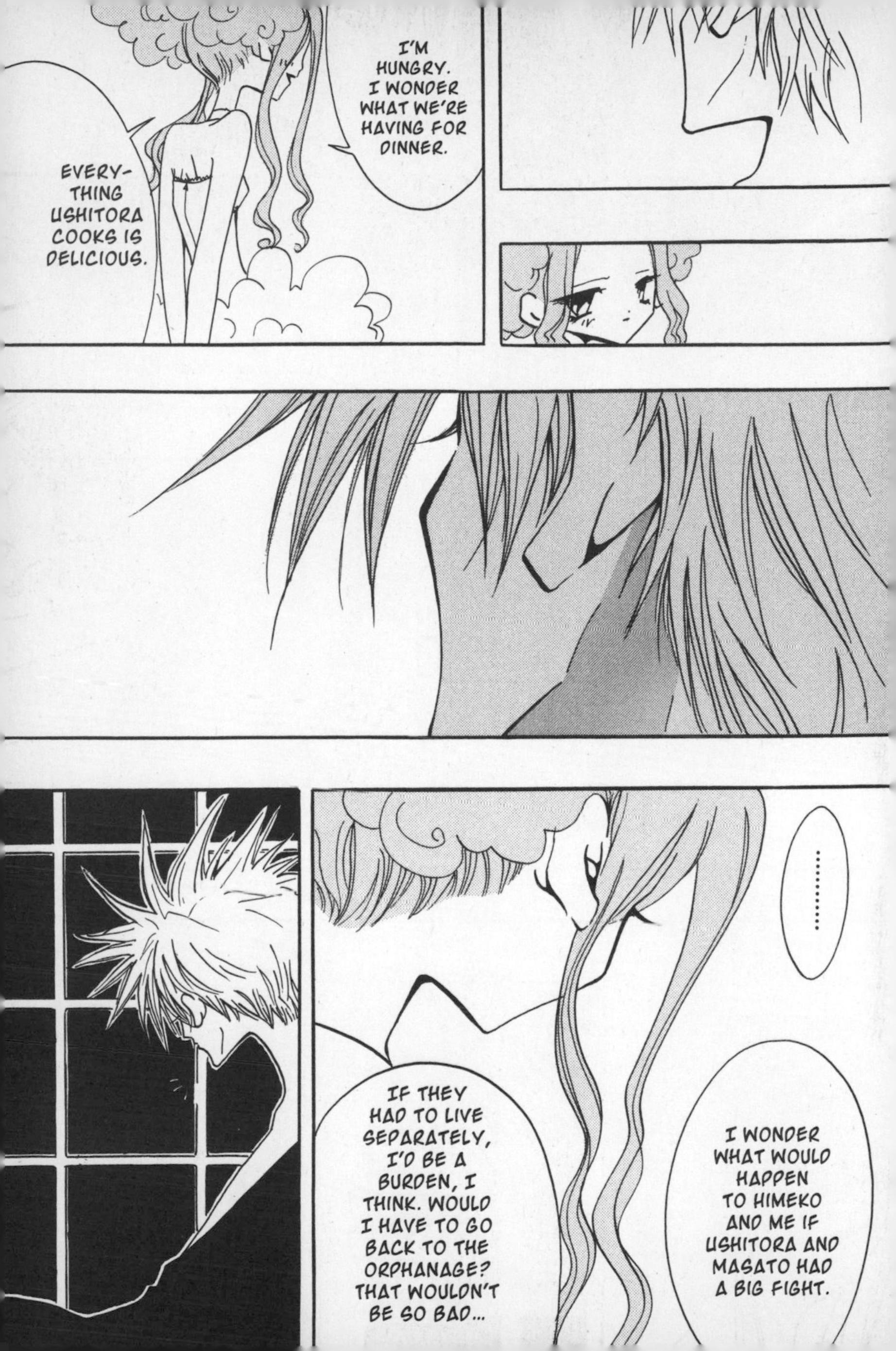
I'M HUNGRY. I WONDER WHAT WE'RE HAVING FOR DINNER.
EVERY-THING USHITORA COOKS IS DELICIOUS.
......
I WONDER WHAT WOULD HAPPEN TO HIMEKO AND ME IF USHITORA AND MASATO HAD A BIG FIGHT.
IF THEY HAD TO LIVE SEPARATELY, I'D BE A BURDEN, I THINK. WOULD I HAVE TO GO BACK TO THE ORPHANAGE? THAT WOULDN'T BE SO BAD...

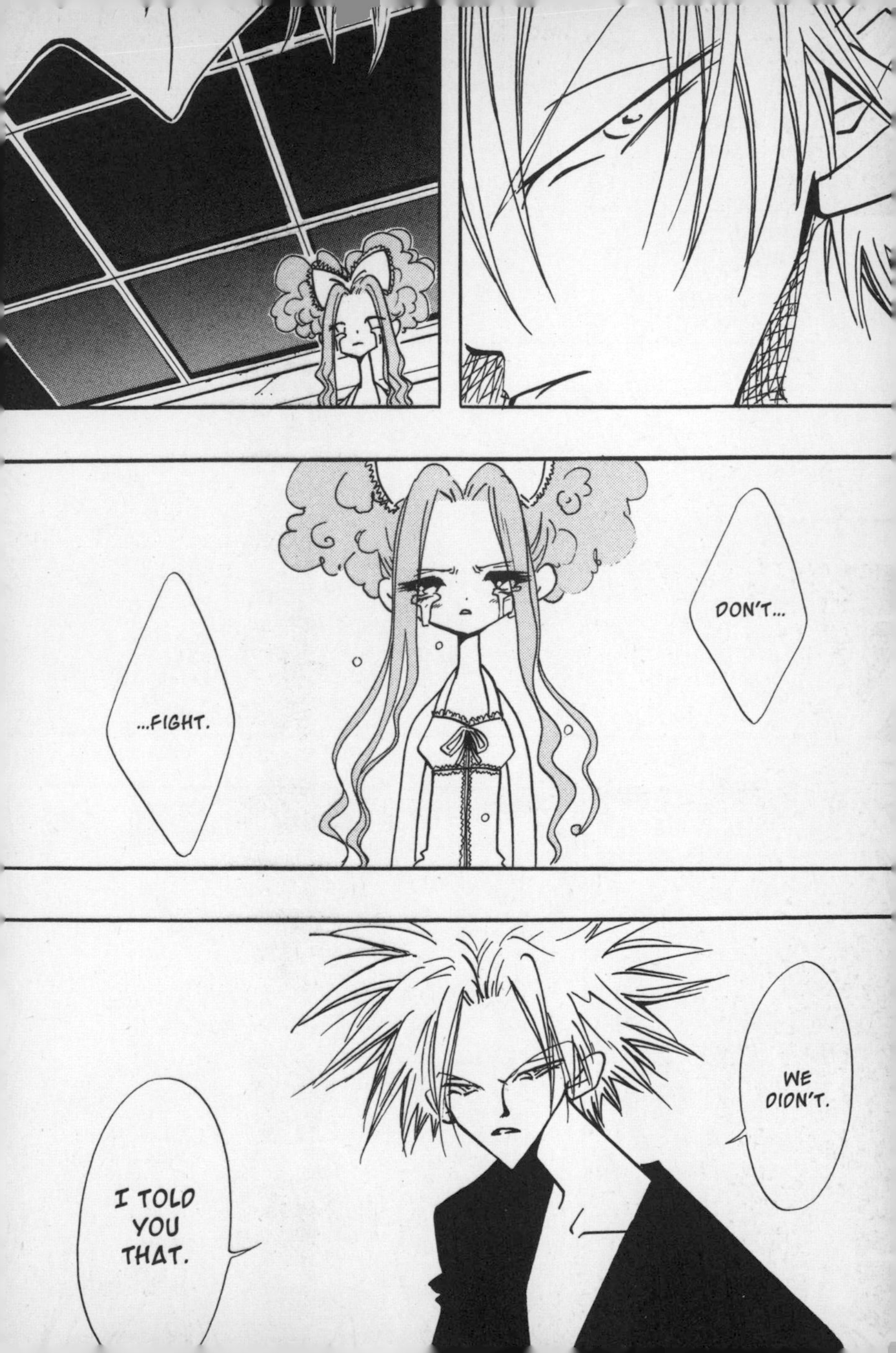
DON'T...
...FIGHT.
WE DIDN'T.
I TOLD YOU THAT.

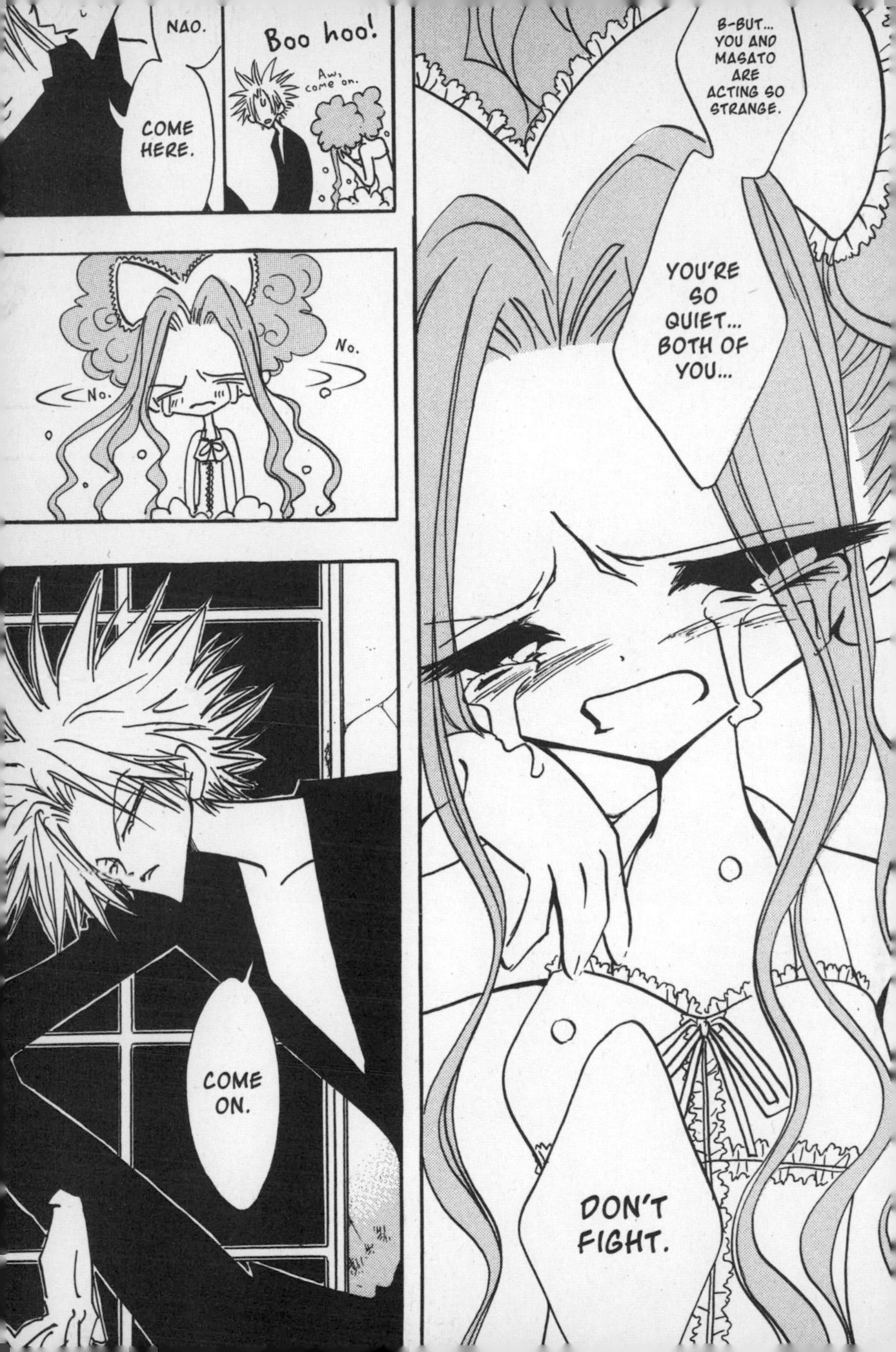
Boo hoo!
Aw, come on.
NAO.
COME HERE.
No.
No.
COME ON.
B-BUT... YOU AND MASATO ARE ACTING SO STRANGE.
YOU'RE SO QUIET... BOTH OF YOU...
DON'T FIGHT.

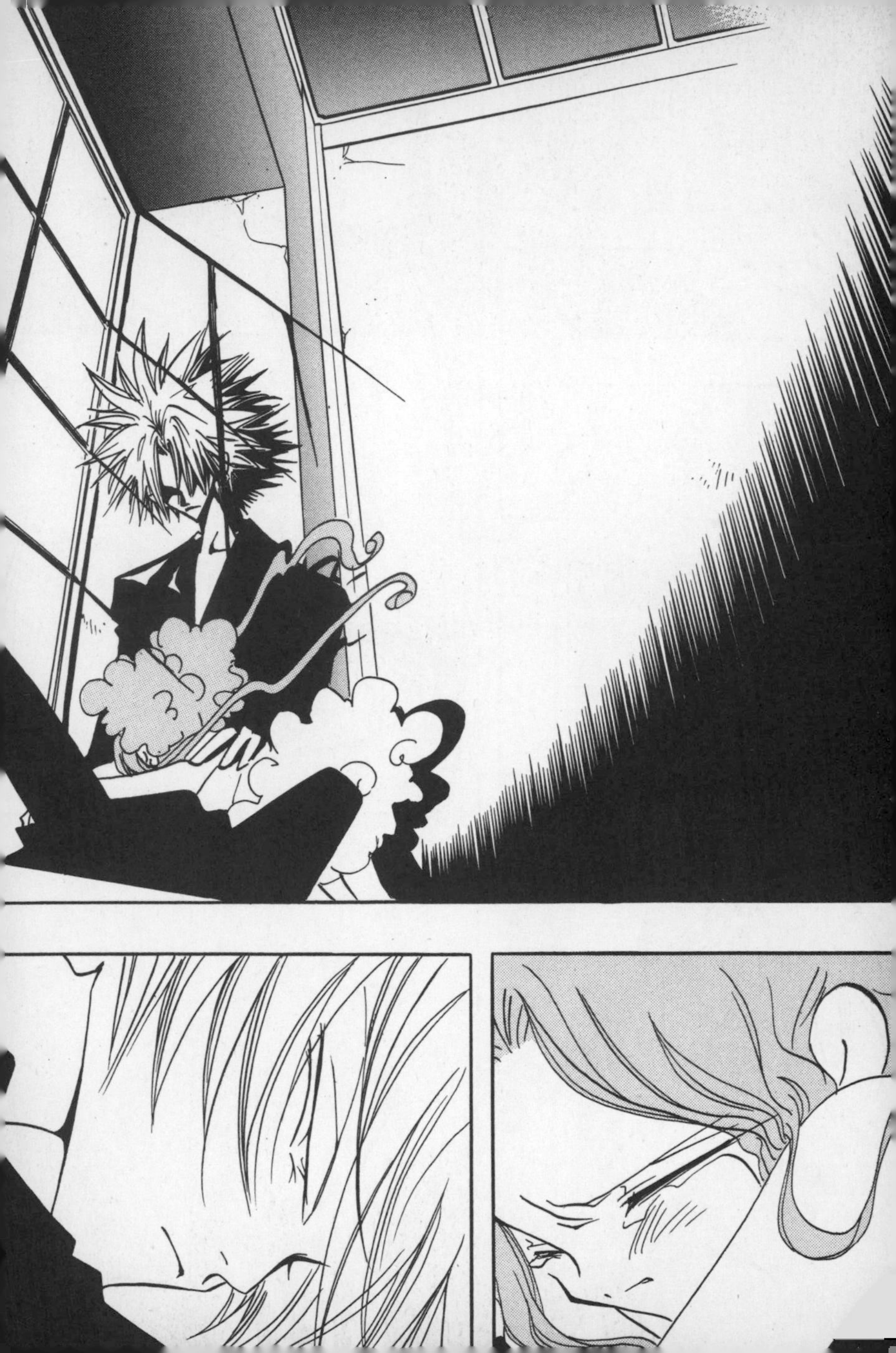

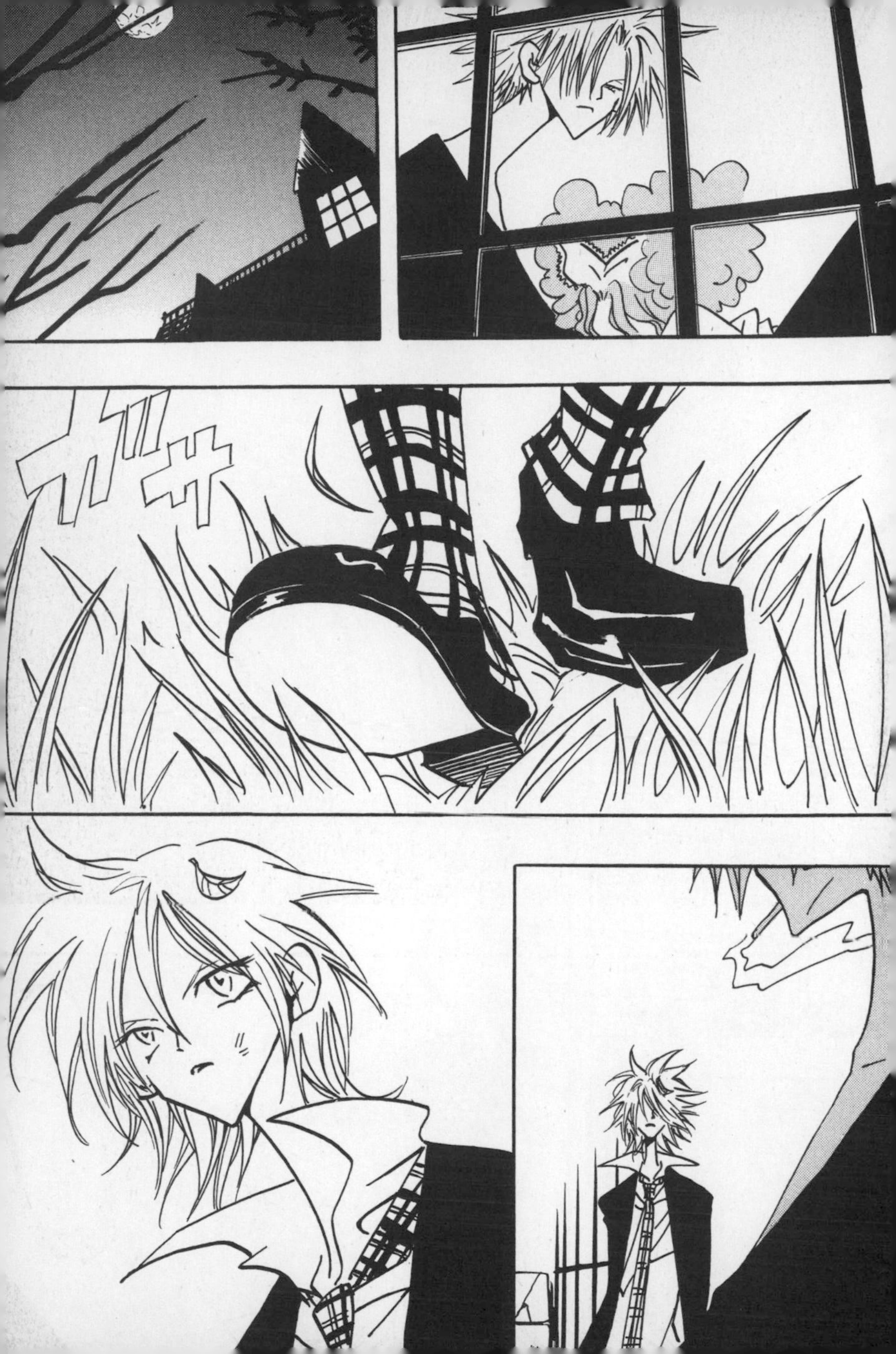
ガサ

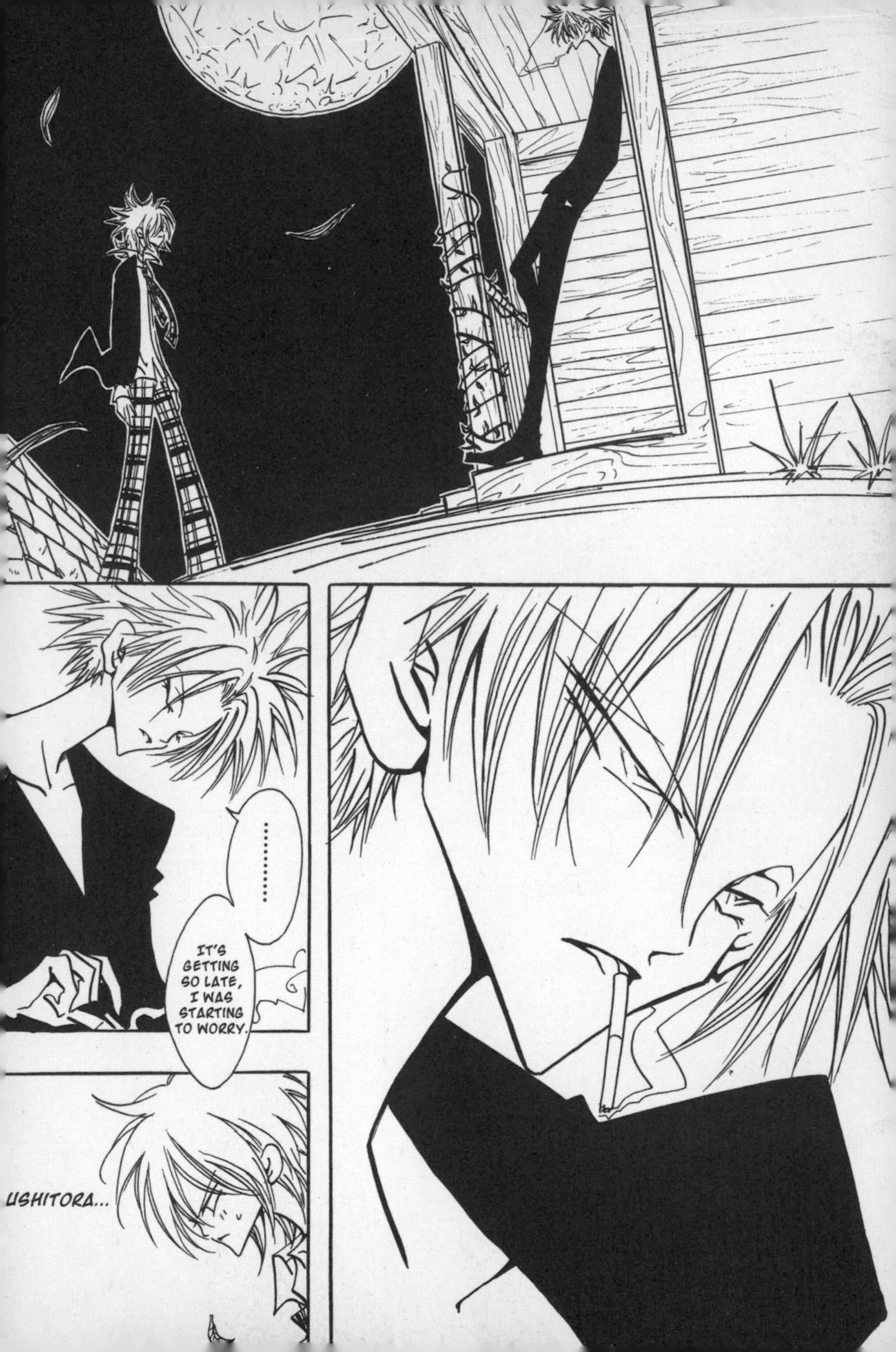

IT'S GETTING SO LATE, I WAS STARTING TO WORRY.
....
USHITORA...

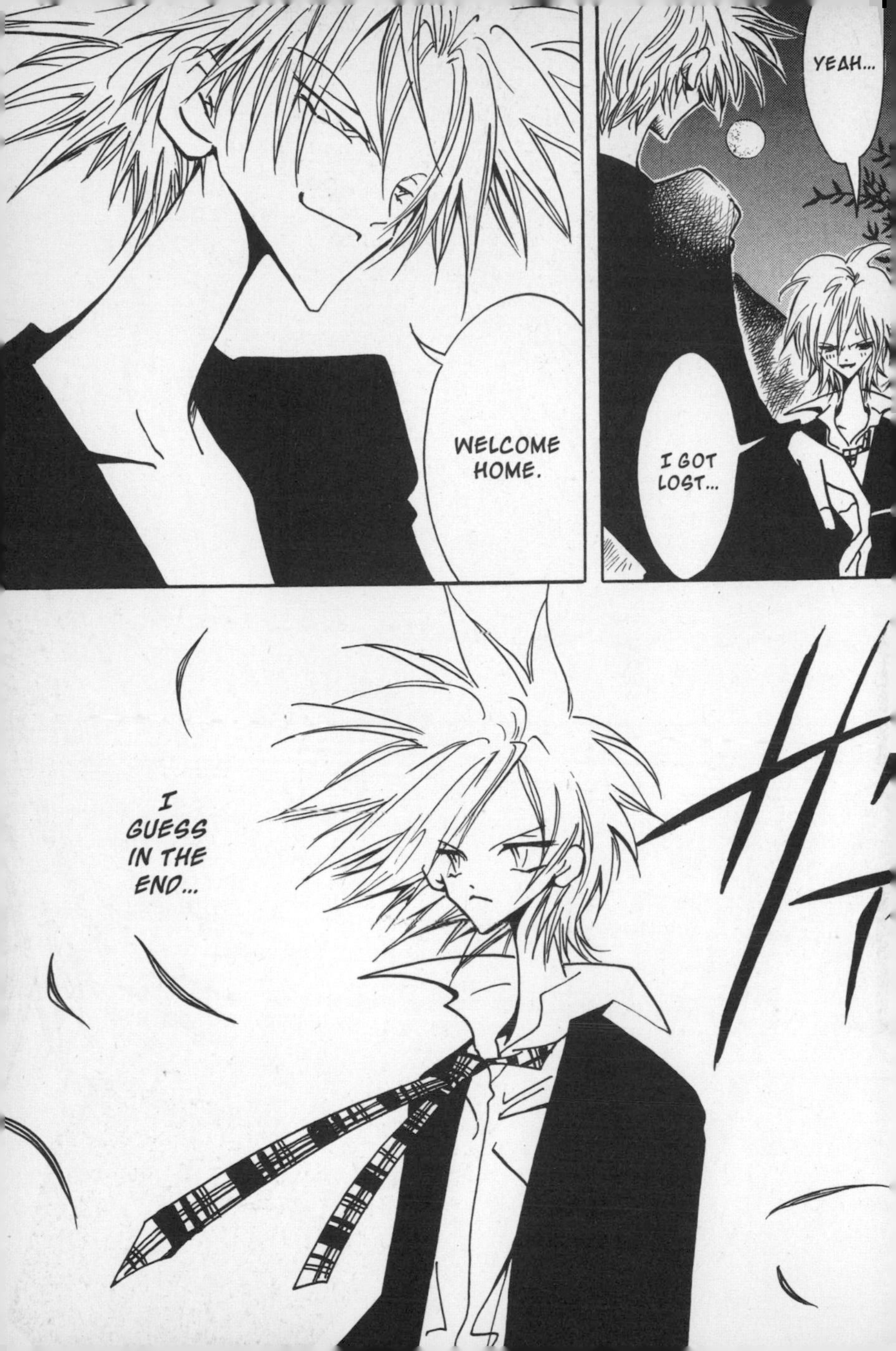
YEAH...
I GOT LOST...
WELCOME HOME.
I GUESS IN THE END...

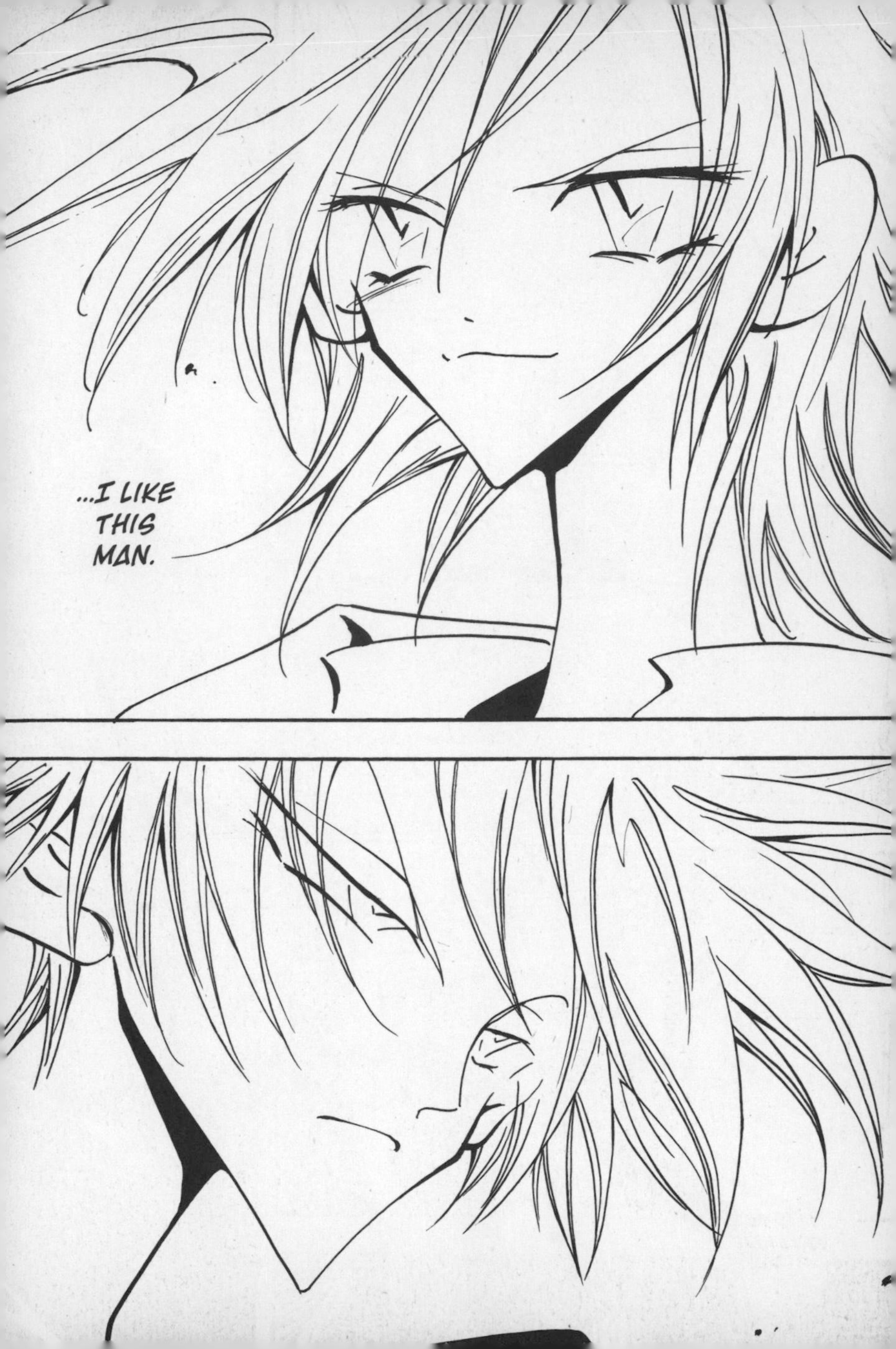
...I LIKE THIS MAN.

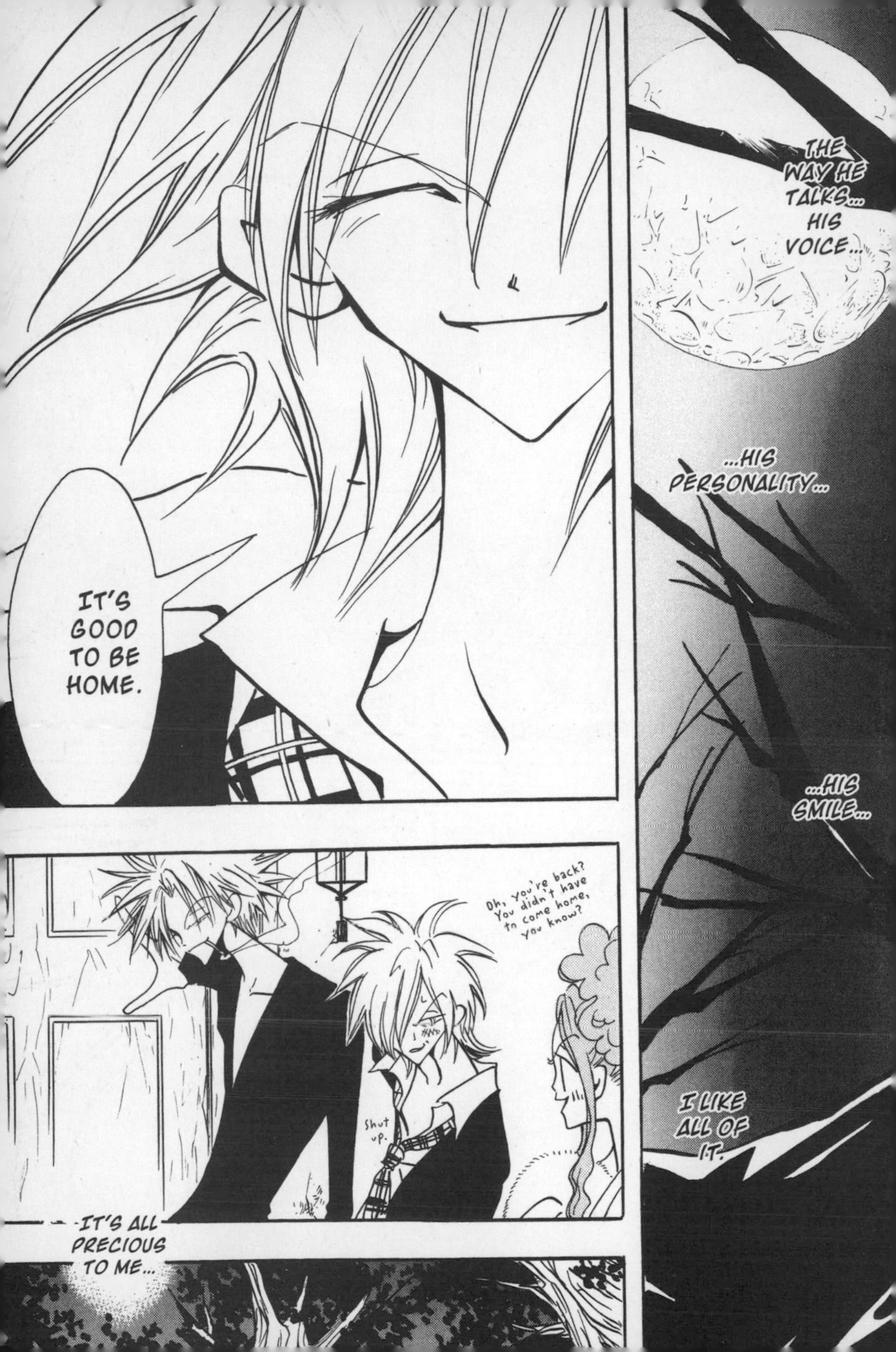
THE WAY HE TALKS... HIS VOICE...
...HIS PERSONALITY...
...HIS SMILE...
I LIKE ALL OF IT.
IT'S GOOD TO BE HOME.
Oh, you're back? You didn't have to come home, you know?
Shut up.
IT'S ALL PRECIOUS TO ME...

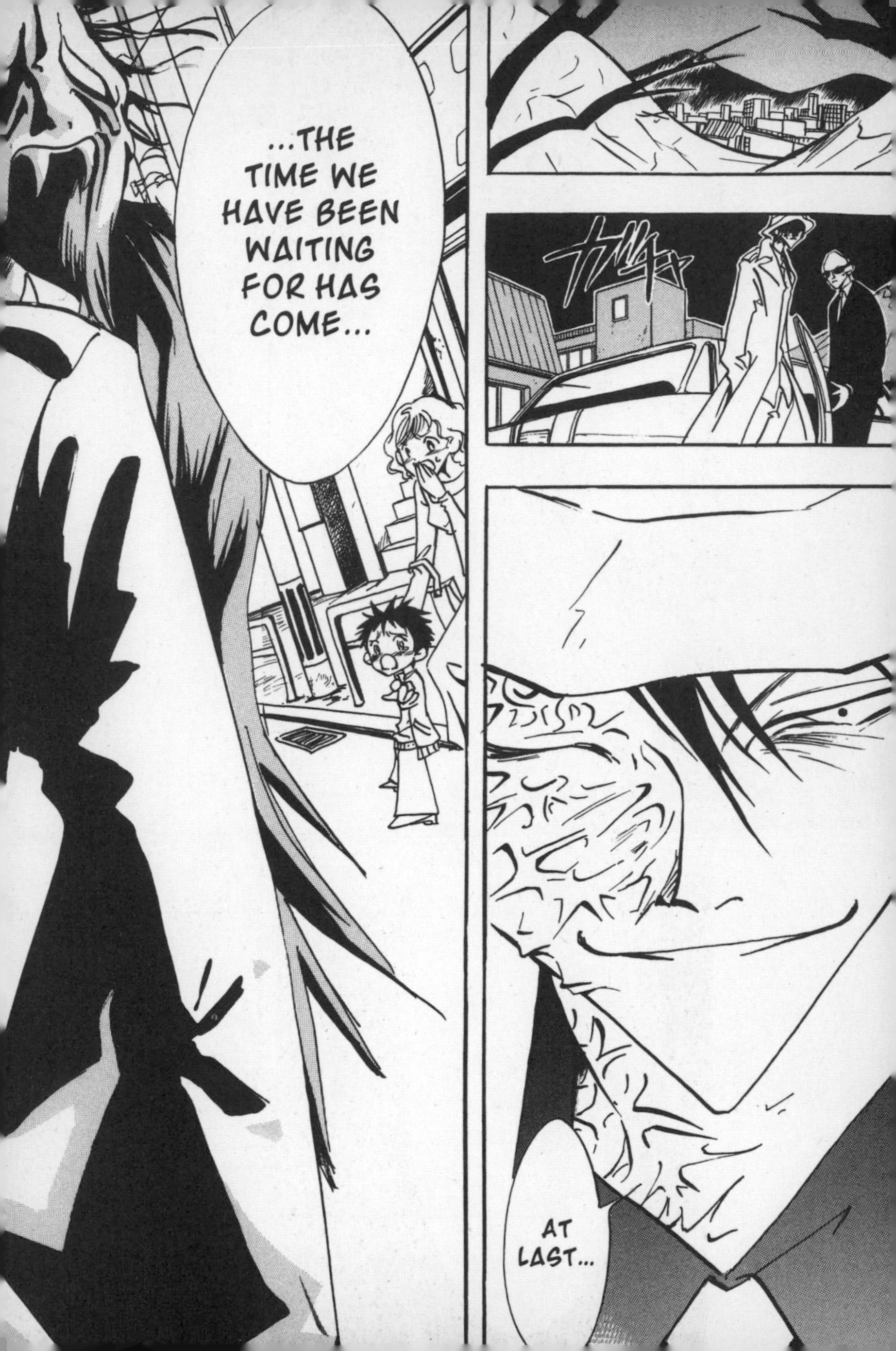
AT LAST...
...THE TIME WE HAVE BEEN WAITING FOR HAS COME...

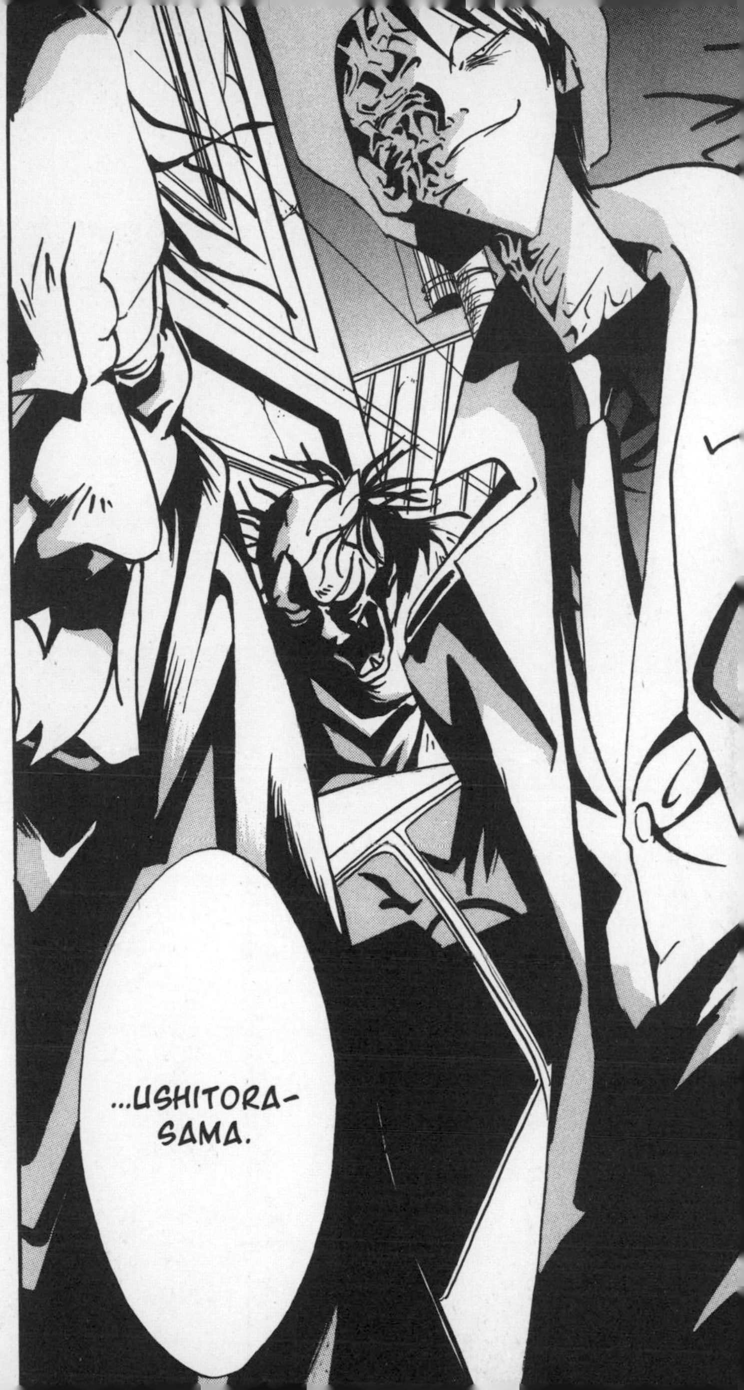
...USHITORA-
SAMA.

I WISH...

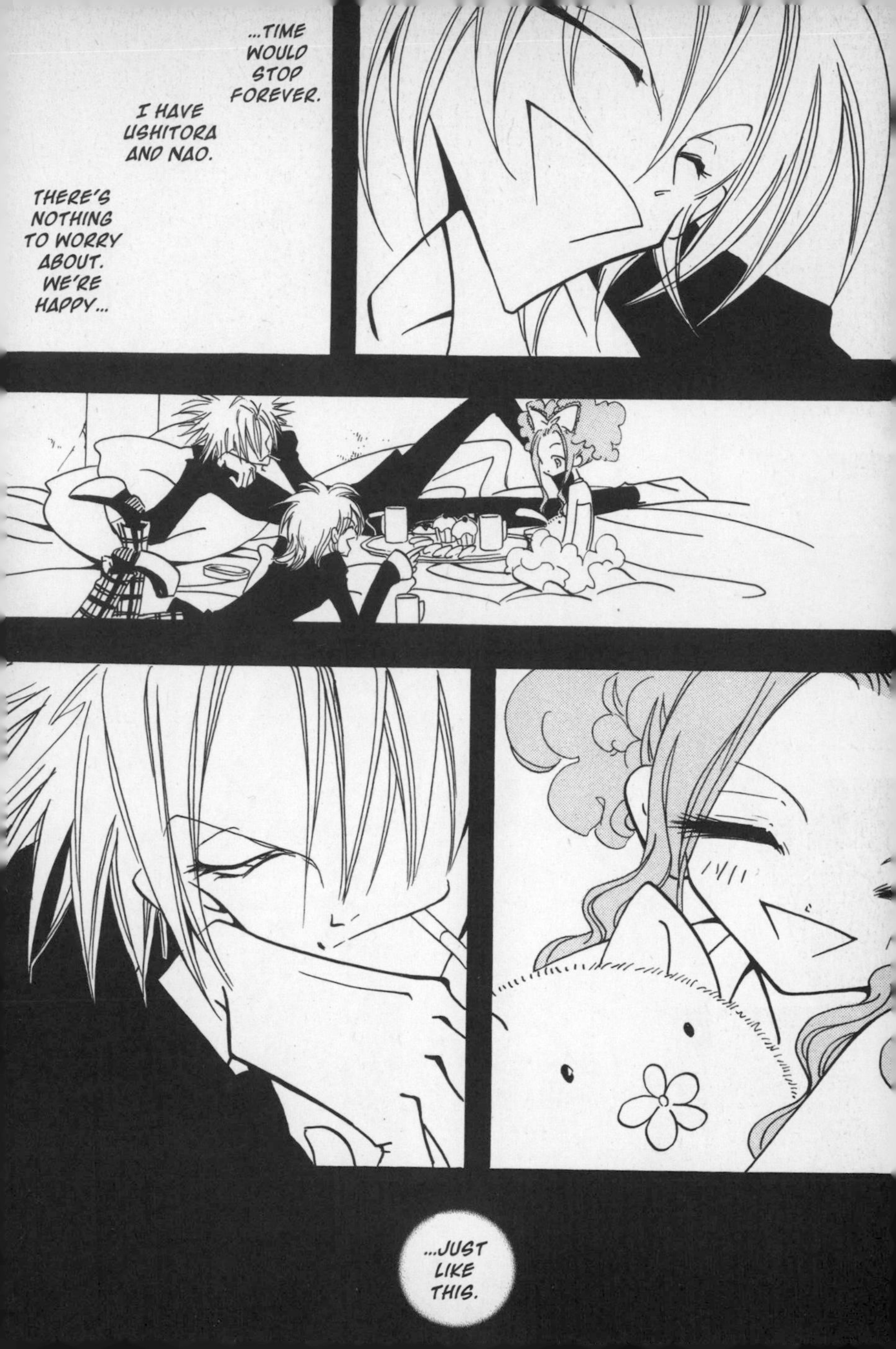
...TIME WOULD STOP FOREVER.
I HAVE USHITORA AND NAO.
THERE'S NOTHING TO WORRY ABOUT. WE'RE HAPPY...
...JUST LIKE THIS.

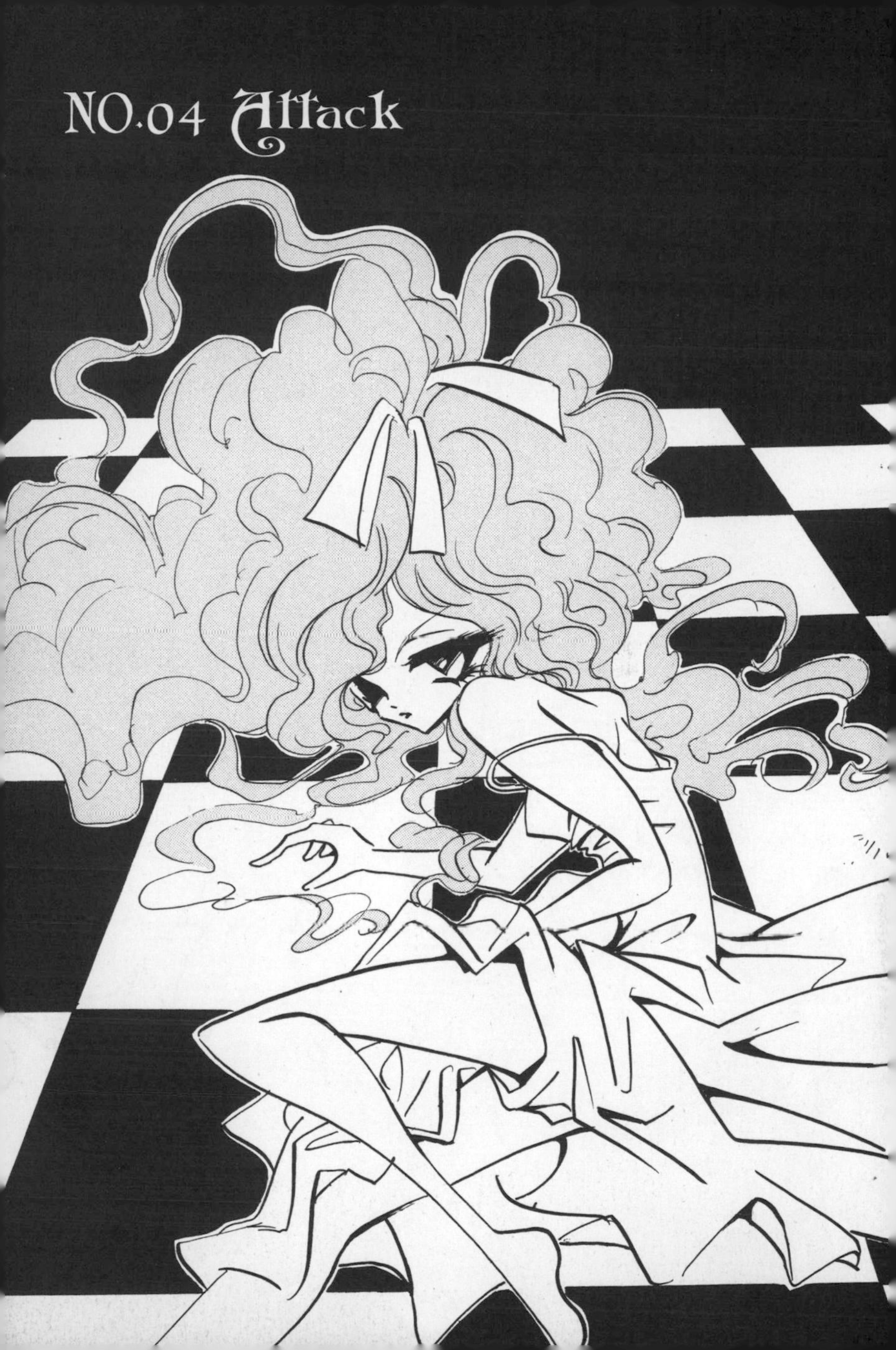
NO.04 Attack

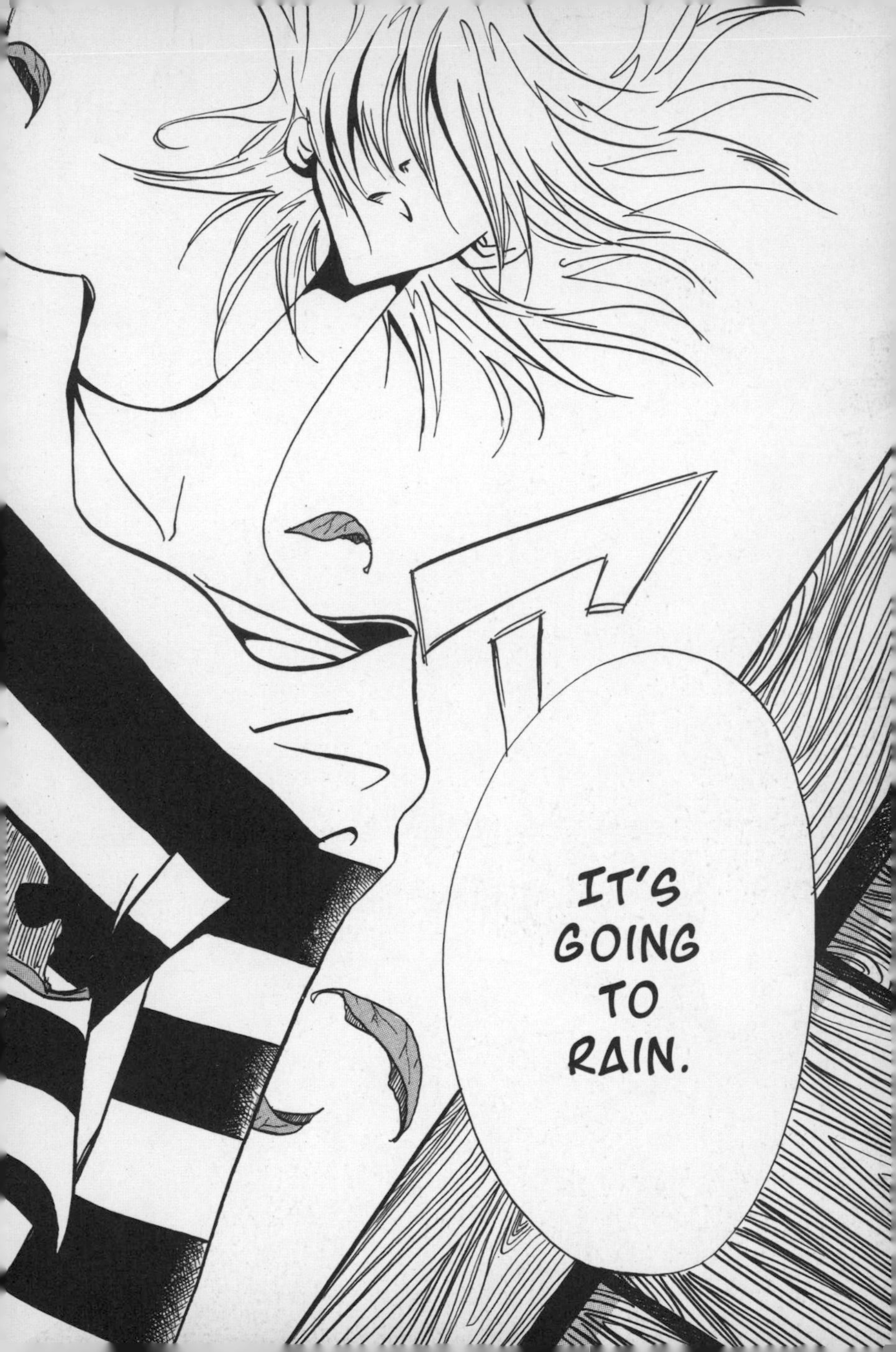
IT'S GOING TO RAIN.

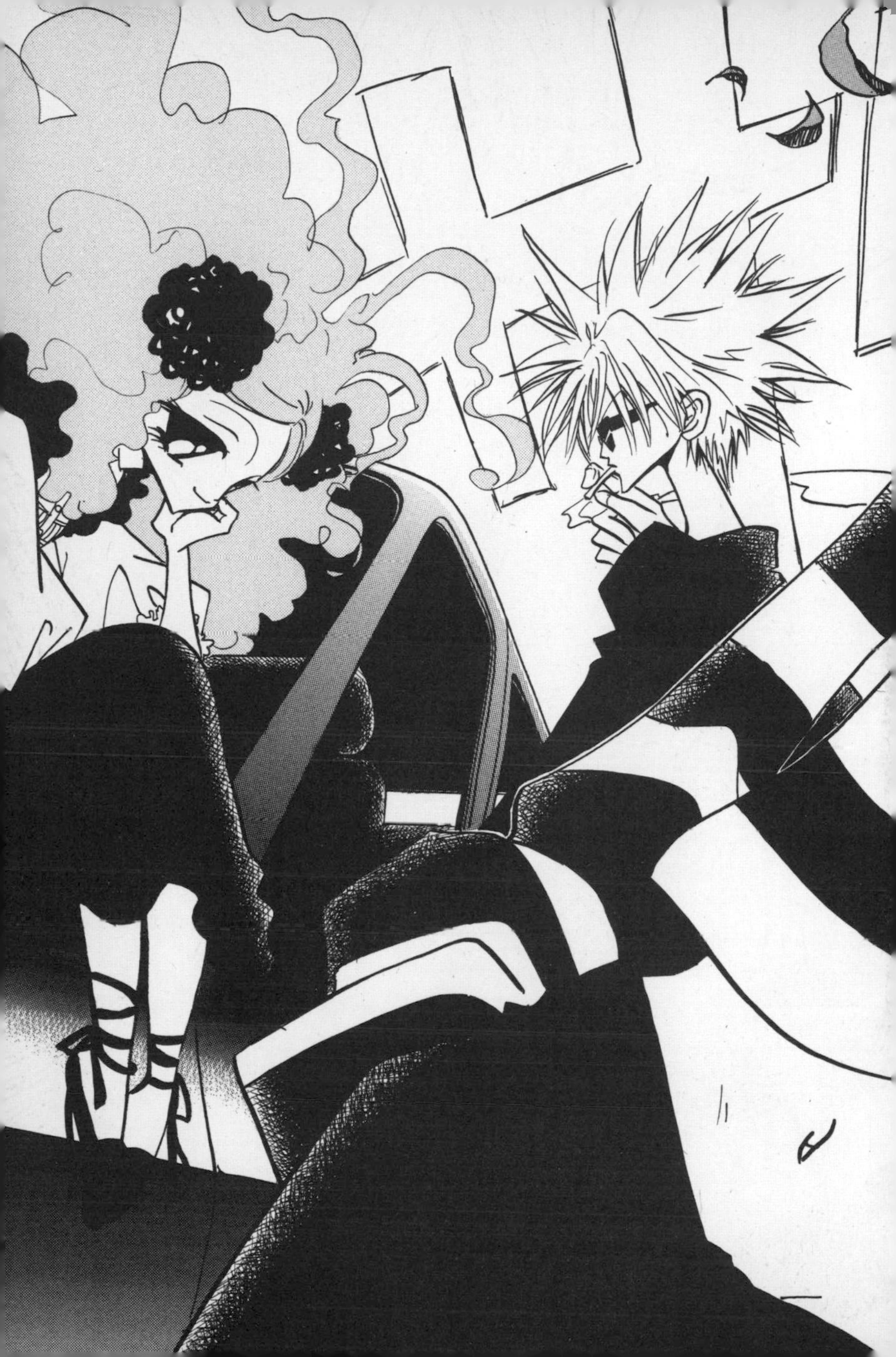

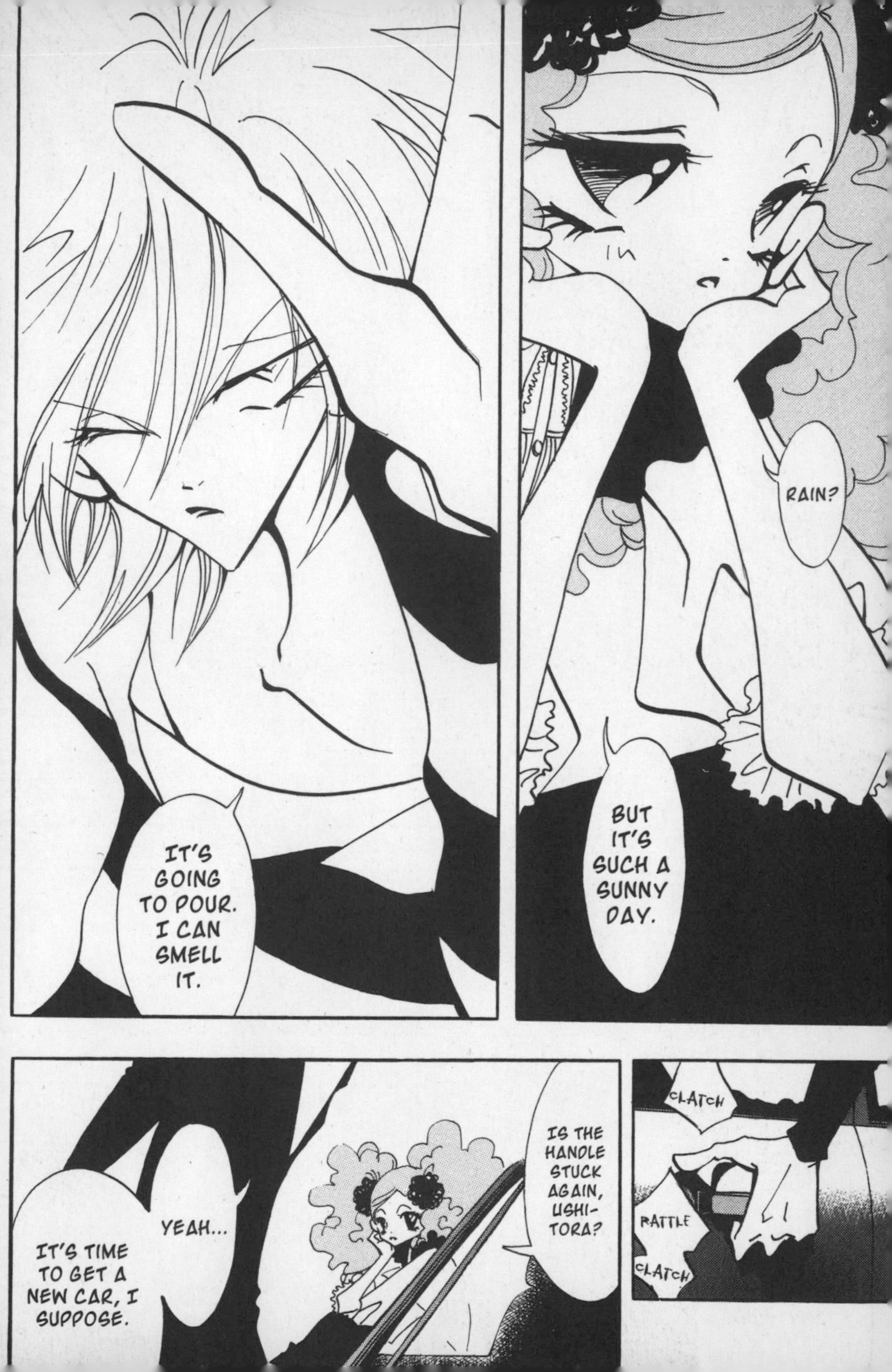
RAIN?
BUT IT'S SUCH A SUNNY DAY.
IT'S GOING TO POUR. I CAN SMELL IT.
CLATCH
RATTLE
CLATCH
IS THE HANDLE STUCK AGAIN, USHITORA?
YEAH...
IT'S TIME TO GET A NEW CAR, I SUPPOSE.

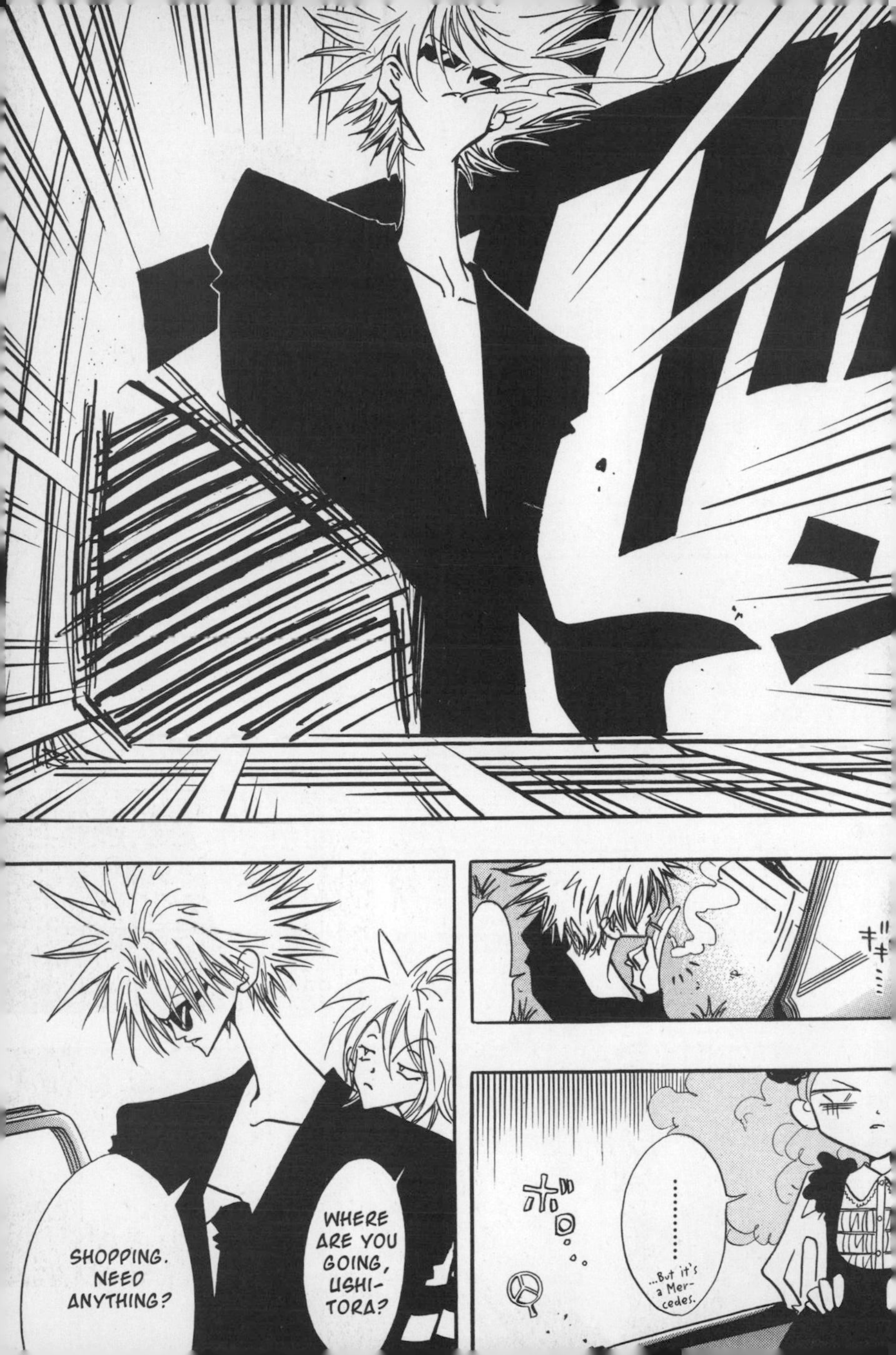
......
...But it's a Mercedes.
WHERE ARE YOU GOING, USHI-TORA?
SHOPPING. NEED ANYTHING?

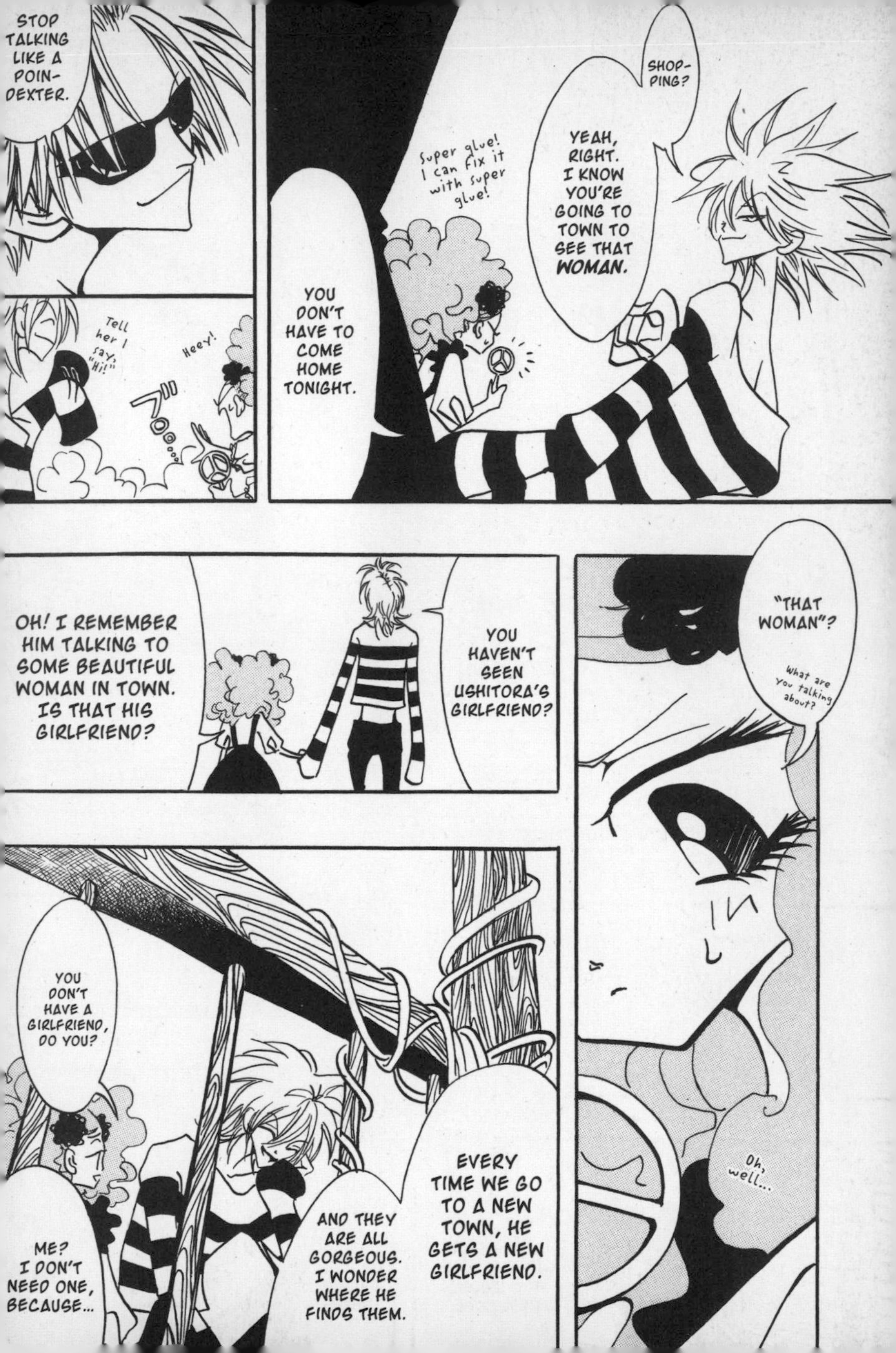
SHOP-PING?
YEAH, RIGHT. I KNOW YOU'RE GOING TO TOWN TO SEE THAT *WOMAN*.
YOU DON'T HAVE TO COME HOME TONIGHT.
Super glue! I can fix it with super glue!
STOP TALKING LIKE A POIN-DEXTER.
Heey!
Tell her I say, "Hi!"
"THAT WOMAN"?
What are you talking about?
Oh, well...
YOU HAVEN'T SEEN USHITORA'S GIRLFRIEND?
OH! I REMEMBER HIM TALKING TO SOME BEAUTIFUL WOMAN IN TOWN. IS THAT HIS GIRLFRIEND?
EVERY TIME WE GO TO A NEW TOWN, HE GETS A NEW GIRLFRIEND.
AND THEY ARE ALL GORGEOUS. I WONDER WHERE HE FINDS THEM.
YOU DON'T HAVE A GIRLFRIEND, DO YOU?
ME? I DON'T NEED ONE, BECAUSE...

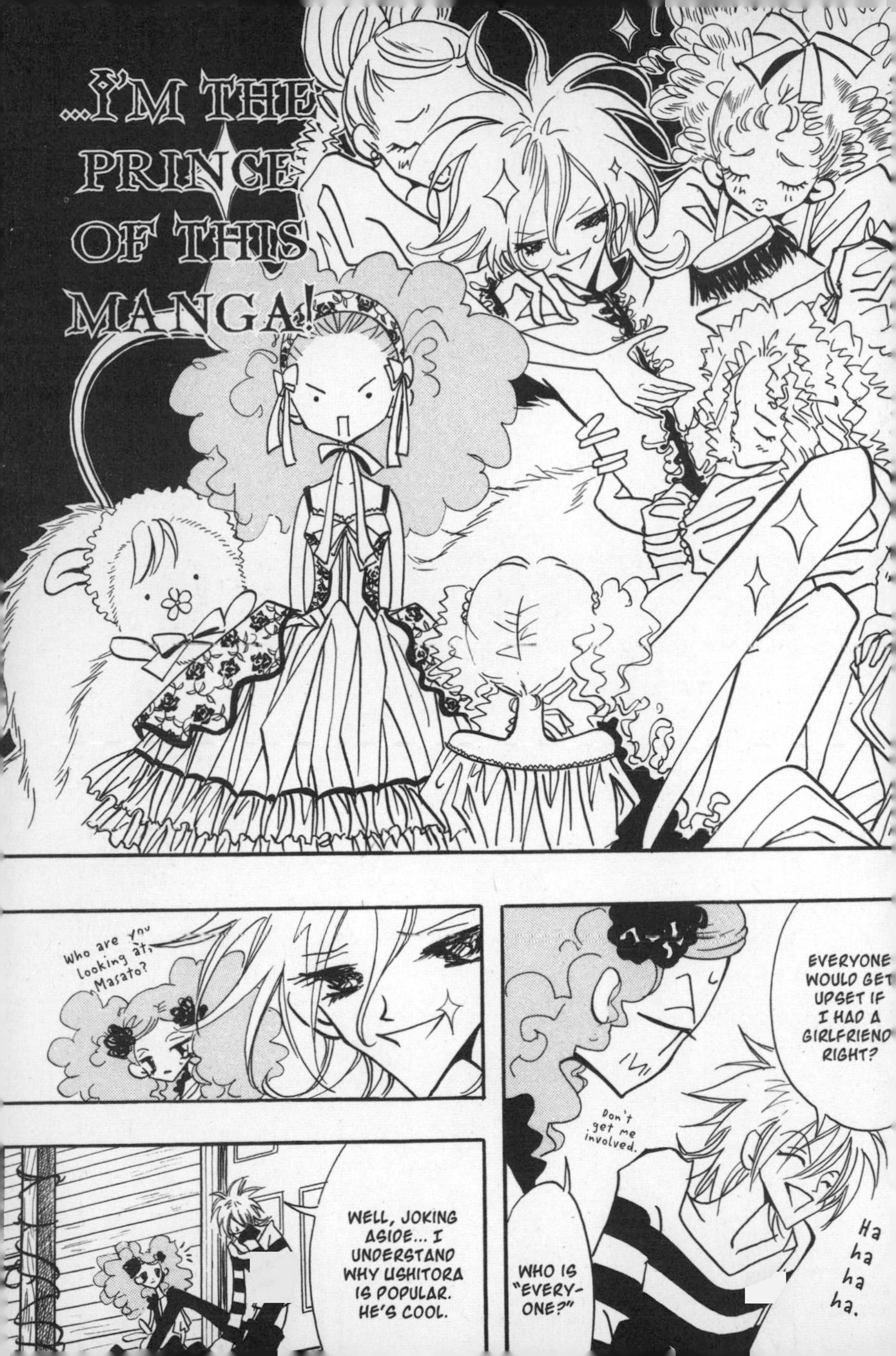
...I'M THE PRINCE OF THIS MANGA!
EVERYONE WOULD GET UPSET IF I HAD A GIRLFRIEND RIGHT?
Don't get me involved.
Ha ha ha ha.
WHO IS "EVERY-ONE?"
Who are you looking at, Masato?
WELL, JOKING ASIDE... I UNDERSTAND WHY USHITORA IS POPULAR. HE'S COOL.

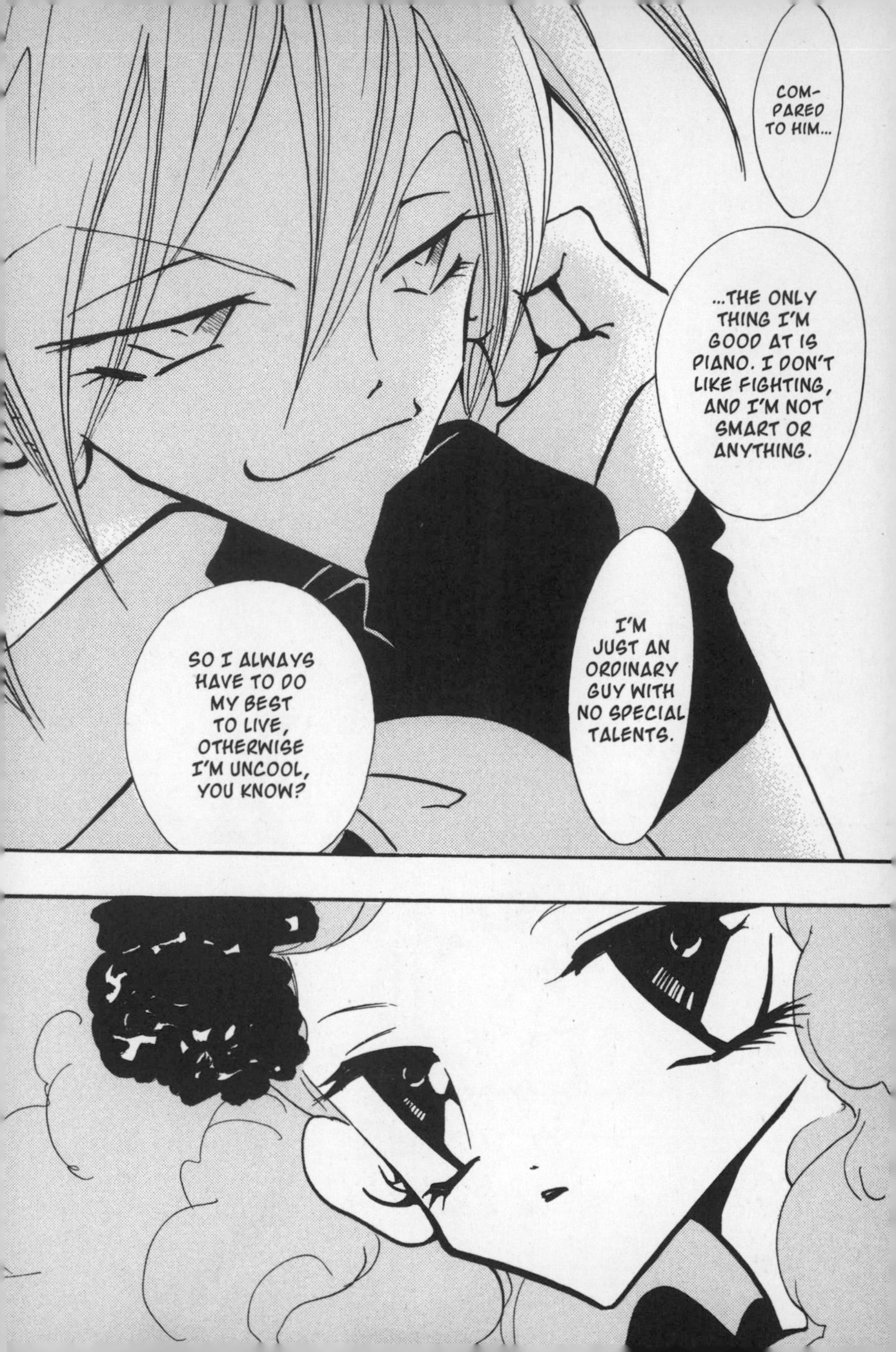
COM-PARED TO HIM...
...THE ONLY THING I'M GOOD AT IS PIANO. I DON'T LIKE FIGHTING, AND I'M NOT SMART OR ANYTHING.
I'M JUST AN ORDINARY GUY WITH NO SPECIAL TALENTS.
SO I ALWAYS HAVE TO DO MY BEST TO LIVE, OTHERWISE I'M UNCOOL, YOU KNOW?

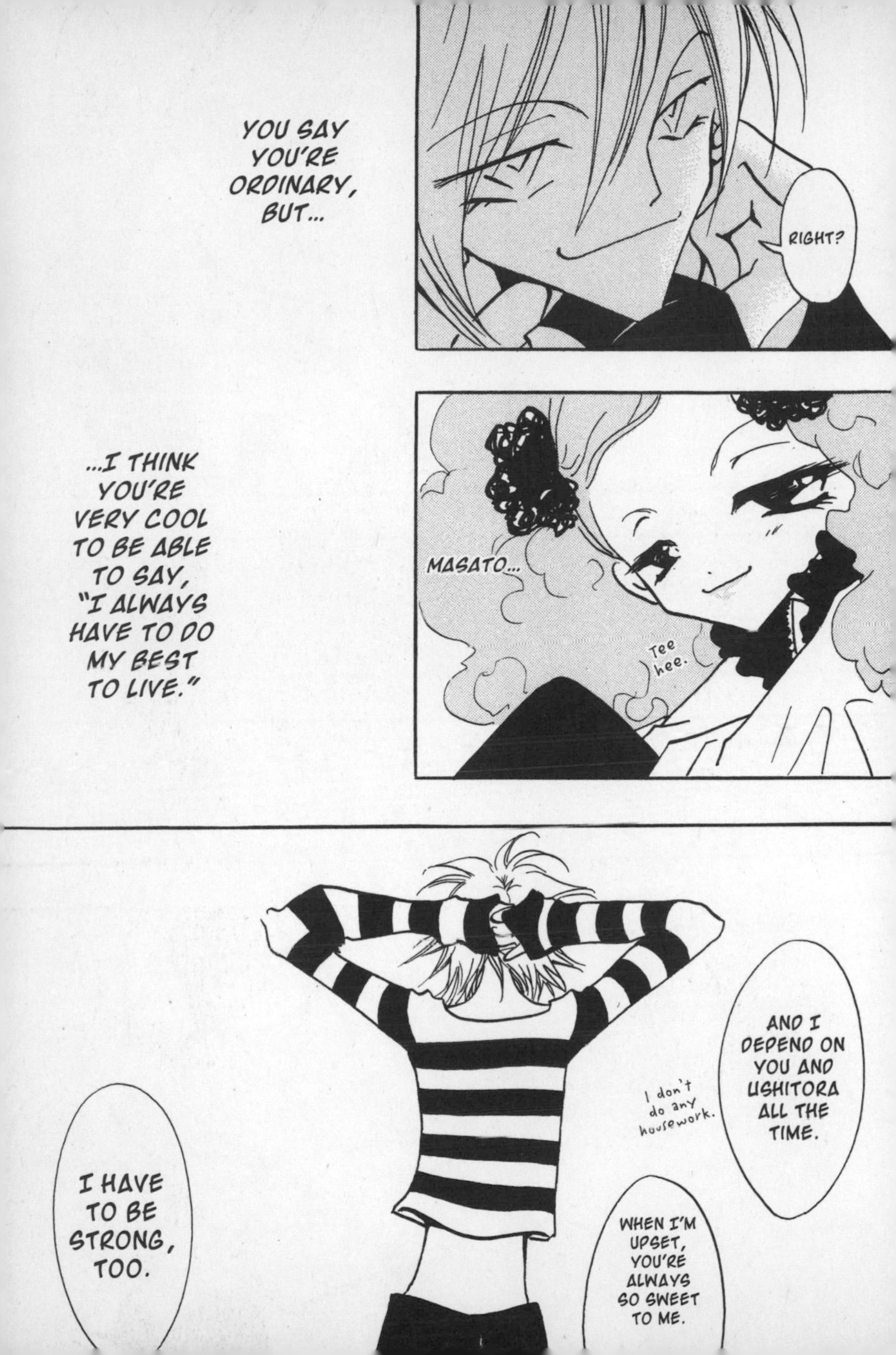

RIGHT?
YOU SAY YOU'RE ORDINARY, BUT...
MASATO...
Tee hee.
...I THINK YOU'RE VERY COOL TO BE ABLE TO SAY, "I ALWAYS HAVE TO DO MY BEST TO LIVE."
AND I DEPEND ON YOU AND USHITORA ALL THE TIME.
I don't do any housework.
WHEN I'M UPSET, YOU'RE ALWAYS SO SWEET TO ME.
I HAVE TO BE STRONG, TOO.

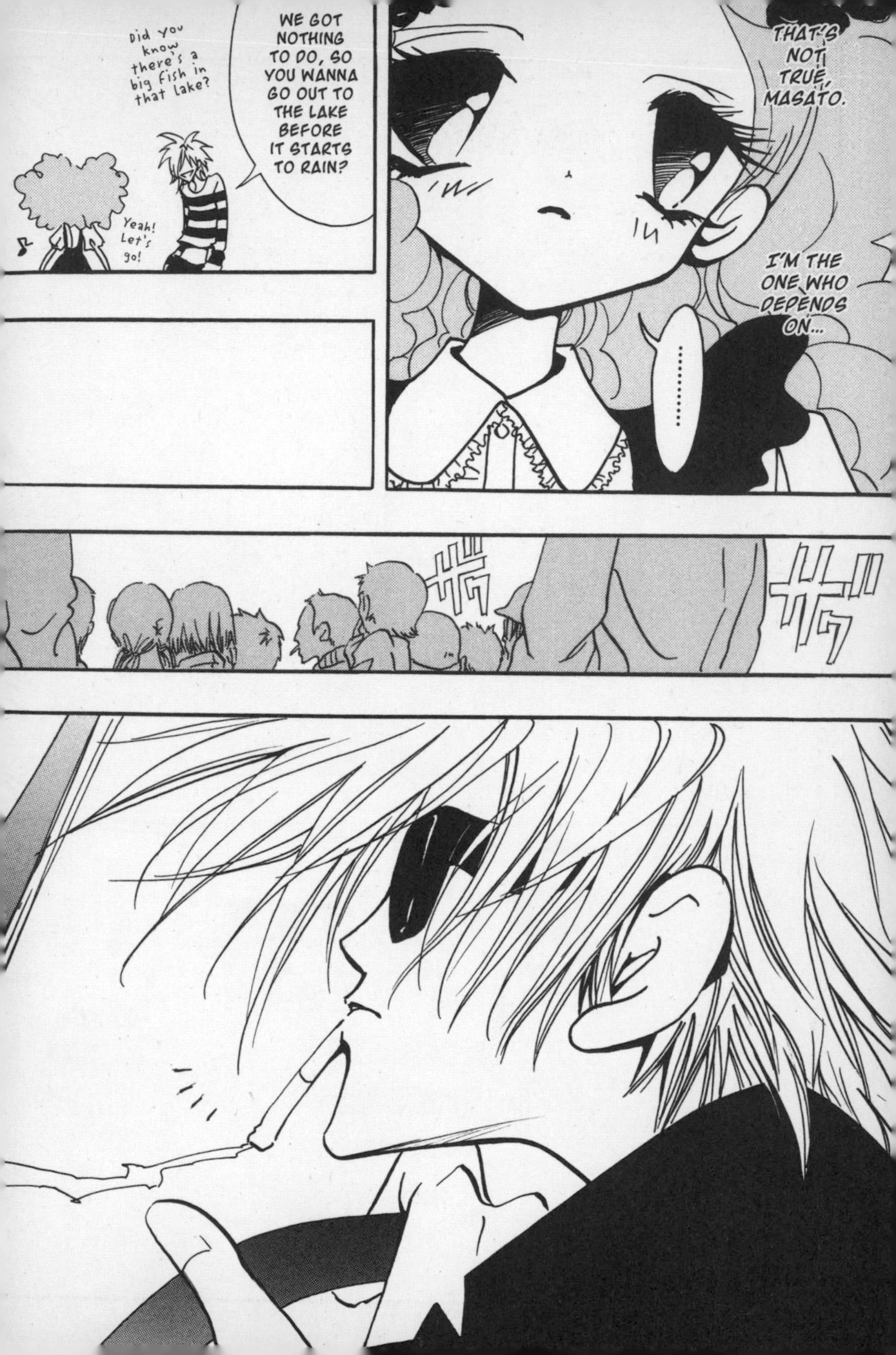
THAT'S NOT TRUE, MASATO.
I'M THE ONE WHO DEPENDS ON...
......
WE GOT NOTHING TO DO, SO YOU WANNA GO OUT TO THE LAKE BEFORE IT STARTS TO RAIN?
Did you know there's a big fish in that lake?
Yeah! Let's go!

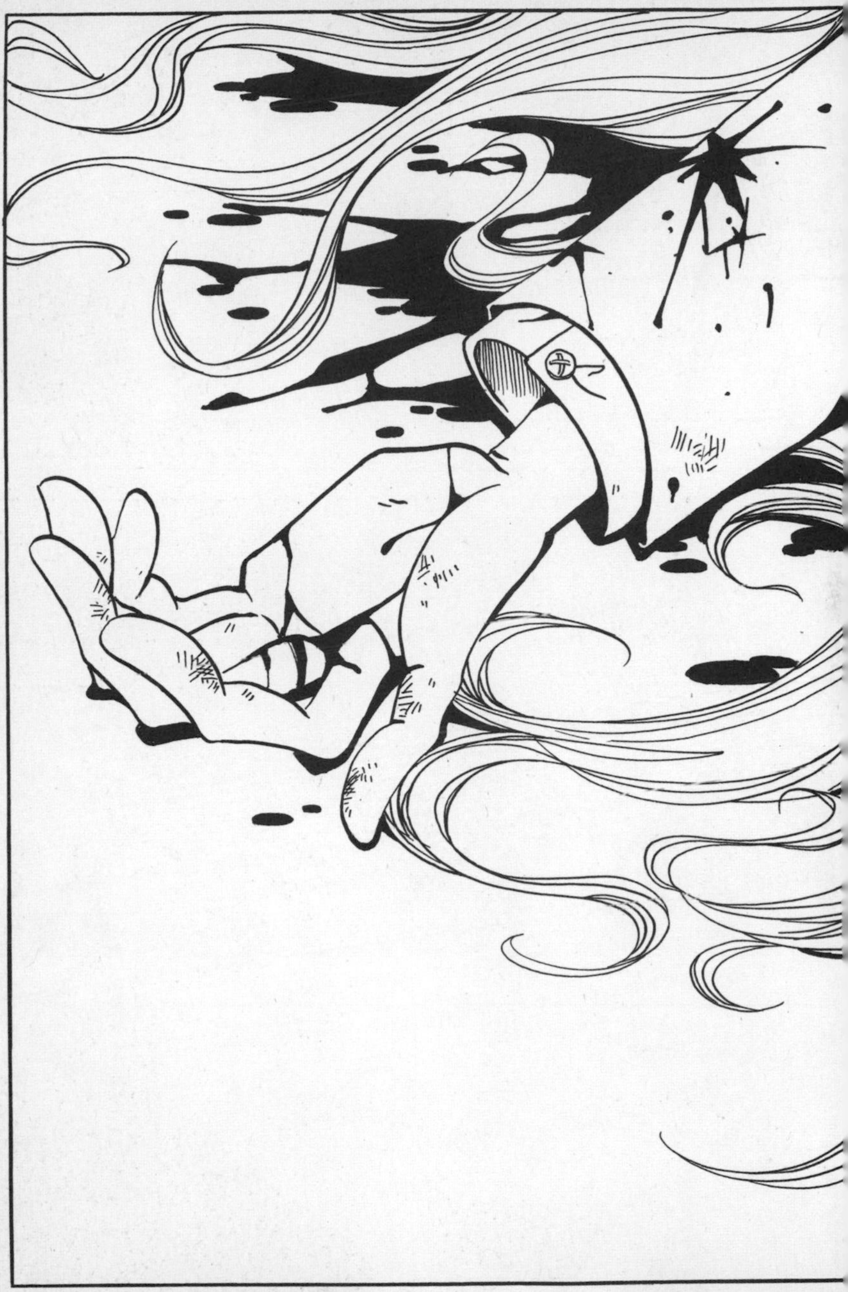

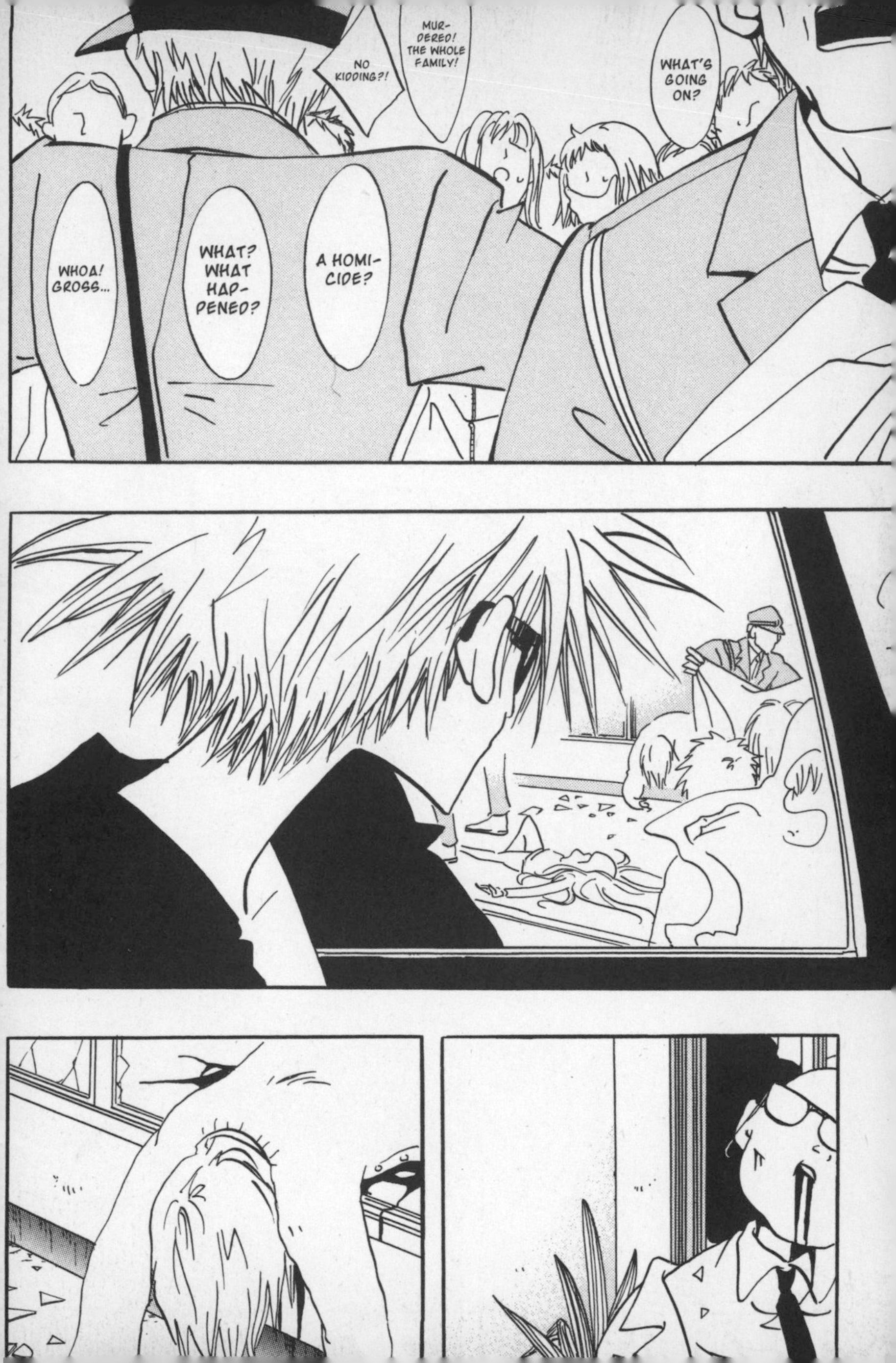
WHAT'S GOING ON?
MURDERED! THE WHOLE FAMILY!
NO KIDDING?!
A HOMICIDE?
WHAT? WHAT HAPPENED?
WHOA! GROSS...

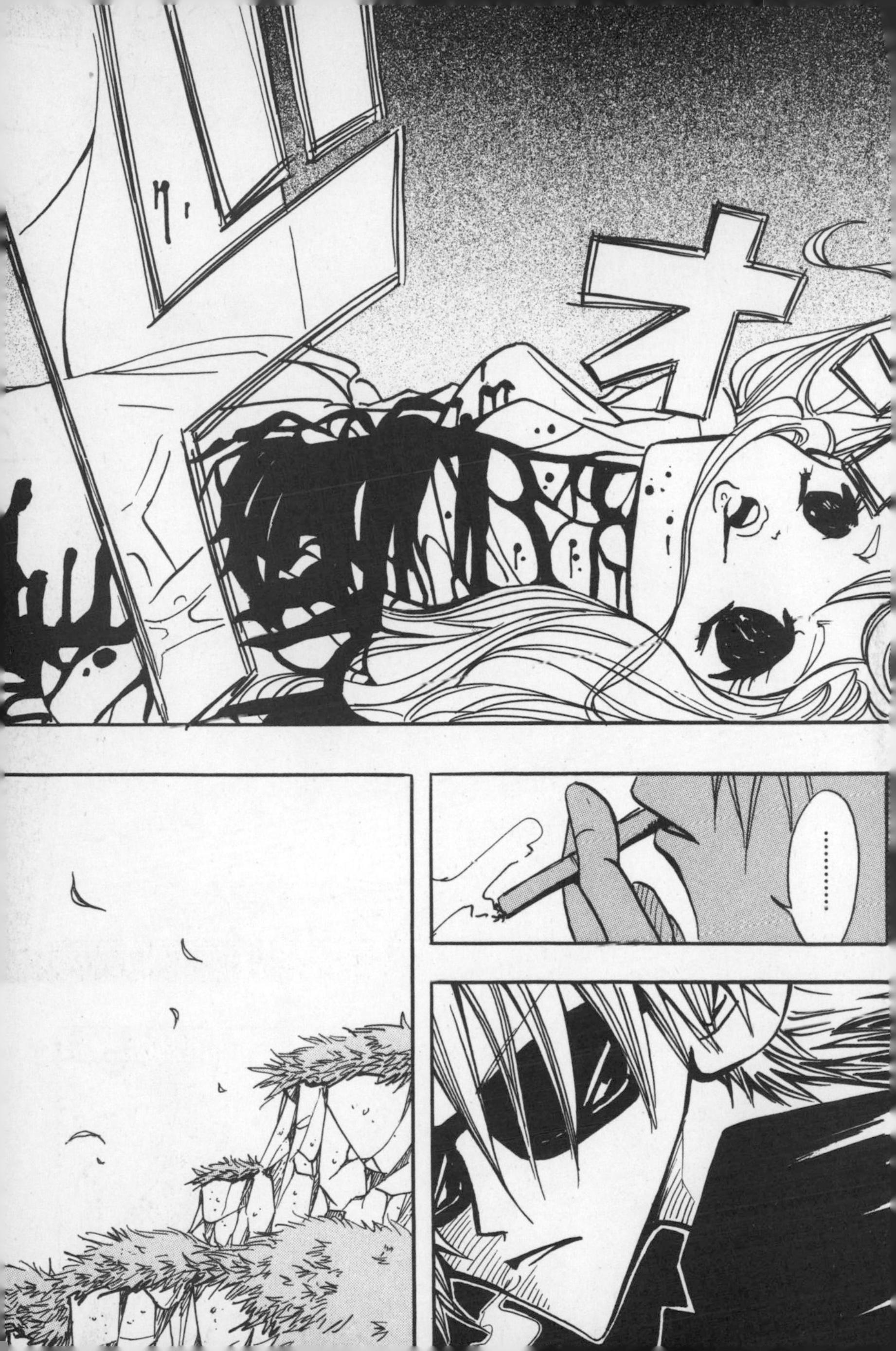

....

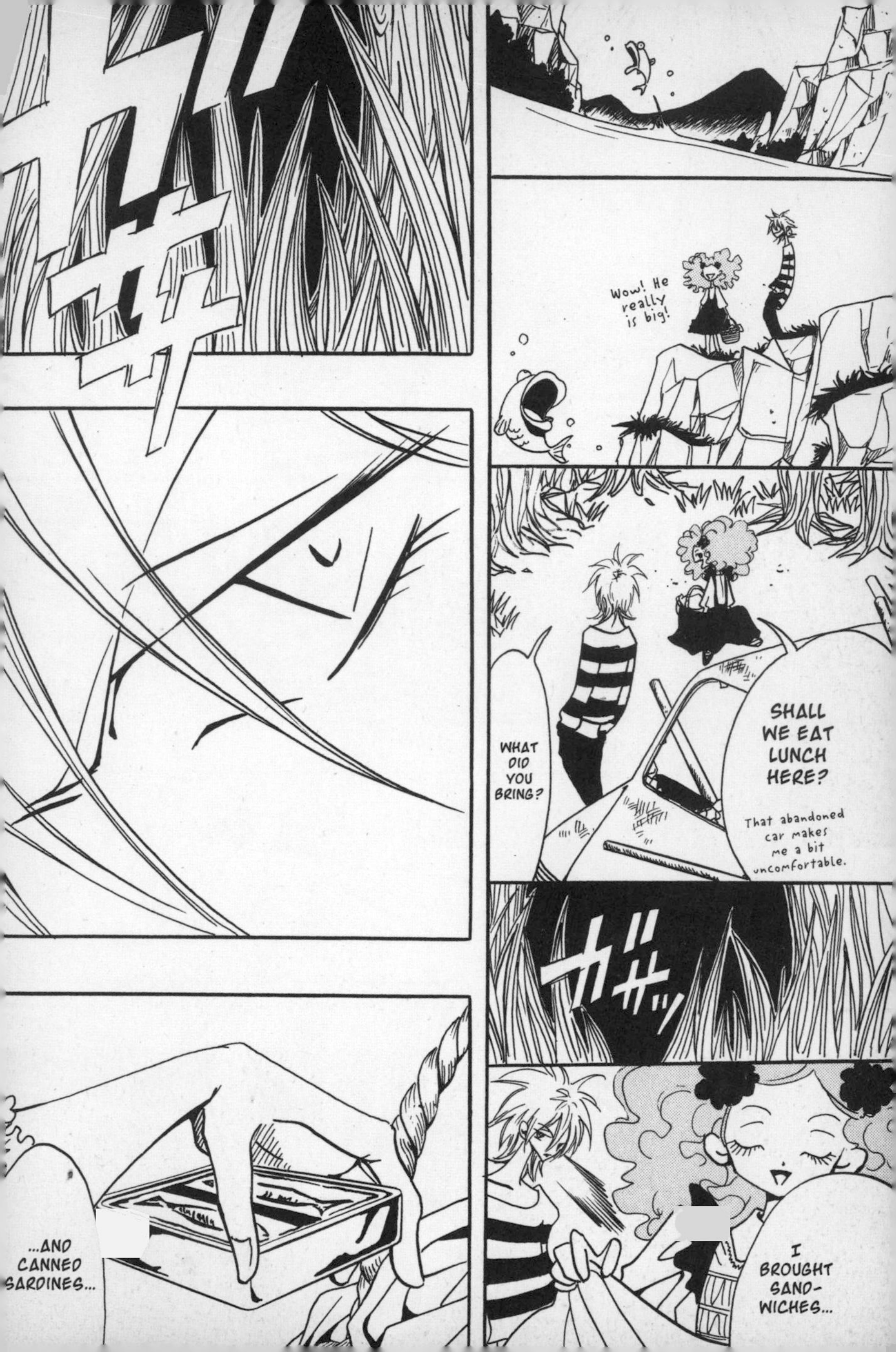

Wow! He really is big!
SHALL WE EAT LUNCH HERE?
That abandoned car makes me a bit uncomfortable.
WHAT DID YOU BRING?
ガザッ
I BROUGHT SAND-WICHES...
...AND CANNED SARDINES...

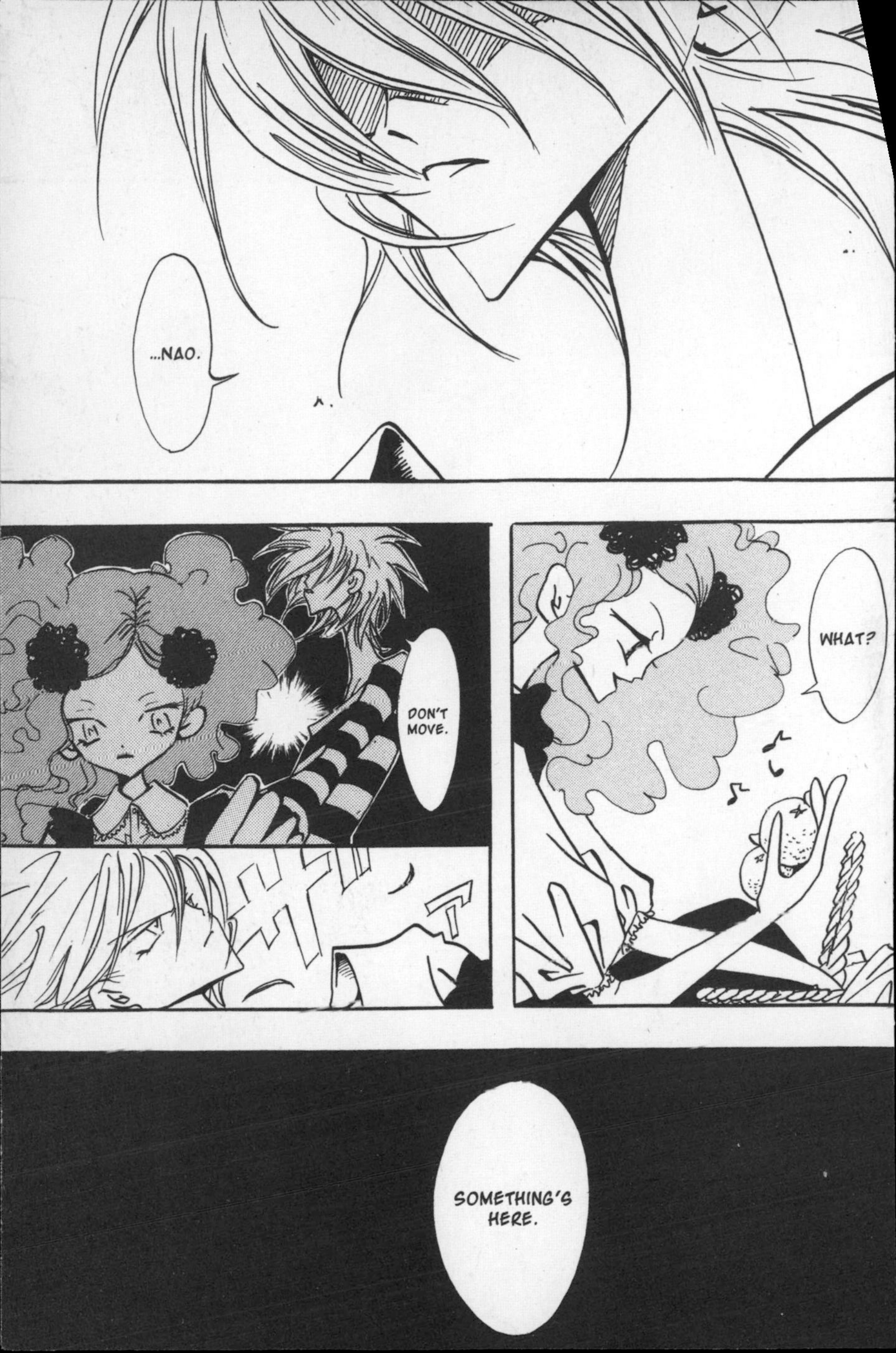
...NAO.
WHAT?
DON'T MOVE.
SOMETHING'S HERE.

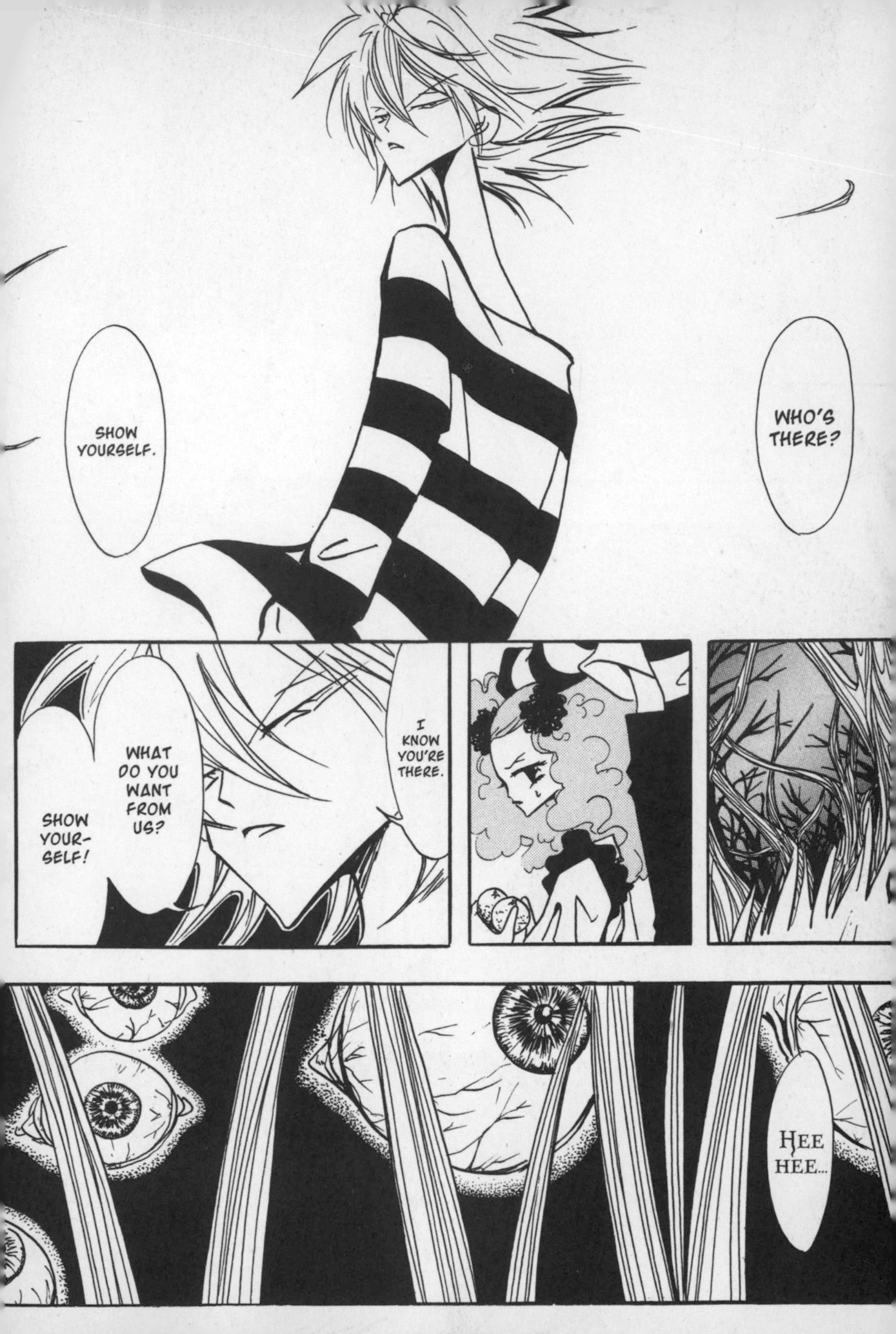
WHO'S THERE?
SHOW YOURSELF.
I KNOW YOU'RE THERE.
WHAT DO YOU WANT FROM US?
SHOW YOUR-SELF!
HEE HEE...

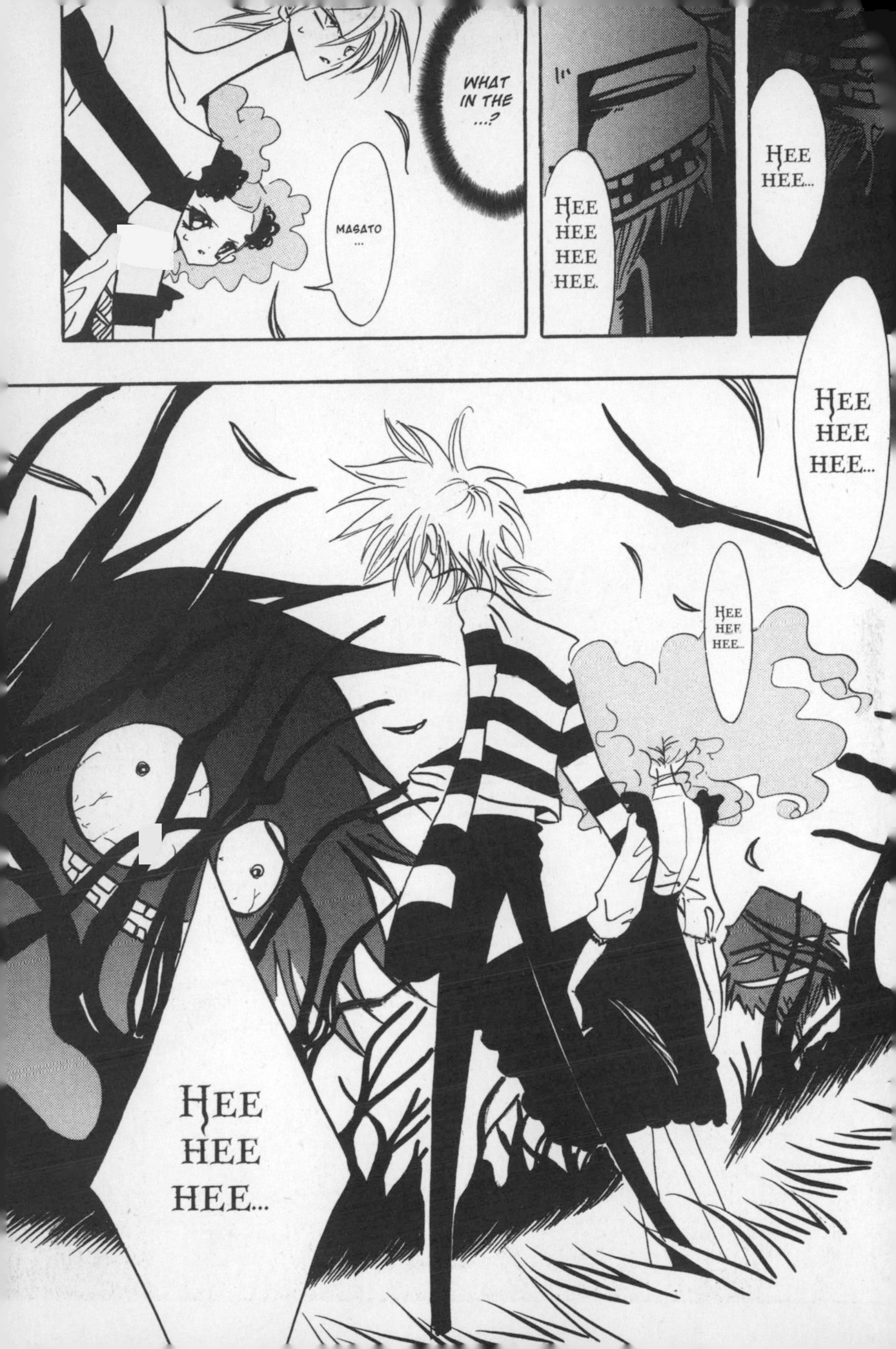
HEE HEE...
HEE HEE HEE HEE.
WHAT IN THE ...?
MASATO ...
HEE HEE HEE...
HEE HEE HEE...
HEE HEE HEE...

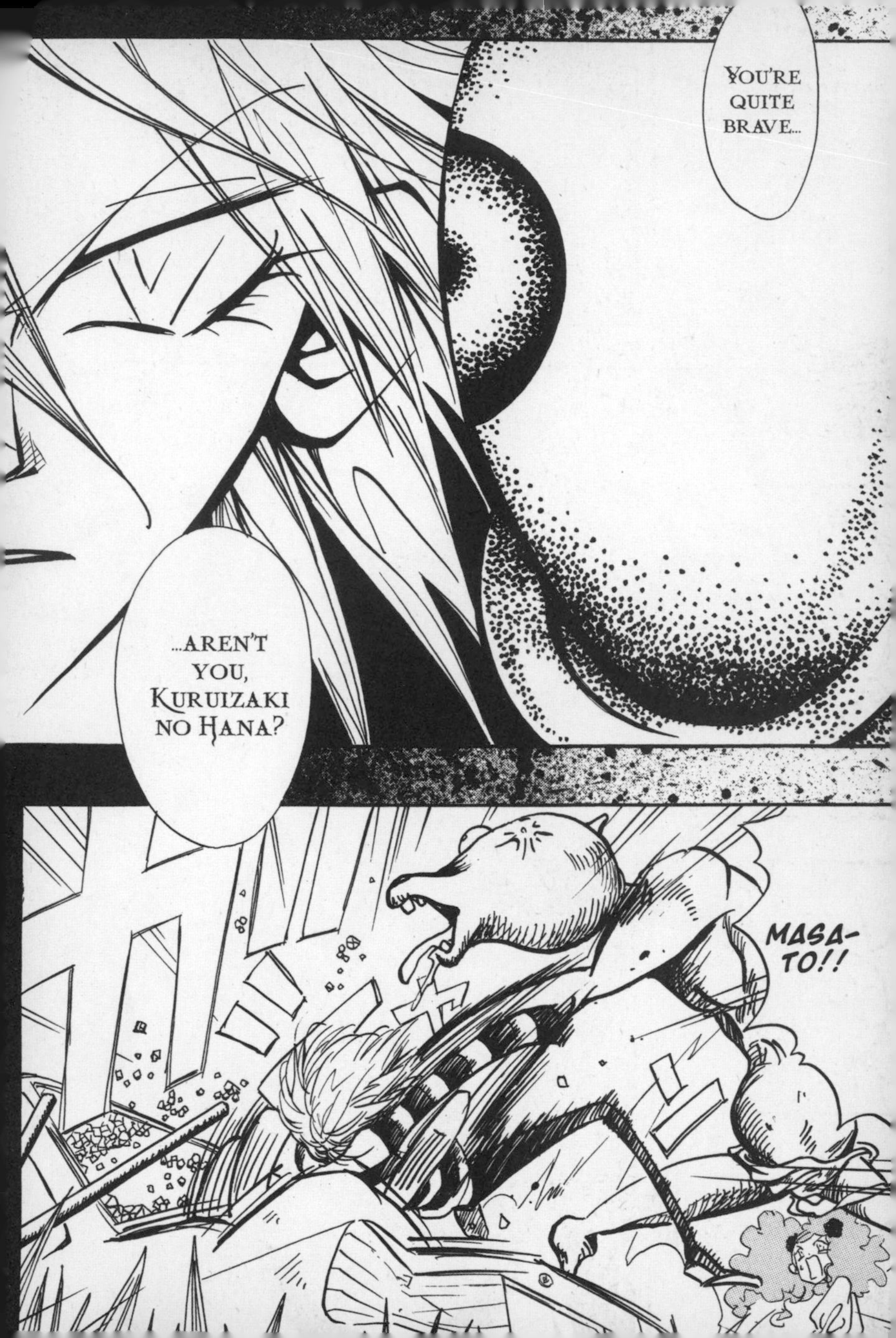
YOU'RE QUITE BRAVE...
...AREN'T YOU, KURUIZAKI NO HANA?
MASA-TO!!

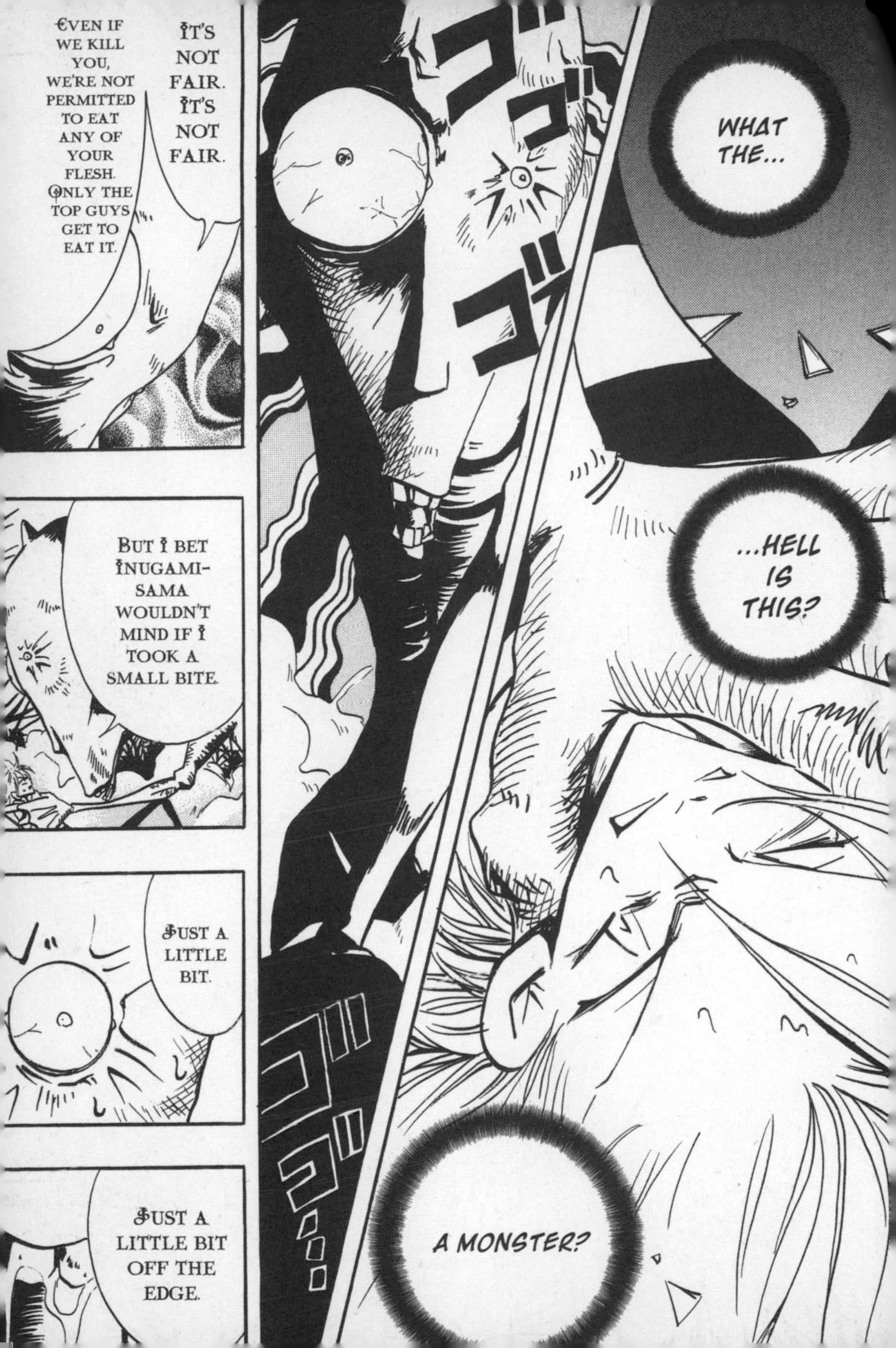
WHAT THE...
...HELL IS THIS?
A MONSTER?
IT'S NOT FAIR. IT'S NOT FAIR.
EVEN IF WE KILL YOU, WE'RE NOT PERMITTED TO EAT ANY OF YOUR FLESH. ONLY THE TOP GUYS GET TO EAT IT.
BUT I BET INUGAMI-SAMA WOULDN'T MIND IF I TOOK A SMALL BITE.
JUST A LITTLE BIT.
JUST A LITTLE BIT OFF THE EDGE.

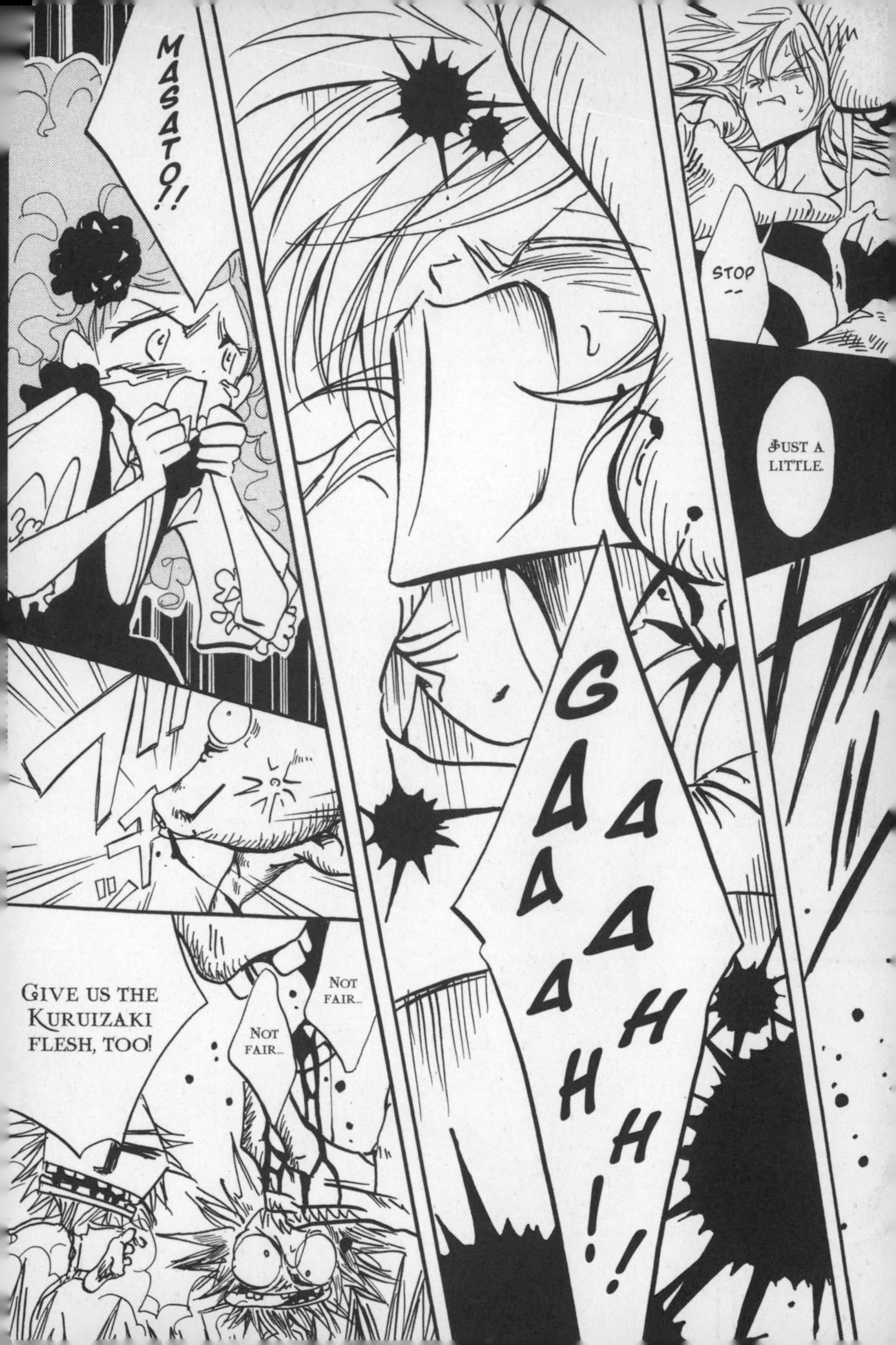
STOP --
JUST A LITTLE.
GAAAAAAHHHH!!
MASATO!!
NOT FAIR...
NOT FAIR...
GIVE US THE KURUIZAKI FLESH, TOO!

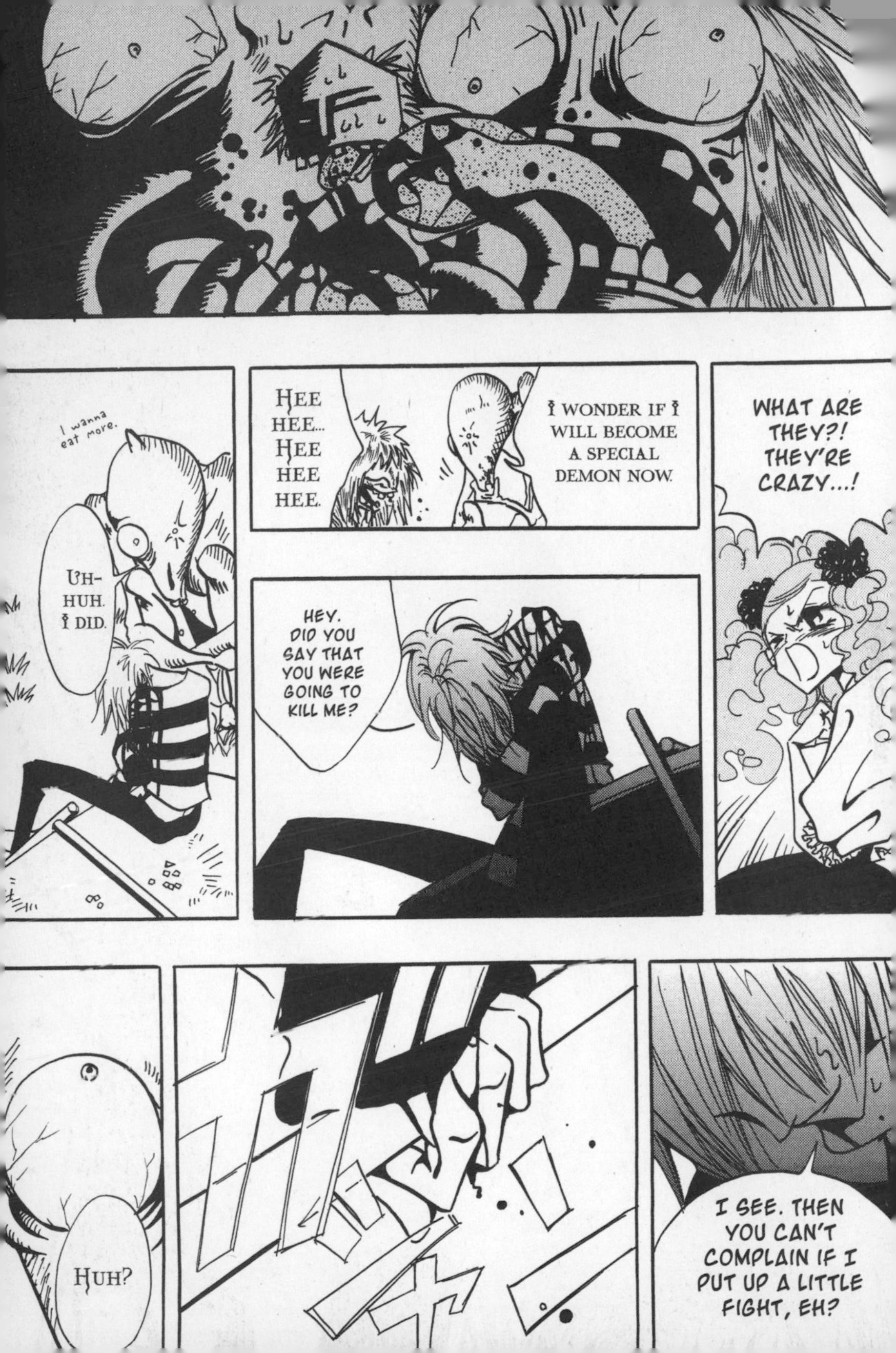
WHAT ARE THEY?! THEY'RE CRAZY...!
I WONDER IF I WILL BECOME A SPECIAL DEMON NOW.
HEE HEE... HEE HEE HEE.
HEY. DID YOU SAY THAT YOU WERE GOING TO KILL ME?
I wanna eat more.
UH-HUH. I DID.
I SEE. THEN YOU CAN'T COMPLAIN IF I PUT UP A LITTLE FIGHT, EH?
HUH?

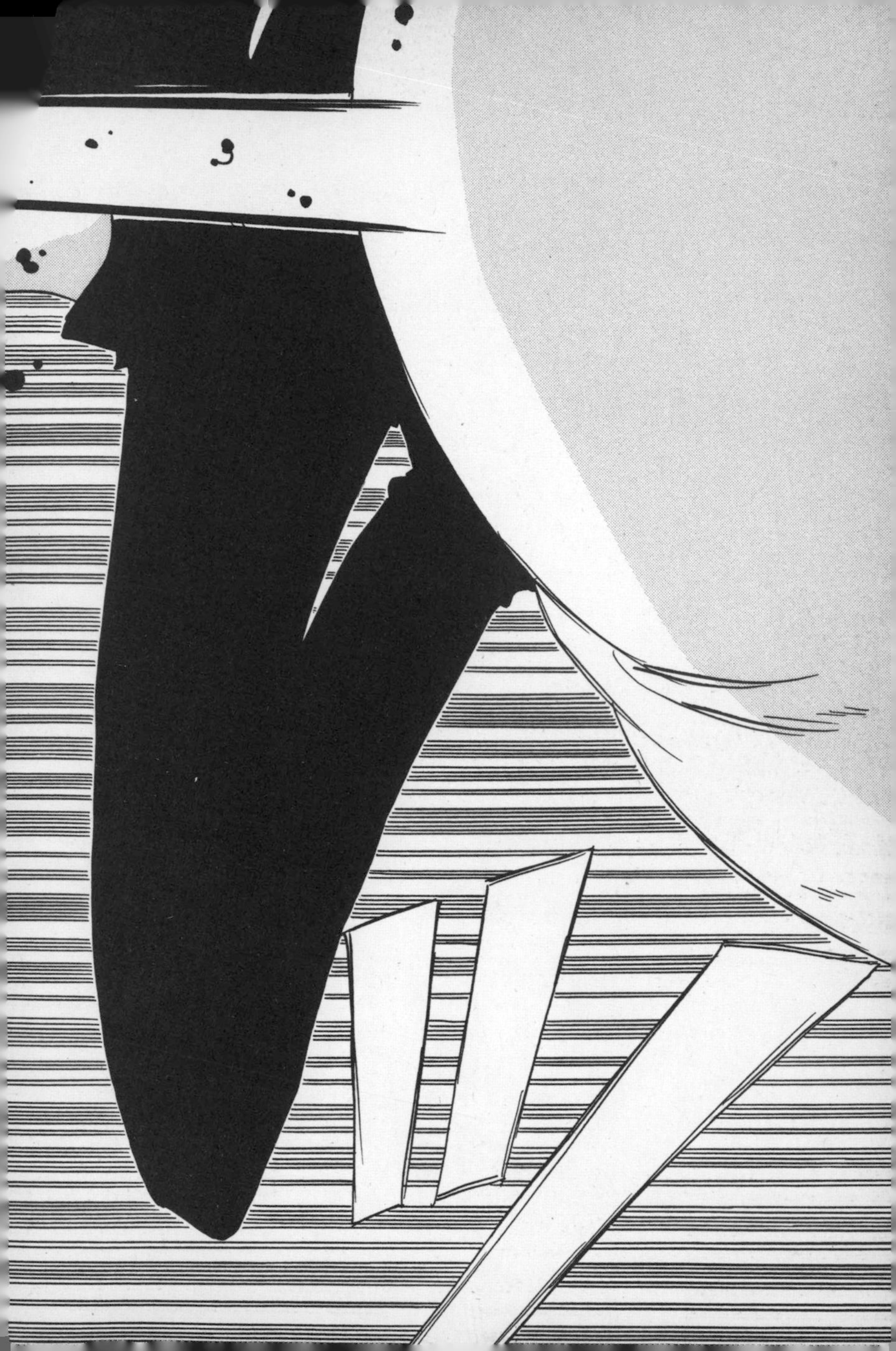

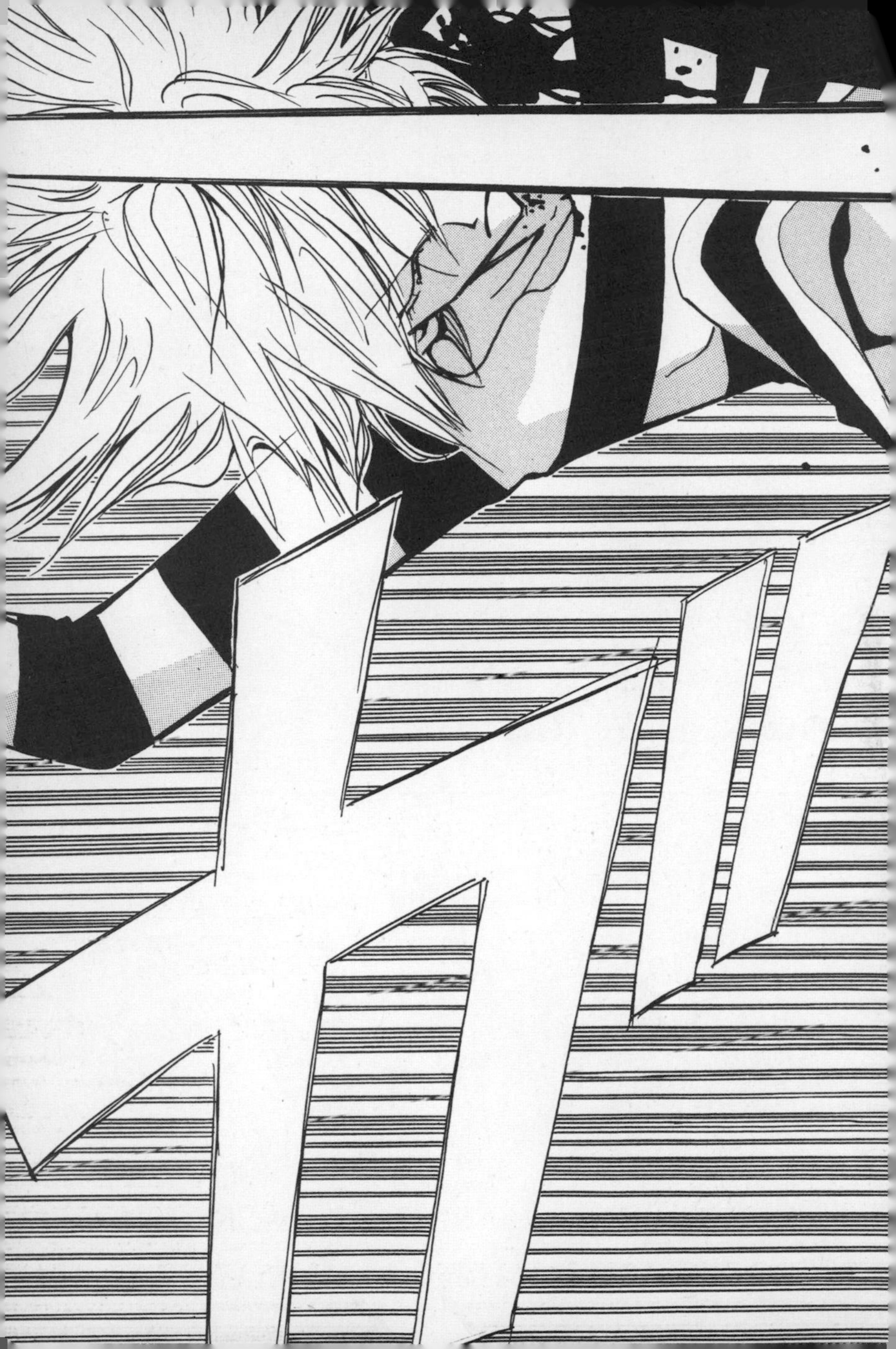

GYAAAAH!!

IT HURTS!

IT HURTS!

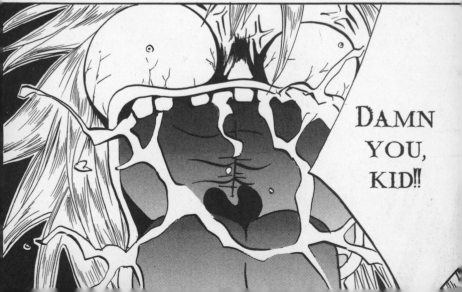

DAMN YOU, KID!!

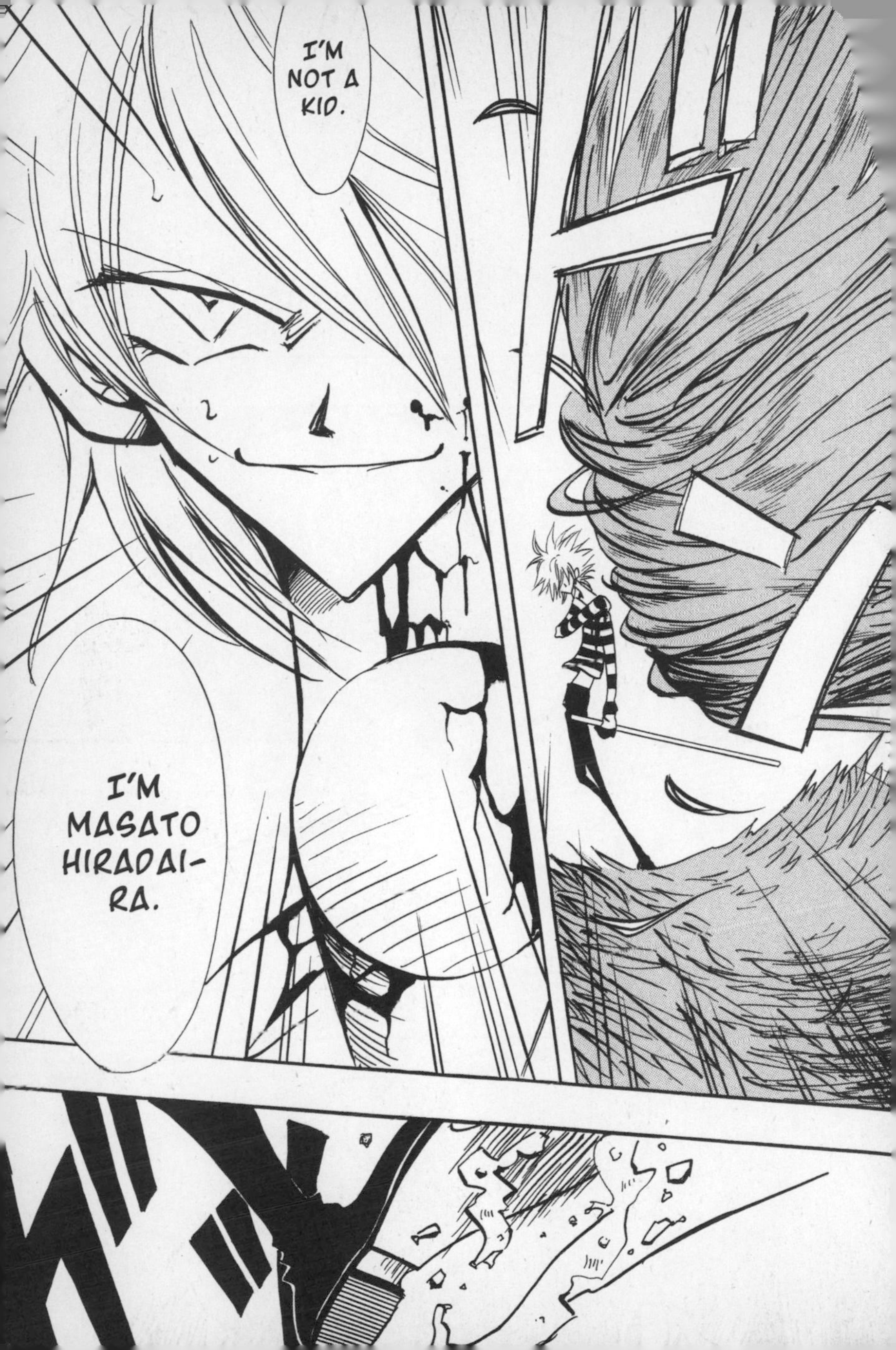
I'M NOT A KID.
I'M MASATO HIRADAIRA.

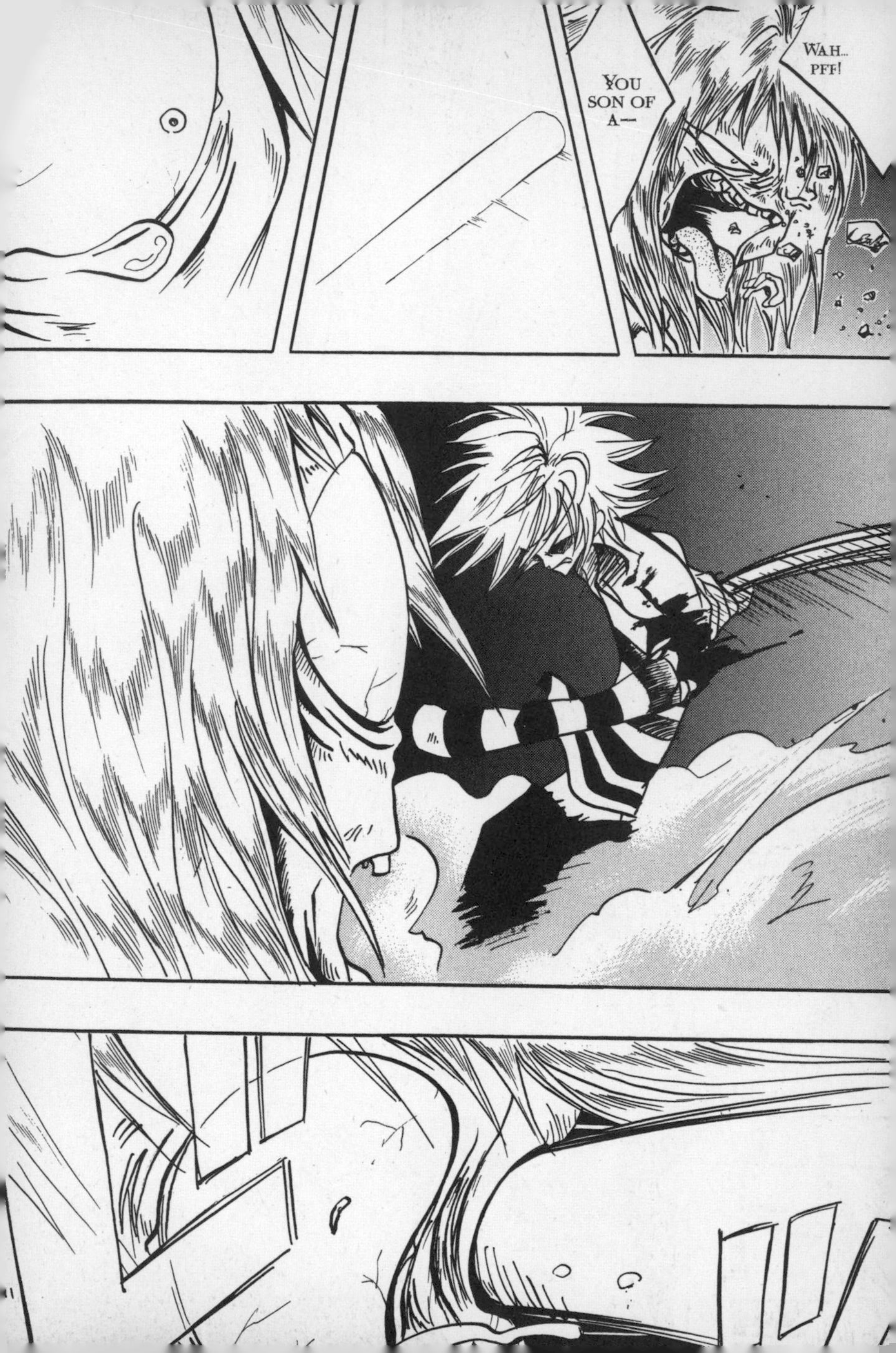
WAH... PFF!
YOU SON OF A—

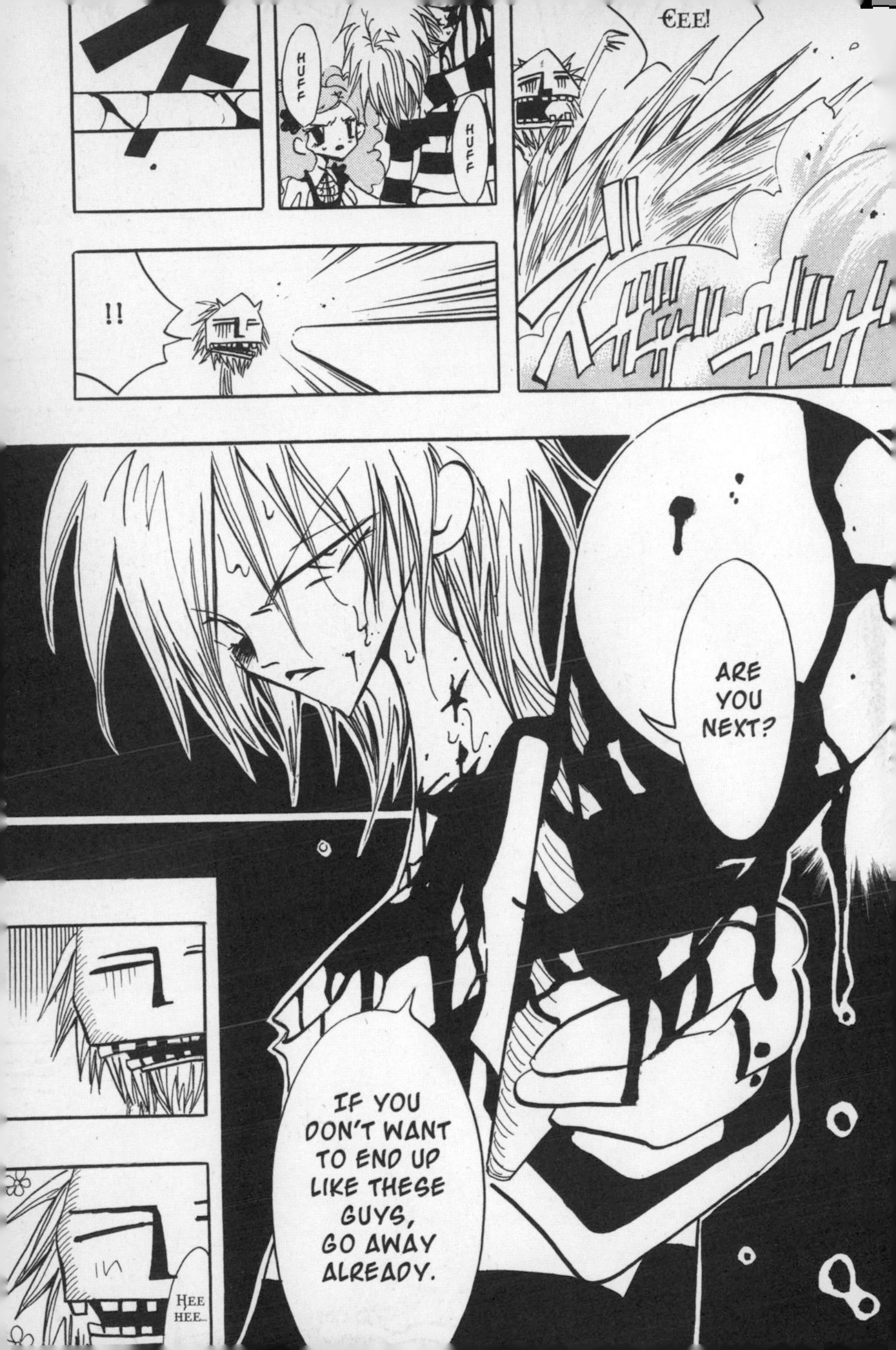
CEE!
HUFF
HUFF
!!
ARE YOU NEXT?
IF YOU DON'T WANT TO END UP LIKE THESE GUYS, GO AWAY ALREADY.
HEE HEE...

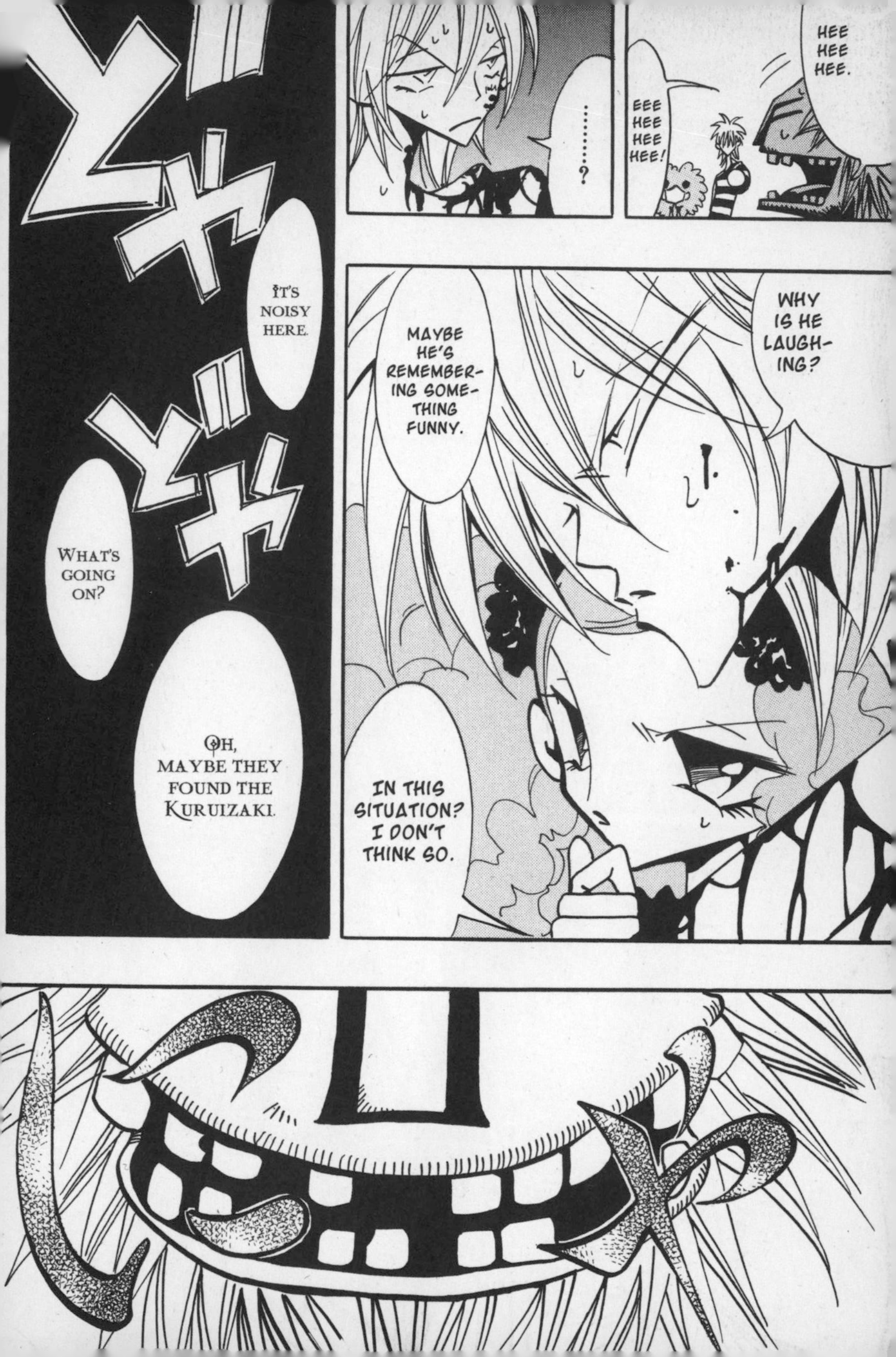
HEE HEE HEE.
EEE HEE HEE HEE!
......?
WHY IS HE LAUGHING?
MAYBE HE'S REMEMBERING SOMETHING FUNNY.
IN THIS SITUATION? I DON'T THINK SO.
IT'S NOISY HERE.
WHAT'S GOING ON?
OH, MAYBE THEY FOUND THE KURUIZAKI.

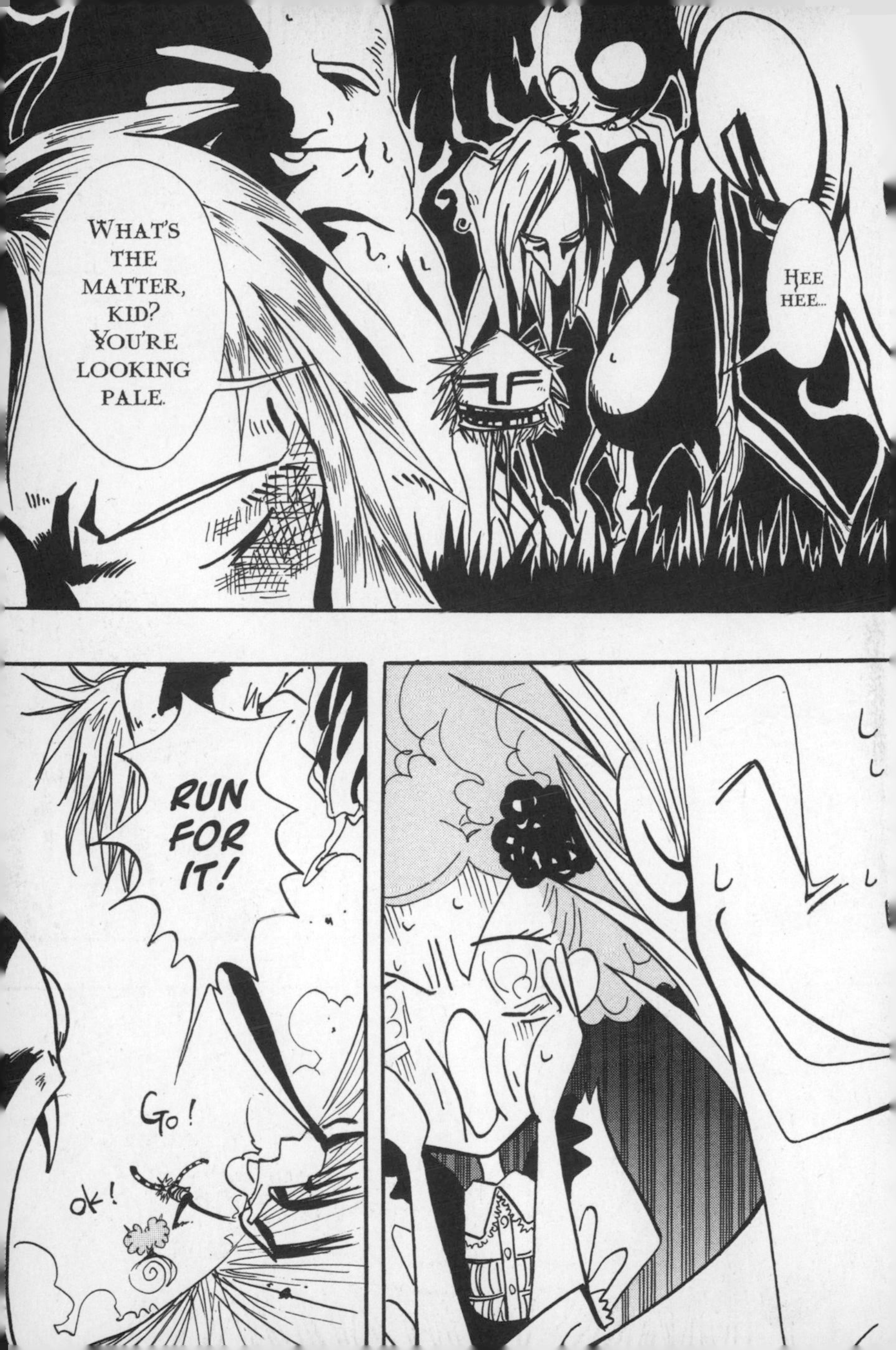
HEE HEE...
WHAT'S THE MATTER, KID? YOU'RE LOOKING PALE.
RUN FOR IT!
GO!
OK!

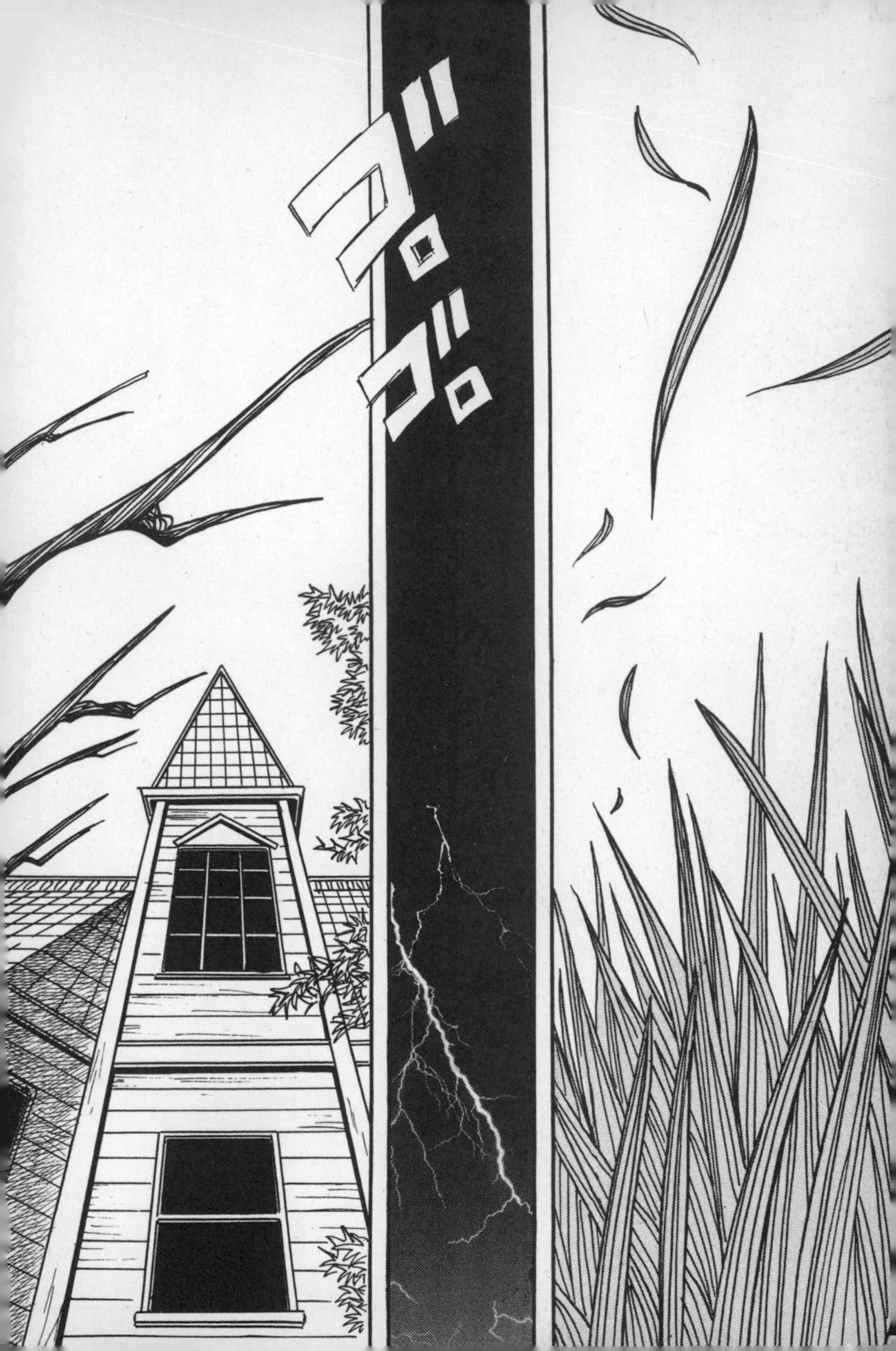
ゴロゴロ

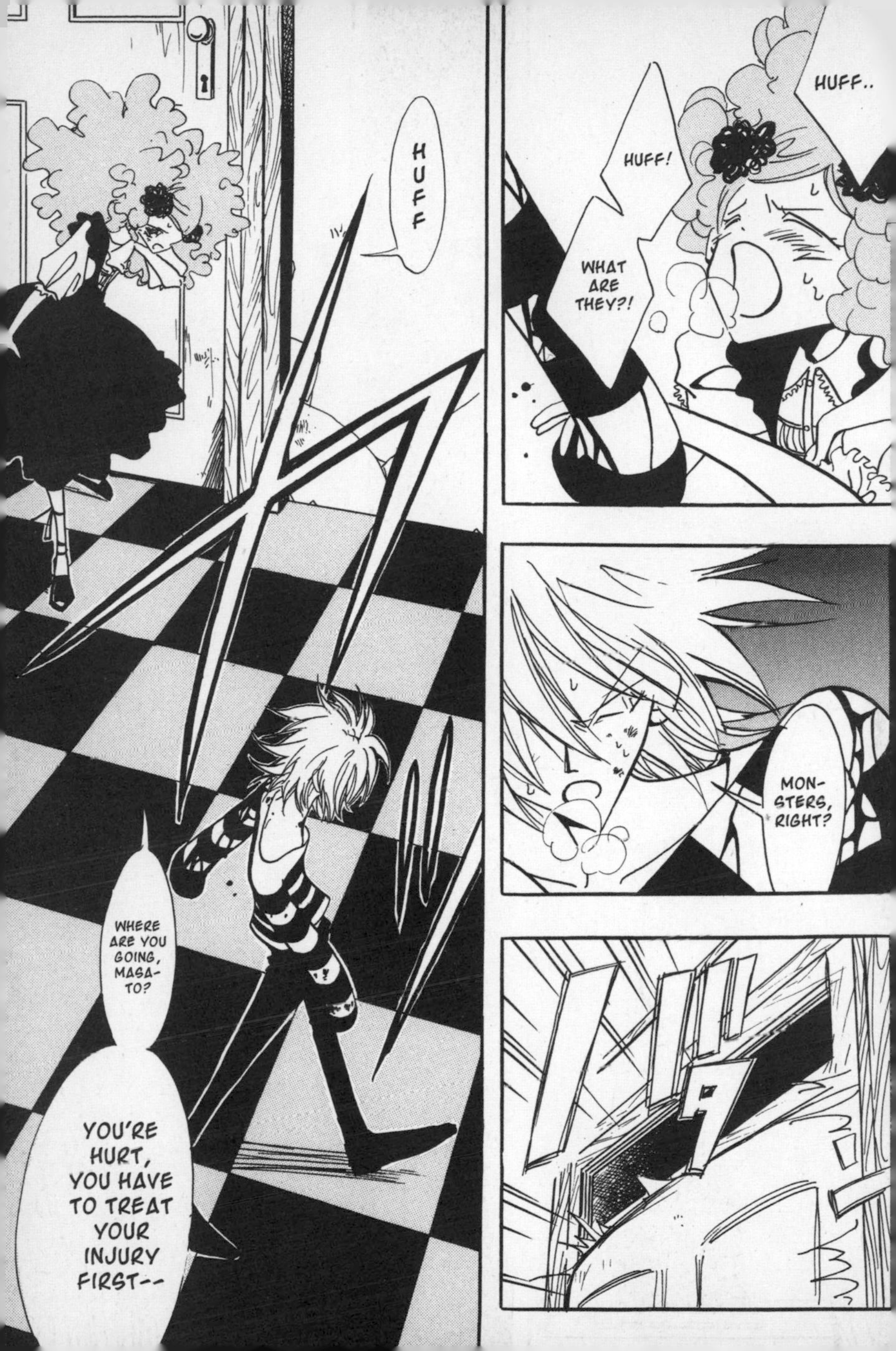
HUFF..
HUFF!
WHAT ARE THEY?!
MON-STERS, RIGHT?
HUFF HUFF
WHERE ARE YOU GOING, MASA-TO?
YOU'RE HURT, YOU HAVE TO TREAT YOUR INJURY FIRST--

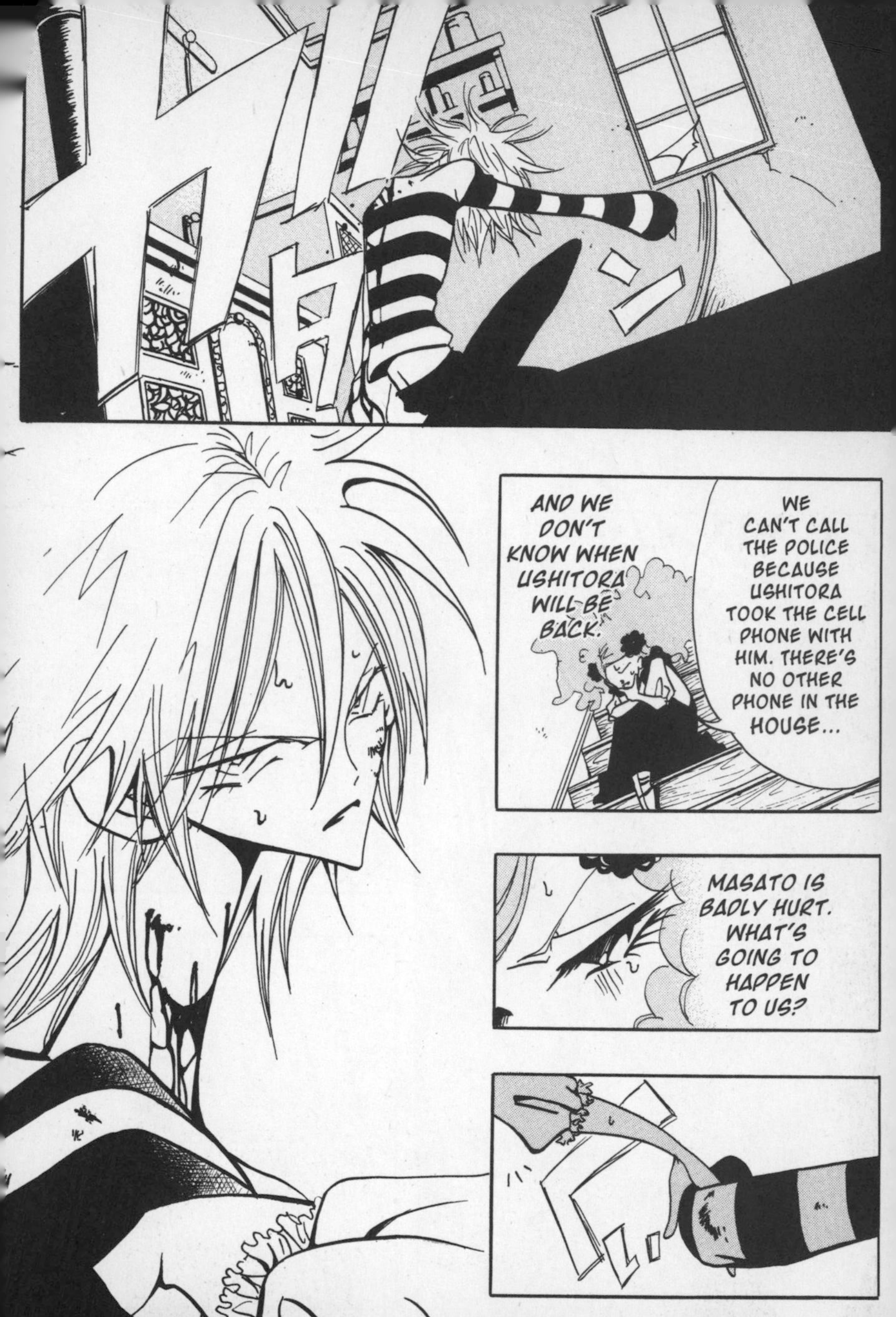
WE CAN'T CALL THE POLICE BECAUSE USHITORA TOOK THE CELL PHONE WITH HIM. THERE'S NO OTHER PHONE IN THE HOUSE...
AND WE DON'T KNOW WHEN USHITORA WILL BE BACK.
MASATO IS BADLY HURT. WHAT'S GOING TO HAPPEN TO US?

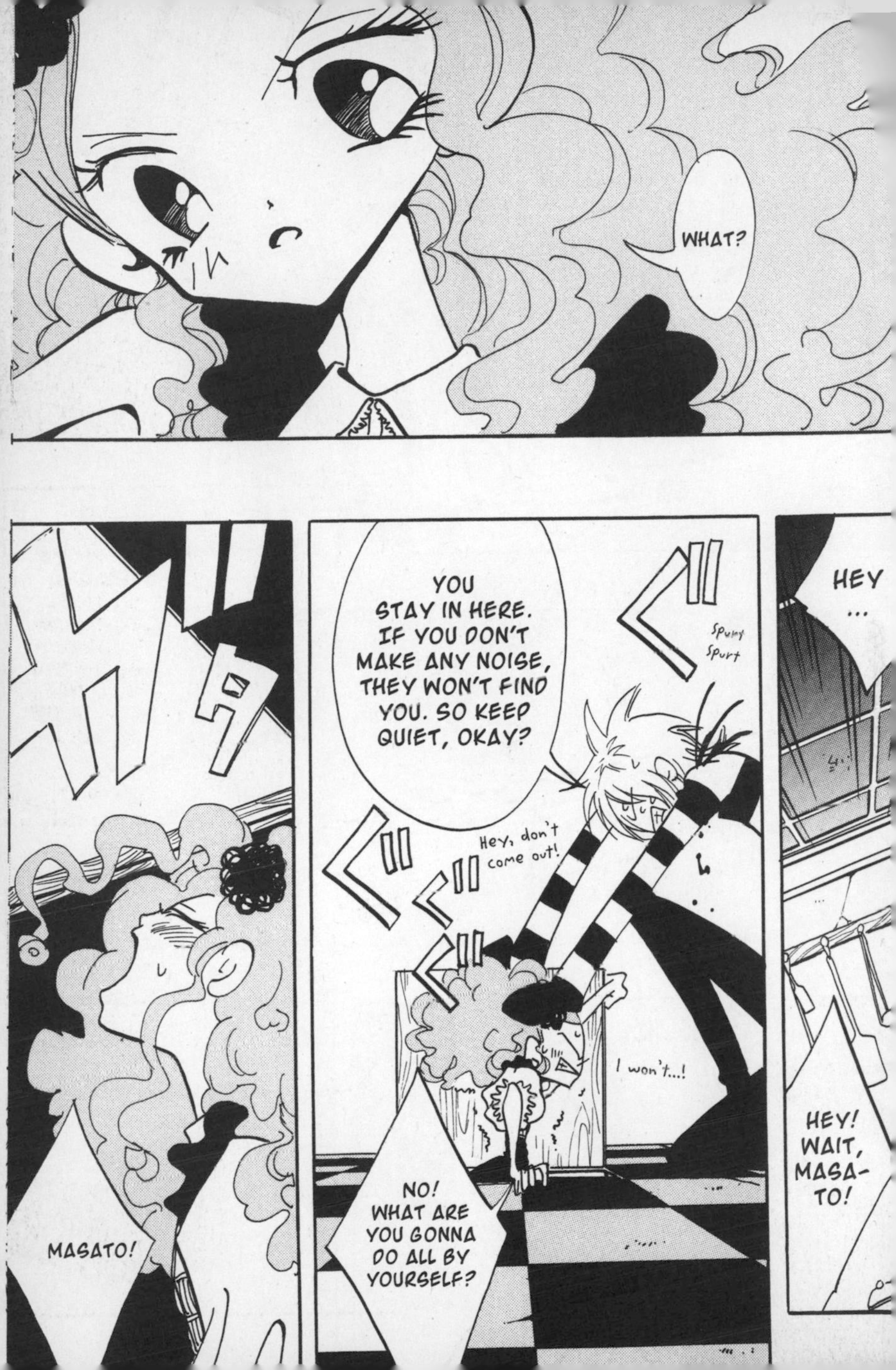
WHAT?
HEY ...
HEY! WAIT, MASATO!
Spurt Spurt
YOU STAY IN HERE. IF YOU DON'T MAKE ANY NOISE, THEY WON'T FIND YOU. SO KEEP QUIET, OKAY?
Hey, don't come out!
I won't...!
NO! WHAT ARE YOU GONNA DO ALL BY YOURSELF?
MASATO!

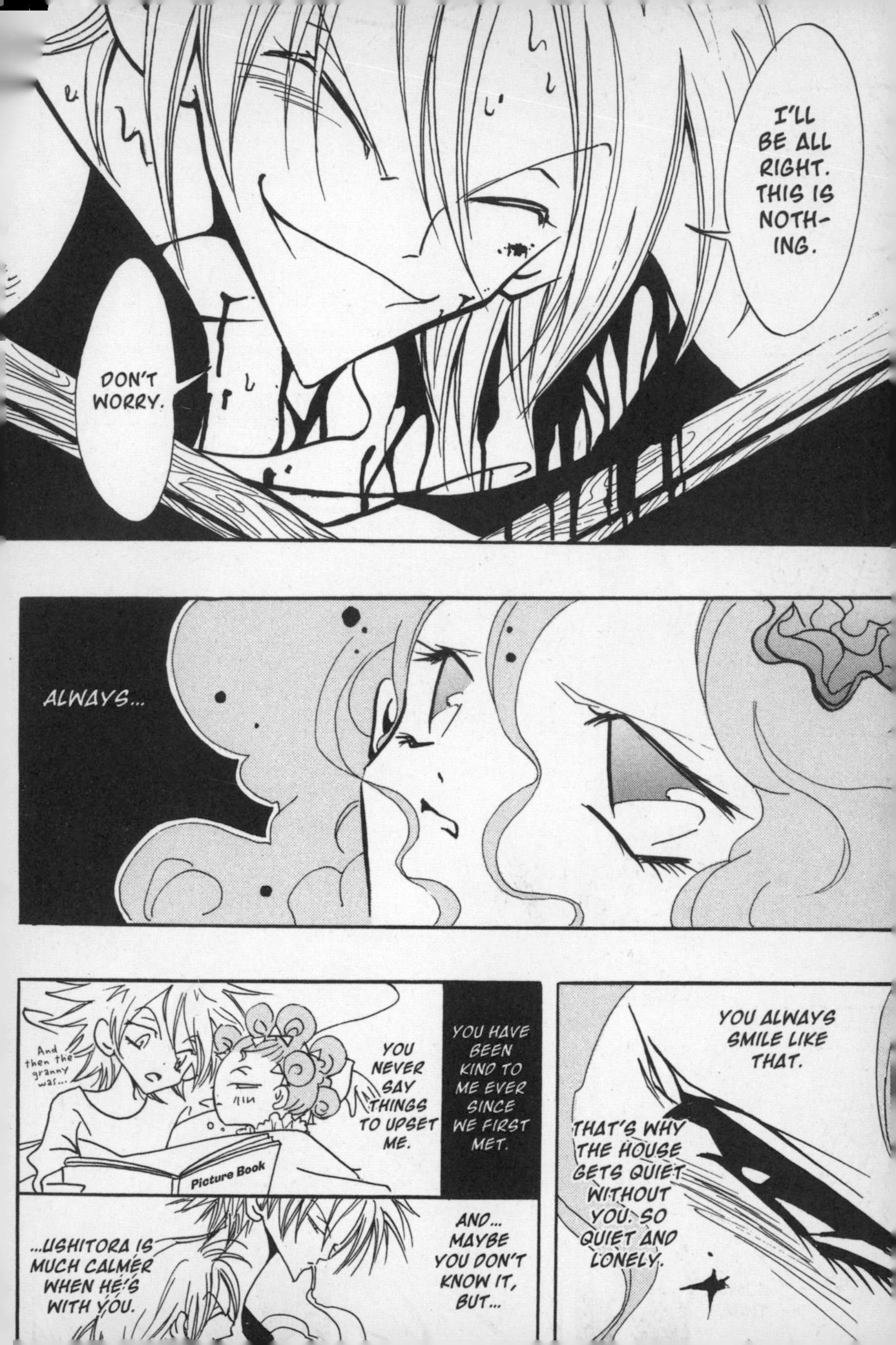
I'LL BE ALL RIGHT. THIS IS NOTHING.
DON'T WORRY.
ALWAYS...
YOU HAVE BEEN KIND TO ME EVER SINCE WE FIRST MET.
YOU NEVER SAY THINGS TO UPSET ME.
And then the granny was...
Picture Book
AND... MAYBE YOU DON'T KNOW IT, BUT...
...USHITORA IS MUCH CALMER WHEN HE'S WITH YOU.
YOU ALWAYS SMILE LIKE THAT.
THAT'S WHY THE HOUSE GETS QUIET WITHOUT YOU. SO QUIET AND LONELY.

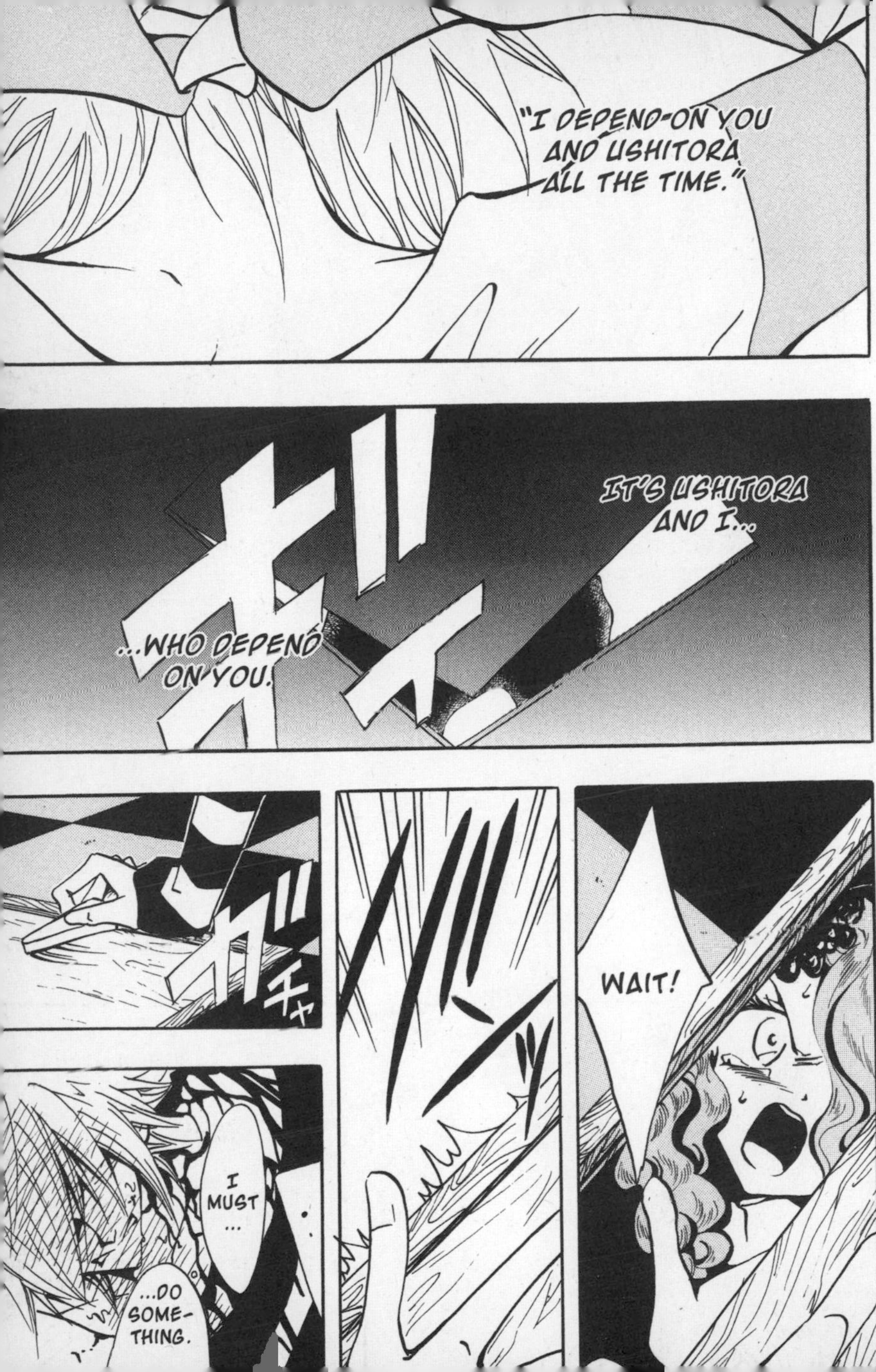
"I DEPEND ON YOU AND USHITORA ALL THE TIME."
IT'S USHITORA AND I...
...WHO DEPEND ON YOU.
WAIT!
I MUST ...
...DO SOME-THING.

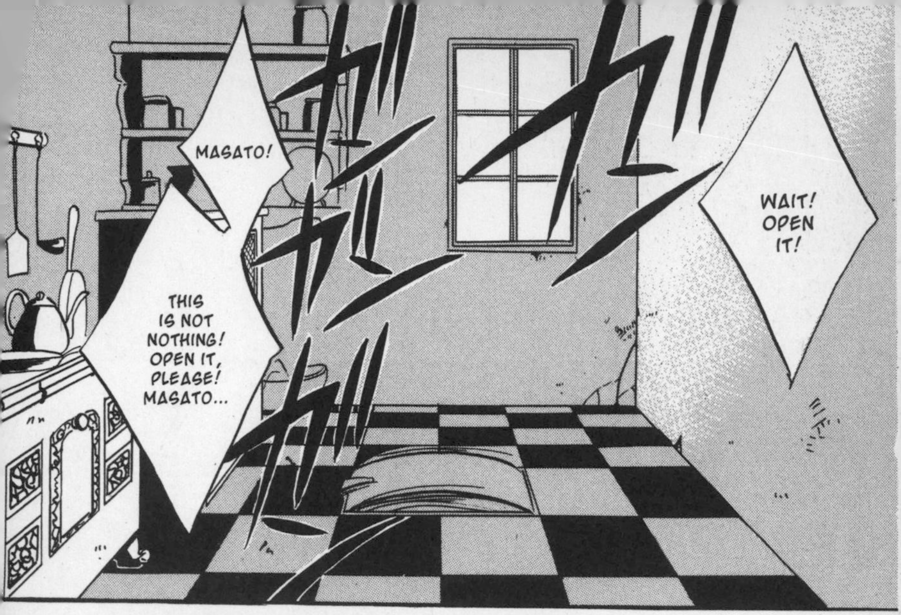
WAIT! OPEN IT!
MASATO!
THIS IS NOT NOTHING! OPEN IT, PLEASE! MASATO...

*YOU'LL BE...
KILLED.*

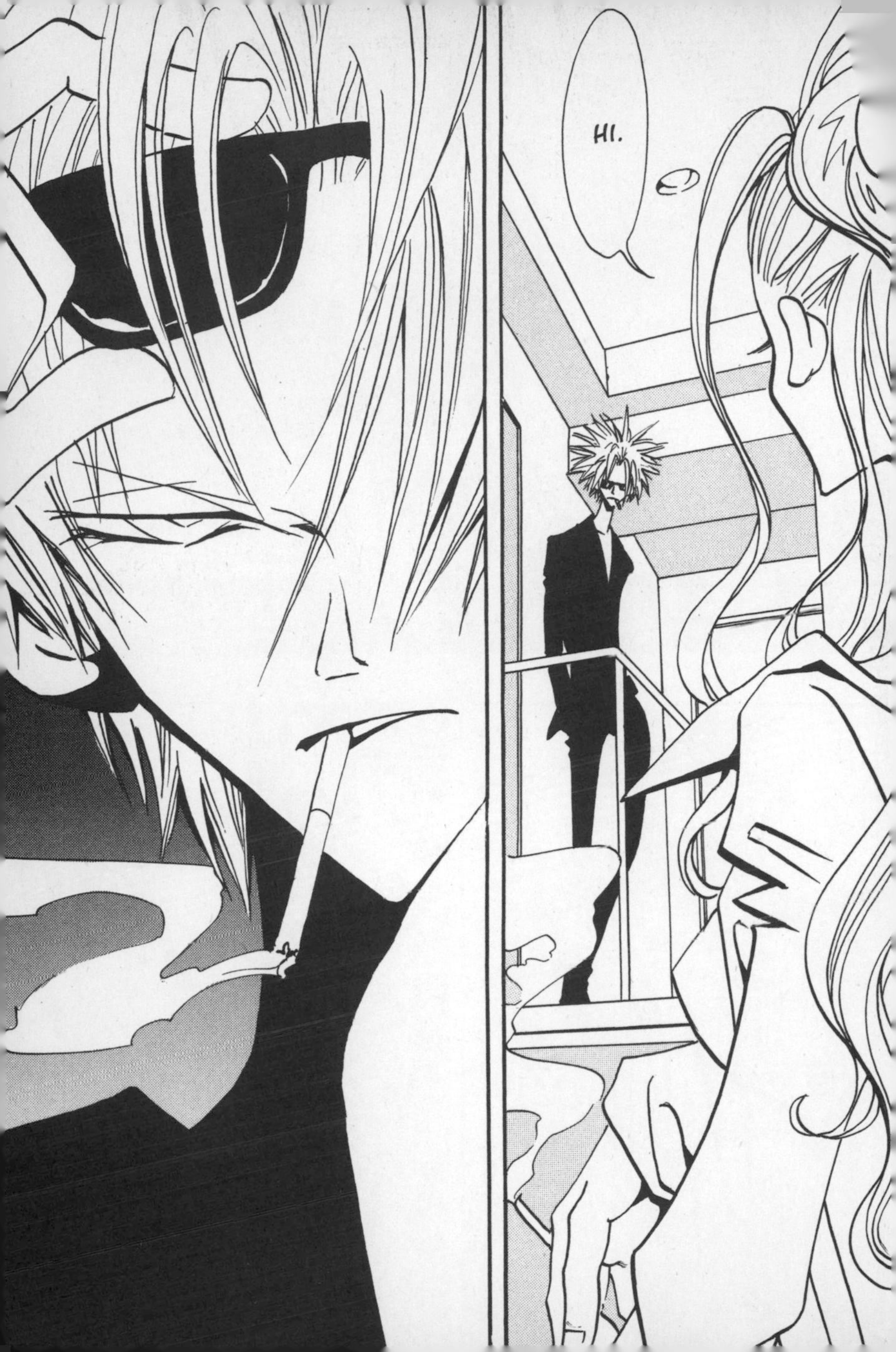
HI.

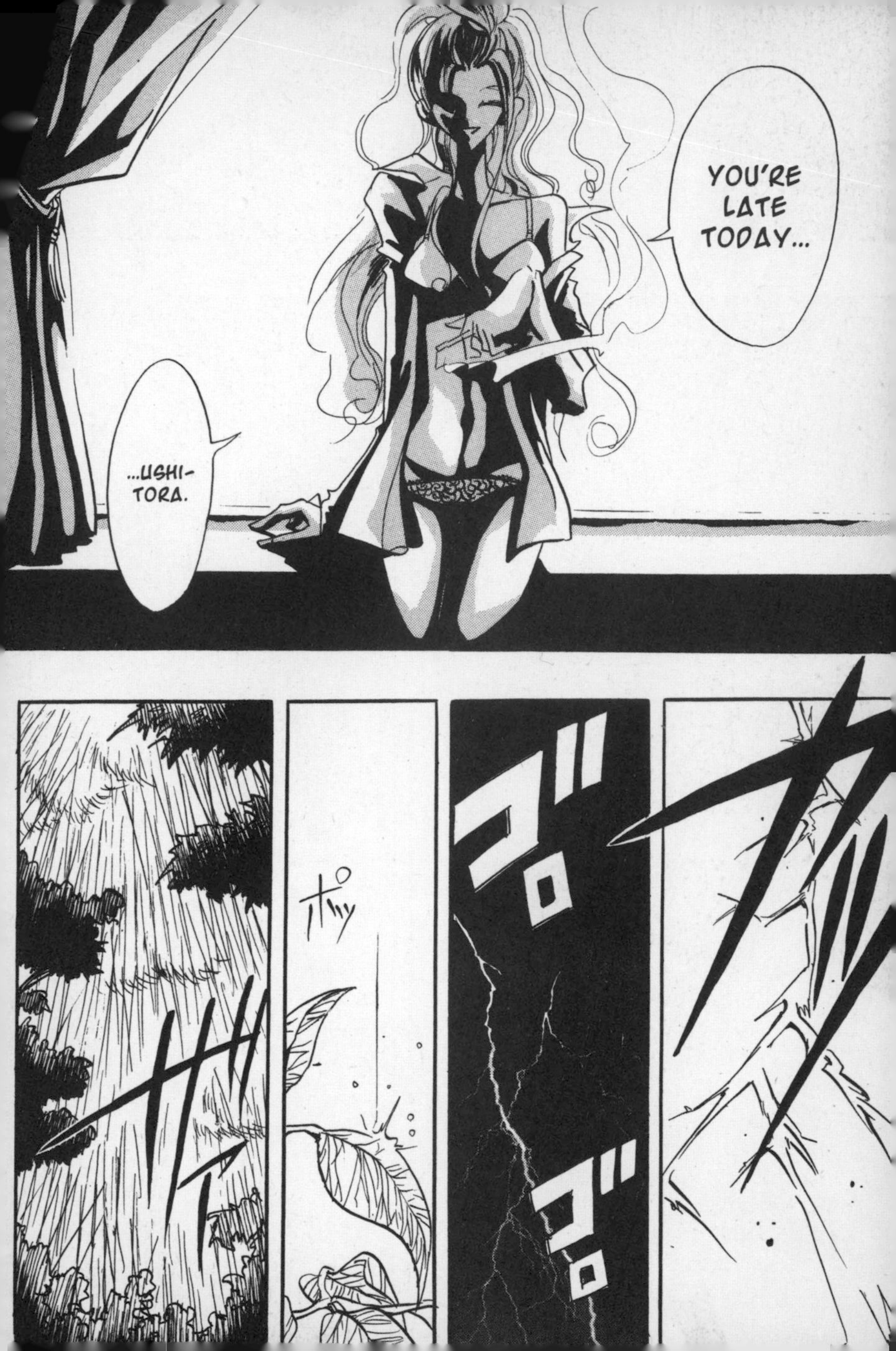
YOU'RE LATE TODAY...
...USHI-TORA.
ゴロ
ゴロ

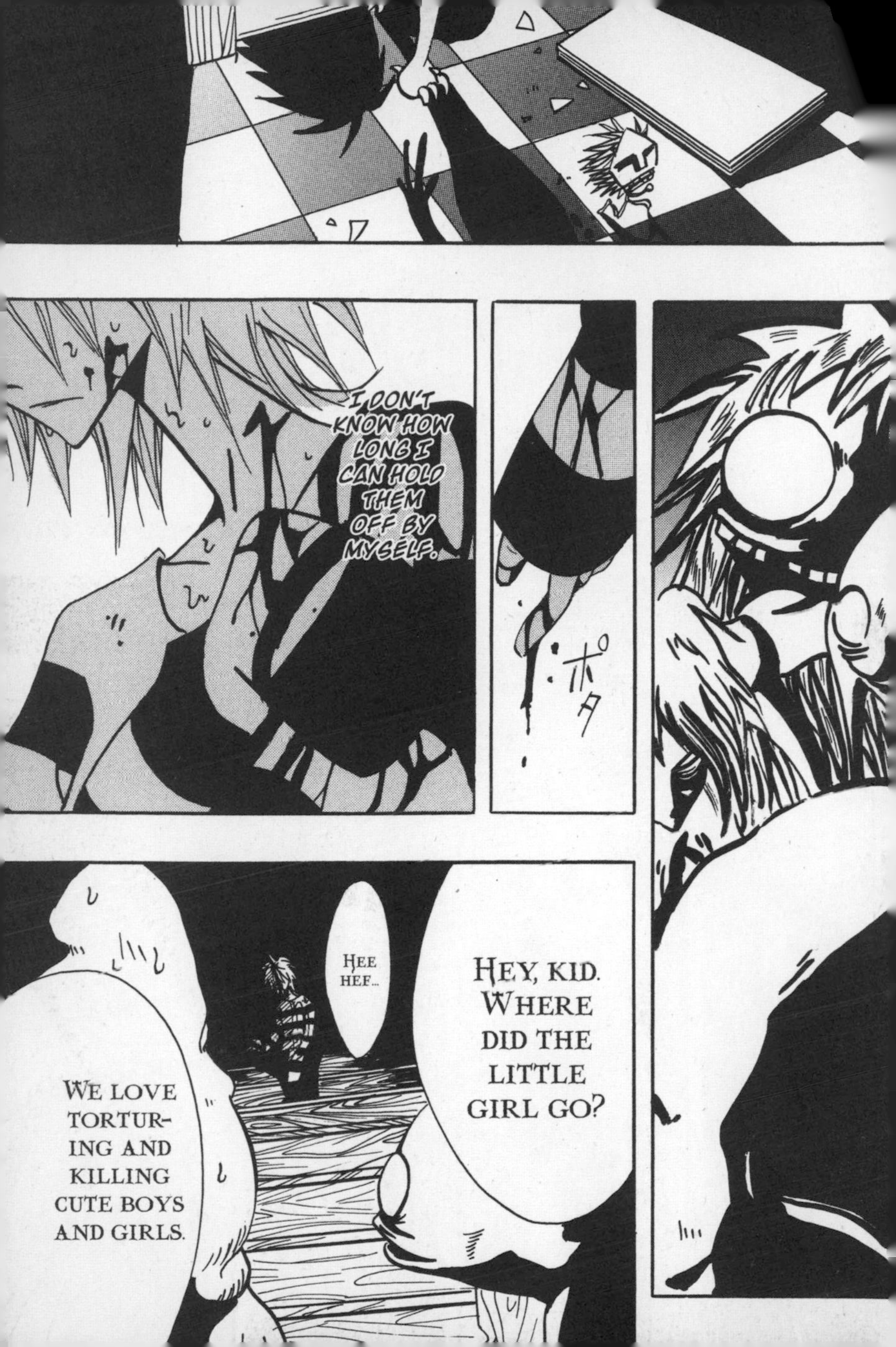

ポタ
I DON'T KNOW HOW LONG I CAN HOLD THEM OFF BY MYSELF.
HEY, KID. WHERE DID THE LITTLE GIRL GO?
HEE HEF...
WE LOVE TORTURING AND KILLING CUTE BOYS AND GIRLS.

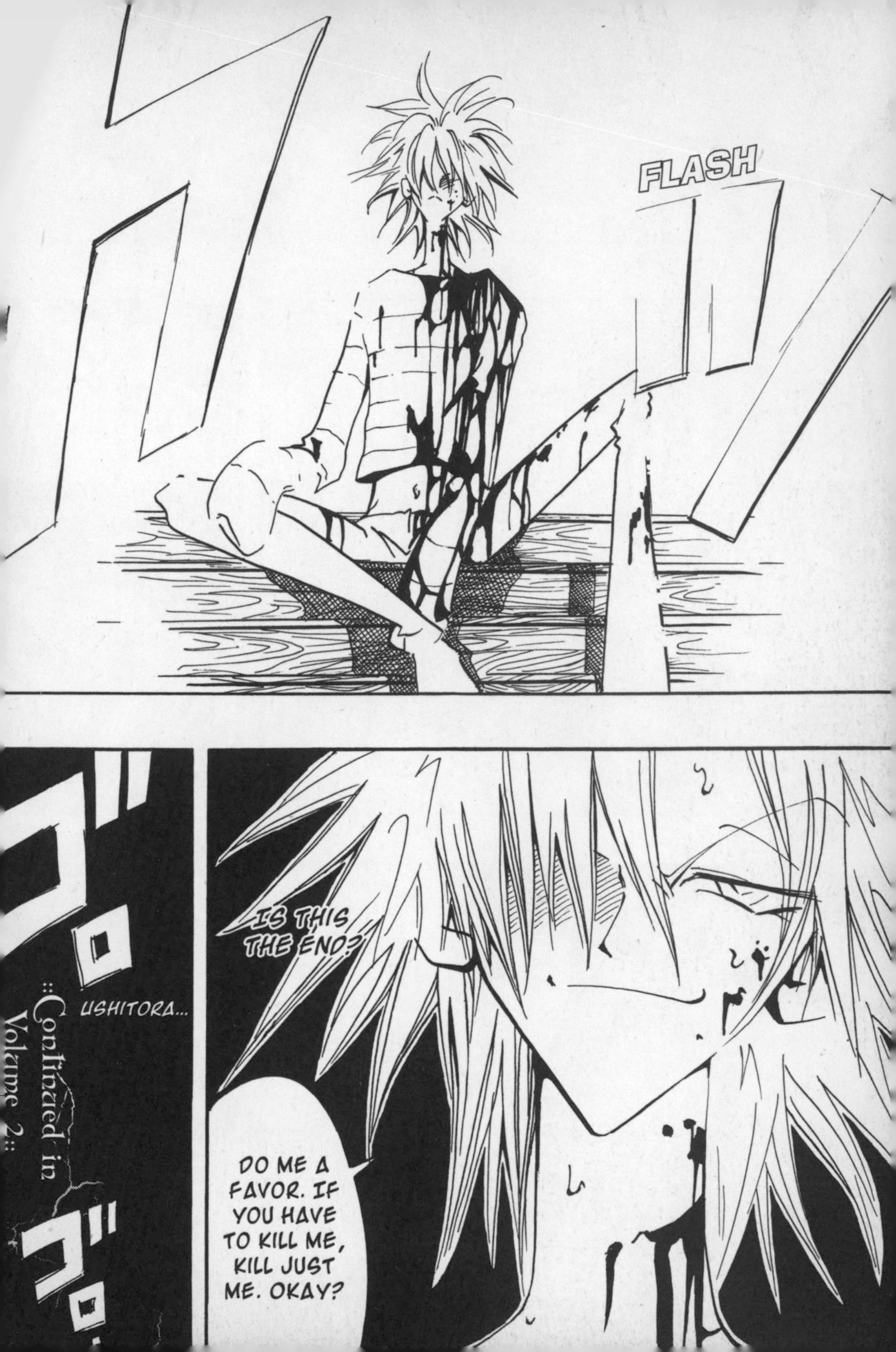
FLASH
IS THIS THE END?
USHITORA...
DO ME A FAVOR. IF YOU HAVE TO KILL ME, KILL JUST ME. OKAY?
::Continued in Volume 2::

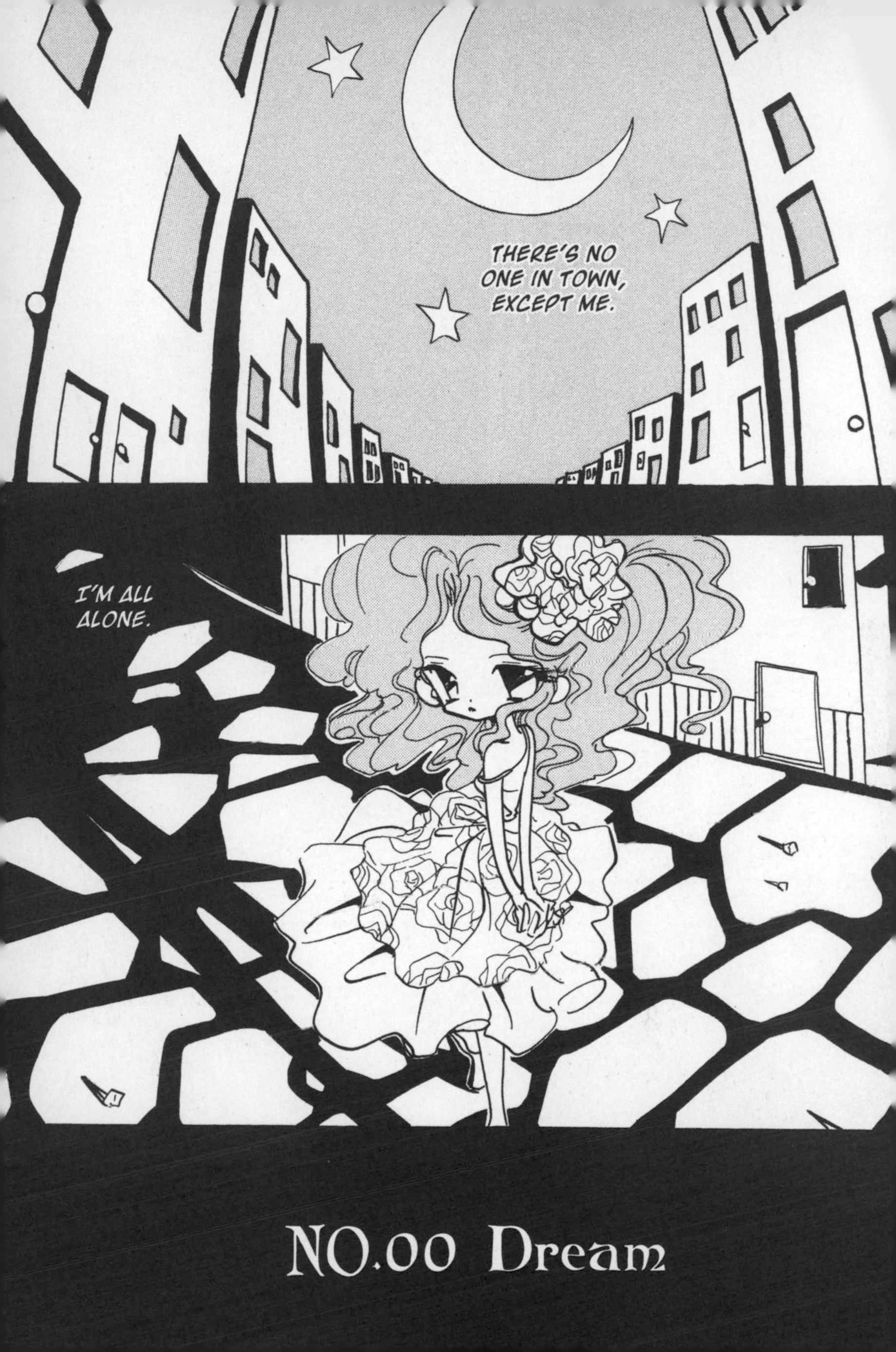
THERE'S NO ONE IN TOWN, EXCEPT ME.
I'M ALL ALONE.

NO.00 Dream

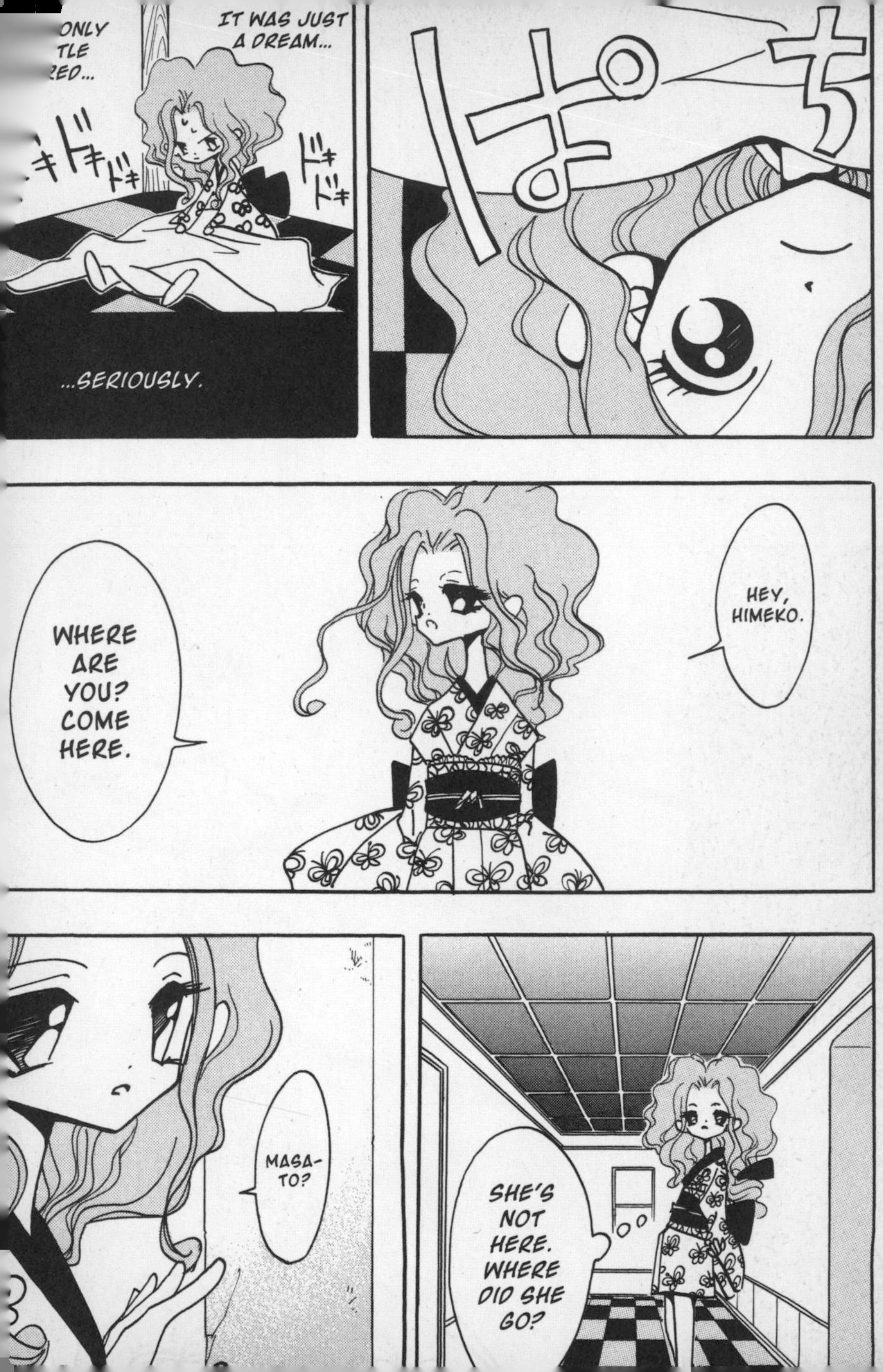
ぱち
IT WAS JUST A DREAM...
ONLY
TLE
RED...
ドキドキドキ
ドキドキ
...SERIOUSLY.
HEY, HIMEKO.
WHERE ARE YOU? COME HERE.
SHE'S NOT HERE. WHERE DID SHE GO?
MASA-TO?

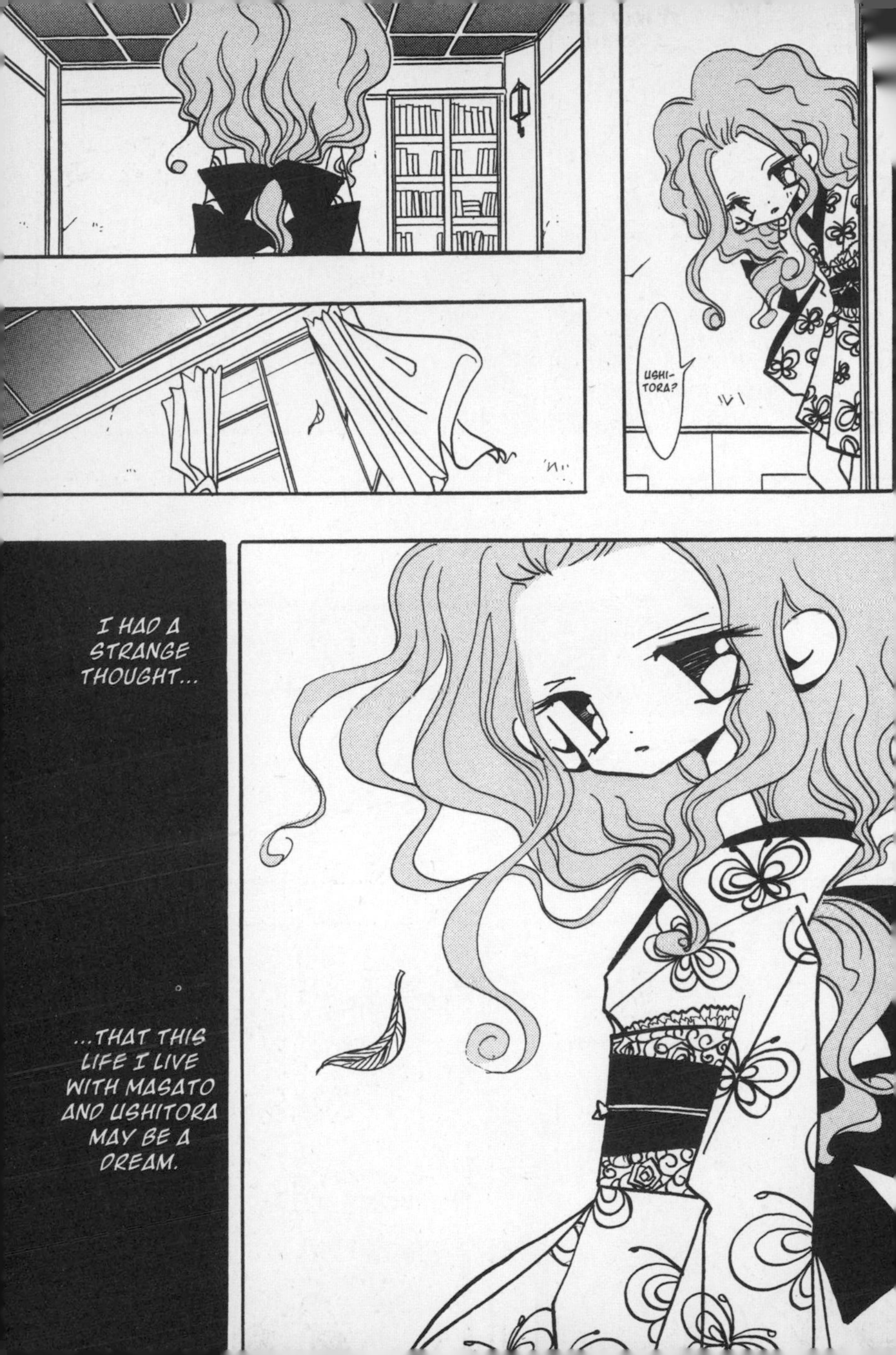
USHI-TORA?
I HAD A STRANGE THOUGHT...
...THAT THIS LIFE I LIVE WITH MASATO AND USHITORA MAY BE A DREAM.

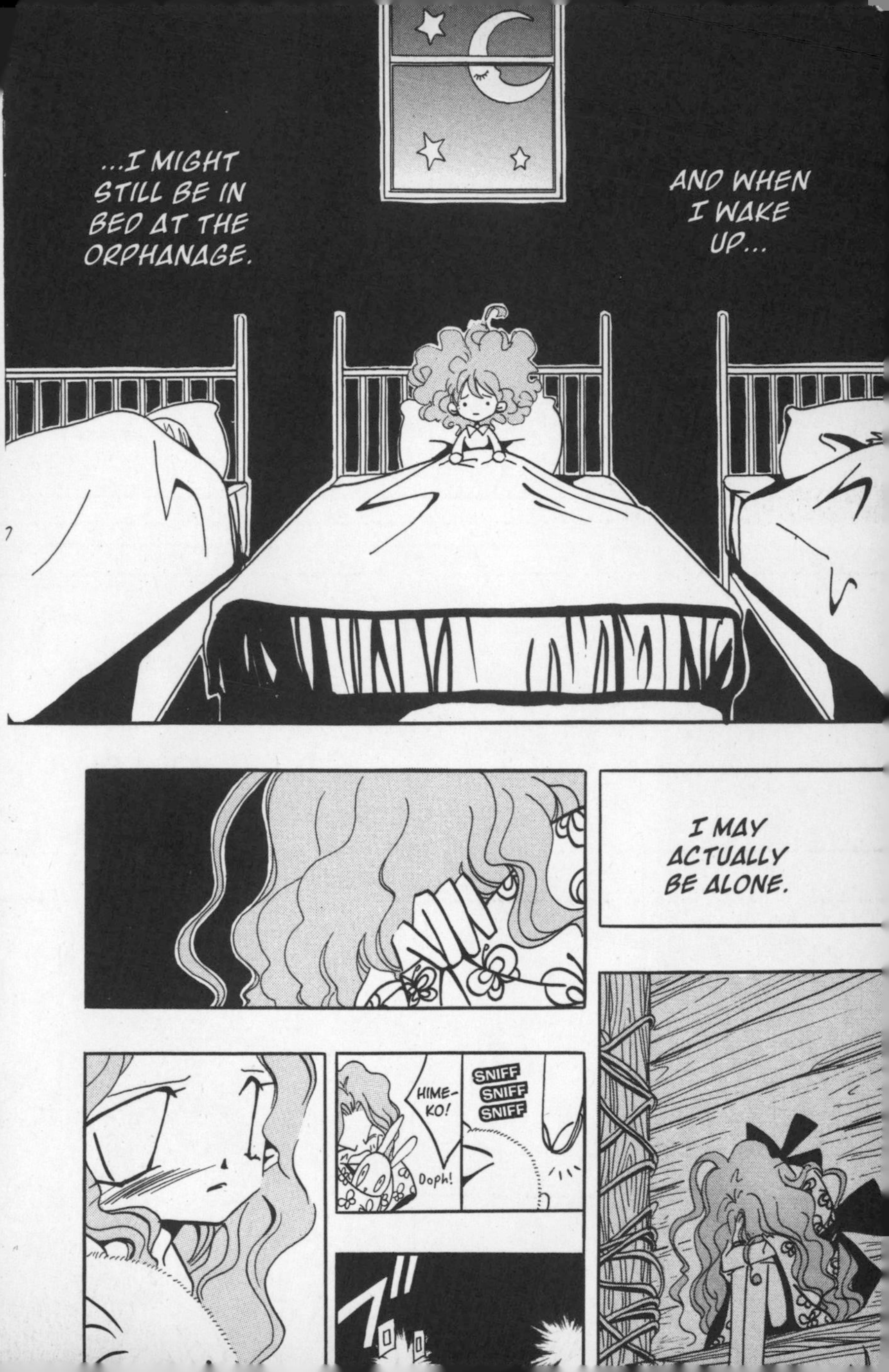
AND WHEN I WAKE UP...
...I MIGHT STILL BE IN BED AT THE ORPHANAGE.
I MAY ACTUALLY BE ALONE.
SNIFF SNIFF SNIFF
HIME-KO!
Ooph!

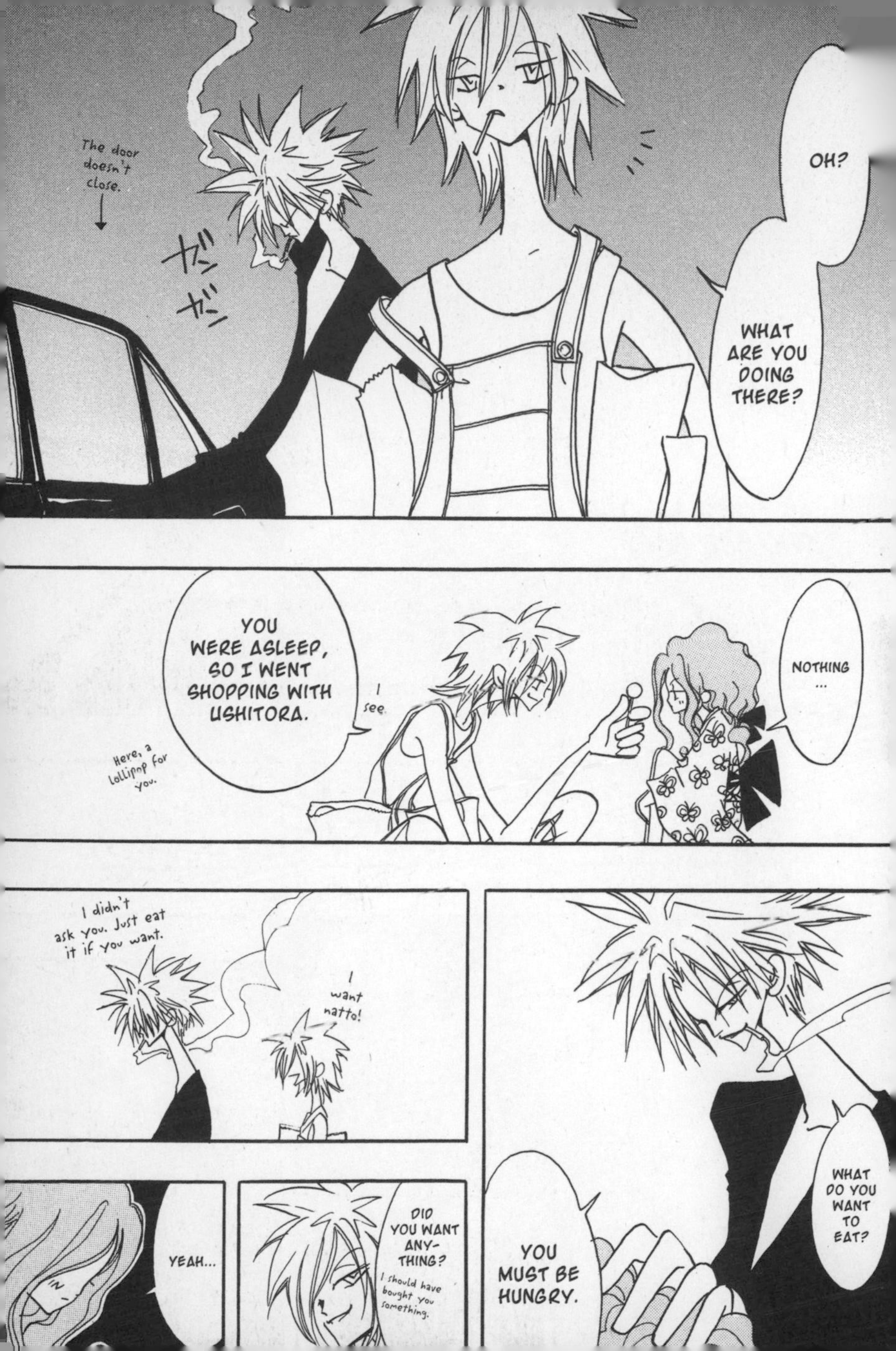
OH?
WHAT ARE YOU DOING THERE?
ガン ガン
The door doesn't close.
NOTHING ...
YOU WERE ASLEEP, SO I WENT SHOPPING WITH USHITORA.
I see.
Here, a lollipop for you.
WHAT DO YOU WANT TO EAT?
YOU MUST BE HUNGRY.
I want natto!
I didn't ask you. Just eat it if you want.
DID YOU WANT ANYTHING?
I should have bought you something.
YEAH...

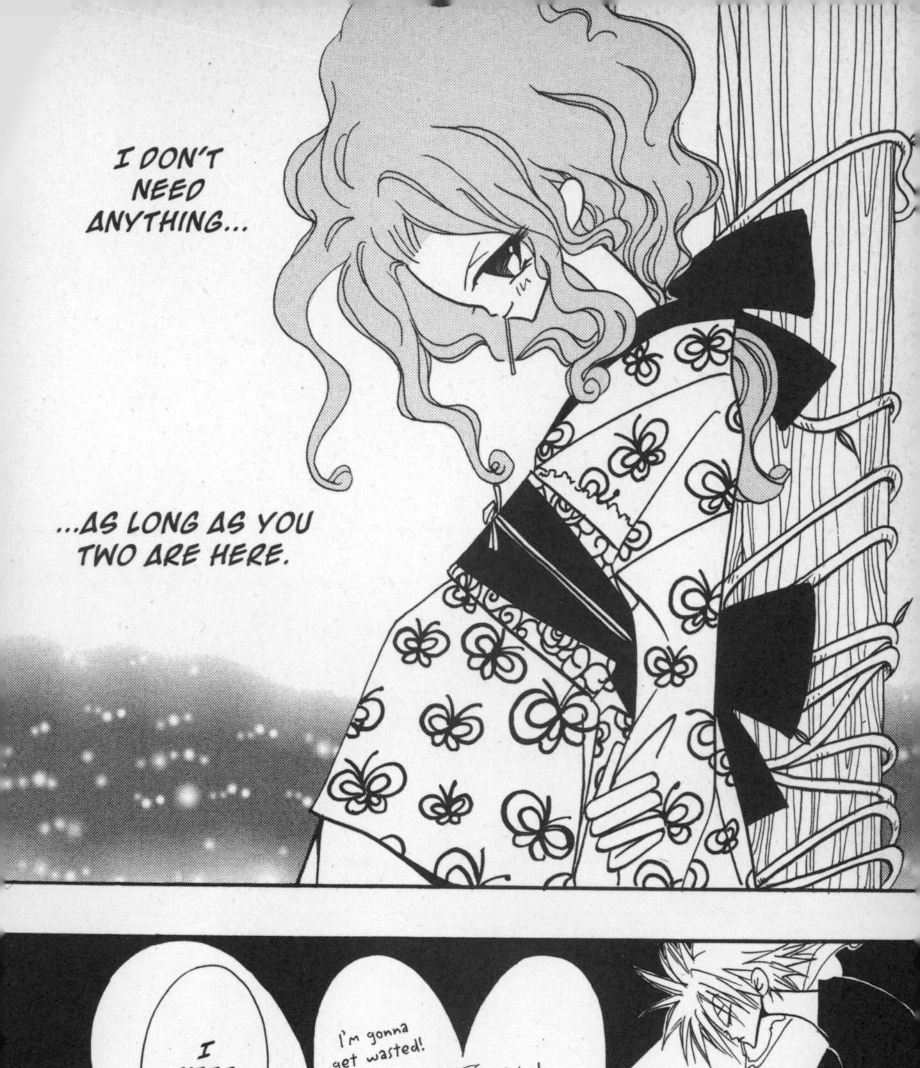
I DON'T NEED ANYTHING...
...AS LONG AS YOU TWO ARE HERE.

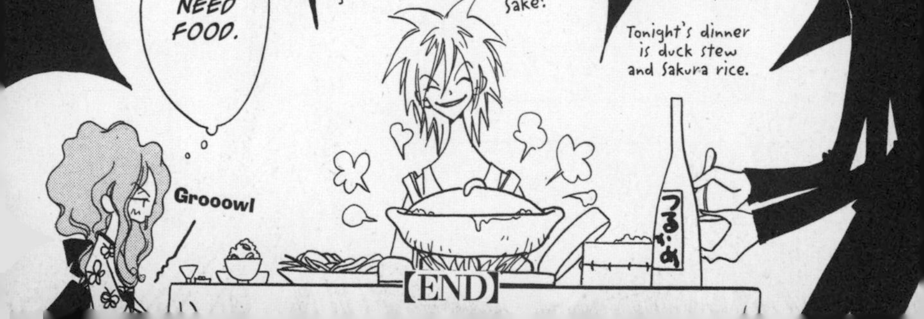
Tonight's dinner is duck stew and Sakura rice.
Sake!
I'm gonna get wasted!
I NEED FOOD.
Grooowl
つるかめ

【END】

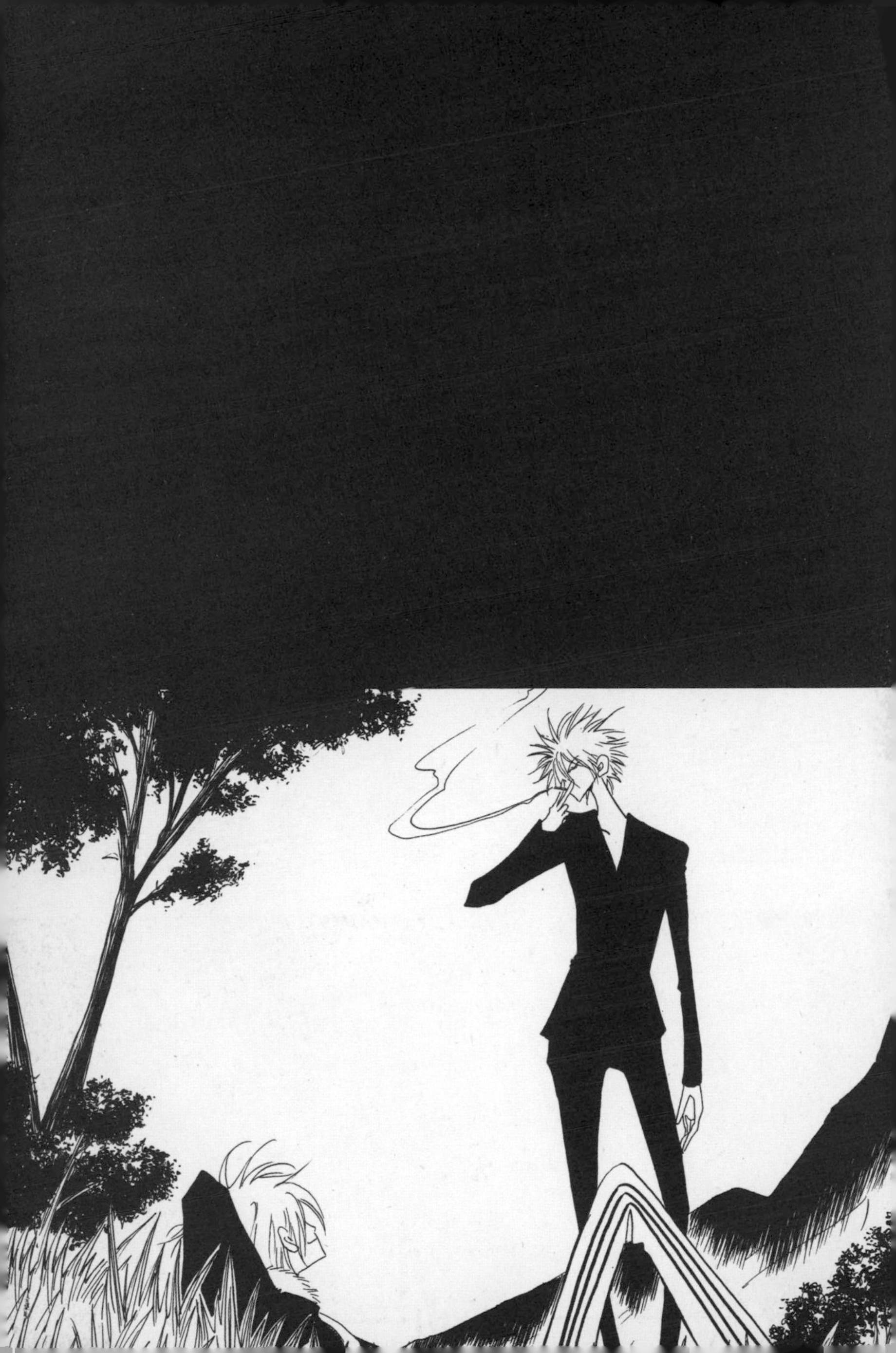

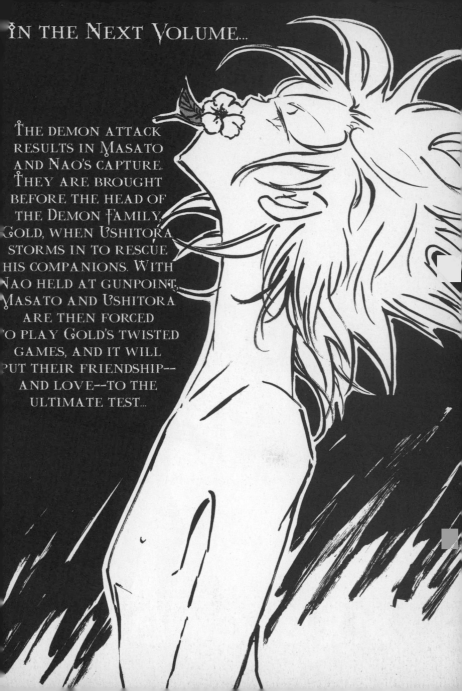

IN THE NEXT VOLUME...

THE DEMON ATTACK
RESULTS IN MASATO
AND NAO'S CAPTURE.
THEY ARE BROUGHT
BEFORE THE HEAD OF
THE DEMON FAMILY,
GOLD, WHEN USHITORA
STORMS IN TO RESCUE
HIS COMPANIONS. WITH
NAO HELD AT GUNPOINT,
MASATO AND USHITORA
ARE THEN FORCED
TO PLAY GOLD'S TWISTED
GAMES, AND IT WILL
PUT THEIR FRIENDSHIP--
AND LOVE--TO THE
ULTIMATE TEST...

AVALON HIGH
CORONATION

VOLUME 1 • THE MERLIN PROPHECY

#1 New York Times bestselling author Meg Cabot's first ever manga!

Avalon High: Coronation continues the story of Meg Cabot's mega-hit novel *Avalon High.* Is Ellie's new boyfriend really the reincarnated King Arthur? Is his step-brother out to kill him? Will good triumph over evil—and will Ellie have to save the day AGAIN?

Don't miss *Avalon High: Coronation #1: The Merlin Prophecy*—in stores July 2007!

MEG CABOT

HARPERCOLLINS & TOKYOPOP
WWW.HARPERTEEN.COM   WWW.TOKYOPOP.COM

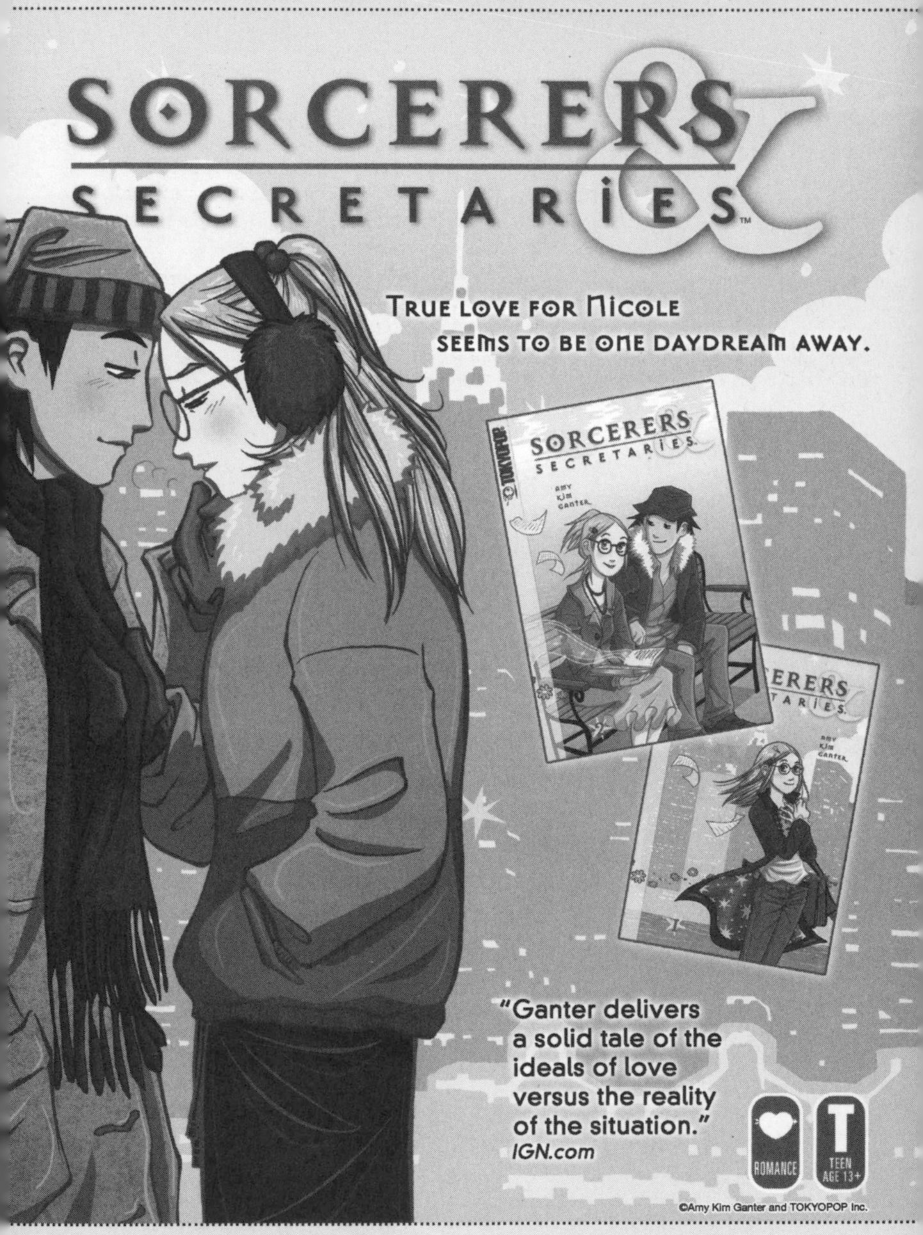
SORCERERS & SECRETARIES™
TRUE LOVE FOR NICOLE SEEMS TO BE ONE DAYDREAM AWAY.
SORCERERS & SECRETARIES
AMY KIM GANTER
"Ganter delivers a solid tale of the ideals of love versus the reality of the situation."
IGN.com
ROMANCE
T
TEEN AGE 13+
©Amy Kim Ganter and TOKYOPOP Inc.

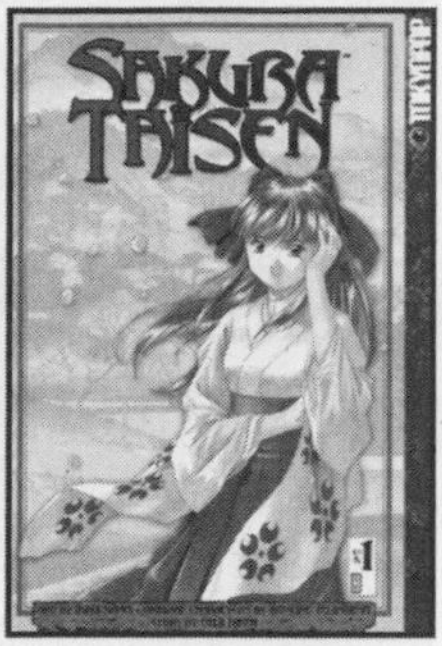
SAKURA TAISEN
TOKYOPOP
1

ACTION

T TEEN AGE 13+

SAKURA TAISEN

BY OHJI HIROI, IKKU MASA AND KOSUKE FUJISHIMA

I really, really like this series. I'm a sucker for steampunk-type stories, and 1920s Japanese fashion, and throw in demon invaders, robot battles and references to Japanese popular theater? Sold! There's lots of fun tidbits for the clever reader to pick up in this series (all the characters have flower names, for one, and the fact that all the Floral Assault divisions are named after branches of the Takarazuka Review, Japan's sensational all-female theater troupe!), but the consistently stylish and clean art will appeal even to the most casual fan.

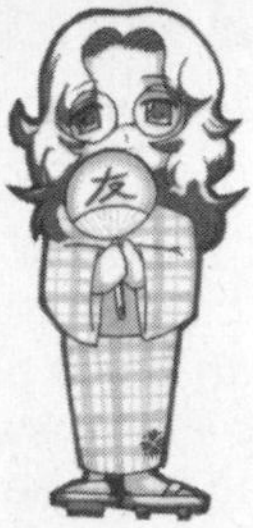

~Lillian Diaz-Przybyl, Editor

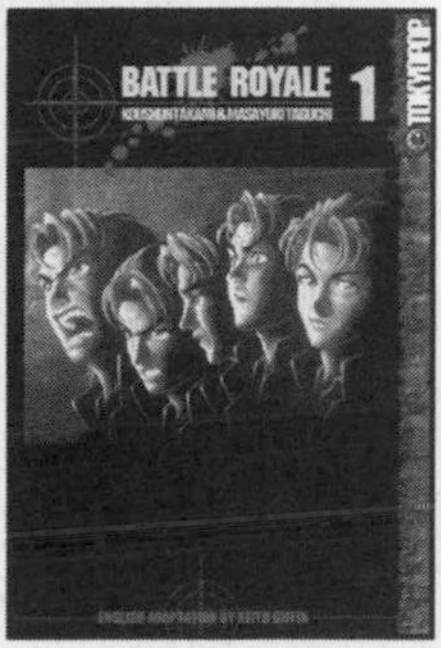
BATTLE ROYALE 1
KOUSHUN TAKAMI & MASAYUKI TAGUCHI
TOKYOPOP

ACTION

M MATURE AGES 18+

BATTLE ROYALE

BY KOUSHUN TAKAMI AND MASAYUKI TAGUCHI

As far as cautionary tales go, you couldn't get any timelier than *Battle Royale*. Telling the bleak story of a class of middle school students who are forced to fight each other to the death on national television, Koushun Takami and Masayuki Taguchi have created a dark satire that's sickening, yet undeniably exciting as well. And if we have that reaction reading it, it becomes alarmingly clear how the students could so easily be swayed into doing it.

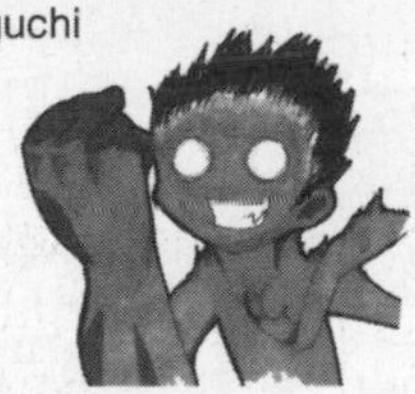

~Tim Beedle, Editor

STOP!

This is the back of the book.
You wouldn't want to spoil a great ending!

This book is printed "manga-style," in the authentic Japanese right-to-left format. Since none of the artwork has been flipped or altered, readers get to experience the story just as the creator intended. You've been asking for it, so TOKYOPOP® delivered: authentic, hot-off-the-press, and far more fun!

DIRECTIONS

If this is your first time reading manga-style, here's a quick guide to help you understand how it works.

It's easy... just start in the top right panel and follow the numbers. Have fun, and look for more 100% authentic manga from TOKYOPOP®!

1
2
3
4
5
6
7
8
9
10

THE MANGA REVOLUTION · LEADING
漫画革命